D0762627

Violence in the City of Women

Violence in the City of Women

POLICE AND BATTERERS IN BAHIA, BRAZIL

Sarah J. Hautzinger

UNIVERSITY OF CALIFORNIA PRESS

BERKELEY   LOS ANGELES   LONDON

University of California Press, one of the most
distinguished university presses in the United States,
enriches lives around the world by advancing scholarship
in the humanities, social sciences, and natural sciences.
Its activities are supported by the UC Press Foundation
and by philanthropic contributions from individuals
and institutions. For more information, visit
www.ucpress.edu.

University of California Press
Berkeley and Los Angeles, California

University of California Press, Ltd.
London, England

© 2007 by The Regents of the University of California

Library of Congress Cataloging-in-Publication Data

Hautzinger, Sarah J., 1963–.
    Violence in the city of women : police and batterers in
Bahia, Brazil / Sarah J. Hautzinger.
        p.   cm.
    Includes bibliographical references and index.
    ISBN-13: 978-0-520-25276-9 (cloth : alk. paper)
    ISBN-13: 978-0-520-25277-6 (pbk. : alk. paper)
    1. Women—Brazil—Bahia (State)   2. Policewomen—
Brazil—Bahia (State)   3. Family violence—Brazil—Bahia
(State)   4. Masculinity—Brazil—Bahia (State)   5. Sex
role—Brazil—Bahia (State)   I. Title.

    HQ1544.B33H38   2007
    364.15′553098142—dc22   2006036211

Manufactured in the United States of America

16   15   14   13   12   11   10   09   08   07
10   9   8   7   6   5   4   3   2   1

This book is printed on New Leaf EcoBook 50, a 100%
recycled fiber of which 50% is de-inked post-consumer
waste, processed chlorine-free. EcoBook 50 is acid-free
and meets the minimum requirements of ANSI/ASTM
D5634–01 (*Permanence of Paper*).

In memory of my mother, Sue O'Brien

CONTENTS

ILLUSTRATIONS

FIGURES

TABLES

PROLOGUE

My eyes filled with tears as I hung up the phone, the dim light of the rising Colorado sun diffusing through my window. Almiro, my beloved godson whose sixteenth birthday I'd missed a few weeks before, said at the end of our conversation that he, too, was *"tudo emocionado,"* all emotional. He gave the typical, prolonged Brazilian good-bye, carefully detailing the people in my life to whom I should pass on hellos and hugs from him and his family.

An odd coincidence marked this call, because Almiro had been trying to call me that morning via the same public phone on which I reached him, and we hadn't spoken for months. What's more, this pay phone (in Brazil, the *orelhão,* the "big ear") had been broken for months. We'd been using other pay-phone numbers, but all of them were out of service. What the heck, I'd thought, and given this one a try.

It was 3 A.M. after a Sunday-morning breast-feeding, and I couldn't get back to sleep. I had gotten up and sat down at the computer to work. Quickly, however, I was overwhelmed by *saudades,* the particularly Brazilian feeling of missing, nostalgia, longing. I decided that even if I couldn't talk to Almiro or his family, I needed to speak to someone in Bahia. It would be Sunday morning in northeast Brazil, a good time to try.

On the couch my newborn daughter was looking around with an alert smile in her eyes, calm and relaxed.

The phone rang for nearly three minutes, and then a girl's voice answered. I asked for Yancí—this phone was closest to Yancí's house—and the girl said she was not there. "Is this the Alto do Mungongo?" I asked. She said it was. I asked her to call someone else, also to no avail; finally it occurred to me to ask her to call Almiro himself. I heard the receiver being knocked about, and background voices, and I was thrilled to hear Almiro say "hello," with a distinct attempt at an American pronunciation. I asked about it, laughing, and he laughed back and said he'd been told someone was calling from the United States. Not for the first time, I was taken aback by his ever-deepening voice, by how quickly the boy was becoming a man. Still, he was unmistakably my *afilhado* (godson).

After declaring my amazement and relief at finally getting through, I asked how things were going. "Going well," Almiro said, which is the obligatory response. He added, "Getting by" *(levando)*. I told him that part of the reason I'd been bad about writing was that he had a new little sister, my second daughter, born seven weeks ago. He received the news with a cheerful "Really? That's great." He was especially impressed that the baby was born at home—"just like in the old days," he said. I told him I had just been reading in my field notes about how his grandmother, now passed on, used to be a midwife *(parteira);* there was a note of pride in his voice as he affirmed it.

I've always felt a little sheepish sharing news about my young children, which has been generally good, with my impoverished Brazilian "kin." The arrival of a new baby in their family is not automatically good news, and not only because new babies are additional mouths to feed in an economy of scarcity. The family despaired, for instance, each time Almiro's older sister Josi was discovered to be pregnant; she had now given birth three times and was still in her early twenties. She is considered "mentally deficient," reportedly from her father's kicks to her mother's abdomen while she was in the womb. Josi was found hitting the first baby when the baby was three months old. Their mother and my *comadre,* Zizi, is now raising two of her grandchildren; one of the fathers' mothers took in the third.

Almiro shared news of a cousin's new baby. The father did have a job, thankfully, and thus her arrival could occasion celebration. Then Almiro's father, my *compadre* by virtue of our being "co-parents" but with whom I am not close, came on the line. He was still unemployed and back living with Almiro and Zizi's family (he'd started another one) for a time. The receiver then went to Almiro's second-oldest brother, who said enough to tell me that he was still drinking too much and possibly still smoking crack. Finally, the four-year-old niece grabbed the phone receiver to ask whether I could give her some special girl shoes *(sapato da safina);* I didn't know exactly what those were; I imagined sequined slippers festooned with the likeness of a TV cartoon character.

Eventually Almiro's mother, my *comadre* Zizi, came to the phone. She sounded exhausted and in poor health, a worrisome croak in her voice. Zizi had never seemed to need to make light of the family's situation to me. She told me that the violence in the neighborhood grew worse all the time, and that you couldn't even walk in the Baixa da Vasco, the neighborhood adjacent to the Mungongo, where I also did fieldwork, anymore. She reported that just yesterday, a little girl she knew I was close to lost her twenty-eight-year-old brother in a shooting there. He left behind a woman with four children, and three more children by a previous partner. I asked whether he had been "involved in something." We both knew what I meant—theft or gangs or drug dealing—and I hoped I didn't sound like I thought he'd deserved to be shot if he were.

"No," Zizi said. "He just knew someone . . ." and trailed off. We both sighed, leaving a moment of dead air on the line.

When I asked, Zizi told of a new bank account I could try to wire money to, something I'd done in the past when able. She also mentioned things Almiro could use for Christmas (the usual new shirt, shorts, and sandals) but insisted she didn't need or want anything in particular for herself. I knew that if I managed to get a box off it would contain presents for fifteen or so different people, with me hoping they provided all with a happy moment, that none of the presents was too cheap and that I didn't inadvertently leave anyone out.

I took a deep breath and asked Zizi whether Jorginho was "keeping his hands" (I didn't add feet, belts, and so on) to himself. We both knew this was euphemistic for his not beating her. I said it almost as if in jest, with the tone of an older sister feigning anger on her behalf. She said he was "behaving himself." Zizi had told me in 1994 that the physical violence in her marriage was a thing of the past, and I was glad to hear her say that this was still the case. All the same, when I asked whether Zizi's current health problems had to do with her old, persistent spinal injury, from when

Jorginho "accidentally" pushed her down some stairs years ago, she affirmed, "Yes, it's that same old thing."

These conversations in Portuguese felt awkward. I figured that I talk more than Zizi, although I speak a nonnative's Portuguese, because she lacks privacy at the public phone, and I probably have more practice chatting on phones than she has (I'd always had one at home, and she rarely did). There were long pauses in which she waited for me to say something. If it were my other good friend, Zizi's more loquacious sister-in-law, Yancí, on the phone, she would talk as much as I did.

"What luck that this public phone is working," I said, explaining that I'd been trying the other number and had all but forgotten about this one.

"Yes," Zizi replied. "The boys in the area vandalized the other one, and just yesterday the man came and fixed this one."

"You mean, this phone wasn't working until yesterday?" I asked. "That's right," she affirmed. I couldn't believe the coincidence.

After a pause she asked: "Almiro called you, right?"

I realized she hadn't understood me before. "No," I said. "That's what I'm saying: I just dialed this number out of the blue, thinking there was no way it would work."

Suddenly the coincidence struck her, too. She explained, "It's just that ever since the phone was fixed yesterday, Almiro has talked of nothing other than trying to call you. It's been months we haven't had a phone, and he has been missing you so much."

"I know," I told her. "I always worry that he'll think I'm not thinking about him, but I do every day."

"He knows that," she told me. "He never forgets you either."

I was relieved to learn that Almiro was back in school, at the early secondary level, and studying at night. I felt affirmed about my role in getting him back in school when he had been nine years old and out of school for almost two years, a role that had led to my becoming his godmother, seven years ago. My nonjudgmental anthropologist's hat had had to come off before I could confront his neglectful and sometimes violent father on his behalf. Almiro had missed odd years of school since then but seemed to find his way back to the books each time.

I found the phone call's coincidence, that each thought one of us had called the other, uncanny, difficult to explain. Although not particularly rational (more likely, sleep-deprived), a sense that my path from anthropologist to Almiro's godmother was not random, but held purpose, filled the morning air.

Fifteen years earlier, my first introduction to Brazil's specialized women's police stations came on a sticky-hot afternoon in the city of Salvador, capital of Bahia, the largest state in Brazil's poverty-stricken northeast. I had been in the city for a few weeks, unsuccessfully trying to locate the *capoeira* (a Bahian martial art/game/dance form) academy and a teacher who taught there, whom I'd trained with previously, back in the United States. I had struck up a conversation with a young man who described himself simply as "a student" in the Praça Municipal, next to the famous Elevador Lacerda, which connects the upper and lower parts of this colonial city across a cliff that separates them. From where we sat upon an ornate but crumbling wall, perched atop the cliff, we had a sweeping view of the vast blue Bahia de Todos os Santos (Bay of All Saints) below.

Exactly how the topic of violence against women arose I am uncertain, but I do recall the student telling me that in Salvador, men thought twice about hitting women because the city had a group of women who beat the pulp out of men who batter their women. I was traveling through Brazil, on my way back to the United States after a year in Chile and other Spanish-speaking Latin American countries, and at the time I spoke no Portuguese. I felt lucky, then, to have grasped this nugget through the ungainly, Spanish-Portuguese pidgin the student and I used. Patient with my slow comprehension, he proceeded to describe an ensemble of women— seemingly avenging, indomitable viragoes—who located and exacted justice from male batterers by using a vigilante, eye-for-an-eye maxim of justice. Relying on their strength as a group, these formidable women were able to impress upon male bullies that the costs of their abuse could be outweigh its "benefits."

But how do they find out about a battered woman? I wanted to know. How are these women able to assault men without someone—the police, opposing gangs of men, whoever—intervening? Is this group organized, and if so, by whom? Only gradually did my queries ferret out another fact: far from being the vigilantes he seemed to intimate, these women *were* police, and their "project" was state-sponsored. The student seemed to treat this critical detail as almost incidental, an afterthought.

Later, back in the United States as a doctoral student in anthropology, I began to look for material about the women's police stations. I located the transcript from a segment on ABC's investigative reporting program, *60*

Minutes, which confirmed the existence of Brazil's specialized police stations. I learned that on average 80 percent of complaints registered in the specialized stations involve some sort of "domestic," gender-based partner violence, be this physical, economic, verbal, or psychological.

Over the ensuing years, while I investigated women's police and the problem of partner violence in Brazil, I often recalled that in my first introduction, the law enforcement, *policing* aspect of these stations' activities got second billing. For the student with whom I'd initially spoken, and for numerous taxi drivers, merchants, and neighbors with whom I subsequently spoke, it was more important to tell stories about *women* taking revenge for other women—by beating up men! For instance, the student might as easily have narrated for me the numerous cases of police brutalizing civilians for untried offenses; instead, his account was of women turning violence back on violent men to avenge other women.

This was my first hint that the divisions of a pitched, gender-based battle were being drawn before my eyes on the streets of Salvador. This was the city dubbed "The City of Women" over fifty years earlier by the North American ethnographer Ruth Landes because she had been so impressed by the authority and autonomy commanded by the African-Brazilian women she studied there in her investigation of Candomblé, the region's foremost African-Bahian religion (Landes 1994 [1947]). Half a century later, I was learning of a quite different kind of institution that onlookers also felt compelled to describe in terms of gendered conflict and power struggles. The student with whom I'd spoken, and gradually I found that many others shared his perspective, had initially thought of the women's police station as arising from battle lines drawn according to gender, between women and men, rather than between civilians and a paramilitary state.

The police stations brought a coincidence I had found as uncanny as my phone call with Almiro's family fifteen years later. Long before I could easily converse in Portuguese, when I had first scraped together graduate student funding to investigate rumors of a new women's police station in Salvador, I learned that Salvador's women's police station had been inaugurated in 1987, on my birthday, October 17. The coincidence somehow comforted me, suggesting that I'd found a foothold on a rock I was meant to scale.

These two conversations, one in 2002 and one in 1987, are the rough bookends for this work. The chapters that follow plumb everything that happened in between, spilling into more recent events as well. The book spans a period of nearly twenty years but also illuminates my journey from the role as academic fieldworker of gender-based violence and Brazil's police-women stations to more personal roles, as friend, *comadre,* and godmother.

As its cover promises, the book is about the criminalization of men's violence against female partners, mostly in one Brazilian city: Salvador, Bahia. But it also deals with men's responses to the notion that violence is no longer acceptable, at least according to recently reformed Brazilian law, but is, instead, criminal. How do ways of being masculine change in response—or do they?

My godson, Almiro, is the anchor for an array of life stories that organize this inquiry. His aspirations and disappointments, his family, his prospects, and the obstacles that plague him all penetrate the narrative, as do the models of masculinity shown to him as possible as he comes of age. The book explores how his father's violence against his mother shaped his childhood and, to some degree, his present and future. Finally, Almiro's story connects the changing theater of the Brazilian state, and the paramilitaries' relationship to violence in particular, with violence of the most personal sort: one-on-one, domestic, partner, gender-based.

ACKNOWLEDGMENTS

I am deeply indebted to the people and institutions who made the various phases of this research possible.

Many in Bahia supported this project over the years: first and foremost, my "NEIMista" sisters at the Núcleo de Estudos Interdisciplinares sobre a Mulher at the Universidade Federal da Bahia (UFBa). Cecília Bacelar Sardenberg, Alice Alcântara Costa, Margaret Greene, Rita Costa, Sílvia Lúcia Ferreira, Sherry Blackburn, Luiza Huber, Jaqueline Leite, Sílvia de Aquino, Neuza de Oliveira, Elizete Passos, Alda Britto da Motta, Enilda Rosendo, and Ívia Alves have been especially important colleagues and companions there. In 1990 I worked with UFBa undergraduates as part of a collective senior thesis on Salvador's women's police station: Ieda Barbosa Pinheiro Franco, Acacia Batista Dias, and Eliene Cerqueira de Melo. I am grateful for their early camaraderie. Between 1992 and 1999, I relied upon my research collaborators Francisco Gomes, Carlos Ferreira Danon, Altair Paim, and Flávio Gonçalves (who generally spoke with men) and Rosimeire Gonçalves and Ana Paula dos Reis (who, along with me, focused on women). Together, this team observed while participating, interviewed, surveyed, administered questionnaires, and held focus groups with Bahians. For most of us, this was the first long-term, immersion-based fieldwork to which we had dedicated ourselves. I count myself immensely fortunate to have shared such beginnings.

While in the Anthropology program at Johns Hopkins University and in the years that followed, I was shepherded especially by Sidney Mintz and Gillian Feeley-Harnik, both of whom were and continue to be inspiring, gently prodding, and generous mentors. Along with them it was my enormous privilege to train under Emily Martin, Katherine Verdery, Ashraf Ghani, and Rolph Trouillot, and next to Erik Mueggler, Eric Rice, Bonnie McElhinny, and Ella Maria Ray, all anthropologists who embody the very best in relevant, committed scholarship, integrity, and friendship. Conversations with Brazilians and Brazilianists Jaqueline Pitanguey, Daniel Linger, John Russell-Wood, Kim Butler, Janaína Amado, Inês Alfano, Sonia Alvarez, Vitória Assis da Boa Morte, Cida Nowotny, Peter Blasenheim, Judy Bieber, Andrea Cornwall, Conni Gregor, Sonia John, J. Lorand Matory, and Heleieth Saffiotti were indispensable. Brazilian feminist activists in Bahia and other cities welcomed and aided me, among whom I would especially wish to thank Lena Souza, Rita Andrea, Cristina Rodrigues, and Kátia de Melo in Salvador; Maria Luisa Heilborn, Schuma Schumacher, Gary Barker, Marcos Nascimento, and Christine Ricardo in Rio de Janeiro; Marcia Dangremon and Cecy Prestrello in Recife; Marcia Farah Reis, Simone Diniz, Nalu Faria, Nilza Traci, and Teresa Virardo in São Paulo; Márcia Camargo in Rio Grande do Sul; and Monica Barroso, Fátima Dourado, and Lila Dourado in Fortaleza. This list is far from complete, but it begins to testify to the energy, openness and, yes, sisterhood that the Brazilian women's movement consistently and hospitably offered. The wealth of material they shared was sufficient fodder for a dozen books; I hope they recognize their experiences in this one.

Stalwart supporters at Colorado College have been Calla Jacobson, Margi Duncombe, Andrea Lucard, Tricia Waters, Mario Montaño, Jean Scandlyn, Amanda Udis-Kessler, Barabara Whitten, and Mike Hoffman; all, in different ways, helped me along on this project. Suzanne Ridings, Heloisa Guerreiro, Inês Alfano, Manuel Savage, Charles Cummings, Ann Brucklacher, and Noah Tamarkin assisted in various preparation tasks with able hands. Colleagues in the Department of Anthropology at Colorado College have been steadfast friends and supporters, and those in the Feminist and Gender Studies department have helped sustain passion for daily labors. The many wonderful students I have had the pleasure of working with at Colorado College have educated me about writing and reading ethnography; in a sense, this book is written with them in mind as readers. Despite so many having aided in the making of this book, any remaining short-comings in this work are my responsibility alone.

To the foundations and institutions that have generously supported phases of this research and writing, my utmost gratitude is due. At University of California Press, Stan Holwitz, Jacqueline Volin, Suzanne Copenhagen, and Randy Heyman have been patient, supportive, and enthusiastic in ways that made a difference. It has been my good fortune to receive the support of a John D. and Catherine T. MacArthur Foundation Professorship, a Charlotte Newcombe Dissertation Fellowship, a National Institute of Mental Health (Division of Violence and Traumatic Stress) National Research Service Award, a Wenner Gren Foundation for Anthropological Research Pre-Dissertation Grant, a Fulbright (Institute for International Education) Dissertation Research Abroad Fellowship, and support for internships from the Brazilian Fundo de Apoio a Pesquisa, through the Universidade Federal da Bahia. In this project's earliest phases, aid came from Ford Foundation Women's Studies Grants, the Atlantic History, Culture, and Society Program of the Johns Hopkins University, and an Institute of Intercultural Studies Research Grant.

Fieldworkers often grapple for words adequate to thank our "informants"—the members of communities that gradually admit us into their lives. Perhaps there are no such words. Because talking and writing about domestic violence can pose risks to victims, I am committed to the strict use of pseudonyms throughout this work; this unfortunately prevents me from thanking by name most of the people to whom I am especially indebted: policewomen and members of the communities I researched. I am able to thank some informants by name because they are public figures: the police *delegadas* Maria Célia Miranda, Isabel Alice de Pinho, and Iracema Silva de Santos, along with officers Tânia Mendonça and Jener Mululo. Each was far more receptive to my own, and I expect many other researchers', fly-on-the-wall presence in their workplaces than they had any obligation to be. Many others go unnamed: the people who fundamentally enabled this work to be carried out, who not only housed and helped feed but also tolerated and humored me. In particular, I would like to thank residents of the community I call Alto do Mungongo, the two adjacent communities along the Avenida Vasco da Gama that I studied, and members of the family I call "Bomfim." Finally, I thank the city Salvador da Bahia itself, where in waiting rooms and at bus stops and in homes and in taxis and waiting in line ad infinitum, people took the time to talk with me, sharing a "culture" with which I became hopelessly enraptured.

My heartfelt thanks go to Timothy Ferguson, my unfailingly supportive partner and generous friend, and to our daughters, Marley and Alair, who have tolerated "Mommy's very important papers" since they could think the words. My appreciation also goes to my father, Jim Hautzinger, who has supported my education and growth in so many ways.

I dedicate *Violence in the City of Women* to my mother, Sue O'Brien. A journalist and editor who bragged that she'd raised her children by the philosophy of "carefully supervised neglect," her highest expression of maternal love was reading and marking up everything I or my brothers ever wrote, from junior high research papers through doctoral work. She was unable to see this manuscript published, and we sorely miss her.

Portions of chapter 2 appeared previously in "Researching Men's Violence: Personal Reflections on Ethnographic Data," *Men and Masculinities* 6, no. 1 (2003): 93–106; and, in earlier form, in *Cultural Shaping of Violence: Victimization, Escalation, Response,* edited by Myrdene Anderson. © 2004 Purdue University Press. Reprinted by Permission. Unauthorized duplication not permitted.

Portions of chapters 4 and 5 appeared in earlier form in the following publications: "The Powers and Pitfalls of Gender Essentialism: Policing Male-to-Female Violence in Brazil," *Political and Legal Anthropology Review* 20, no. 2 (1997): 34–46. "Calling a State a State: Feminist Politics and the Policing of Violence against Women in Brazil," *Feminist Issues* 1–2 (1997): 3–30, © 1997 by Transaction Publishers; reprinted by permission of the publisher. "Criminalising Male Violence in Brazil's Women's Police Stations: Flawed Essentialism to Imagined Communities," *Journal of Gender Studies* 11, no. 3 (2002): 243–251 (http://www.tandf.co.uk/journals).

In the introduction, excerpts from Matthew Gutmann, "Trafficking in Men: The Anthropology of Masculinity"; Heleieth Saffiotti, *Gênero, Patriarcado, Violência*; Erik Mueggler, *The Age of Wild Ghosts*; Ruth Landes, *The City of Women*; Teresa Caldeira, *City of Walls*; and Allen Feldman, *Formations of Violence,* appear by permission.

In chapter 4, the excerpt from Cecília MacDowell Santos, "Delegacias da Mulher: Percursos e Percalços," appears by permission. In chapter 5, the excerpt from J. Lorand Matory, *Black Atlantic Religion: Tradition, Transnationalism, and Matriarchy in the Afro-Brazilian Candomblé,* appears by permission.

Brazilian states and regions

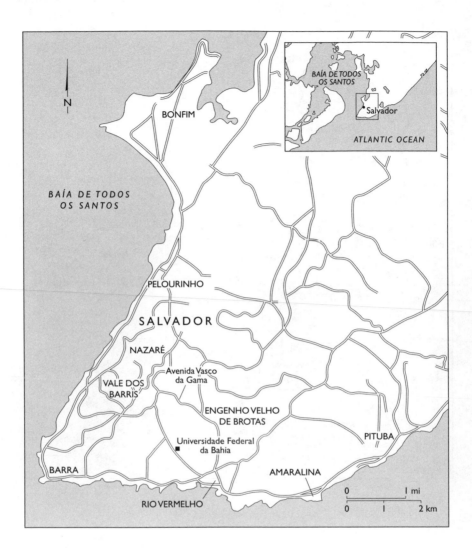

Metropolitan Salvador

Introduction

Violence in Salvador da Bahia, City of Women

Contrary to the assertion that men are made while women are born
(albeit "in the native's point of view") is the understanding that men
are often the defenders of "nature" and "the natural order of things,"
while women are the ones instigating change in gender relations and
much else.

MATTHEW GUTMANN
"Trafficking in Men: The Anthropology of Masculinity"

The people involved in a violent relationship should desire change.
For this reason, it's difficult to believe in a radical shift in a violent
relationship when you work exclusively with the victim. She suffers
through changes, while he remains as he always was, maintaining
the *habitus*—the relationship can even grow more violent. Everyone
perceives that the victim needs help, but few see this need on the
part of the aggressor. Both require assistance to promote a true
transformation in a violent relationship.

HELEIETH SAFFIOTTI
Gênero, Patriarcado, Violência

BEFORE THE ADVENT OF ITS women's police stations, Brazil suffered an
international reputation as a country where men who battered and even
murdered their wives could get away with it. This began to change in 1985,
when the newly elected state government of São Paulo created the first all-
female police station expressly for the purpose of registering, investigating,
and prosecuting diverse forms of male violence against women. At that
time, a variety of Brazilian women's groups, both feminist-identified and

not, played watchdog over courtroom processes and judicial decision making. They succeeded in installing multiple shelters, counseling services, and legal advocacy centers throughout the country through a combination of new governmental, nonprofit, and nongovernmental organizations' services. On a mass scale, these efforts rejected men's rights to hurt women physically, threaten them with violence, force them to have sex, or restrain their free movement. By 2004, stations specializing in attending to women numbered 339 (Santos 2004), having been installed in all twenty-three Brazilian states. However, 90 percent of the country's municipalities lacked specialized stations; and 61 percent of the women's stations were concentrated in the southeast, the country's wealthiest region, with the state of São Paulo alone claiming 125 (40.7 percent) of them. The state of Minas Gerais, just north of the states of Rio de Janeiro and São Paulo and also part of the southeast region, ran a distant second, counting 13 percent of the total number of stations.[1] Although the actual names of Brazilian all-women police stations vary from state to state, I will refer to them all as DMs, short for Delegacias da Mulher (Women's Police Stations) or, where context allows, simply *delegacias*.[2]

The principal rationale for instituting the DMs was to intervene in the impunity that male offenders typically experienced in the Brazilian law enforcement and legal system. For charges ranging from murder to sexual assault, wife-beating, and battery, scores of men in the 1970s had been absolved, and the feminist population was becoming ever more outraged. Ensuring that women were attended by female police, it was hoped, would alleviate the predominant male bias among police that kept complaints—the starting point of any criminal proceeding—from being taken seriously.

The women's *delegacias* are but one thread in the fabric of changing gender relations in Brazil. In the two decades plus since 1979, when the Brazilian feminist antiviolence project began in earnest, women's status has changed in staggering ways; women's groups have struggled for, and won, grudging gains in an impressive array of areas.

Even the military government (1964 to 1984), which tended to instrumentalize women as conservative reproducers of "tradition" and the status quo, responded to demands of the women's movement by making day care available as early as 1973, and family planning services by 1977 (Marques-Pereira and Raes 2005: 75, 78).[3] In the 1980s, feminist groups built on lessons learned under authoritarianism to seize the opportunities that democratization afforded. From the legal or extralegal extension of reproductive rights;[4] to the establishment of legal protections against violence, sexual harassment and assault, and double standards on adultery; to women's participation in the creation of women's councils at city, state, and national levels, women took hold of the decade. Between the International Year of Women in 1979 to Brazil's first democratic elections in 1984, the women's movement had emerged as the most organized and successfully opportunistic sector in the grassroots civilian opposition. This positioned feminist activists advantageously for the drafting of the National Constitution, ratified in 1988, in which women's groups succeeded in having 80 percent of their proposals written into law. Brazilian women moved to the forefront of international leadership in the women's movement in part through watershed conferences held in Rio de Janeiro in 1992 and Cairo in 1994. As women's groups worldwide prepared for Beijing's world conference on women in 1995, Brazilians held more than ninety events representing more than eight thousand organizations (Marques-Pereira and Raes 2005: 82). This level of preparation helped cement the international leadership role of Brazilian feminists and paved the way for the "NGOization" of the movement seen currently, in which municipal, state, and national councils contract out research and action projects to nongovernmental organizations (Alvarez 1998).

In virtually every area where women's rights activists have made inroads, however, the changes they achieved on paper or in policy continue to confront practical and ideological battles over implementation, enforcement, and regulation. Economic rights, long a hot-button issues for women's groups, present a prime example. Between 1976 and 2002 in Brazil, women working for wages outside the home went from 28 percent to close to 50 percent of the eligible female population, while men's participation stagnated at a problematic 75 percent of the eligible male population.[5] Protections against sex discrimination written into the 1988 National Constitution boldly asserted women's legal entitlement to economic equality. Nonetheless, the rise in remunerated labor has neither improved nor stabilized the situations of poor women, who still predominate in the lowest-paying work in both the formal and informal sectors and are subject to horizontal segregation (i.e., pink-collar jobs) and vertical segregation (glass ceilings, discriminatory practices against mothers, harassment). Currently, the statistically average Brazilian woman can expect to earn just 54 *centavos* to her male counterpart's *real,* the Brazilian currency (about one *real* to two U.S. dollars). In sum, activists have achieved many gains, but these are largely confined to policy, legal, and institutional changes, marshaled by intellectuals. To fulfill their potential to transform Brazil at its foundations, women of all echelons of the society require still more information about their rights, more experience in agitating for them, and greater volition to take greater leadership in governmental and civilian sectors.

The women's police stations, then, are merely the most novel result of women, as a group, producing analyses, generating demands, and exercising levels of agency unprecedented in Brazilian history. This book's assessment is that even after more than twenty years, Brazilian antiviolence institutional measures remain at their incipiency. With regard to gender-based violence, women have seen reforms in laws and policies that once ensured men's impunity, but they have barely begun to confront long-entrenched codes and scripts of machismo that reproduce patterned syndromes of violence against women on a cultural level, particularly within educational settings. The *delegacias,* however, have created contexts where this critical conversation can become focused and intensified.

One result has been to load expectations for DM policewomen with multiple contradictory meanings. Regardless of who the actual policewomen serving in the DMs were or what they believed or practiced, as representatives of executive state authority they came to symbolize feminized, newly democratic power in the public eye. They represented the possibility of the state's monopoly of force being put in service of some of Brazil's most vulnerable citizens. The experience of the women's *delegacias* chronicles a power shift in which women as a group articulated the need for a form of citizenship informed by their gendered position in society. The *delegacias* thereby created a precedent for the articulation of citizenship as non-"neutral," which pioneered pathways for other marginalized constituencies—Afro-Brazilians, the landless peasantry, the urban homeless—to use as well. By expressing women's rights first as human rights, and more recently as citizens' rights, women have repositioned themselves to make possible the exercise of authority, self-representation, and justice (Marques-Pereira and Raes 2005: 92).

When women question the violence and domination that many men seek to enforce, they strengthen the potential for genuine social transformation in the gendered organization of labor, space, and power. And yet, women's politicized questioning of their personal relationships simultaneously generates interpersonal conflict. When people are culturally conditioned to inherently link conflict and violence (as are most Brazilians and North Americans), more conflict inevitably translates into more violence. Therefore, the women's *delegacias* in Brazil present us with a problem of circularity. The DMs appear destined to be simultaneously a part of calling men's violence into question, and of the very questioning and contestation that can foment outbreaks of violence, particularly domestic violence. The story of the women's *delegacias,* then, puts Brazilians' relationship with violence itself on trial. It is about a people deeply disenchanted with the deadly costs of violent conflict searching for ways in which conflict can effect transformation toward social justice and gender equality, rather than merely sparking violence that further deepens oppression and inequality.

SITES

Much ethnographic writing finds place to be a container for social being or a surface on which social life is played out.

ERIK MUEGGLER
The Age of Wild Ghosts

This book is a tale of two places in one city: Salvador da Bahia, capital of the state of Bahia, the largest state in northeastern Brazil.[6] The first place, where my research began, was the city's sole all-women police station. I spent fourteen months of fieldwork in that *delegacia* between 1990 and 1999, collaborating with six student researchers. Together we administered a questionnaire to police officers, then followed up with dozens of interviews and informal conversations with police. Later in the research we concentrated on listening to complaints being lodged and depositions being held, as well as on interviewing women complainants and accused men, some of the latter through jail-cell bars. Since my stints of full-time fieldwork in the *delegacias* I have continued to pay long visits, observing hearings and catching up with police through 2006.

The research began in the DM, but the book begins with the second place, where I focused my later fieldwork. This place, a "popular" (nonelite) poor urban neighborhood I call the Alto do Mungongo, first became my home in 1993, when I moved with my partner from a middle-class setting into the community. For nine months then, and for additional months over four subsequent visits, I focused on understanding women and men "on the ground," locked in violent relationships. Three neighborhoods were in fact involved: the Alto do Mungongo, where I lived; an adjacent, similarly poor community; and a nearby housing development, where lower-middle and middle-class residents predominated. In 1993 and 1994, my Bahian collaborators and I employed rather formal methods, undertaking a long survey of twenty-five households in each community, and following up with semistructured interviews with individuals we believed had histories involving domestic violence. In 1995, we convened all-women and all-men focus groups, seeking general feedback about our findings. During later trips in 1999, 2005, and 2006 (and many phone calls throughout this period), I continued as a participant observer of these communities.

Viewing violent relationships in these community contexts, and especially observing how individuals in households, families, and neighborhood networks position themselves in relation to a couple's violence, showed me discernible patterns through which violence could escalate to the point that women sought out police intervention or, as they say, to "take providence" (*tomar providência*).

RUTH LANDES'S SALVADOR DA BAHIA AS "SETTING"

I know by now that women [in Bahia] are the chosen sex. . . . I take it for granted just as I know in our world that men are the chosen sex.

RUTH LANDES
The City of Women

Salvador da Bahia has been called the "Black Rome," because for many it represents the Afro-Brazilian capital not only of Brazil but arguably of the Americas as well. As such, the city itself becomes an undeniably influential "personality" in this inquiry.[7]

The anthropologist Ruth Landes, student of Franz Boas, conducted fieldwork in Salvador in 1938 and 1939 and eight years later published the monograph *The City of Women*. Landes's book took the form of a descriptive memoir, full of dialogue and personal reflection. She focused on how the ritual lives of women involved in Candomblé, an Afro-Brazilian spirit-possession religion, brought meaning and resources that helped them withstand the poverty and military repression of the period. She asserted that she had found a "cult matriarchate" (Landes 1940) in which "women ruled in the religious affairs, and therefore the most important affairs, of Bahian blacks" (Matory 2005: 191). Although in many ways her account anticipated by decades the literary turn in anthropological writing, at the time *The City of Women* was deemed at best a "very intelligent travel work" (Honigmann 1947) and a "tourist account" (Mishnun 1947). At worst it was vehemently "rejected as unscientific by the anthropological profession" (Melville J. Herskovits [1948], quoted in Cole 1994: viii).

Arguing that the work deserved a contemporary rereading, Sally Cole credits Landes with refus[ing] to produce an ethnographic portrait of candomblé (and Afro-Brazilian culture) as homogenous, integrated, and static, the then-standard approach among her professional peers. Instead, she described internal conflicts, dialogues, and contestations of meaning in a context of change and fluidity, and she situated Afro-Brazilian culture in the past—the history of colonial and nineteenth-century slavery and of the urbanization and proletarianization of Brazil. These characteristics, which located the book on the margins of anthropology in its day, are the very reasons we have for turning to it again at the end of the twentieth century. (1994: viii)

As Cole anticipated, Landes's view of Salvador indeed resonated with my own forays into the city fifty years later, as a later-generation North American anthropologist. In particular, Landes's conviction that there was something distinct about black Bahian women's relative autonomy, status, and power within the Candomblé networks she studied, while acknowledging the profoundly sexist and patriarchal backdrop of Brazilian society as a whole, has significance beyond Afro-Bahian religions for networks of marketers and street vendors, where women's control calls attention. Images of Landes as woman-tourist ethnographer similarly resound for me in cautionary ways, as I am ever conscious of myself as an outsider-anthropologist in many respects: a middle-class North American studying mostly working-class Brazilians, a white face in human landscapes of mostly brown faces, a woman often turning her focus to men. There are a number of Brazilian anthropologists (and other researchers) concerned with gender-based violence and the DMs who, as native anthropologists, write with more cultural intimacy than I can. Nonetheless, I hope to contribute a unique angle to a multivocal literature.[8] This is not meant apologetically: were I not convinced that outsider-insider perspectives productively synergize into the most holistic body of understanding possible, I could not embrace anthropology as my discipline.

What inspired Landes to dub Salvador "The City of Women"? She recounts a conversation with Nestor Duarte, a professor of law in Bahia: "He was writing a book on the history of the Negro woman in Brazil, and his studies had deeply impressed him with her independence and courage. . . . In his opinion, the Negro woman was an ennobling and modernizing influence in Brazil. She had always been self-reliant economically, in Africa as in slaveholding Brazil, and that combined with her eminence in the candomblé to give a matriarchal tone to family life among the poor. This was a desired balance, he thought, to the harsh dominance of men in all Latin life" (Landes 1994 [1947]: 75). Shortly after this conversation, Landes met renowned *mãe de santo* (Candomblé priestess, *iyalorixá*) Dona Menininha, who embodied all she could expect in a self-determining woman. As Duarte put it to Landes, though Menininha had a husband, a lawyer who was "as fair in complexion as she [was] dark," she was in no way dependent: "Dona Menininha supports herself, and I am sure her daughters will do the same even when they are married. That kind of woman has been independent for so long—for untold generations—that I cannot visualize her becoming dependent and shut in even after she climbs into middle-class life" (Landes 1994 [1947]: 76).

Landes's now-historic book anticipates many of the themes of this work, though my focus is on violence and not religion. I view Landes's impulse to elevate and romanticize women's roles, however, from critical perspectives. Although this work shares her concern with the significance of independent and indomitable women for men, masculinities, and violence, I do not assume that equating it with female dominance—matriarchy—even within micro-institutional settings, is necessarily accurate, or necessarily a good thing for men or women. I take seriously that the influence of Landes's proclamations led ethnographer J. Lorand Matory, in his recent work *Black Atlantic Religion: Tradition, Transnationalism, and Matriarchy in the Afro-Brazilian Candomblé,* to describe contemporary Bahia as "[t]he gendered minefield of post-Landean Bahia" (2005: 262) and to concur with criticisms that Landes constructed a "primitivist cliché" in her rendering (2005: 191).

In brief, Matory charges that Ruth Landes's work, alongside that of her Bahian colleague and collaborator Edison Carneiro, ignored evidence of the historical predominance or equivalence of male leaders in Candomblé (Butler 1998b; Harding 2000), and that she wrote dismissively about the significant number of important male priests who were their contemporaries, stating that these men were all passive homosexuals of secondary rank and importance (Matory 2005: 192). Carneiro, in Matory's reading, absorbed this homophobic perspective from Landes; having "apparently [felt] embarrassed by the pathologizing gaze of this powerful transnational visitor," he shifted from an earlier position of acceptance of and admiration for the male priest who could become possessed to "condemning them for 'giving themselves up to homosexuality, where they take the passive role, dropping into the small gossip typical of lower-class women'" (2005: 197).

The influence of Landes's depreciation of men to elevate women "has placed the Candomblé priesthood within the force field of Western feminism, powerfully affecting the options and life chances of Afro-Brazilian men and women," Matory writes (2005: 205). He builds on the life story of Candomblé *pai de santo* (male Candomblé leader, *babalorixá*) and his own close personal friend Pai Francisco to illustrate the real marginalization of men to which the Landean legacy has contributed. Pai Francisco is disadvantaged by his "dying" Jeje nation (a Candomblé subgroup), as well as his light skin (despite family involvement in Candomblé going back to his Afro-Bahian great-great-grandmother [2005: 232]). Unlike the "great Quêto mothers," who have capitalized on opportunities for state and wealthy patrons' sponsorship through promoting the matriarchal exclusivity of Candomblé (2005: 204, 259), Pai Francisco has struggled materially to fulfill the calling of his *orixá* Xangô because of his increasing marginalization as a male possession priest. Pai Francisco himself happens not to be "a viado" (gay; 2005: 234), yet like all male priests he has unjustly suffered, in Matory's reading, from the homophobic images Landes and Carneiro propagated and the resultant feminization of many Candomblé temples in the service of immensely effective strategic claims of greater authenticity, purity, and Africanness.

The force of Landes's matriarchal imagery has been fomented in part by subsequent transnational feminist texts, such as those by historian Kim D. Butler (1998a, 1998b) and religious studies scholar Rachel Harding (2000), which emphasized Candomblé's power as "an exemplar of black women's power in particular" (Matory 2005: 200). In asking about the significance of Bahian women's power for gendered violence, this work inevitably engages such transnational feminist discourse, and in some ways amplifies it. But like so many authorial decisions, my choice to invoke Landes's vision of Salvador as the "City of Women" has polemical elements. My strategy is no more to enshrine Bahian women as matriarchs than it is to ratify portrayals of Bahia as a place especially advantageous to women. Salvador da Bahia might be just as reasonably be called *no* city for women— not to mention children and men—particularly from empirical materialist or feminist perspectives. Women's "powers" in a place like Bahia might just as reasonably be termed survival strategies, particularly when they are measured primarily in terms of men's marginalization and disempowerment. (Households led by women or reliant soley on women's earnings, for example, are hardly "empowered" when their children remain destitute and undereducated.) Rather, I do seek to plumb the diverse meanings and effects of women's autonomy and relative power, which I believe stand out as legitimate issues in Bahian culture. Referring to Salvador da Bahia as the

City of Women, then, might be called a romanticization, but I would argue that this is less a *false* romanticization than one that is self-conscious and selective, begging questions about how specific forms of feminized power, fueled by cultural practices, may serve as resources for resisting men's violence and domination.

In light of these historical currents, Salvador may be viewed as a setting where two currents of feminized power converged through the 1990s: The first was relatively new, an artifact of the contemporary feminist movement and measures to criminalize violence against women during redemocratization. The second, to the extent it is valid, had much deeper historical roots, grounded in an alchemy of African influences, the effects of centuries of slavery, and continuous struggles for survival in the midst of chronic poverty, racial discrimination, and social marginalization. Matory's (2005) treatment reminds us to be attentive to how transnational feminist scholarship itself can have a role in constructing, and reifying, Bahian gendered relations. Each of these discourses about women's empowerment might be considered versions of what Freire [1978] optimistically called the "power of the oppressed." The most intriguing question, perhaps, is why, or whether (and under what conditions), these survival strategies function as "power" at all.

SALVADOR AS A CITY OF WALLS

Can we conceive of a model that can leave space for the proximity of bodies and sensuality and yet enforce respect for privacy, individuality, and human rights? . . . Is there a model that protects people's bodies and enforces individual rights while maintaining the indeterminacy of borders that constitutes the democratic public space?

TERESA CALDEIRA
City of Walls

Today, Salvador is a city increasingly known to tourists, and is now second only to Rio de Janeiro as a destination for international travelers.[9] Brazilians flock there in search of the essence of Brazil's colonial past, as though pilgrimages to Bahia were a key to knowing what it is to be Brazilian. Salvador's *carnaval* rivals the fame of Rio de Janeiro's: it is considered more participatory and *popular,* of the people and of the street, and less identified with pageantry, samba clubs, and exclusive balls (Dunn 2001). The city also draws international travelers for its renowned history and for regional festivals for important local saints such as Bonfim, Conçessão, São João, and

Figure 1. Centro Histórico (Historic City Center) of Salvador. Photo by Sarah Hautzinger.

Sant'Ana. Candomblé, the spirit possession-based religion, is far from the only distinctively Afro-Bahian cultural practice of note: food made with African *dendê* palm oil such as *moqueca, acarajé,* and *caruru* epitomize Bahia's taste and smell. *Capoeira,* the now internationally recognized martial art/dance form, is thought to have developed first among slaves on Bahian sugar plantations, and the number of academies continues to grow rapidly in Salvador, elsewhere in Brazil, and internationally.

The name Salvador da Bahia is shortened from Salvador da Bahia de Todos os Santos, Savior of the Bay of All Saints. During the colonial era, Salvador served as capital of the Portuguese empire for over two hundred years, from 1549 until 1763, when the crown moved the royal court from Lisbon to Rio de Janeiro as a protection from Napoleonic forces. Painted tiles, ornate ironwork, and ceramic rooftops fill the city's colonial districts, widely thought to evidence the best seventeenth- and eighteenth-century architecture of the New World. Today, in the *cidade alta* (high city), where the Portuguese built the city's first buildings atop a cliff for protection from seafaring marauders, sixteenth-century walls and foundations can still be found. Even the geographical fortressing of the city on the cliff did not secure it, though, for over Brazil's first three centuries post-contact,

Salvador would come under Portuguese, Dutch, French, Spanish, and British control, not to mention that of pirates of diverse nationalities.

The icon most readily associated with Salvador is arguably the *baiana de acarajé*. Whereas a *baiana* is simply a female Bahian, a *baiana de acarajé* peddles *acarajé* and *abará*, fried and steamed bean cakes, respectively, served with shrimp and a cashew paste, tomatoes, and onions. Often, these peddlers sell a sweet of coconut or peanut-brittle as well. The archetypical *baiana de acarajé* is a quite plump and dark-skinned woman, but I have seen transgendered *baianas*, white *baianas*, and emaciated *baianas*, and the occasional man's-man *baiano*, selling *acarajé* and *abará* on the streets of Salvador. They set up shop on street corners in every neighborhood, rich or poor. In the relatively elite neighborhood of Amaralina, *baianas de acarajé* may sit in an arc of seven or eight along the beach wall, their sumptuous, white skirts of lace and linen billowed out by the petticoats and hoops beneath, and on their heads turbans of richly colored silk, often woven with glistening metallic threads. *Baianas de acarajé* in humbler neighborhoods may wrap their heads in plainer cloths, and their skirts may dispense with the lace, hoops, and petticoats; still, the white linen and covered head are ubiquitous.

Regardless of neighborhood, *baianas* wear long strands of beads about their necks, known as *guias* (literally, guides). In theory, the *guias* reveal which *orixá* (god) of Candomblé is the *dona/o da cabeça*, (the owner of her head), or which god she serves and, perhaps, is possessed by during a Candomblé *festa* (celebration/ritual). Thus, the *baiana de acarajé* by day is typically a *filha de santo* (daughter of saint; a Candomblé devotee) in her home life, or perhaps even a *mãe de santo* (mother of saint; a Candomblé leader).[10] For Brazilians, the element of Candomblé is as important an association with Salvador as the *acarajé* itself.

I describe the *baiana de acarajé* at some length here because these visual icons of the city also embody many of the structural features that afford women unique positions in Salvador. *Baianas* control aspects of the informal economy that, while highly lucrative only in exceptional cases, provide ongoing, relatively constant income. Aside from the predominantly female merchant networks, *baianas* involved in religious networks such as those of Candomblé create for themselves another buffer from being isolated by or wholly dependent on a male partner (cf. Burdick 1990). Finally, the cultural prestige Bahians accord *baianas*, the appreciation of their grace, work ethic, and ability to literally feed the city through the years, derives from a distinctly Afro-Bahian aesthetic and pride. As I will discuss at length, all of

Figure 2. *Baianas de acarajé* selling food at night. Photo by Sarah Hautzinger.

these factors tie into the so-called "matrifocal" kinship features of many Bahian families.

In the late 1980s and early 1990s, when I began traveling to Salvador, one could have described the core of the city as spatialized by class (excluding the ever-expanding *periferia,* made up largely of migrant newcomers). The old, upper city included the crumbling walls of the old Pelourinho (literally "whipping post"), where slaves were once sold, and adjacent Maciel, where 70 percent of the adults of working age have been documented as participating in the sex trade (Espinheira 1971, 1984). Back then, these neighborhoods were abject slums by night and much of the day. The middle class lived in newer neighborhoods: Barra, Graça, Rio Vermelho, Pituba, and Itapoa, generally on the ocean side of the bay where the better beaches were found.

The spatialization of the poor in the older neighborhoods and the wealthy in more recently built places changed dramatically through the 1990s, as the historic district of the *cidade alta,* high city, passed into a dramatically accelerated phase of globalization. Beginning in 1992, a massive renovation and preservation project, funded with state and international contributions, was launched to make over the historic district. The preservation effort fell under much criticism, however, when the Bahian state governmental agency in charge permanently removed over six hundred indigent families, offering minimal aid in relocation. The renovation has benefited many local cultural groups, *blocos de carnaval* (carnival clubs), and other artists, but also multinational retailers, as large stretches of real estate are devoted to ubiquitous chains such as United Colors of Benetton, Betel Electronics, and L & M Gem Wholesalers.

In Bahia, as in other "cultural showcase" cities in developing countries that depend on international tourism amid highly visible poverty, a gaping divide exists between spaces secured for the comfort and safety of the middle class and the spaces where the poor retreat to their humbler homes. During carnival this line becomes the ropes that keep the paying partiers in their *blocos* and those who cannot pay pushed to the edges of the street. During the rest of the year, the class line—an invisible wall—falls between Salvador's historic district and elite beach communities, the *bairros nobres* (noble neighborhoods) on the one hand, and working-class neighborhoods and *favelas* (slums) on the other.[11] This wall traverses the "two Brazils," the extremes of wealth and poverty, and it can be found in every Brazilian city.[12] Poor and rich intermingle because there are many places where *favela* and "noble" spaces interpenetrate, but especially because so many poor work as service providers in the homes and neighborhoods of middle-class employers. Workers' movement into noble neighborhoods is not reciprocated, however; most middle-class employers have never visited the homes of their domestic and other service providers, who typically live in distant, marginalized, and often improvised and semilegal neighborhoods.

In the humbler neighborhoods, shopping is more likely to take place in an open air *feira* (fair) than in a newer *supermercado* (supermarket). Goods and services for sale become far more homogeneous, as large packages of everything are broken up and sold individually at slightly higher prices to accommodate hand-to-mouth consumers. Where "have-nots" scale muddy paths up hillsides to reach their homes, "haves" use driveways with access by car, often in well-protected apartment house garages. Have-nots may work as security guards behind walls cemented with broken bottles, placed shards up, all along the top; haves are the ones guarded and escorted, and the wealthiest of these are aware of themselves as potential kidnapping targets for ransom (Brazil leads the world in financially motivated kidnappings). The have-nots must know how to survive "off-grid": to make *gatos*—illegal hook-ups (but literally, "cats") into power and water lines, or to make dozens of calls on a live calling card that a friend turns up. The alternative, usually, is to do without these resources.

Figure 3. Self-built structures and high-rises intermingled.
Photo by Sarah Hautzinger

In Brazil, the term *marginal* is commonly used in the newspapers'
sections on crime to mean "criminal." *Marginalidade*—marginality—is
broader, including those who are marginalized from society, disallowed
from participating in "normal" life, whether this means the formal economy, social respectability, or lawful citizenship. The ambiguity in the word
prefigures endemic conflict, wherein poverty itself is frequently criminalized. Salvador, where the spaces showcased for outsiders' eyes are often false
fronts, is a city where the *marginais* (the plural of *marginal;* those living in
the margins in the class-based sense of the term), depending on what one

means by the term, could represent the numeric majority.[13] As I have been reminded each time a poor friend has had to go into a *bairro nobre* (noble neighborhood) to pick up a parcel I've sent through someone traveling to Brazil and has been questioned with hostility, people who "look like" *marginais* (generally looking both more indigent and darker-skinned) may be automatically suspect in middle-class spaces. It is not surprising that many poorer Bahians self-protectively prefer to stay on their side of the invisible wall that crisscrosses the city.

FIELDWORK ON THE OTHER SIDE OF THE WALL: ALTO DO MUNGONGO AS TWENTY-FIRST-CENTURY QUILOMBO

Moving to the Alto do Mungongo was a leap from one side of the wall to the other, a distinct vantage point from which to understand Bahians' lives. From the once-elegant old house, a respectable address on a named street where we had lived with other foreign researchers and students, Tim and I moved into a *morro* (a hill-neighborhood). Our friend in the next neighborhood joked that we'd joined him in the *güeto* (ghetto). If they used the term *favela*—slum—as much in Salvador as they do in other parts of Brazil, it would have been used for the Mungongo.

I'd been looking for the right neighborhood for months, visiting many all across Salvador and its periphery. When a neighbor we knew decided to make a break from her mother's home and rent out a little house in the Alto do Mungongo, within walking distance from where we had been living, I called off the search. She knew of another one-room dwelling we might rent out there. Suddenly, the undistinguished, close-by little neighborhood made more sense than the places I had been visiting. The cross-over from what political scientist Guillermo O'Donnell (1993: 1359) has called a "blue zone," where the state's high degree of presence effectively sustains the rule of law and regulates behaviors and economics, to a "brown zone," where illicit markets, vigilante law, improvised housing, and illegal taps into electricity and water are the norm, literally entailed crossing an avenue and a short walk.[14]

Despite the residents' sense that the place they lived was unique, the Alto do Mungongo could have been any of the dozens of small communities, most of them nameless clusters of houses, along the Avenida Vasco da Gama. Vasco da Gama was a thoroughfare that, although one of the most important in the city, was considered an eyesore. The once crystalline stream that ran between its opposing lanes of traffic was now little more than an open, reeking sewage canal. The Avenida's eyesore status was confirmed when city officials conspired not to let foreign dignitaries drive through when the Ibero-Latin American talks were held in Salvador in 1993. In 1995, a large supermarket chain opened a store right across the avenue from the traditional marketplace. Most residents thought that the traditional market would not survive for long, although it continues to limp along. More recently, people in the Alto make frequent references to being bought out at less-than-replacement prices for housing, or simply being forced out by bulldozers preparing the ground for middle-class high rises. Somehow, an unconscious consensus has been reached that their time there is almost up; poor people can scarcely keep a foothold in such a desirable location, close to downtown and to the beach.

From the beginning, I found it significant that the avenue concentrated many of the city's auto-service shops. Alhough only a small fraction of the zone's humble residents could afford cars themselves, a significant number of the area's men were employed fixing the cars of the city's better-off inhabitants. For the middle class, neighborhoods along Vasco da Gama were conduits through which to get from one place to another, but with little "placeness" of their own.

Neighborhoods elsewhere in the city I'd considered featured well-defined boundaries and often impressive internal organization, with *associações de moradores* (neighborhood associations), *clubes de mães* (mother's clubs), multiple churches, and neighborhood health clinics. They were also much larger, some with populations into the tens of thousands. By contrast, the Alto do Mungongo was little more than a tumble of some three hundred houses, built one atop of another at ever denser and more inventive angles. Wealthier Brazilians, falling prey to none of the mystique that foreigners like myself may initially harbor about such places, ranged from wary to repulsed at the prospects of life in such a setting. On several occasions elite friends entered such communities for the first time in their lives to visit us, the resident gringos. During the long days of summer, when water pressure was insufficient to reach the houses uphill from our own, such friends might witness an endless parade of girls as young as three years old (joined by only the youngest boys) having to trek down and up, down and up again, portaging water in buckets, pots, and used plastic soft drink containers. During the wet season, when the inadequate system was swollen with heavy rains, they might scramble to avoid raw sewage flowing down the paths. Like us, they tried not to balk at babies' skin ravaged with scabies, their lingering coughs that went untreated, or the many older children who sat home for lack of books to take to school, often locked indoors as their mothers boarded buses to clean homes or wash clothes for middle-class families. Hardships outweighed delights in such a place. Despite the thrill of booming, late-night samba band sessions or the delights of *caruru* feasts honoring children, any temptation to romanticize poverty was quickly squelched. Still, as outsiders, we experienced feelings of discovery as once-foreboding, twisting pathways disappearing into the dark gradually grew familiar.

The choice of the Alto do Mungongo seemed a good one for a neighborhood study, but I remained apprehensive. How did I expect to approach people and talk about an issue as sensitive and explosive as domestic violence without being seen as intrusive, and alienating the people I wished to come to know? It was one thing to begin conversations about women getting beat up in the *delegacia,* a place designed to attract such cases. But would such conversations be feasible in a place where I was living day and night and where everyone knew one another?

As would no doubt have been the case in whatever other hamlet I might have chosen, one family came to especially capture my participant-observer attention. This family, whom I here call the *família do Bomfim* (literally the family of the Good End), was by any account the central family of the Alto do Mungongo. All of the houses surrounding the tiny central plaza—itself little more than a clearing with an old, contaminated well—at one time belonged to one or another in the Bomfim family, many of which were rented out to tenants. This family had been in the area the longest—for at least six generations, counting today's children—and had once claimed the entire plot of approximately ten acres. Other Mungongo residents who owned the plots upon which their houses were built had, without exception, at some point purchased them or gotten permission to build from members of this family. Often, residents newer to the Mungongo, who built larger, well-constructed houses up hill, seemed to prosper through the years beyond members of the Bomfim family, whose internal divisions did not aid their individual fortunes.

The widow's dance hall, a *barracão* (literally "big shed") of plaster and lath and a ceramic-tiled roof, adjoined the bar run by her only daughter, and doubled as a *terreiro de Candomblé* (Candomblé temple). A central place was given to the *peji* (altar) where figures of the *orixás* (Candomblé deities) were kept, along with their respective *otás*—stones dedicated to each *orixá,* through which the deities are "fed" with blood from animal sacrifices or foods to their liking. As the widow aged and the bar seemed to become a stronger focus of social life than was the *terreiro,* the saints' houses outside the *barracão* grew more and more neglected, the roofs falling in and debris piling on the altars.

Adults who had grown up in the Mungongo remembered Almiro, after whom my godson was named, as the patriarch of the family, as "a real African from Africa itself, who spoke African to you all day and you had no idea what he was saying." Other family members corrected the story by specifying that the *babalorixá* (a revered *pai-de-santo,* priest of Candomblé) Almiro was born in the Mungongo, as was his father before him. It was this elder Almiro's grandfather who was "the African" who first settled in what is now the Mungongo.

Stories of the neighborhood's early origins varied. One of the widow's sons held fast that his great-grandfather—the "real African"—was one of the survivors from a famed shipwreck that had occurred off the coast off Rio Vermelho not far away. He had been destined for the slave markets of Salvador but because of the shipwreck was able to escape to what is now the Mungongo. He took an indigenous Tupinambá woman as a wife, and set about producing children at the site where his descendants remain to this day. The accuracy of this story is in doubt, given that the shipwreck he refers to occurred between 1509 and 1511 and involved a French trading ship that was unlikely to be transporting Africans being sold into slavery.[15] Moreover, the widow's husband died at the age of eighty-four in 1970, an age that placed his birth just two years before Brazilian abolition in 1888. Therefore, many more generations of Bomfins would have had to have lived in the Mungongo to place the family's origins back into the early sixteenth century than the reported two generations thought to have preceded the elder Almiro.

One family member specifies the ethnicity of the founder ancestor as Jeje Marrim, I was also told Jeje Mundombé; both are difficult to reconcile with sources that suggest that all the early *terreiros* of Candomblé in the area were of Quêtu origin, but all agree that today the widow's Candomblé is Quêtu.[16] Memories of the Jeje ancestor include that of a being of "superior, more developed" stock: "They were *kings* in Africa, not just common folk," the widow's son told me. This, he claimed, endowed the Afro-Brazilians of this part of the city with exceptional beauty and abilities, especially with respect to artistic talents. They were able to build a powerful culture here because their culture in Africa had been especially distinguished. He spoke of the "*auto-poder da cultura*" (the culture's own potency), and indicated that the tenacity of this Jeje culture was exceptional. "Walk around this city, and you don't see the kind of developed *negros* (Afro-Brazilians, the preferred term) that you see in this zone, all up and down the *avenida*." The son's arguments may presume more future continuity with his co-ethnics for one escaped Jeje than seems plausible; today the area is noted for its unrivaled number of the city's Quêto ritual specialists, who comprised the earliest cluster of uni-ethnic Candomblés in the city (Verger 1993; Rego 1993; Butler 1998b; P. Johnson 2002; Matory 2005).

The widow's daughter's account of the neighborhood's past and how it involved her family jibes more easily. She understood that long ago (she could provide no dates) two Africans were being delivered to the slave market at Concessão, when they escaped. One of them absconded to what is now the Mungongo, which then was *puro mato fechado* (completely closed jungle), even though today the growth of the city has engulfed it and it is now fairly close to the city center. As in her brother's account, the fugitive ancestor married an indigenous woman and established the *aldeia* (village), along with the *terreiro* (temple) of Candomblé, where they stand today.

She affirmed that her father, the *babalorixá* Almiro, did in fact speak fluent "Africano," but he also spoke Portuguese without an accent.[17] Eventually, the family gained legal title to the land, and although developers had tried to buy them out several times, they had always refused.

Although I've had difficulty reconstructing historical details about the Alto do Mungongo, I mention the widow's children's accounts for their significance as family and neighborhood "myths of origin," revealing a proud collective identity centered around defiance of, and indeed as a specific exception to, the history of enslavement and subjugation that infuses most Afro-Bahian family histories. The major point on which the siblings' accounts concurred was that the Mungongo was founded by a free African, a refugee from slavery. Such exceptionalist stories can be so common that it is prudent to remember that they understandably hold revisionist appeal to many black Bahians; although many may not be based upon historical fact, assuredly some are. Neither brother nor sister offered terms such as *quilombo* (a Brazilian maroon community, or settlement of escaped slaves) or *mocambo* (a *quilombo* around old Salvador; Schwartz 1996: 211; Bastide 1996), but when I asked whether the word described the community's derivation, both excitedly affirmed that, yes, the Mungongo's origins were along such a line. The straw house shown in figure 4 is sug-

Figure 4. "Casa de Palha" (straw house) near the Alto do Mungongo, ca. 1900. Photo reproduced with the permission of the Bibliotcca Juracy Magalhães Jr., Rio Vermelho.

gestive of how the community may have appeared in the decades following the Alto do Mungongo's founding.

GENDER-BASED VIOLENCE IN A "WOMAN'S" CITY

Ruth Landes's World War II–era assessment of Salvador's gender relations in *The City of Women* (1994 [1947]) was not out of keeping with perceptions of later anthropologists and historians, who have also commented upon the power and autonomy its black women commanded, almost always through their association with Candomblé or women's marketing networks (Lima 1977; Graden 1998; Wimberly 1998; Butler 1998a). Some anthropologists have even viewed Bahian women as problematically emasculating to men, as when anthropologist Klaas Woortman argued that Afro-Bahian women's relative economic and social autonomy may exacerbate a sense of failed masculinity in their male partners, thus leading at times to their violently lashing out against their spouses. In metaphorical terms, Woortman observed, "Here the cock does not crow, for he is not the lord of the land"

(1987: 21; also Neuhouser 1989). He found poor Afro-Bahians in general to share a sense of "subjective marginality" that exacted a particularly heavy toll from men, "strongly inhibit[-ing them] from fulfilling roles of masculinity as defined in the dominant culture" (1987: 21). The poverty of these men disallowed aspects of their ability to "be macho"—for their wives earned more consistent income, fed and clothed their children, and called their men weak—"she talks just to talk, to humiliate him, because she knows very well that good jobs are few." With firm footing in neither the labor force nor the family, poor men's identities could be especially destabilized and precarious. Reports such as Landes's that trumpet black women as dominant matriarchs can, as we have seen, further undermine men's roles and importance in their communities.

Paradoxically, the northeast region is stereotypically that which produces the most macho, bullying, and abusive of Brazilian men. Without negating Woortmann's basic intention, my research supports an alternative proposition, more in keeping with clashing machos and indomitable women: it is precisely when a "rooster" feels his masculine identity threatened that he may begin to "crow" and puff, and that part of this performance may involve assaulting his female partner, resorting to violence as a compensating "resource" for power and control.[18]

How does one resolve the seemingly contradictory trends of resistant, indomitable women on one hand, and domineering, bullying men on the other? Much of the violence between men and women in Bahia arises not solely from men's use of violence to dominate, I argue, but also from men reacting to women's contestation and rejection of male dominance. Salvador's strong women and its association with some of the highest per capita indices of registered incidents of domestic violence in the country appear as irreconcilable facts, but only when one assumes that violence is *always* ultimately a question of female subjugation. Viewing violence, at least in part, as a problematic *symptom* of changing gender roles resolves this contradiction.

During the 1990s, Bahian "roosters" appeared particularly under siege. In Brazil, a key ingredient to successful masculinity, and to cementing women's dependence, is men's role as primary breadwinner for families. However, between 1981 and 1998, the percentage of women considered economically active rose 111 percent, whereas that of men rose just 40 percent. New jobs went to women four times to men's one (Nogueira 2004: 9).

Thus, Brazilian women's gains in the labor market could, in part, be read as men's losses. However, as discussed earlier, in Brazil as in other Latin American countries, the benefits of the expanding labor market for women are hampered by women's comparatively low wages, the fact that women's jobs are disproportionately part-time and with minimal or no benefits, and the continued tendency to see women's income as supplemental to the presumed primary wage of a male-partner breadwinner (Safa 1995, Elhers 1991, 2000; Stolcke 1991: 97). In Brazil, over half of new jobs going to women between 1983 and 1998 were low-paying positions, and just under half were considered "extremely low" (*baixíssimos;* Noronha 2004).[19] Again, Brazilian women still earn just 54 *centavos* for each *real* paid to men. Black women's income is doubly damned, as a recent study of São Paulo's workforce showed: In 2001, the average monthly income of white men was R$874 (R$ = Brazilian *reais*); for white women it was R$583; for black men it was R$422; and for black women it was R$296. The average monthly income for families with children that had a black woman as the primary earner was R$162.00, with 71.3 percent of women and 55.1 percent of men receiving up to two minimum-wage salaries as income (Nobre 2003). Women workers remain concentrated in three sectors: 46 percent of the female labor force is composed of domestic, rural, and commercial workers (Marques-Pereira & Raes 2005: 87).

Thus, although women may be gaining footholds compared to men, and women's jobs, including those in the informal market, have proved to be more resilient (Palazzini 1995), these "gains" have come at a cost. They don't necessarily translate into greater security to meet basic needs, but rather into more women working longer hours for scarcer total family wages. The loads of working women's "double day" *(duplo jornada)* are far from lightened: women still shoulder the majority of domestic work and child care, even as working mothers often leave their children unsupervised in unsafe conditions in the absence of adequate child care. Wage-earning women may be less subject to direct male control or violence, something particularly true for the 37.5 percent of households in Salvador headed by women.[20] Still, considering women's low pay, income differentials by sex, and the difficulties involved in providing for and raising children in female-headed households, caution should be exercised before celebrating such households as a remedy or corrective to traditional gender hierarchies (Stolcke 1991: 100; Machado and Noronha 2002).

Many Bahian men practice polygyny, sustaining long-term unions with more than one woman, which may contribute to keeping them on the periphery of matricentric households, where they become undependable, and eventually nonessential, members. Afro-Bahian polygyny often goes hand in hand with so-called "matrifocal" kinship organization, evident throughout Afro-Caribbean populations and including former plantation-based slavocracies such as northeastern Brazil, where the dyadic bond of greatest importance is that between mother and child, rather than that between conjugal partners (Smith 1973; Monagan 1985). In these families, where women "attain a central position by default," analysts have underlined how "men fail"—to support the family, to sustain a strong presence in the home—while "women make due" (Kerns 1997: 3).

Historically sensitive analysts agree that African institutional structures could not survive the ravages of slavery intact (Mintz and Price [1976] 1992). At the same time, on an ideological level the continuation of models of African-influenced kinship is plausible. For Salvador, Woortman (1987) points to the polygyny (and agnatically based lineages) of Yoruba-Nagô groups (the most important of which, in Bahia, was Quêto). Polygynous family structures, he argues, have a predisposition toward matrifocality, particularly where women command significant power, as in historic reports of Yoruba women (Matory 1994; Mintz 1971a). It remains an open question as to what degree the matrifocality in the African American diaspora bears imprints of Africa. What we do know is that current kinship patterns result at least in part from slavery having forced a certain matrifocal component upon Africans and their descendants in bondage, because the paternity of slaves never received juridical recognition, among other factors. Factors such as the laws pre- and postabolition regarding marriage and family preservation, inheritance laws, the freedom of movement afforded men versus women, and access to remunerated work also merit consideration. It is likely that the current patterns evident in Bahia result from some combination of the effects of the recent history of slavery and cognitive or ideological West African influences. Bahia's distinct combination of men's multiple unions *and* matrifocality, against a Brazilian mainstream that rejects such arrangements, creates a climate particularly ripe for conflict and contestation between men and women.

There is some evidence, however, that Afro-Brazilian men, alongside their Afro-Caribbean counterparts, possess ways of conceiving of their masculine identities that are less reliant upon female dependence than are those of their Euro-Brazilian counterparts. Sidney Mintz, for example, proposes that women's power need not pose inherent threats to men and masculinity. He postulates that in diverse Caribbean locales where Afro-Caribbeans comprise the majority, economically active women and men operate through "separate risk structures," noting that this allows "men to accept women's independent participation in a separate risk structure without feeling threatened *as men*" (1981: 530, also 1971a). In other words, a powerful or economically successful woman need not automatically imply some deficit in her male partner's masculinity. Regardless of their origins, masculinities that allow for women's autonomy and success may provide a critical resource in reshaping men's ways of being powerful that do not rely upon violence.[21]

RACE AND AFRO-BRAZILIANS IN BRAZIL

Race and racism in Brazil present complex problems whose scope extends from Brazil's historical self-idealization as a "racial democracy" on the one hand, and on the other its notoriety as a place where racism is pernicious and dialogue on race is repressed (Goldstein 2003; Sheriff 2000; Twine 1998; Hanchard 1994).[22] The anthropologist Darcy Ribeiro asserts that for Brazilians, nationality itself provides the foremost "ethnic" identity: "When one says: our *negros*, the reference is to skin color; when one speaks of *mestiços*, one points to this secondarily. But the relevant thing is that we are Brazilians, a general quality that transcends its particularities" (1995: 133). Many a guidebook or film for popular audiences extols the blend of European, African, and Indigenous into Brazil's counterpart to Mexico's *raça cósmica* (cosmic race). Despite the sense of three equal parts harmoniously blending, my ordering of the terms—first European, second African, and third Indigenous, is not arbitrary. Rather, it reflects how most Brazilians themselves represent their racial composition as majority-white and Euro-Brazilian, when alternative readings are equally plausible.

In the 2000 demographic census 53.7 percent of Brazilians report themselves as *branca*, white. Although just 6 percent of all Brazilians self-report as *preta*, black, it is instructive to note that when the *preta* category is added to that of *parda*—meaning brown or mulatto—the national figure for Brazilians of at least some Afro-Brazilian descent reaches 44 percent (see table 1).

By summing the two categories that include descendants of at least partial African ancestry, I do not wish to imply that such calculations reveal some "racial actuality" of significance. In fact, simplistic typologies ignore the complex, shifting, and context-sensitive terminologies for color and features that Brazilians employ. Up to 116 racial or color terms were recorded outside Salvador in 1971 (Sanjek 1971), and 492 terms were collected in the 1960s in multiple sites (Harris 1970). Many of these terms are still in use, as are practices that may categorize the same person by multiple "racial" categories or assign full siblings to wholly different "races" (cf. Kottak 1992: 13). Similarly,

TABLE I
Regional distribution of population "by color" *(por côr)*
In percentages

Region of Residence	*Branca* (White)	*Preta* (Black)	*Parda* (Mulatto)	*Preta* and *Parda* (Part African-Brazilian)	Other (Asian and Indigenous)
Brazil	100	54	6	38	44	<1
Northeast[a]	28	33	8	58	66	<1
Southeast[b]	43	62	7	29	36	<1
South[c]	15	84	4	11	15	<1
Other regions[d]	15	39	5	54	59	3

SOURCE: Censo Demográfico 2000, Instituto Brasileiro de Geografia e Estatística.

NOTE: Percentages are rounded to the nearest whole number.

[a] The northeast region comprises Bahia, Sergipe, Alagoas, Pernambuco, Paraíba, Ceará, Piauí, Rio Grande do Norte, and Maranhão.

[b] The southeast region comprises São Paulo, Rio de Janeiro, Espírito Santo, and Minas Gerais.

[c] The south region comprises Paraná, Santa Catarina, and Rio Grande do Sul.

[d] This table omits the two least populated regions: north (seven states, 7.6 percent of national population) and central west (three states and Federal District, 6.85 percent).

although early assertions that racial discrimination was merely an epiphenomenon of classism have been discredited, long-standing observations that racial identity and identification is bound up with class, as in the expression that "money whitens," may still hold relevance (Goldstein 2003: 106).

A one-drop, hypo-descent rule of reckoning an African-descended population, as is commonly employed for African Americans in the United States, whereby "one drop" of African descent makes a person "black," has not been traditionally used in Brazil. In showing how much higher the percentage of African descendants could be were the criteria more open-ended, my point is simply to recognize how the positive value of historically afforded whiteness, and to whitening one's family through time, can function to bias census numbers and underrepresent "blackness" (Skidmore 1974; Twine 1998). Now "blackness," of course, has no fixed, transnational meaning. However, research on Brazilian racial discrimination tells us that although Brazilians' self-identifications lean opportunistically toward lighter categories, racism functions in the opposite direction, such that there is no measurable advantage to being lighter-skinned: being *preta* and being *parda* function to raise one's liability for racial discrimination in the same way. While a "mulatto escape hatch" theory once held currency in Brazilian studies, which posited that mulattos could "escape" from racial discrimination through miscegenation because of Brazilian acceptance of *pardos* (Degler 1971), subsequent research found that no such escape existed (N. V. Silva 1985). Mulatto parents who had achieved upward class mobility were as unable to pass on such advances to their children as were blacks; by contrast, whites were able to "efficiently" transmit class advancement to younger generations (Hasenbalg 1985; Hasenbalg and Silva 1999). In a country where "good appearance" in ads euphemizes a preference for whiteness, or where a state governor's daughter could be assaulted for having the audacity to delay an elevator in a middle-class apartment building (her dark skin color led assailants to assume she was also poor and out of place; Hanchard 1994: 178; Goldstein 2003: 107), racial bias is a formidable force that can and should be studied, analyzed, and confronted as distinct from classism.

The northeast region, in which Bahia is the largest of nine states, is the only one in which those of at least partial African descent form a clear majority. In the northeast as a whole, only 32 percent claim whiteness as their color, and in Bahia many of these, as Bahians commonly joked to me, were *brancos da Bahia,* Bahian whites, with at least *"um pé na África,"* one foot in Africa. Once a group of North American blacks arrived in Bahia for an international symposium on racism, and my Afro-Bahian friends wondered to me in politely whispered asides, "But, they're white!" for folks of that color would have self-identified as white in Bahia, except the minority whose politicization and social positioning lead them to self-identify as black. Whereas in the majority-white south and southeastern regions a dirty-blond like me may be taken for Brazilian until proven otherwise, in Bahia my kind of whiteness appears distinctly foreign in a non-Bahian way that some Bahians apply equally to their southern European-Brazilian compatriots (cf. Linger 1992; Schneider 1996: 184). As Jeferson Bacelar has argued, Bahia is so pervasively Afro-Brazilian that to be anti-black is equivalent to being anti-Bahian, for in terms of symbolic representation, Bahia is ethnically African (1989: 82). Livio Sansone (2003) provides another take on this question in his book *Blackness without Ethnicity,* highlighting how Afro-Bahianness permeates all that can be considered distinctively Bahian, but is neither limited to dark-skinned Bahians nor primarily grounded in oppositional identity politics (for better or for worse; cf. Butler 1998b).

Establishing the importance of Afro-Brazilianness for Bahia, both demographically and culturally, holds critical significance for this work. Despite the subalternity born of racism, poverty, and marginalization of the region within the national arena, I find that aspects of Afro-Bahian religious practice, kinship, social organization, and economic enterprise have broad salience, permitting alternative gender dynamics that differ from those of mainstream, middle-class, Luso-Brazilian culture. Namely, I argue that Afro-Bahian cultural settings offer women a form of relative power and autonomy that can serve as a resource for resisting domination and violence. This is a cultural argument, often applying to lighter-skinned Bahians as much or, in individual cases, more so than darker-skinned counterparts, depending upon details of heritage, community, social positioning, and so on.

"FACTS" VERSUS REPRESENTATIONS OF VIOLENCE

The event is not that which happens, but that which can be narrated.

ALLEN FELDMAN
Formations of Violence

I went to Bahia expecting that violence would be nearly impossible to study directly in a systematic way: to some extent, wouldn't the work have to rely on ways people represented violence after the fact, rendering most "facts" difficult to pin down?[23] This indeed proved true. At the same time, however, violence had a way of flinging itself into my life, casting me in the role of witness.

The most literal example of this was the first day of *carnaval* in 1994, when a victim of assault literally hurled herself into my path. We were descending our shantytown's muddy hill, heading downtown for the festivities, bedecked in our carnival *fantasias* (costumes) from the *bloco afro*, the Afro-Bahian carnival block or club, we had just joined. Just as we reached the busy avenue below, a door flew open from a passing station wagon and a long-haired woman, dressed completely in white, appeared to leap from the vehicle, rolling roughly on the gravel-strewn pavement before us and speckling her white clothes with red blood at the knees, hips, shoulders, and elbows. We saw that her face was bruised and a black eye, which did not appear to have been caused by her jump from the car, was beginning to swell up. She immediately scrambled to her feet and moved away from us, trying to evade the driver, who dogged her in the station wagon in whatever direction she walked, screaming for her to get back inside.

Before anyone could reach her to see if she needed help, she relented and climbed back inside.

Then there was the time when my husband and I were sitting at our makeshift table in our one-room, clay-block house, and perceived the approach of our next-door neighbor's lover as he strode furiously away from the *briga* (fight) we'd been unavoidably overhearing for the last hour. He passed our open door, and whirled impulsively, casting a sharp steak knife down onto our table. "Keep this away from her!" he commanded, and continued on his way.

In the neighborhood context, many *brigas*-in-progress caught my attention, through overheard voices, raised in anger or the high pitch of panic, the sounds of crashing objects penetrating thin walls, and the thud of bare feet racing past my door as brawlers fled or neighbors raced over to see what was going on.

Further occasions where violence found me without my seeking it out included an injured, disoriented young homeless woman who sat next to me on a bus, saying she was in search of the women's *delegacia* after being beaten. I took her there and remained with her for the next twelve hours to ensure she didn't fall asleep and never awaken, because the police believed she had a serious concussion. I helped a neighbor and battered woman leave her husband and, as told in the prologue, became the *madrinha* (godmother) of a little boy from a violent home, making me the *comadre* (comother) of his battered mother and his batterer father.

Although there were times, as these passing tales show, when male-female violence in Bahia simply inserted itself into my day-to-day life—as it would for any Bahian—these kinds of events were relatively rare. More often, my access to the *brigas* depended on narratives offered to me by the people involved, or by those who were party as witnesses or links in chains of gossip, in both the *delegacia* and the neighborhood. Like the woman's clothes after she jumped from the station wagon, blood, bruises, and fractures mark my interview transcripts:

> Once he grabbed me around the middle, and it was with so much violence, with so much real malice. Then he broke both my legs! Until this day that one is broken; it swells and aches.
>
> [Another time,] the neighbor lady sees me and screams, "Put some ice on her face! Get some ice!" Because my face was really a mess, with pieces falling off. I got myself up, and I got a club, and I called the street to

attention. I got all their attention, then I gave him my best with the club. There was no one who could hold me—three men tried and no one could keep me down.

Josara

This was a little fracture he did, here in the tibia [holds out bruised and cut forearm]. And the other arm up here. . . . He's never mistreated me in front of the children, and that's why now they think the trouble he's in with the police is all my fault. They cry for him. . . . And that's why I'm here today: To ask them to set him free [from jail] and drop the charges.

Maria do Carmo

At first it was just words, but then one day he slugged me. When the kids came along it just kept getting worse. He's given me bruises, but he's never drawn blood or knocked me out. One time he pushed me down the stairs and hurt my arm. It started that he rapped me hard on the head. Then, I grabbed an iron and everyone was trying to get me to stop and not hurt him. That's when he belted me with all his might *(com vontade),* and I started to have the beginning of a seizure in my eyes. I went off to the hospital . . .

Deca

I went to the beach one day, and when I came back he began to attack me. He threw me inside the house, and first he slapped me. . . . He was ready to kill me *(me esticou);* he locked everything and started to beat me until there was blood on the walls. And the other day, in the street, he held me down by force—see the bruises on my arms? He was "wanting to talk . . ."

Lena

If I hadn't run he would have burst my head open with a bottle. Only you seeing could you believe it. . . . He won't talk about it; he just beats me. There are times when my entire body is covered with marks; I turn this color of purple when he beats me. This eye of mine, last year he beat me so much it just . . . I don't have anything to compare it to. It just stayed red, the white part was just red, red, red.

Jacilene

Perhaps I place these harrowing words and events in the introduction in a futile attempt to get something out of the way. When international journalists have interviewed me, I've frequently become aware that I was not providing the material they were seeking from someone parked in a Brazilian police station or a slum, studying violence. It became clear that they had hoped I would regale them with tale after tale of bloodcurdling, brutalizing horrors, confirming their expectations of the exotic barbarity of Latin American men and the overall gravity of gender-based violence in Brazil that could necessitate all-female police stations.

My emphases have been elsewhere. Where the voices above conform with the horrific images of dominance-driven, man-to-woman battering with which publics are most familiar, in this work I highlight a different dynamic, one that has often escaped attention: ways women resist men's domination, availing themselves of resources to avoid becoming victims— their own agency to refuse, community support, cultural delegitimation, and state sanctions against violence. Mutual violence, where women may themselves use violence as a way of asserting themselves or refusing domination, as well as men's compensatory violence, where violence is used more as damage control than to secure dominance, also require attention. This work approaches violence's significance for gendered power relations as being far more complex than has commonly been recognized and advocates distinguishing between contrasting dynamics of violence, as well as how these fit into global, national, and regional historical processes. Similarly, I claim that the creation of the *delegacias* has brought to light not only shocking levels of partner violence against Brazilian women (similar to levels in developed nations such as the United States, the United Kingdom, or countries of continental Europe) but also the advanced state of Brazil's women's movement in confronting gender-based violence and men's impunity.

Something about violence remains, for me, impenetrable. Despite my Foucaldian convictions that violence not only destroys meaning but also produces its own, or that violence not only severs social relationships but also constructs them, I am left without much insight about hurting others per se. Far more arresting for me have been efforts that actively assert antiviolence and nonviolence as options and that advocate ending violence whenever possible.

To aide myself in continuing this work, I have dedicated myself to the part of the account I find hopeful and have avoided viewing my task as the compiling of one nightmarish story after the other. Some of this was not conscious: I often repressed actually thinking through, or emotionally "processing," all I was hearing and seeing. More than once I have read back through week-old field notes and had no recollection of having recorded the traumas they described. Or I have left the *delegacia* to get a bite for lunch and found myself on the bus headed home when I'd intended to return. Of course, the horror stories are important. Even as I do not relish subjecting readers to the gruesome details in the above transcripts, I place some of them up front to inoculate against any impulse on my part to gloss over them.

GENDER-BASED VIOLENCE IN BRAZIL FROM A CROSS-CULTURAL PERSPECTIVE

Nonviolence doesn't set out to obliterate violence. Rather, it seeks to invite it in. If nonviolence destroys its enemies, it has lost.

BRUCE CORIELL
from his lecture "Nonviolence and Light"

Activists against gender-based violence in Brazil often despaired over the difficulty in sustaining a focus on a specific form of violence, when they perpetually felt their society as a whole awash in new and unprecedented waves of epidemic violence. Massacres of street children and indigenous people; gang versus paramilitary shootouts that claim bystanders' lives; low-intensity wars over land between entrepreneurial miners, ranchers, plantation owners, and loggers on one side and peasants and indigenous tribes on the other; kidnappings for money that often end in deaths; police torture and killings of civilians—the list goes on and on.

To dwell on a specific form of violence in one time and one place, to stay the impulse to let the multifarious violences wash together in a horrific, paralyzing flood, it might serve first to suggest some premises about gender-based partner violence, informed by cross-cultural research.

Premise one: gender-based partner violence, although it is alarmingly widespread across contemporary societies, is not a universal phenomenon. Numerous scholars have recorded cases, usually in small-scale or peasant cultures, where such phenomena are rare or unknown (Levinson 1989; Campbell 1999; Boulding 2000; Mitchell 1999; Gilmore 1990; Krauft 1987). In the sixteen societies Levinson discusses where family violence is relatively absent, helpful factors include husbands and wives sharing in domestic decision making, wives having some control over the fruits of their labor, wives being able to divorce as easily as husbands, marriage being monogamous, an absence of premarital sexual double standards, divorce being relatively infrequent, husbands and wives sleeping together, men resolving disputes with other men peacefully, and immediate intervention in wife-beating incidents (1989: 103–4).[24]

Lepowsky (1999) provides an example of a small-scale, egalitarian society, the Vanatinai in Melanesia, in which wife abuse is virtually absent; and in the few instances of violence she was aware of (five over ten years), four of the five were instigated by women (cf. Burbank 1999). However, her conclusion that "the example of Vanatinai offers evidence that the rarity of intragroup violence, especially of attacks of men on women, is a characteristic of egalitarian societies" certainly needs to be called into question in light of examples such as the egalitarian (except in terms of gender) Yanomami, where interpersonal violence and spousal assault are notoriously frequent.[25] Thus, although the statement that those societies with relative absence of family violence are almost exclusively small-scale and egalitarian, the converse is not true (unless by egalitarian we mean that they are also gender-egalitarian; conventionally, egalitarian refers to absence of rank or class stratification).

Refuting the often-presumed universality of wife beating fortifies those who seek to stop gender-based violence, in Brazil and elsewhere, with vital prospects of hope. If partner violence is not a fixed, inevitable part of "human nature," but rather relies upon a culturally conditioned responses to conflict, supported by specific values and social processes, then it can be changed.[26]

Premise two: although violence—here defined as the arguably illegitimate injury of another (Riches 1986; Stewart and Strathern 2002: 35–51)—is necessarily destructive, it is not exclusively so. For many Brazilian men, violence is also a key resource for the performance of masculinity. Violence need not always be a masculinizing resource: accounts exist where women initiate more violence and such force is associated, culturally, with forms of femininity, but that is generally not the case in Bahia. The destructive-yet-productive paradox requires that those seeking long-term prevention of gender-based partner violence ask what "positive" functions violence serves for men and what alternatives exist.

Premise three: distinctions can usefully be made about different forms of violence and accompanying institutional responses. Gender-based violence is not "one size fits all." Many of the truisms perpetuated by battered women's movements, in the justifiable interests of championing sanctions and creating sanctuary for women victims, do not hold up empirically. One such truism reads: man-to-woman violence (always, everywhere) secures masculine power and control, reinforcing patriarchy. In fact, men's violence can symptomize men's lack of control and women's increasing access to power. It is mistaken to assume an a priori correlation between societies with high levels of male-to-female violence and sharper degrees of male dominance or of gendered power asymmetries favoring men (Burbank 1999: 43–52). Rather, research suggests that during rapid shifts toward gender egalitarianism, temporary increases in violence may occur (Levinson 1989: 75; Straus 1993; Yllö 1983, 1984, 1993). Criminalization undermines cultural tolerance for male violence, thus lowering the utility of violence as an acceptable masculinizing resource. Loss of this resource, however, can raise men's insecurities, paradoxically catalyzing their "need" for redressive violence. It follows, then, that a very different kind of violent domestic incident may be on the rise, one potentially fueled by the delegitimating discourse on male violence. Contemporary Brazil offers a promising opportunity to explore such transitional dynamics; these cannot be understood, however, without attention to the criminalization and delegitimation of male violence as historical processes.

Battered women's movements have frequently perpetuated a second truism, for political purposes, that cultural influences and socioeconomic class background are insignificant in shaping social patterns of violence, because violence cross-cuts all class and cultural groups. In fact, the presence of domestic violence in all strata in a violent society does not translate into even distribution of violence into all contexts, nor does it diminish the variable patterns that emerge in particular historical processes and sociocultural contexts. In addressing issues of poverty, racism, and social marginalization as they relate to domestic violence, the present work breaks from a certain orthodoxy that defines much of the scholarship in this area. The valid assertion that domestic violence cross-cuts all class, ethnic, or racial groups has, in an atmosphere of politically correct circumspection, too often translated into what has been called "the myth of classlessness of domestic violence."[27] In Brazil, as elsewhere, there is an understandable sensitivity to any suggestion that domestic violence might assume more severe or frequent forms in poorer socioeconomic groups. A central reason for this is that the societal tendencies to naturalize class-as-race or class-as-culture are altogether too common, thus hazarding that discussions about domestic violence as influenced by poverty may be read as racist, on the one hand, or as stigmatizing and deterministic "culture of poverty" arguments, on the other. This work recognizes these hazards and stands with Brazilian scholars who reject culture-of-poverty explanations in favor those grounded in a culture of machismo (M. Azevedo 1985: 27).[28] That said, this work also acknowledges that the stresses that poverty generates hold significance for the patterning of domestic violence. In claiming that we must take these stresses seriously, I would point out that poverty does not resemble ethnic identity. It is an experience, a process, and an obstacle that individuals and families strive to overcome. Poverty creates anxieties, uncertainties, insecurities, and desperation. Although attempting to attain or maintain middle-class or elite status generates particular concerns and insecurities as well, the frequency and degree of crisis may be less. People struggling in poverty, in a society with entrenched patterns and prescriptions about violence, may find themselves in the kinds of situations in which violence tends to arise more often than do persons whose socioeconomic circumstances subject them to fewer stresses, insecurities, and uncertainties.

Finally, premise four: preventing violence requires more than punishment. Public policies that deal with male violence on an exclusively punitive level, as do most of Brazil's women's police stations, are insufficient. Laureen Snider (1998) makes the critical point that overreliance on criminalization stems from a tendency to misidentify penalty with social control. Moreover, criminalization-centered responses are inadvertently elitist, benefiting white and middle-class women at the expense of poor and working-class women and women of color, who are more reluctant to involve police because of perceived bias and a higher probability of police abuses against partners from subaltern social backgrounds. Feminists and other progressives need to look to more broadly based, preventive approaches to ameliorating violence and hegemonic masculinity.

BRAZIL IN A GLOBAL CONTEXT

Brazil has become emblematic of a "culture of male violence," as a recent collection of anthropological essays on violence against women demonstrates (Counts, Brown, and Campbell 1999). Here, Brazil, together with India, is held up as an example of the kind of society in which "neither wife-beating nor wife-battering is disapproved, and even the murder of a wife may go unpunished" (Brown 1999: 5). However, Brazil's notoriety in this regard may have more to do with the high-profile intensity of feminist vitriol, and the novelty of institutional responses such as the DMs, than with higher incidence per se. Against the backdrop of international data, Brazil's levels of partner violence, although they are as worrisome as in most places, do not appear exceptional.

A good baseline for the ubiquity of male-to-female violence comes from a compilation of nearly 50 population-based surveys from around the world: between 10–50 percent of women reported being hit or otherwise physically harmed by an intimate male partner at some point in their lives. Worldwide, an estimated 40 to 70 percent of homicides of women were committed by partners, frequently in the context of an abusive relationship (Heise, Ellsberg, and Gottemoeller 1999). More limited studies in Africa, Latin America, and Asia report even higher rates of physical abuse among the population—up to 60 percent or more of women, for example, in (low-income sectors) of Ecuador (United Nations 2000: 158).[29] For Latin America in general, a range of 25 to 50 percent of women report at least one assault. Although women assault their partners as well, they do so less frequently and seriously, and usually in self-defense (Anderson 1997; United Nations 2000; Campbell 1999: 264). No cultural cases are on record where female-to-male violence appears part of a pattern of coercive controls underwriting women's social dominance in the way male-to-female violence can, in case after case.

According to a study of 138,000 women in fifty-four countries, 23 percent of Brazilian women had been subject to physical violence by a partner at least once in their lives (Harazim 1998). A multicountry study on women's health and domestic violence against women, carried out in 2000–2001 through the World Health Organization, compared urban and semirural women. In São Paulo, it was found that 27.2 percent of women who had ever had a partner had suffered physical violence at his hand at least once, whereas this figure was 33.7 percent for residents of the Forest Zone of Pernambuco, a state to the north of Bahia (d'Oliveira and Schraiber 2005).

These national figures for Brazil do not differ appreciably from those for the United States, where one in four women can expect to experience violence from an intimate partner in her lifetime (Tjaden and Thoennes 2000), or from others of the world's most developed countries, where figures range from just 13 percent of Swiss women experiencing partner violence, to Canada's 29 percent, the United Kingdom at 30 percent, and Australia, where 22 percent of women had been abused within the last twelve months. Nor is Brazil a standout within the Latin American region, where 48 percent of Puerto Rican women, 28 percent of Nicaraguan women, and between 27 and 40 percent of Mexican women (in Guadelajara and Durango City, respectively) have reported experiencing partner violence (United Nations 2000: 154).

Brazilian men who assault partners are more likely than other men to be violent with children in the home as well (41 percent); 66 percent of homicides of women in Brazil with known perpetrators are committed within families (Dijaci, Geraldes, and Lima 1998). A World Bank study found that one in five absentee days for women from work was due to domestic violence (Harazim 1998); the overall cost to Brazil's gross domestic product was calculated to be 10.5 percent.[30]

Research carried out under the auspices of the Pan American Health Organization presents opportunities to consider Salvador, Bahia, in the context of other Brazilian data (from Rio de Janeiro) and broader Latin American and international data.[31] Salvador stood out as having higher rates than all the other samples in both men's and women's self-reports of beating or slapping of a partner.[32] Salvador's men scored the highest agreement with the statement, "An unfaithful woman deserves to be beaten," among nine population samples (19 percent). Although in Salvador women's approval of beating for female adultery, 11.3 percent, was higher than the women's average of 8.3 percent, the discrepancy between men's and women's approval was by far the greatest in Salvador.[33] This finding prefigures my assertion in this book that Salvador presents an especially fertile social context for male and female contestation of gendered norms and of violence.[34]

Significant sectors of Brazilian society correspond positively with the general predictors for greater occurrence of violence against women in cross-cultural research: wife beating is most likely when men control family wealth and decision making, conflicts are solved by means of physical force, and women do not have equal access to divorce. Other Brazilian sectors, however, including the largely Afro-Bahian urban enclaves of concern in this book, feature the very characteristics that inhibit violence against women, such as all-female work groups and female control of wealth (Brown 1999: 9; Levinson 1989: 102). Although these features do not appear to correlate with lower reported levels of violence in Bahia, where incidences appear relatively high, they may indicate that violence here is less exclusively indicative of male dominance than a mixture of men using violence to gain power and men using violence to prevent, or protest, the loss of power to which they feel entitled.

ON PSEUDONYMS AND MYTHOLOGICAL ALLUSIONS

When Bahians learned I was an anthropologist, I joked that I didn't do "*antropologia folclórica*" (folkloric anthropology). So saturated was the literature on Bahia by ethnographic and historical accounts of *carnaval* (carnival), *capoeira* (the Bahian dance/martial art), Candomblé and Umbanda, *acarajé* (the Afro-Bahian street food), and *travestis,* that violence against women seemed, by contrast, a rather sober and mundane topic.

Because my concern was violence, the Human Subjects Review Board (HSRB) at Johns Hopkins University, where I began this research as a doctoral student, required stringent use of identity protection, confidentiality, and anonymity for participant subjects, particularly in the focus group phase, where I could not control content in a quasipublic context I had created. In response, the Human Subjects Review Board required me to use pseudonyms extensively for all participants who were not public figures, regardless of subjects' personal preferences. However appropriate, my efforts to conduct responsible research inadvertently muffle and undercut the accuracy of the portrayals written here. Attempting to minimize risks and maximize potential benefits to those with whom I work prevents me, in small ways, from sharing with readers how much more striking truth can be than my necessary fictionalizations.

In an effort to compensate for the absence of undisclosable, always more compelling truths and to preserve factual connections, in places I take modest license in the book. For example, in choosing a pseudonym, such as Yancí for the defiant and bold sister who condemns her brother and sister-in-law's violent history, I spin an intentional association with the *orixá* Iansã. I would not trouble with such an allusion, however, were not the real person's actual name still more suggestive of an indomitable, feisty woman, tied to Afro-Bahian history and Candomblé. Iansã enters as a way of capturing the spirit of Yancí's censored name.

Similarly, for the surname of the extended family that is the focal case study in the opening chapters, I use the pseudonym Bomfim, an alternate spelling for one of Salvador's most important patron saints, Nosso Senhor do Bonfim (Our Lord of the Good End). Bonfim is tied to Oxalá (father of all *orixás*) and to Jesus in their revolutionary, justice-rendering senses (Silverstein 1995; Butler 1998a: 164–165). The actual surname, which would fit far more seamlessly into this ethnography but cannot be disclosed, invokes similar themes.[35]

On a still more metaphorical note, in epigraphs and chapter discussions, I share myths about *orixás*—gods or saints from Candomblé and other Afro-Based Brazilian religions—that relate to gender conflict and violence. The intent here is to reflect on distinct, multiple versions offered by selective Candomblé archetypes on how to be women or men. In particular, for distinct versions of violent men I cite both Xangô (god of thunder) and

Ogum (*orixá* of iron and war); for defiant, indomitable women, Iansã (*orixá* of storms); for dispassionate, "if looks could kill" mother-in-law widows, Naná Buruku (*orixá* mother of all and sometimes of death). Finally, I draw upon a specific aspect of Iemenjá (*orixá* of the sea), Yemanjá Assaba, to represent abused and embattled wife-mothers.

The objective of such allusions, once again, is to draw upon the gendered diversity offered by the Candomblé pantheon and to highlight the polysemic possibilities offered by this aspect of Brazilian culture. I wish to invoke a Candomblé perspective on the "dynamic tension between genders, which sets the world in motion" (P. Johnson 2002: 43) as a commentary on material about partner conflict and violence.

J. Lorand Matory, in his ethnography entitled *Sex and the Empire that Is No More: Gender in the Politics of Metaphor in Oyo Yoruba Religion* (1994), calls upon rival *orixás* Sango (Xangô in Bahia, god of thunder) and Ogun (Ogum in Bahia, god of war, mobility, and technology) as explanatory devices to contrast two historical ages, as well as two distinct gender ideologies, for early modern Nigeria. To summarize, he associates power and governance in the Age of Sango (sixteenth through early nineteenth centuries) with metaphors of marriage—"not the subordination of females to males but of horses to riders and *wives* to *husbands*," where wifeliness could include cross-dressing men who acted as wives of gods or monarchs, and where the monarch himself was a "wife" of Sango. During the Age of Ogun, which took hold in the mid- to late nineteenth century, British colonialism and effects of the slave trade favored the rise of nonroyal, military republics. Although the Age of Sango brought many women to power, their politico-ritual legitimacy was strictly tied to wifeliness and subordination to the "sexually redolent" (1994: 7) husband/god Sango by violent possession. The Age of Ogun, by contrast, was marked by "vast human mobility and warfare, and de-emphasis on marital and kinship metaphors in the constitution of the state" (1994: 15–16), and favored power divorced from possession, which was largely associated with women (in Yorubaland Ogun, unlike Sango, does not possess or penetrate in ceremony). "Ogun's relations with wives are clumsy," Matory writes. "Ogun fails to recognize the complementary distinctness of the wifely role" (1994: 18). In Bahia, Ogum stories show him clashing with independently minded Iansã and losing her companionship, and as easily insulted and fated to destroy that which he loves (Verger 1993: 247). But in Malory's Nigerian past, whereas the most powerful women in the Age of Sango were wives, in Ogun's male-centered organizations women were on their own: "Corollary to Ogun's pathbreaking . . . is the escape and autonomy of women," the most successful of whom were unwifely, militaristic, and "legendarily antireproductive" and who "enriched and empowered themselves" through commanding slaves and controlling trade (1994: 19). Women's relative power and autonomy did not signal their ascension as a group, however: "The inescapable reality of the Nigerian national political economy is that the sons of Ogun rule and women do not" (1994: 25–25).

Matory's Sango and Ogun complexes represent "ancient mythic models," which he claims do "not simply belong to different times and places" but also to "rival gendered outcomes of problems and potentials continuously recognized—and even contemporaneously personified—in Oyo-Yoruba politics" (1994: 23, 25). Although he is careful to underline the limits of these models and cases where they cannot apply, he also argues for their "very *suitedness* of that symbolism to . . . those Nigerians, Béninois, Cubans, Brazilians, Trinidadians, and U.S. Americans who still implicitly regard Oyo as a divine prototype of world order" (1994: 240).

This study concurs about the suitedness of these gendered metaphors, structured around Xangô and Ogum, for contemporary Bahia. It draws upon the contrast between women tied to wifeliness versus those who have "escaped" into separation and autonomy as a way to analytically tie the neighborhood and police station ethnographies together. Women tied to legitimacy through wifeliness, who tolerate husbandly forcefulness, might be thought of as symbolically linked to Xangô. Women who "escape" into "autonomy"—*delegacia* complainants ready to separate, policewomen in gender-segregated stations, and other women who reject tying their lots to "wifeliness"—echo the defiance of Iansã and the separation of men and women under Ogum-style, failed husbandry.

My sources for Candomblé are largely literature-based, and my goal is not to make claims about actual Candomblé practices in Bahia. Rather, my use of Candomblé epitomizes what Paul Johnson calls "public Candomblé." He cites myriad Candomblé-derived references in popular culture, expropriated from *terreiros* and actual ritual practice. Concerned with "meaning, symbolism, cosmology, and philosophy," such references depart from the secretive, ritual enactment of Candomblé, used instrumentally to effect one's desires or destiny: "[I]ts language is not that of the hand, of ritual" (2002: 166).

Although I did live in a small neighborhood that was anchored, historically, by an old family *terreiro,* Candomblé was not my main focus as a participant observer. It was my privilege to experience over nearly two decades, however, the typical forays into Candomblé of a foreigner in Bahia, visiting *festas* big and small at various nations' *terreiros* and getting several readings through the casting of cowrie shells *(jogo dos búzios)*.[36] The research team made similar short investigations of other religious communities, including Catholic, Protestant *(crente),* Spiritist, Umbanda, and even Jehovah's Witness groups. But none of these (with the exception of Umbanda, whose general use of some *orixás* parallels that of Candomblé) seemed to offer "archetypical" figures with such currency in Bahian culture, or with themes so in line with my concerns, as Candomblé. Catholicism becomes equally polysemic through the trinity and the saints, but unlike divine personages in that faith, the *orixás* can themselves be violent, destructive, and angry, even as they also heal, empower, and bless. In short, the repertoires of feeling and action in Candomblé are immeasurably more diverse, "morally" checkered, and human, thus offering unsurpassedly fertile language for thinking about, and acting in response to, violence.

The tendencies discussed earlier to underrepresent Afro-Brazilianness, even in Bahia, manifest in widely varied forms, including the elevation of classical "Western" traditions above those tied to Afro-Brazilian culture. One memorable presentation by an esteemed feminist scholar, given at the Universidade Federal da Bahia, impressed this upon me. She analyzed data on Bahian women's attitudes and behaviors by drawing on archetypes of Greek goddesses: Athena, Aphrodite, Artemis, and so on. Although the method did not seem unproductive, I did wonder why we sat in a tropical ivory tower invoking ancient Greece. Mindful that Bahian popular culture throughout the 1990s drew far more frequently on the "saints" or *orixás* of Candomblé and other Afro-based Brazilian religious practices (such as Umbanda, Quimbanda, Macumba, and Tambor de Mina)—complete with astrology-like newspaper features detailing the welfare of one's *orixá* and its significance for a devotee—I pondered whether these closer-to-home personages might not illuminate diverse Bahian experiences equally well, if not better.

Ultimately, it was one of my interviewees, loosely involved in Umbanda, who convinced me that it was reasonable to explore how Bahians might draw upon their *orixás* as resources for understanding and navigating conflict. Lisabete shared with me how, as her marriage grew stormy and she started to be hit regularly, she had managed to stand up to abuse and death threats from her husband. She "allowed" fiery Iansã (goddess of storms), who in her personal pantheon normally occupied a secondary position, to temporarily take the lead ahead of the more gentle, less bellicose goddess

Iemenjá (*orixá* of the sea), who normally was her *dona da cabeça* (the owner/ruler of her head), meaning her foremost *orixá* and the one who would "descend" or "incorporate" were Lisabete to be possessed. Lisabete was a white, working-class Bahian married to a dark-skinned, middle-class man. Tellingly, as he drew upon class superiority to demean her, she drew upon racist stereotypes to depreciate him, even as she invoked Afro-Brazilian models to empower herself as a woman.

Another time, a man summoned to the women's police station following a charge filed by his wife swore that he had acted in self-defense: it was not his wife who had attacked him, but the formidable Oxossi (masculine *orixá* of the hunt), who at that moment was possessing his wife's body, investing it with a preternatural strength. In this case, both complainant and accused appeared white. Just as Lisabete drew on an Afro-Brazilian *orixá* as an empowering resource, this man appealed to another to argue that his use of force was defensive and should win him impunity.

The point of these stories is not to argue that Candomblé or other *orixá* religions enjoy an exclusive, primary place in the bedrock of Bahian culture.[37] Rather, this work attends disproportionately to Candomblé, and not to Catholicism, Espiritismo, or Evangelismo, for two reasons. The first is practical: the neighborhood and the family I came to know best was marked by the presence of a long-standing *terreiro* in its center, such that residents felt forced to stake out positions in relation to it (the Evangelicals in the neighborhood assiduously avoided the compound in the center). The second is that, as I will detail, Candomblé appeared to offer Bahians, and women in particular, distinctly helpful resources for navigating relationship conflict. In the marketplace of religious, ideational options from which Brazilians pick and choose, the historical defiance in the face of domination that Candomblé signified for enslaved and postemancipation Africans and Afro-Brazilians has a gendered component of significance for women.

GENDER-BASED VIOLENCE: SUMMARY OF THE FIELD

As sociocultural anthropology, this work reaches for two opposing poles: to be both ethnographic—illuminating for readers a certain time and place—and ethnological, asking how a particular case compares against the known spectra of human experiences. In the effort to set ethnography about Salvador da Bahia against ethnology about comparable contemporary accounts of criminalizing gender-based violence, each chapter in this book finds its own, rather particular theoretical concerns. In respective chapters, these range from reproducing victimization between women kin, to "threatened" or "thwarted" masculinities and compensatory violence, to sharpening the distinction between domineering battery and what I have called "contestatory" patterns. In later chapters on gender and policing violence, I address the significance of all-women policing in a developing nation's state formation, and of the occupational shaping of gender identity in the relationships between policewomen and feminists.

But these are quite specific. In closing this introduction, I provide a wider backdrop for this work by reviewing important currents of thought in the field of gender-based violence. From amid the cacophony of interdisciplinary conversations about interpersonal violence, those concerned with power, social structure, and gender are of special significance. Here I consider four general explanatory models in the gender-based violence literature of particular relevance: they are resource theory, exchange theory, ecological theory, and feminism. Of these, the first three tend to be employed for positivistic, hypothesis-testing purposes. By contrast, the approach of this work is feminist and interpretivist, or concerned with how gender elucidates the patterning and logics of relationship conflict and violence.

Resource theory is based on the notion that "the more external (outside the family) resources one controls, the less likely one will be to use . . . violence to maintain control" (Levinson 1989: 15; also Campbell 1999: 238). Resources can be either material (i.e., income, contribution to subsistence, inheritance, dowry), organizational (i.e., kin ties, political allegiances), or ideological (i.e., nonviolence, feminism). Most applications have concentrated on men's deficits and their use of violence as compensatory (Okum 1986: 90; Levinson 1989: 15; Anderson 1997; Melzer 2002); rarer variants have accounted for women's resources as helping them escape or avoid violence (cf. Cubbins and Vannoy 2005; Anderson 2002), and virtually none at women's violence as a resource itself. Resource theory's relevance for this work takes on historical, descriptive dimensions as I explore how the criminalization of men's (but not women's) violence, the advent of pro-women police stations, and Afro-Bahian gendered social dynamics fortify women's positioning vis-à-vis couple conflict.[38]

In interpretive anthropology, the closest counterpart to resource theory is cultural reproduction theory, also called practice theory. An outgrowth of Marxist thought, *cultural reproduction theory* expands the materialist notion of capital into more abstract realms of practice, speaking of symbolic, social, cultural, linguistic, political capital, and so on. As with resource theory, cultural reproduction theory then traces how individuals or groups deploy their respective capitals as power, converting what they already have into desired outcomes. Cultural reproduction has been employed with masterful results in anthropology (Bourdieu 1977, 2001; Bourgois 1995; Ortner 2003; Goldstein 2003) and may be considered a more comprehensive version of resource theory.

Exchange theory postulates that "people hit and abuse other family members because they can" (Gelles quoted in Levinson 1989: 15). The theory is often presented in economistic terms resembling cost-benefit or risk assessment analysis. Violence between family members will occur as long as the benefits outweigh the costs. Exchange theory is useful for evaluating the efficacy of negative sanctions in preventing violence, especially in circumstances of rapidly rising cultural awareness of criminalization, as in Brazil and India. Some observations by exchange theorists parallel those of social evolutionists in pointing to increasing isolation of family groups in the Western industrial nations and an accompanying disappearance of traditional social sanctions such as neighbor or extended family intervention. A pivotal factor can be whether institutional responses replace informal interventions as relatively isolated nuclear families become predominant in changing societies. Anthropologists and other social scientists have produced strong evidence in support of the argument that negative sanctions work to prevent violence (Campbell 1999: 244; McCall and Shields 1986; Ventura and Davis 2005).[39]

Ecological theory may most accurately be considered a methodological framework, emphasizing interrelationships between concentric levels of analysis, generally moving from individual, to interpersonal and community, to societal or national, to global (Kirk and Okazawa-Rey 2001: 3). Heise's (1998) application of ecological theory to violence against women demonstrates the utility of distinguishing between causal or correlative factors operating at different levels of interaction.[40] Although the present work, again, does not attempt the predictive and causal assertions of applications of ecological theory (Flake 2005; Dasgupta 2002; Oetzel and Duran 2004), the theory/method parallels my efforts to conjoin the micro-to-macro, ethnographic-cum-ethnological analyses that mark sociocultural anthropology

Feminist theory, finally, informs this work on a fundamental level. For present purposes, it may be understood as the rejection of inequality between men and women as natural, in favor of seeing male dominance as a product of historical and sociocultural processes that produce and sustain patriarchy. For understanding gender-based violence, feminism prioritizes gender in explaining why male-to-female violence is more prevalent than female-to-male violence, and why the two forms of violence differ in their social significance.[41] As is elaborated at length in chapter three, feminist approaches to gender-based violence have often been exclusively identified as those that elaborate the social and cultural ways in which violence disproportionately underwrites women's oppression, whereas those concerned with women's own violent agencies have often been categorized as something other than feminist. This work expressly revises such a dichotomy, claiming the concern with men's compensatory violence in response to men's losses and women's gains as an equally feminist preoccupation. In accordance with the perspectives of pro-feminist men, the feminist approach forwarded here attends to men's dispositions regarding women's equality, with the expectation that lasting gender egalitarianism cannot be stabilized through conflict-based, adversarial, or punitive models.

CONTRIBUTION TO ANTHROPOLOGY

This study joins a growing body of anthropological studies of conflict and violence whose accounts have grown increasingly successful at revealing the linkages between violence at interpersonal, community, national, and international levels (Riches 1986; Feldman 1991; Tuzin 1997, Daniel 1996; Stewart and Strathern 2002; Das et al. 2000). With few exceptions (Seremetakis 1991; Caldeira 2001; Goldstein 2003), treatments of interpersonal and gendered violence have been dealt with separately from diverse forms of civil and state violence, and this work strives to bridge that gap by concentrating on their interrelationship. This research finds its closest counterparts in a network of international, feminist legal anthropology that chronicles an array of experiences resulting from new mandates for states to champion women's human rights and safety in the home (Merry 1994, 2000; Lazarus-Black and Hirsh 1994; Lazarus-Black 2001; Adelman 2003; Adelman, Erez, and Shalhoub-Kevorkian 2003; Torstrick 2000; London 1997). By tracing state interventions back into the community, as well as portraying state representatives as community members themselves, I try to follow Michel Foucault's admonishments to trace power out to its "capillary ends," with all the variability and messiness that that entails (see Oliven 1984b). If a degree of schizophrenia of voice and of perspective results, I hope that it significantly reflects the back-and-forth tacking of social change itself, which is never an even or unidirectional process.

In the anthropology of gender and feminist studies more generally, recent years have shown a growing commitment to studying men and women together, and both in non-reductive ways. In particular, here I aim to avoid reducing gender to what *women* do or experience. In studying conflicts between men and women, I pay attention to the role of man-to-man and woman-and-woman relationships, and how these are shaped by kinship, economics, ideology, and social change (Gutmann 1997, 1996, 2003; Goldstein 2003; Moore 1988; Safa 1995; McClusky 2001). To study gender from a sociocultural perspective means to think about gender systemically and politically, including but not limited to seeing gender as a collection of individual performances. In locating this ethnography amid the complex and specific historical process of criminalization, I attempt to illuminate how men experience their options for performing masculinity as constrained and produced by history and culture, but also by institutional and social changes. In this way, violence becomes a new performance of an old masculinity (or the only way for many men to perform a traditional masculinity in the face of contemporary changes). Combining committed feminist activism with serious ethnographic work poses immense challenges; often it has meant insisting on cautious comparativism that contradicts politically expedient truisms. The balance I have sought is to explore men's violence empathetically and without demonization, while at the same time never letting men "off the hook" or losing sight of what I unambiguously deem the wrongness of violence, men's and women's alike.

STRATEGY OF THE BOOK

Chapter 1 presents a triangle of three Afro-Bahian women kin, residents of the Alto do Mungongo neighborhood. The first, Dona Alegrina, referred to as "the widow" earlier in the introduction, is the great-grandmother and Candomblé priestess *(mãe de santo)*. She orders her son to beat his wife, appearing to conspire in re-creating the kind of oppression she suffered herself as a young wife. Second, readers meet Alegrina's daughter, Yancí, an indomitable mother and grandmother in her own right, who has eschewed formal unions with men, given her children her own surname, and derided and refused to sympathize with battered women—arguing that they must "like" it if they allow it. Finally comes Zizi, the daughter/sister-in-law, a long-abused, semi-abandoned, and desperately poor mother of five. The stories of these women kin and the violence that selectively intertwines their lives breaks up the tendency to study couple violence as exclusive to dyads of male abusers and female victims. Similarly, considering how Zizi is able to break from violence, without leaving her home or relationship, under-lines battered women's agency, and how this agency's effectiveness is con-tingent upon broader circumstances.

Chapter 2 compares the varied perspectives of these three women to those of the family's men, as expressed in interviews and focus groups with other neighborhood men. Men's conversations about conflict in unions, in stark contrast to women's, revolved around key scenarios of hypothetical female adultery and compromised male honor. Younger men, in contrast to their older counterparts, were less ready to accept that a man had to be willing to threaten or use violence in order to prove his manhood. This rein-forces the notion that cultural tolerance for violence is changing but begs the question about how younger men recreate strategies for "being men" when a critical masculinizing tool—violence—becomes untenable. Particu-larly for young men such as these, whose poverty and Afro-Brazilian iden-tities already relegate them to relatively marginal positions in racist and clas-sist Brazil, the difficulty of maintaining identities as successful men is compounded by the criminalization of violence. In concluding, the chap-ter contextualizes these stories in terms of historical changes that favor women's rising status, power, and autonomy, heightening the degree to which men's masculinity itself appears to be on the defensive, paradoxically fueling violence as a way for men to reassert power and control.

Chapter 3 follows women desperate for intervention from their neigh-borhood settings to the city's Delegacia da Mulher, or Women's Police Station. Two relational dynamics—domination and contestation—were observed to underlie most conjugal conflicts between complainants and accused. Both dynamics are ordered by a "between slaps and kisses" ideol-ogy that sees violence and love as inextricably linked, and naturalizes vio-lence by tying it to romance, passion, and jealousy, as well as to models of essential gender difference. Such notions, in turn, support the naturaliza-tion of male violence as part of "normal" masculinity but also lay the groundwork for women's resistance. This tension is traced through an eclectic sampling of cultural practices: folk dancing, popular aphorisms and phrases used to discuss violence, and literary maxims that have passed into popular wisdom.

In chapter 4, the book shifts gears to a more institutional focus, where the mission of the specialized police station is examined against visions held by the feminists instrumental in its founding. Beginning with an interna-tional focus, a survey of the countries that have created all-women police stations highlights that this route seems to have appealed exclusively in less-developed countries, remaining notably absent in those most developed. The chapter explores why this might be the case, asking about the opportunities feminizing the police creates in rapidly democratizing or gender-reformist settings.

The policewomen articulate more personal perspectives in chapter 5, including the dilemma of feeling stereotyped to do (feminized) "social" work rather than (masculinized) "real" police work. Policewomen hold firm to a particular version of the "police have no gender" ethic they were taught in conventional police academies; this heightens their reluctance to champion victimized women. Since their masculinized occupational identity combines with their frequent down-playing of identification as women, they are poorly positioned to identify with either vulnerable complainants or women's movement activists, the two groups of women with whom they most closely work (cf. Martin 1989; McElhinny 1994).

The book's conclusion and epilogue bring readers up to date on the actors with whom they have grown familiar, as well as recent developments in institutional responses to domestic violence in Bahia and Brazil in general. I explore connections between policewomen and other anti-victim women, and make a case for sustaining analytical attention and political action to gender-based violence specifically, even as it is inextricably interpenetrated with other forms of violence.

ONE

Womanly Webs

In-Laws and Violence

Invocation for Naná Buruku
eldest female orixá, mother of all,
tied to sea depths, mud, and good deaths.

Proprietária de um cajado
Salpicada de vermelho,
sua roupa parece coberta de sangue.
Orixá que obriga os Fon a falar Nagô.
Minha mãe foi inicialmente do país Bariba
figua parada que mata de repente.
Ela mata uma cabra sem utilizar a faca.

Owner of a cane
Splattered with red,
her clothes seem to be covered in blood.
Orishá who obliges the Fon to speak Nagô.
My mother was initially of the Bariba nation.
Still water that slays without warning.
She kills a goat without using a knife.

PIERRE VERGER
"Orixás da Bahia"

THE FIRST VIOLENCE I EVER witnessed wrack Zizi's body was rendered not by her husband, Jorginho, but by his mother. The formidable Dona Alegrina issued this psychological lashing in the form of a mere glance in Zizi's direction, across a courtyard, from twenty-five yards away.

That afternoon I'd been talking to Zizi and her friend Diana, the new next-door neighbor who inhabited the room next to mine and Tim's. Diana seemed to be in her late thirties; she had lovely olive skin, wispy black hair that was *liso* (smooth), and very nice, sexy clothes, appropriate for her work as a nightclub singer. Zizi was her buddy from down below, a mother who I knew was somehow part of Dona Alegrina's family. Zizi washed Diana's clothes for pay and helped her hang the lingerie and sheer blouses on the line.

It was Diana's lover who had shocked us a few days before by flinging the sharp knife he'd wrestled from her grip onto our table, ordering us to "keep it away from her!" When I'd returned the knife a few hours later she had looked at me ruefully, keeping silent. Today, though, she wondered aloud to Zizi and me how many more times in her life knives would slash their way into her romances.

Diana pointed to a deep scar on her neck I hadn't noticed before. With her jaw slightly clenched from an anger that seemed permanently lodged there, she told me, "This one was from my last love affair." That time, the knife had been taken in hand by her ex-lover's wife, who in a jealous rage had lunged at her neck, trying to damage her throat and destroy the singing voice by which she earned her livelihood. Though the wife missed her larynx, Diana had spent ten days in the hospital. Her lover had never even come to visit. But Zizi had, Diana added, with an appreciative glance at Zizi.

Diana's tallying of knife wounds was not yet over; this was actually the *third* blade in her romantic history, she told us. All her "bad luck with men" seemed to end with knives. The first knife had killed the "one true love" of her life, her only fiancé, in a bar fight when she was eighteen. Just before, oddly enough, they had agreed that if one of them died they would come back and take the other with him or her. Diana, who said she didn't like Candomblé, nonetheless once went to a *festa* (celebration), where she was told that her love was lingering about in her life, preventing her from loving again. Diana claimed to both believe and disbelieve this, seeming more comfortable than I could be with the contradiction.

I was easily drawn into Diana's reverie. For a change, I was hearing about how violence had stabbed its way, repeatedly, into just one person's life. I'd spent so many days before this, during the nine months I spent in the Salvador's women's *delegacia*, recording case after case of the city's daily harvest of violence. On a given day I might have heard ten to twenty cases, many of them involving crises coming to a head in the lives of bruised or bloodied women, most of whose faces I would never see again. By the time

I sat with Diana and Zizi, I still felt a little punch-drunk myself. The prospect of being able to talk to a few people more than once struck me as welcoming, even if the stories were still distressing to hear.

Suddenly, in the middle of one of Diana's sentences, Zizi whipped her body away from the ledge of Diana's balcony, where she had been watching the courtyard below. She flattened herself against the house wall with enough force to produce a thud. With stiffened shoulders, panicked and hiding, she told us in a conspiratorial whisper: "There she is, there's my *sogra* [mother-in law]."

It was the first time I'd actually seen the widow Dona Alegrina, reigning "matriarch" of the Alto do Mungongo, in the flesh.[1] Zizi was married to her third son, Jorginho, whom I had met along with various other members of the family in the neighborhood (see figure 5), but until now Dona Alegrina herself had remained elusive. She was heavyset, though not so bountiful as many older Bahian women, and gave the impression of resting uncomfortably on her feet, probably because of the telltale white bandage wrapped around one ankle. Dona Alegrina was lighter-skinned than her children whom I'd met (five lived in the Mungongo), her skin color suggesting perhaps more indigenous ancestry than her children had. Her son Zumbi later confirmed that she was "half *índio*." Her faded cotton dress, accompanied by a light sweater despite the heat of the day, somehow contradicted the expectations of grandeur I only then realized I'd held of her; from my first acquaintance with this community, I'd been hearing about Dona Alegrina, formidable *mãe de santo* of Candomblé.

Later, when I knew her better, Dona Alegrina would show me photographs of herself in ritual dress for a ceremony at her *terreiro* (temple), in which her elegant adornment more than fulfilled my expectations.

But now I asked Zizi why she was hiding.

"She hates me, and so I don't like her either, and we don't talk. Just 'Good day, good night,'" Zizi said.

I asked, "Does Dona Alegrina have any daughters-in-law that she *does* get along well with?" I'd already noticed that Aldagisa, wife of Valdinho, Dona Alegrina's eldest child, seemed to live cooped up in her tiny house, and that her husband was gone more nights than not. Zizi smiled wryly and said only one, who doesn't live here. She didn't get along well with any of the three daughters-in-law who lived in the Mungongo.

Zizi said that Dona Alegrina had never liked her, in all the years since she'd been with Alegrina's son, which was almost since she had left her family in São Felix. Though Zizi came to live with Jorginho at the Mungongo

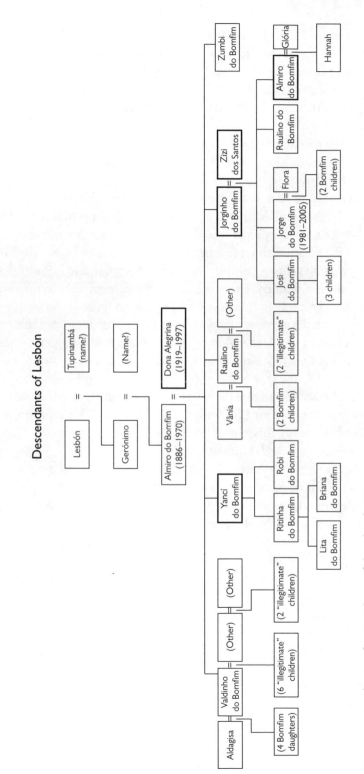

Descendants of Lesbón

Figure 5. *Família Bomfim*: Residents of the Alto do Mungongo.

at the age of eleven, she actually left home to work in Salvador at just seven, following her father's abandonment of her mother with eleven children. Zizi was the oldest girl, and so had to leave to find work; she was essentially fostered out to a lighter-skinned, more well-to-do family than her own, becoming a "created daughter," or *filha de criação*. Researchers have documented these Brazilian "daughters" as unpaid servants, often left uneducated and without access to family patrimony compared to their "siblings," the families' blood offspring (Twine 1998; Goldstein 2003; Scheper-Hughes 1992). Apparently, men of the Bomfim family regarded girls in such circumstances as appealing prospective partners: I could now count three generations (Dona Alegrina, daughter-in-law Zizi, and granddaughter-in-law Vani), each of whom had "escaped" *(fugiu)* to the Mungongo with Bomfim family men, all at ages well younger than twenty.

The day that Zizi revealed her problem with Dona Alegrina was also when she first intimated in my presence that Jorginho's philandering had led to explosive fights between them. I asked at the time if the arguments had gotten "rough" *(duro)*, euphemistic for including physical violence. This was a question I became practiced at working up to asking women in the neighborhood, but of course I never felt comfortable posing it and never knew what reaction it might provoke. Zizi's neighbor Creuza, long-suffering from her husband's battering, had sighed heavily, sunk into a long silence, and eventually begun to weep silently. Cândida, another neighbor locked in chronic conflict with her husband, let out a raucous, barking laugh. Sônia, whose domineering husband scarcely allowed me to interview her and may have been listening from the next room, simply ignored the question, even though I'd asked in hushed tones, and quietly changed the subject.

For Zizi's part, she merely lowered her chin and looked at me with eyebrows raised and lips pursed, her silence seeming to answer loudly in the affirmative. Later, this would be more than confirmed through Yancí and others. Although Yancí detested the way all five of her brothers treated their wives, "poor Zizi" had it the worst; she was "really a case that could use some help."

The triangle of closely related women kin around which this chapter turns comprises Zizi, Dona Alegrina, and Yancí, Zizi's sister-in-law and Dona Alegrina's only daughter. Their histories, I found, displayed staggering differences in position, power, experience, and attitude regarding gendered violence. Jorginho, the husband, son, and brother through whom the women are related, does not come into focus until the next chapter. Beginning with the women helps illuminate an oft-ignored aspect of violence against women: that conflict, victimization, and resistance may have as much to do with women's relationships to one another as with women's relationships to men.

Yancí, the daughter and sister-in-law, is accorded a prominent position for a work about domestic violence, considering that she was about as far from being victimized by male violence as any woman I met in Bahia. Where both Yancí's mother and her sister-in-law Zizi have been, in different ways, subject to what their family members consider "abuse" from their husbands, Yancí represents the significant number of women I met in Bahia who were bossy, brash, and indomitable. I intentionally cast Yancí as spokeswoman for all the "anti-victim" women I encountered, with the hope that her presence will keep readers aware that even in a book about wife-beating, most women are *not* victims of such violence, nor do many of them see themselves as vulnerable in this respect.

Listening to women from the Bomfim family talk about violence reveals a distinctively Afro-Brazilian ideology of female superiority. Many Bahian women's views of their own power and freedom cast the male privilege and dominance generally associated with to male-to-female violence in a paradoxical light. By showing how women like Dona Alegrina can be, at times, complicit in the abuse of women like Zizi, I seek to situate man-woman dyads in the context of larger kin and community networks that also influence and shape violent dynamics. By highlighting how some women instigate violent incidents, despite their greater vulnerability to serious injury when a conflict turns physical, I explore how gender-based partner violence need not always be about men securing or maintaining male domination. Rather, it may frequently reflect women questioning, rejecting, and rebelling against beliefs, norms, or behaviors that enforce their subjugation.

THE WIFELY WASHERWOMAN

Zizi and I exchanged our first shy hellos across a clothesline that extended along the short ledge where three "houses," the middle one ours, were constructed atop an older dwelling. The houses on the ledge began as one long room, which was then divided into three, with doors added to give each a separate entrance. Each residence consisted of one room, with water plumbed into a corner for a sink, shower head, and a "self-flush" toilet, meaning you filled a bucket and poured it in yourself. Raw wiring extended along the central beam of a common roof made of asbestos siding, to which a single light bulb socket and plug had been wired for each house. From the *prazinha* (little plaza) below us a labyrinth of a half-dozen muddy paths, *ladeiras* (literally, ladders) snaked up the hillside in different directions, toward dozens of houses above. Most of these were humble, but a few were grandiose; all were fashioned in an improvised, one-room-at-a-time process that spanned many years. From the shelf where Tim and I lived, Zizi's chestnut-brown face could frequently be seen cresting the ledge as she climbed the muddy dirt path to visit Diana, whom Zizi declared her "only friend in the world."

In return for the cut-rate laundry services Zizi supplied Diana, Diana was helping Zizi with the arithmetic for her new mail-order business, for which Zizi seemed overwhelmingly grateful. Beyond the laundry and the mail-order business, informal sector activities of the sort many Mungongo women undertook to make ends meet, I came to realize that just getting out from under her mother-in-law's watchful eye was a relief for Zizi. I watched the two friends, struck by Zizi's small body, taut and muscular in its petiteness, with the wiry strength of an adolescent boy. She managed also to resemble a ballerina, in the way her long neck seemed carefully held above open, squared shoulders, collarbones defined under tightly drawn flesh.

Just as I watched them, Zizi and Diana watched the gringos who had moved in next door.[2] The first thing that the neighborhood found notable about us was that Tim could be seen as regularly as I could hanging up laundry on the line outside. Not only would he pin up his own, hand-washed clothing but also household linens like sheets and towels, and occasionally even clothes of mine. On top of the fact that he did too much laundry for a man, the children who came to gaze into the windows of our room reported back to their mothers that Tim (who had over ten years experience as a professional chef) was often seen *cooking!* Soon the children were reporting back to me what their mothers had said: If I wanted to take good care of my husband and keep him, he should not have to do laundry or cook. They seemed genuinely concerned to help me, generously reasoning that I must merely be misguided. Understandably, all the sitting around talking to people, the interviewing, didn't quite conform to their notions of work. Most people didn't see me sitting with an assistant, transcribing, or making field notes, because I closed the door first, as I didn't like to advertise having a computer; I suspect they wouldn't have counted it as work, either, if they had seen me. I was aware that I resembled one of those "bad" women, the type people described as setting themselves up for their hard-working partners' rage, and even deserving of violence.

I had never washed quantities of clothing by hand before, and as I hung out my less-than-spotless efforts I was keenly aware that I lacked critical skills for being a passable Mungongo woman. (In particular, the little speckles of blood found each morning on our bed sheets, only on whichever side I'd been sleeping, defied my scrubbing efforts. The mosquitoes seemed to prefer my blood to Tim's, and would become too engorged to fly away, getting crushed whenever I rolled over.)

Probably after being prompted by Zizi, Diana politely suggested that Zizi would be happy to help with our washing, as she took in clothing to augment the salary of her husband, Jorginho, who worked as a bus driver. Diana enthusiastically vouched for Zizi: "She's the best; I wouldn't let anyone else touch my clothes." We had thus far resisted hiring any domestic help in Brazil, but quickly decided to allow ourselves the luxury of a washerwoman. Besides, my domestic ineptitude would help me to get to know Zizi better. I began dropping off my clothes at her house.

One night, Zizi came to deliver Tim's laundry and pick up mine, her eighteen- and seven-year-old sons in tow as usual, along with a visiting twelve-year-old nephew. She stood respectfully in the front door, and I invited her several times to come in and sit before she accepted. She opted for the chair right next to the door rather than sitting on the covered tackboard mattress serving as a couch toward which I'd gestured, but her seven year-old son Almiro was more courageous, tromping in and sitting in the center of the mattress. Upon sitting, Zizi began to explain, "I'd told Tim I'd get the clothes to him by Monday—"

"Yes, but he told me he hadn't been around all day Monday, so don't worry about it," I cut in, hoping to spare her the need to apologize.

But it became clear she had a story to tell. "See, Sarah, it's that I don't have an iron, and I usually borrow other people's. I borrow Diana's iron a lot, and she's cool, she never minds. But there are other people. . . . You know how sometimes you borrow something of someone's and then she needs it and asks for it back in a way with her face closed to you, almost like she's mad at you? I always feel bad, and I hate to have to be borrowing.

"So, that's what happened: on Monday I couldn't get an iron. But you know what? The next day my husband came home from work, and I saw a package on the table. I looked at it, and he said, 'Why don't you open it?' I did, and I got an iron for a present!" She finished with a victorious nod of her head. "These clothes of Tim's are the first ones I ever pressed with it!"

I asked, "Did you have one before, that broke or something?"

"No," she shook her head. "This is the first one I've ever had."

For ten years, Zizi had been washing people's clothes and, somehow, returning them ironed, without what was an essential tool of the trade, especially for Bahians, who almost uniformly iron even cotton T-shirts and jeans. "Was it your birthday or anything?"

"No, no, he just gave it to me. See, I didn't receive anything on Mother's Day, or my birthday, or for Christmas, so . . ." Zizi spoke without a sense of deprivation or self-pity; she was focused on how lucky she had indeed been today. She repeated the Brazilian equivalent of the saying in English "God helps those who help themselves" (*Deus ajuda a quem cedo madruga;* literally, "God helps those who rise with the sun").

I was moved by Zizi's sense of being "blessed," in circumstances that for many would appear only as a slight respite from hardship. I was also curious about her relationship to her husband. He had a full-time job as a bus driver, but apparently had not been in a position to help his wife obtain a piece of equipment essential to her trade before now.

By the time I returned to the Alto do Mungongo two years later, I had come to understand better how Zizi could have gone without an iron all those years. Zizi and Jorginho's bright and beguiling youngest child, Almiro, then nine, had been out of school for a year and a half, I learned. The incredible part was that Jorginho's employer, the bus company, would have paid Almiro's tuition to go to any reasonably priced private school in the city. Jorginho told me he had simply been "too busy" to get around to completing the necessary paperwork. Meanwhile, other family members assured me, Jorginho had been paying the tuition for his other woman, Gabriela, to attend English classes, which by any Bahian's measure are an expensive luxury. The allocation of resources between Jorginho's two "wives" was starting to add up. The concern I showed about Almiro's education led, perhaps, to my eventually being asked to "baptize" Almiro and become his *madrinha* (godmother). This connection helped me ensure, or at least attempt to, that he would never stay out of school for long again.

ROMANCING VIOLENCE

Finding time to hear more about Zizi, Jorginho, and his mother wasn't easy. Though Zizi never presented herself as less than willing to talk with me, she also seemed unable to free herself from household duties long enough to allow for an extended conversation. Instead, the conversations through which she unfolded her story of life with Jorginho came in snippets. The first of these came as Zizi cut onions, bell peppers, and hot *malagüeta* peppers, along with a freshly caught red snapper, which she boned with a worn, rather dull knife.

According to Zizi, the principal reason for her problems with her mother-in-law was the same for her problems with Jorginho: it all revolved around Jorginho's extramarital involvements and Zizi's unwillingness to accept them.

"Fights between *marido e mulher* [husband and woman] happen," she explained, "even more so among the poor class, like me, generally because of other women *[mulheres na rua]*. I used to get jealous a lot. He did too, but he didn't demonstrate it as much. But at the very beginning our fights were about that, about some woman in the street, who many times would even come *here* looking for him. They didn't come here to the house, but they looked for him here in the neighborhood—that's what they told me. You know how neighbors are." I remembered repeatedly having been told that the only reason one would tell a woman that her husband was betraying her was because one wished her ill.

Zizi continued. "I cried, argued, said I was leaving him, everything. Then, with time, I started letting these fights alone, thinking more about my children . . ."

"And right after you married," I asked, "you said that you never accepted that he had other women, and that Dona Alegrina thought that you had to accept it?"

"She accepted it—she still accepts it. And not only me—it's the same with all her daughters-in-law—she still accepts it, and she gets along well with her sons' lovers," she said. Zizi spoke at length of the "*falta de moral*" (lack of morals) this presented, reminding me of what has been called the "amorality" (but not immorality) of Candomblé (Prandi 1991; Greenfield 1994).

"Why, do you think?" I asked.

"I don't know. I guess it's because she suffered so much with their father, so she wants to take it out on *[descontar]* us . . . She thinks that this is like the old days when women tolerated that kind of thing, but I'm not going to put up with it.

"That was my conflict with her. She suffered a lot with their father."

Zizi paused, as if considering whether to go on. What she said next turned out to be sensitive information, indeed. "Would you believe he even put another woman to live together with her, Sarah? He divided the house right in two, and put the other woman in one part and Dona Alegrina in the other! So, she was *revoltada* [disgusted, offended], and she didn't fight like me. She stayed quiet all those years." Only years after this conversation, after Dona Alegrina had passed away, would both Zizi and her sister-in-law Yancí confirm that Alegrina, the teenager who married the *pai de santo* in late maturity, had shouldered her own share of slaps and punches, especially in the early years.

But now Zizi took a slow breath, then continued. "He got old, went blind, and Dona Alegrina kept taking care of him, keeping all that resentment inside.

"Most of her daughters-in-law don't care about this problem of hers. I, when I was younger, didn't try to understand either, because of the way she treated us."

Zizi lowered her voice and confided with intensity. "Often I think that if Dona Alegrina hadn't entered in the middle of our fights, they wouldn't have reached the level of aggression they did. But she got right in there. . . . At times we'd be arguing and she'd say, '*Beat* her!'" Zizi raised her voice to act it out. "'That's just what she deserves, to get beaten!' And then I would turn on her: 'No! It's *a senhora* [you, formal] who deserves to be beaten!'" Despite her sense of who deserved what, Zizi always ended up taking the brunt of blows. Even if the fists and feet were Jorginho's, she held her mother-in-law equally responsible.

Zizi summed up the way she was treated, in later conversations as well, as Dona Alegrina "*descontando*" on her daughters-in-law. Here *descontar* refers to "taking it out on someone," but a more literal gloss could be "discounting," as in debiting from someone else's figurative "account." She also used a phrase I heard from others: "paying in the same coin." The coin, it was clear, could be conceived of as abuse, its different denominations ranging from verbal to psychological to economic to physical.

Ultimately, I identified several similarly quasi-economistic slang terms for "to beat" someone, including *dar conta* (to give account), *cobrar* (to charge; in Bahia, this was used most often as meaning to "nag," to "demand," or to "expect," but could also mean to "beat,");[3] to *baixar* (or *meter*) *pau em* means to give a beating, but *pau* (literally wood; also a beating) has also served as slang for diverse principal units of currency: the *cruzeiro (novo)*, the *cruzado (novo)* or since 1995, the *real*.[4] Of special note is *dar porrada* for "to beat," literally "to give semen," where *porrada* derives from *porra*, or "penis."

From the first time I heard such references, I wondered how such a political economy of abuse, wrongful force, or violence might work. Had Dona Alegrina, having advanced to widow-matriarch, somehow been able to recoup for her own "account" what had once been wrongly debited, when her husband caused her suffering?

I was struck by how neatly Zizi's description of her mother-in-law fit with women who have been called "token torturers" in anthropological literature. Typically an older woman, frequently a mother-in-law, a token torturer reproduces oppression and abuse, reinforcing the same patriarchal values used to subjugate her in her youth (Campbell 1999). She is a "token" in that she advances, by age and often widowhood, to be able to stand in for the same forces that socialized her into feminine constraint, thus serving as the ultimate hegemonic agent for patriarchy and working against a social category of people—women—to which she belongs. Whether or not the token torturer concept would prove helpful in understanding Zizi and Alegrina, I knew the situation would be unlikely to be that simple, neatly conforming to the model. Specifically, I was interested in what agency and resources Zizi could exercise to prevent the reproduction of such a cycle.

Zizi mused about how she came to sympathize, over time, with her mother-in-law. "Later, Sarah, I sought to change my life and my children's lives; then I started to understand her problem also. I do know I'm not going to be that way with my daughters-in-law. I'm going to try to help, and I already told my sons: When you all get married I don't want to see you mistreat your wives in front of me—I'll grab a broom and you all will get it! That cracks them up."

From where we sat, in the corner of the main room of their old *taipa* (lath and plaster) house, I could see that the room served multiple functions: kitchen, dining room, living room, and den, as well as being the place where everyone except Jorginho and Zizi would unroll a strip of foam rubber to sleep on at night (that is, the four children and, at this time, two nephews). Adjoining rooms seemed perpetually in construction, never quite yet usable, appearing given over to the encroaching tropical wet and vegetation. On a wooden, paint-chipped cabinet, an old television and stereo set had been optimistically placed; neither was working. The only other furniture in the room was a Formica table with some mismatched chairs. A newly captured monkey, about the size of a large man's outspread hand, chattered furiously from atop its cage on the wall, broadcasting its resentment of the string around its neck. Household members and others looked in every few minutes, asking Zizi if she'd finished washing some article of laundry, or when lunch would be ready.

I noticed a simple shrine in the corner, to Cosme and Damião (Cosmos and Damian) and the *ibejis*—twin Catholic saints and twin spirits of

Candomblé, respectively. Not long after this, Cosme and Damião would become an embarrassing, annoyed-at-oneself association for me. As I came to know Dona Alegrina and Yancí better, I gave Dona Alegrina a Cosme and Damião; she indirectly passed on a curt message about the work that receiving such a gift would make for them. Foolishly, I hadn't considered that if one gives an image of a saint as a gift for a *terreiro,* one obligates the recipients to "seat" it properly, which can be expensive and laborious.

Zizi saw me studying the shrine, and allowed that she liked Candomblé. But, she added, she thought it important to recognize its limitations. Dona Alegrina, after all, was considered a powerful *mãe de santo,* and Zizi was certain she had tried to use her sway—she had indeed "found *trabalhos*" (works, spells for the Candomblé *exus, orixás,* or other entities) intended to see her son with one of the women she preferred over Zizi. Despite Zizi's fear of Dona Alegrina's abilities, she could afford to view neither her mother-in-law nor Candomblé as all-powerful. So, she concentrated on their limitations.

This came up when Zizi mentioned Jorginho's other women coming, at times, to visit Dona Alegrina.

"You really think they do?" I asked. "Why would they?"

"To do malice. She never did accept me being with Jorginho, you know. So they would work with Dona Alegrina. Jorginho gave them her telephone number, and they called."

"You mean, to do a spell [*trabalho,* here meaning sorcery] to help the woman conquer [*conquistar*] Jorginho?"

"Exactly." Zizi nodded indignantly. "I've found my name several times on a piece of paper," as part of a *trabalho,* she assumed. "But I never got too concerned, because even though I like Candomblé and everything, I think that the first person above all else is God, and my faith is in God. A lot of women have done things, and she [Dona Alegrina] has done things, to see if he'd leave me. But she must have done it wrong, or they never worked. She would only do things to see if he'd leave me. She could have done a *trabalho* to see if we could stop fighting, but she never did *that.*"

Zizi looked up from her fuming memory, suddenly seeming concerned that I would form the wrong impression. Despite all of the discord, her overall view of her relationship with Jorginho still resembled an epic romance, wherein lovers withstood opposition and adversity to be together. She recounted the beginnings of their volatile love, and how he already had "various other girls—I think he had eight. He told me that he had broken up with all eight of them, just to be with me. . . . Sometimes they would come, wanting to beat me up, and I was younger and smaller. So, he said he was finished with all of them.

"But he went on as he was, going out with a woman and sleeping in the street. . . . I fell in love *[eu me apaixonei]*. They say that poor people don't fall in love, but my case was different."

I wasn't sure who "they" were here, and again wished I'd realized buying a television to watch *telenovelas* would have been the most responsible thing for a fieldworker in Brazil to do.

"The majority of poor people are ignorant to think that way," Zizi went on, "Because the way I felt when I saw him for the first time . . ."

Zizi got pregnant at the age of eleven. Jorginho brought her to meet his mother, and together Dona Alegrina and Zizi decided to terminate the pregnancy, over Jorginho's objections. Dona Alegrina, who in the past had served as a *parteira* (midwife) for many births in the neighborhood, performed the abortion herself. After this first time—Zizi's abortions would eventually total ten—Zizi became terribly ill: "almost paralytic." She was convinced, nonetheless, that it was the right thing to do, "Because I was so young, and he was worried. We were in no circumstances to have a child. We didn't have anywhere to live together; I slept on the beach behind the church, and he took care of me. From the breakfast that she—" Zizi nodded her head in the direction of Dona Alegrina's house, "—gave him, he gave me half, and lunch as well. He wasn't a bad person. He took care of me."

From the beginning, Zizi's feelings for Jorginho were marked with jealousy, but she reflected that if she could only reconcile herself to this, she might still be allowed her passion. After all, she would ask, "Aren't infidelities and fights to be expected? But love is not." Particularly for poor people like her, she again reminded me. "People think love is only for soap opera people from São Paulo."

The first fight with physical aggression occurred in the beginning of the relationship, years before they legalized their marriage. Then and thereafter, she confessed laughingly, she was more likely to be the initial aggressor.

"I was very young," she reminded me. "Anything could happen and I would cry. I fell in love too hard. I was a little child! I'd never had a boyfriend. The way he treated me right in the beginning, when I found out he was going out to get together with another woman, it seemed like—I don't know—I got mad because I knew that he was betraying me and I wasn't betraying him. I wasn't that way, even when we were courting, I never even smiled at another guy. I was full of that insane, possessed *[alucinada]* passion, my first affair *[namoro]*. So when he came back home I fought, I cried,

I wanted to leave. I got aggressive and so he did too," Zizi finished, laughing wryly at the memory.

"So was it something that you usually started?" I asked.

"Almost always. I went off on him *[eu ia em cima dele]:* I scratched him, everything; so he also got aggressive, and there you had a fight. Many times he didn't even get to the point of beating me; he told me to quiet myself down. He'd get a switch from a guava tree, and with this little stick he'd hit my legs and say: 'You're going to quiet yourself. I'm raising you *[lhe criando].* I'm your father,' I don't know what else." Again, Zizi laughed.

"He said *that?*" I was incredulous.

"He did."

"And you responded?"

"I said: 'You're not my father! My father's in São Felix!'"

"But really, I never thought of hurting him, like to the point of him having to go to the hospital. And he even came to me to say, at one point, 'Zizi, this jealousy of yours is going to hurt you *[lhe prejudicar],* someday. Because you are very aggressive: You attack me, you curse me—the one provoking these fights is you! Now, I am of the moment. So I could give you a slap, and hurt you or even kill you. Because I am man. I'm not even going to feel one of your slaps.'

"He used to joke with me: 'Where is your strong hand?' He grabbed my arm: 'Where is the arm to be hitting me? I'm stronger, Zizi. Let's just end with that. Because this is getting ugly. Our children are getting older. We need love, to help each other and not do this anymore.'"

As involved as she became in telling me the story, I still thought Zizi seemed anxious: Was she feeling all right? It was her back, she told me. An old spinal injury. It was hurting more than usual this morning. Also, she hadn't finished washing all the linen for the restaurant next door, and the woman had had a fit.

I asked how the injury had happened. "Well, it was in one of my fights with Jorginho, years ago." Her voice changed, conveying a degree of shame about this admission, closer to the voices of Creuza and Sônia and other women who had been savagely battered and found it humiliating to say out loud. She was careful to assure me, "He didn't really mean to hurt me." At the same time, "But" she sighed, "my spine will never be the same.

"It happened because of the children," she elaborated. "Because they didn't want to go to school or study—he beat up on them too much. I didn't want him beating them that way, so I went to get him off, and he kicked me to get me away from the kids and let him beat them. I lost my balance there on the stairs, and I fell down below. When I fell he went running to help me, saying he was sorry. With time, I started to feel a pain in my spine, in my spinal column, in this bone," she indicated a place below her ribs. "I used to always fall when I was straightening up the cupboard . . ." Zizi's voice trailed off. She shook her head as if to dispel the image, then declared in a voice lowered with resolve, "I'm going to see if I can take it until my children don't need me anymore."

I remembered this statement with greater poignancy when later Josi, Zizi's mentally deficient daughter who was judged incapable of raising babies alone when found slapping her first at three months old, went on to have four babies, against everyone's objections. Zizi is raising three of them, and will be needed not only by her children but by her children's children as well, for years to come.

AFTERNOON IN YANCÍ'S BAR

Invocation for Iansã (Oya-Yansan)

Oyá, courageous woman who, on waking, grasps her saber,
Oyá, wife of Shangô,
Oyá, whose husband is red,
Oyá, who dies bravely with her husband.
Oyá, wind of Death.
Oyá, whirlwind that shakes the trees of the leaves all about.
Oyá, who is the only one who can hold the horns of a buffalo.

PIERRE VERGER
"Orixás da Bahia"

Not long after, I heard about Jorginho's violence from a different, and much less tolerant, perspective than Zizi's.[5] But Yancí, Jorginho's only sister, and I did not start our chat about violence against women with Zizi; Yancí worked her way there slowly.

"Oh Sarah, you don't have to go to the Delegacia da Mulher [Women's Police Station] to hear about that," Yancí declared dismissively when my research came up. "The stories I could tell you, things that happened right here, you wouldn't believe." She chewed raw coconut as she spoke, pausing to suck the fiber dry of milk and spit out the remaining roughage into a trash can beside her.

I sat on a wobbly wooden stool in her kitchen, helping peel potatoes for the midday meal and occasionally swatting at the tiny *muruím* fleas that relentlessly bit my ankles. The fleas didn't seem to bother Yancí quite as much; she said she was used to them. I was capable of wincing, though, watching them settle greedily on the open sore, an uncontrolled ulcer, on her ankle. Like her mother Dona Alegrina, Yancí wore a white bandage around her ankle when she left the house. I had come to see these, which one saw throughout the city, as naggingly symbolic of the inadequate health care available to Salvador's poor. In addition to ulcerated varicose veins and infected sores, uncontrolled diabetes seemed particularly rampant. Given the amount of sugar nearly every Bahian piled into *café* morning, noon, and night, the legacy of the state's history of sugar cane still exacted dearly from descendants of the enslaved Africans brought to Brazil to produce it (Schwartz 1986; Mintz 1985).

Yancí was the mother of two adult children and newly a grandmother. Good-looking and still a vigorous woman in her late forties, Yancí had dark-cinnamon skin and an intelligent, inscrutable brow that set her apart. Her beauty is what some Afro-Bahians I'd interviewed would have called "the type of beauty that doesn't fall," usually in reference to themselves as a way to elide classifying themselves according to cruder "racial" or color categories when asked how they identify by "color" or "race." Such women felt it would be uncouth to actively declare themselves black, but were willing to point out that their darker skin is thought to hold up better under the tropical sun. Yancí shared none of the internalized racism, or presumptions of the interviewer's racism, that such euphemisms often implied—she declared herself "*negra*" without the slightest hesitation when surveyed. I attributed this at least in part to the distinctive history of her family; she never downplayed or seemed ashamed of her background, but in fact was keen to use it as cultural capital whenever possible. She called herself an independent businesswoman with similar pride, and generated a reasonably steady income, albeit modest, through the bar and other improvised, informal-economy enterprises.

Rei was Yancí's friend, sometime lover, and drinking companion. He was in his early thirties, and when working alongside Yancí in the bar he frequently called her his *patroa*—boss—for all to hear, seeming to enjoy the unusual implications of a young, attractive man willingly looking up to an older woman who is also his sexual partner.

I was now getting to know Yancí, Alegrina's only biological daughter, better every day, in part owing to my weakness for buying single cigarettes from her bar. I understood that Yancí had "had her head made," or been initiated into Candomblé, by her own mother. Still, compared to the majority of *filhas-de-santo* (daughters-of-saint, Candomblé initiates), this didn't currently appear to be a central part of Yancí's identity—she had told me that she didn't want to be a "prisoner" of Candomblé, perhaps referring to the level of obligation to the "saints" one takes on when deeply involved. Too, perhaps her lukewarm interest simply resulted from the family *terreiro* growing less and less active as Dona Alegrina aged and struggled with health problems.

Most striking so far in conversations with Yancí was her indignation toward women victimized by men's violence. She dismissed men who are violent as no good, as "without shame" *(sem vergonha)*. But she also saw their worthlessness as unremarkable, as natural: what can you expect? But the *women* who *put up with it*—these required commentary! Yancí declared that she would "never consider allowing" herself to be hit. She had absolutely no sympathy for women who did allow it more than once, insisting that if they stick around they "must like it" on some level.

This lack of sympathy for a chronically beaten woman fit into a belief system that many *baianas* elaborated for me about intrinsic gender difference and vast areas of behavior—moral, intellectual, emotional—where women are simply superior. Yancí easily and repeatedly launched into a litany of ways women outdo men. Her personal version of female superiority was most glaring in her conviction that she was so much more capable of raising her two children than their biological father that she never once considered registering them under "any man's name," but gave them her own surname. Rei's role as her consort and junior further complemented Yancí's defiant profile. Overall, Yancí enacted her roles as mother, *companheira*, boss, daughter, businesswoman, and *filha-de-santo* as no one's subordinate.

Once, she explained to me how she cultivated her distaste for marriage. "I never wanted to marry because the men I had in my life, I always had more than they did, and what I've earned is not to give to them." This would not be the last time I would hear her disparage men's insolvency, which she attributed to their "inability" to muster a work ethic.

Yancí's diatribes made me wonder if I weren't hearing an Afro-Bahian version of the ideology some observers of Latin American women have called Marianismo, or beliefs asserting that women hold specific, generally spiritual and moral, areas of superiority over men. Marianismo is an academic discourse initiated by Evelyn Stevens (1973a, 1973b), who adapted the term, liberally, from practices surrounding diverse devotional "cults" to the Virgin Mary in Catholic history. For Stevens, Marianismo of the Hispanophone Americas referred to covert female control of domestic domains (while still allowing the man to *feel* sovereign), self-abnegation and self-sacrifice in the interests of offspring and other kin, and displays of moral fortitude and level-headedness that calm volatile men's temperaments (Stevens 1973b; see also Stevens 1973a). More recently, the conceptual employment of Marianismo has been sharply criticized: Ehlers (1991) and Navarro (2002) take Stevens to task, rejecting the elevation of Marianismo (by cultural actors and analysts such as Stevens alike) as false consciousness that reinforces women's economic subordination and that is not to be celebrated. Other critics, such as psychologists Mayo and Resnick, express concerned with Marianismo as a learned behavior, whereby women internalize "the culture's expectations of them—to be passive and to accept unconditionally men's right to own them and men's legal right to discipline them through corporal punishment and emotional violence" (1996: 14). They conclude that this results in many Latin American women "act[ing] against themselves and limit[ing] the development of their expectations." In this sense, Marianismo is arguably an ideology that reproduces patriarchal hegemony among Latin American women, getting women to participate in their own oppression by enforcing "natural" differences.

Upon reflection, neither the romanticizing nor the falsification of Marianismo seemed to apply usefully to someone like Yancí, or to a multireligious, Afro-Brazilian context. The fact that many *baianas* did actively profess a form of female superiority is probably the only significant parallel. In order to distinguish an Afro-Bahian ideology of female superiority, perhaps in Bahia such an ideology might be better conceived of as *"Iansá-ísmo,"* (yan-saw-IZ-mo), for the Candomblé goddess Iansá. Iansá is the fierce controller of storms, taker of multiple lovers, and is subordinate to no man. Not incidentally, she is also the *orixá* that "owns" Yancí's "head," as well as being one of the three *orixás* with ties to her mother Alegrina. Far from the self-abnegation of various Virgin Marys and Marias, Iansá (Oyá Iansá) is renowned for leaving her husband-*orixá*, Ogum, for another more elegant, Xangô (Verger 1993: 220, 252). Afterward, Iansá and Ogum exchanged blows that splintered the universes of both men and women. Unlike the women Steven's critics find harmonized and hegemonized by Marianismo, Yancí is hardly self-abnegating, nor accepting of a behind-the-scenes form of power.

If Iansá illuminates much about a strong woman like Yancí, she is not the only model for powerful Bahian women. Surrounding her in the Mungongo and up and down the Avenida are women whose authoritativeness and leadership in their families, communities, and work networks were nourished from endlessly diverse sources—Eliene, who organized the teenagers for trash picking and recycling, Mona and her tight circle of evangelicals, Creuza and her work through the Domestic Worker's Union, or Sandra, the formidable Jehovah's Witness mother of five who ruled absolutely at home, despite outwardly having ceded to husbandly leadership. In complicated and variable ways, each of these women could be understood as individuals as relatively immune to falling victim to male violence as Yancí herself is. At the same time, of course, merely because a woman possesses the passion and defiance of a Yancí does not prevent her from getting beat up by a man. If Yancí were to have her say, however, she would assert that someone truly "of" Iansã would never allow it to happen twice.

SICK LOVE (AMOR DOENTÍO)

Iemenjá Assabá—limps, constantly spins cotton, is willful and sometimes dangerous.

MIKELLE S. OMARI-TUNKARA
Manipulating the Sacred: Yorùbá Art, Ritual,
and Resistance in Brazilian Candomblé

Although formidable Bahian women like Yancí may abound in Bahia, of course not all *baianas* can be described in this way. In point of fact, the Yancís of Bahia construct themselves in opposition to "pitiful" women who permit themselves to become victims.[6]

That afternoon, Yancí told of women she has known whose entire sexuality was wrapped up in being beaten: "There are women accustomed to blows *(pancada)*. They just get used to it. She's beaten up one day, and ten days go by, and she's getting it again. There are women who will only go to bed with beatings!" Yancí used the slang *porrada* for beating, which literally means "semen," thus seeming to group together things that men visit upon women. "I know of several women like that," she finished.

Yancí then recalled for me a story from when she was a young girl that encapsulated for her the idea of "sick love" *(amor doentío),* where passion and violence become fused. It concerned an elderly widow named Filomena, whose deceased husband had battered her bloody, day in and day out, for the duration of their marriage. Finally he got sick and died, and Filomena went into traditional mourning *(luto),* wearing all black.

"About two or three months had passed when it started," Yancí narrated, putting on her reading glasses and sorting her receipts as she talked. "It seemed like Filomena couldn't hold in her grief anymore. She went and got that same heavy mill sprocket [pilão] he used to beat her with. She hurled it up into the air while standing underneath, letting it crash down on her head and shoulders. All this time, she was wailing his name, 'Gilbeeeeerto! Aiiiiiii!,' again and again, along with, 'Bate mais!' [Beat me more]!"

Filomena sobbed and ranted as she grew more and more bloody and bruised, but incredibly, did not die. "In a few days, she was out there doing it again! 'Gilbeeeeeeeeeeeeeeeeeeeeerto!' Every three days or so. We would all go and watch—it got so it was kind of funny."

For Yancí, Filomena's story showed how victims could get so habituated to abuse that they become actively complicit, even recreating it themselves. Like many of her fellow Bahians, Yancí saw abuse and affective attachment as things that become linked, leading victims at times to collaborate to their own detriment. Because they accept the package, despite the agony of some parts, women in love with violent men are said to "like" (gostar de) violence.[7]

Yancí's notions of how a woman could "like" violence were not confined to eroticized masochism, however. Once a woman was pathetic enough to tolerate violence, Yancí found her to be so reprehensible as to actively warrant abuse. After repeatedly hearing other Bahians say things like, "Well, then, she must like being beaten; she has to like it," we began to ask nearly everyone we talked to about the expression, "All women like to be beaten." This was a shortened popularization of the author and playwright Nelson Rodriguez's much-quoted statement, "Not all women like to be beaten, only the normal ones. The neurotic ones fight back" (Nem todas as mulheres gostam de apanhar, só as normais. As neuróticas reagem; Rodrigues 1974). True to his famed pessimistic realism, Rodrigues's phrase implied a kinky, sexualized, and sado-masochistic connection between "liking" and "violence." When informants alluded to sexual connotations along the lines Rodrigues points toward, it was nearly always in association with this kind of habituation. In this context, Rodrigues saw women as "neurotic" because they both desired violence for erotic purposes, and also reacted against it.

However, I came to believe most Bahians understood the connection quite differently. Most commonly, they responded to this question by asserting it wasn't true, as in "They say women like to be beaten, but all I know is that I don't," or, from a man, "No, no one likes to be beaten; of course not." They could go on, though, to entertain the idea that a woman could be seen as "liking" being beaten, usually in the guise of one who tolerated an abusive situation and took no measures to change it.[8] These contrasting conceptions of how oneself would experience fear and pain and how someone else might do so echo the observations that Nancy Scheper-Hughes (1992) made in a related urban setting in northeast Brazil. In the Alto do Cruzeiro, hunger and malnutrition was an open secret, meaning that everyone knew it took an unacceptable toll, yet it was never viewed as the primary cause by the immediate family members of starving babies, overmedicated children and adults alike to quell hunger, or fetishistic obsessions about expensive, commoditized, and advertised foods out of the Cruzeiro's reach. In both cases, objective generalization and subjective particularism diverge in problematic ways, perhaps acting as defense mechanisms in the face of denials and trauma.

Affirming that the woman who sticks around for more amounted to liking being hit, Yancí declared: "She deserves to get beaten more! I'm in favor of men who beat." She went on to qualify how beatings might be deserved.

"I know many women who deserve to be beaten, and they *really* deserve to get it! Now, there are women that get beaten up unjustly, but these are the ones that should get themselves out of the situation."

"And the women who deserve it?" I asked.

"In the neighborhood we have one who's a good example. . . . The husband is a man that works; he's a real worker that provides everything she needs [corresponde com tudo] at home. He helps her, he takes her everywhere she wants to go; he's not lacking in any way, and she wants for nothing. Now tell me, with all that, couldn't this woman wash clothes, or clean house, or cook? If she can't help out her man, then she also can't just go around doing whatever she wants: This no-good [descarada] just stands in other people's doorways, gossiping."

I am again aware of how I can be found "gossiping in other people's doorways" far more than most. "And getting beaten would resolve this?" I wondered.

"To see if she can take shame [toma vergonha], Sarah!" Yancí entreated, her voice intense. "Let's say her man gets home, and he's revolted with this kind of thing. Well, then he needs to give her some smacks [dar de pau]! Because when he goes and complains to her—'Why didn't you do this or that?'—she gives him whatever answer she wants to: 'Oh, I was at so-and-so's house,' or 'Oh, I was gossiping with Fulano, Beltrano, and Ciclano,'" the Brazilian equivalent of Tom, Dick, and Harry.

"An analysis I do here in the Mungongo where I live, Sarah, is that the women here who are beaten are well deserving. Because her father and mother can't hit her anymore, so her husband beats her to set her back on track. But as soon as the woman won't accept this kind of deal, she only gets beat up once." Only upon such a refusal, it seemed, did a woman claim a kind of adulthood many women never reached. Yancí's analysis also places the impetus for refusal directly at the feet of the individual, corroborating arguments that women's emancipation relies on individualization, upon which citizen's, women's, and human rights all necessarily rest (Marques-Pereira and Raes 2005: 92).

"Because if he beats me," she explained, "*one* time. Because, I'm like this: I'm with him. He says he *loves* me. Love is a word that doesn't have any compensation. Love is just itself. Within love exists everything that is good. Within the love I know it's so. . . . Love compensates for all. But why would he beat me? Because there is nothing, no love, nothing."

"But then how can you be *in favor* of men who beat?" I persisted.

Yancí sighed. "Because, Sarah, then she has to take her punches." Again, she used *porrada*—semen—to say "punches."

"So, if I'm a man who provides everything for the home, and my wife doesn't do her share, she deserves to be beaten?"

"Right," Yancí nodded once, decisively. Then she held up a finger, qualifying, "But also, a woman who's getting beat up and doesn't leave is even worse than the man that's beating her. She needs to make a change, or she deserves it twice as much."

"But," I countered, "don't you think that some women aren't in a position [*não tem condições*] to . . . ?"

Yancí was in no mood for such excuses. "We all have family, Sarah. Especially women have family: she has a sister, an aunt. And say you have two or three children. If you can't be a civil servant, or work at Petrobrás [the local petrochemical complex] then you wash laundry, you set up a bar on the beach, you sell bananas and oranges, and you raise your children."

For Yancí, the roles of men and women were distinct and complementary, requiring compliance on both parts. If the woman failed to fulfill expectations, she effectively forfeited her adulthood, and it then became appropriate for her male partner to resort to authoritarian measures, including corporal punishment. If a woman who was doing her part and was otherwise undeserving of abuse continued to put up with this, and didn't leave, in Yancí's eyes she was doubly deserving of beatings. In both cases, physical aggression took the form of punishment meted out at a man's discretion. Because Yancí saw such a measure as a justified, legitimate enactment of authority on the part of the man, it ceased, in her view, to qualify as "violence," or something wrong that merited intervention. Interpretations like Yancí's are difficult to register in single-scale measures comparing levels of tolerance or acceptability of violence against women in different societies, where Brazil may be misleadingly ranked as a society that does not disapprove (Counts, Brown, and Campbell 1999: 5).

The ghostly tale of Filomena's masochism was not the last Yancí had to tell.

"What about the lady with the hair?" Yancí asked rhetorically of Rei, who had been sitting in, listening. She continued, "That lady had hair that was so long, I'd never seen anything like it. And her man was the most jealous I've ever seen—and meaner than he was jealous. I thought I was going to get shot, and I was just a *moça* [maiden]! He grabbed that pretty wife of his and wrapped her long braid three times around his fist, like a dog's leash. He yanked her out of their house out into the *praça* right here in front. I thought her neck would break. His other hand had a revolver, and he was shooting at anyone who tried to get in the middle. . . .

"Then, Sarah, there was the one who lost her fingernails. She went to the beauty salon to get her hair done and her nails painted, to get ready for a party here. She put on a low-cut dress that showed her cleavage. When her husband came and saw how she looked, he took some shears and cut off all her hair, and tore the dress so it was ruined. Still not satisfied, he took some pliers and pulled off two of her fingernails! *É mole?*" Her finish literally meant: "Is it soft/weak?" by which Yancí means, "Can you believe it?"

I scarcely could.

Yancí continued on into other stories, stopping to sell the odd shot of *cachaça,* the liquor made from sugar, or single cigarette to the neighbors appearing in the doorway and tossing the crumpled bills into a small pile on the table. Despite the heaviness of the topic, she recounted the horrors she had witnessed with flourish, in an almost festive, dramatic tone, aided by occasional encouragement from Rei. She acted out the scenes in flamboyant motions, throwing her head back and laughing when the brutality surpassed belief, then gravely fixing me with her eyes, peering above her glasses, asking, "*É mole, Sarah?*"

Eventually, the stories grew closer to home, as Yancí arrived at the history of her younger brother, Jorginho, and his wife, Zizi. By now I'd realized everyone in the neighborhood seemed to treat the couple's violence as common knowledge, but I had never I been privy to the graphic description Yancí now shared with me.

"There's no kind of punishment Zizi hasn't gotten from Jorginho, Sarah—if you can even *think* of it, so could he, and he's used it on her. That woman has been beaten with a shovel, she's been beaten with a big belt, and whipped with a vine *[cipó]* until she *rebocou por dentro* [was plastered hard from the inside]. You know that when they got together, Sarah, she was just a girl; her breasts hadn't even started to grow. Well, he never let them, with all this beating: You see how she doesn't have breasts today?" I thought Zizi did have breasts, just small ones, but said nothing. "Her sisters are small like her, but they have breasts. He just wouldn't let them grow. You know how she is supposed to be of Iemenjá?" Yancí asked me, referring to the *orixá* of the sea, fecundity, and fierce motherhood, renowned also for vanity and jealousy. "We say she is of Yemanjá Assaba, because that's the Iemenjá that limps, and is always working." She leaned forward and whispered the piece she found to be a cruel joke with a smirk, "But, Sarah, did you ever hear of an Iemenjá without breasts?" Iemenjá is typically depicted with enormous breasts, or with just one massive breast, such that she is self-conscious and unwilling to be touched.

Yancí continued to narrate Zizi's suffering. "Every single one of her pregnancies she was battered, Sarah! Kicks to the stomach! She lost more than one of them because of this, and that's why Josi," Zizi's oldest and only girl, then twenty-one, "is retarded, and why Jorge," the second oldest, "has problems too. Kicks to the stomach! She lost more babies than she ever gave birth to this way." Again I thought of the irony that, through Iemenjá, Zizi was tied to maternal fecundity in a way that, just as with her breasts' emergence, her actual life denied.

"Jorginho couldn't even let Zizi make herself pretty! You know how I used to do people's hair for a living? I remember one time I had straightened and permed Zizi's hair, and Jorginho came home and took one look at her and poured a bucket of water on her head, ruining her hair! And then, he tore the shirt she'd borrowed. He knew she only wanted to be pretty for him, but he couldn't let her.

"You don't know the things I did to help that girl. Once I was working in São Paulo, and I had a great job in the house of a very rich Japanese executive. I called Zizi and told her to get away from him, to come to São Paulo and I'd set her up. I was going to give her that great job! She wouldn't have had anything to worry about ever again, and she wouldn't be still living in that miserable hovel. Even Creuza," Yancí referred to the battered woman who went silent then wept when I asked if things got rough, who in the meantime had left her husband, "let us help her get away! But no. You can't help someone who doesn't want anything better for herself.

"He never let her work anyway. Just washing other people's clothes here at home. But every time she gets something else set up, he says no. And she can hardly wash clothes anymore; do you see how she is?"

In fact, I did. Right then Zizi was going through yet another "bad phase" with her spine, limping with more visible pain.

DONA ALEGRINA'S "IANSÃ-ÍSMO"

I was anxious to know what Dona Alegrina might have to say about such matters. However, speaking *with* Dona Alegrina at all for any length of time turned out not to be an easy matter.

A few times, I managed to gain audience in the old woman's kitchen, usually when I was brought in by some family member. The first time I watched, fascinated, as Dona Alegrina gently force-fed rice to a favorite hen who'd fallen ill. The next time was when I so obliviously delivered the statue of the twins to celebrate their approaching saint day. Each of these encounters involved a very brief exchange of small talk, and concluded with something like, "And now I am going to send Sarah on her way [dispensar]; I have things to do." I might venture, "Would there possibly be a time I might be able to talk to the *senhora*"—I used the polite term of address— "with more calm?"

"I'll call for you," she would answer brusquely. She never did. I was intimidated, and thought it best to avoid being any more pushy than I already was.

One of the first substantive encounters with Dona Alegrina came when my research collaborators Carlos and Chico first contacted Jorginho to conduct the survey that preceded longer, one-on-one interviews. Because everyone in his small house was napping, Jorginho suggested that they do the survey next door in his mother's house. The encounter did not get off to a good start, for as they entered, Jorginho announced that they would even have the honor of inaugurating his mother's new dining room chairs. Even though she had said nothing, both interviewers perceived Dona Alegrina to be visibly annoyed *(chateada)* by this.

Dona Alegrina asked Carlos and Chico if this research "had any significance." They answered that it had to do with conflicts in marriage. She responded, quite forcefully, "No one understands anything," adding that it would be impossible to fulfill the objective of the research.

Dona Alegrina explained, "For example, we have four people here. Each one has a different heart and a different head: How can you understand what is happening inside?" Carlos responded, trying to be respectful and humble, that this was precisely why we felt we needed to try to seek out a little understanding. "Well, you might be able to understand a little, but *only* a little. If you are talking to a person like me, no one will be able to understand, because I don't like to talk to anyone." The old woman then announced she would go and do her dishes, but in fact hovered about throughout the survey, interjecting at multiple points. (We attempted to interview people alone, but often this was not possible.)

Carlos asked Jorginho his age, and he responded that he was forty-two. Immediately, Dona Alegrina was upon him: "Forty-two? Who is forty-two? You are forty-three, boy!" Carlos and Chico felt aggression emanating from her and feared she would strike Jorginho. Dona Alegrina seemed to want to show them that she, at least, paid attention to such things.

Carlos and Chico were very concerned that "inaugurating the chairs" uninvited constituted a lack of respect or invasion of some sort, and expedited their work. They omitted questions of a personal nature and opted instead for those involving opinion, such as, "Some people say that a woman's life always has suffering. Is this true? More than men?" Jorginho paused, pensive, and Dona Alegrina supplied a response: "The correct answer is that they both suffer, the man and the woman." She gave an illustration, and Jorginho commented, "You suffered a lot with my father, didn't you *mãe?*" She agreed, but discounted it *(descontou),* and seemed irritated he had volunteered it.

"What has to be done to not suffer is this," she told them, putting her extended thumb to her upraised palm, and pivoting it about with an open-fingered, gathering sweep into a close fist. She asked each of the three men in turn if they knew what the gesture meant. No one did, not even Jorginho. "This is a *redução* [reduction]." She explained herself no further.

Jorginho was asked what he thought about the current gains *(conquistas)* for women in Brazilian society. Dona Alegrina spun about and vehemently took the floor: "Current? *Current?* No, always. She has *always* been superior to the man. Woman *allows* man to believe he is better, but beneath this she does what she wishes. He pretends he is not seeing, in order to keep going. For the relationship between a woman and man to do well, and for the good of the children, it helps for her to work and be strong herself."[9]

Hearing this was my first indication that, like her daughter Yancí, Dona Alegrina subscribed to some version of an ideology of female superiority.

The rest of the interview with Jorginho continued without significant comment from Dona Alegrina: She only chortled when he recounted how a colleague at work saw his wife in the *rua* wearing a suspiciously new *biquini* when she hadn't said she was going to the beach. The man tore the *biquini* off, leaving her nude in the street, and slapped her. Dona Alegrina laughed out loud when he told about the slap, but had no comment when Jorginho said the man had later been arrested for it.

At some point during Carlos and Chico's visit, they mentioned that they worked with me. (They would, of course, have told Jorginho when they requested the interview.) Dona Alegrina reportedly said, "Oh, with Sarah? I adore her." I was surprised to hear this, as I'd had a falling out with the friend through whom we had come to the Mungongo—soon after this, in fact, the friend would accuse me of having performed witchcraft against her, and say that Dona Alegrina had confirmed this—and she had told me that Dona Alegrina had told her I was not a person to be trusted. But maybe the friend was not to be believed; perhaps Dona Alegrina did not dislike or mistrust me after all?

Despite this realization, it was not until a month before I was to leave Brazil in 1994 that Dona Alegrina consented to sit down and talk with me one-on-one. One day, when I stammered out my request, she narrowed her eyes and peered at me. "What do you want to know?" By then I was sure that she seemed more comfortable with the idea of my approaching her in her capacity as *mãe de santo* than to ask her anything about her family life. I was, naturally, very curious to understand how she had managed when her husband brought his other family to live inside the Bomfim household, literally dividing the house in two. I said I wanted to ask her about the kinds of consultations she was asked for that involved conflicts between husbands and wives.[10] She showed herself willing to be asked a question. I explained the project, that I was writing about what people in Brazil thought, and therefore liked to be able to quote people in their own words: Would she mind if I ran quickly to fetch my tape recorder?

Upon returning, I asked Dona Alegrina to tell me the kinds of people that came looking for help, and for what kinds of things.

"They are people," she said, settling more easily than I'd expected into interview mode, "people who feel bad. They [are people] who arrive at the conclusion the doctor can't help them. They come here and do a *consulta* [a *jogo dos búzios* consultation, the divination by multiple casts of cowry shells] to see what path we are going to give. If it's a person being confounded by someone deceased, we'll do one thing. If it's something else, like an influence the person picked up on the road—maybe it's a dirty trick [*pulice*] from some [deceased] slave—our course of action is elsewhere." She proceeded to lay out categories of afflictions—from a slave, a saint, or an *orixá*—and the fundamentals about how one might deal with each.[11]

Pointing at the door, she said, "Now, let me tell you about this girl who just left," referring to a young woman I'd seen go. "Because she was feeling bad, someone sent her here. When she arrived last week, I gave her a consultation, and look what I told her: It's a persecution from a person who is desiring her husband. And what's happening with her? It's that this person went somewhere [bateu para algum lugar], and started to do something." I understood she meant a *trabalho:* a work that enlisted a spirit to act.

"Now what happens?" she asked rhetorically. "The thing that the person did starts to infiltrate into her, the woman. She starts feeling a headache, and dizziness, soon she's losing days at work. The doctor didn't help, so someone eventually sent her to me. I throw the *búzios,* and do a *redução* to find out what it is." I now began to better understand her use of this cognate of the English "reduction": it means make a reading, an interpretation.

Dona Alegrina explained how a *mãe* or *pai de santo* of equal or greater strength could block such a work, returning the client to well-being.

I wanted to steer her toward domestic violence, and changed the subject. "Now, what if I come to the *senhora* and I say, "Shoot, Dona Alegrina, I'm sick with passion about Fulano. He's married, but I think he's not doing well with his wife."

She didn't need to pause to think. "But there's a way to do it for him to stay with his wife and to like you also," she said, holding up an index finger.

"There is?"

"There is, there is," she affirmed, head nodding.

"And the *senhora* would help me with such a thing?"

No hesitation: "I would."

"So, the *senhora* thinks that this wouldn't be right, or wrong? . . . Like some people might say, 'Oh! But that's adultery!'?"

She seemed surprised I could be so misguided. "Adultery? I don't think so."

"It just depends on the happiness of each?" I guessed.

"I think so," she answered, shifting to place a palm on each thigh, elbows in the air. "You see, I'm completely disconnected from this story of adultery. Because I'm a rather experienced [bastante vivida] person. I've already passed through all I had to pass through, to my very limit [até o chão] . . . very experienced."

It was the first time Dona Alegrina made reference to her personal history. Given her reported assistance to Zizi's rivals for Jorginho's attentions, her suggestion that a *mulher da rua*'s (woman of the street's) interests were not inherently antagonistic to those of her lover's wife wasn't wholly unexpected. Still, it was hard to reconcile her view with reports of her own suffering at being thrust into a polygynous "marriage" against her will.

"So, the *senhora* thinks Fulano can stay with me and also the *outra* and be happy?"

"I do and he can," she answered.

"So, the *senhora* thinks that a man can do this—seek out a woman other than his wife—and the *senhora* wouldn't have a problem helping each person find a solution, in a difficult situation?"

"It can happen," she nodded. "No, there's no such thing as a difficult situation. There's such a thing as each person minding his own business. This is what I think.

"Do you know why? I'm going to explain to you what I think." She leaned back, regarding me, one eye almost closed. "It has to do with love. There's no such thing as love outside of the truth. Love is a very free thing. What do you think of love? It's a spontaneous, free thing. And it is a thing with which condemnation does not exist." Dona Alegrina reminded me of her daughter, Yancí, speaking of love as a force with its own agency, not to be bridled by external, moral strictures.

Her philosophical turn showed a softer side, and we grew quiet for what became an awkward interval. I mustered, "The people that come to you looking for help, as in such a case of love, is the majority women or men?"

"Men and women," she answered.

But are there more of one than the other?"

"More women."

"Now, if I were a man, and if I came to the *senhora* and I said, Dona Alegrina, I'm in love with her, but she's with her husband. Are there a lot of men who do this? Trying to take her away *[tirar]*?"

Dona Alegrina nodded, just once.

"Now," I continued, "would the *senhora* do it for him, for him to take her?"

I'd found a line she would not cross. "No," she shook her head, "I don't work to hurt *[prejudicar]* anyone. I prefer the truth. I like the clean path." She went on to list the kinds of works she will do that do not cause harm: prescribing baths, linking a saint with an initiate, giving gifts to the sea.

I wondered if she privileged men's involvement with multiple women over women's, and later asked, "And in the case of a woman with two men? Some people call her loose or a slut *[uma piranha, uma galinha]*. What does the *senhora* think of that?"

"No, I disagree with this," Dona Alegrina answered, shaking her head. "I don't connect with this story of the *galinha*. I think life is . . . *normal* [normal, natural]. That each follows the path they want." It seemed it was not the multiple-partnered woman's sexuality that was the problem for the *mãe de santo,* but one man trying to *prejudicar* another's interest. And a man's interest involved claims on a woman in a way that a woman's interest could not bind a man, apparently. Still, I was confused; these versions appeared structurally irreconcilable, contradictory.

The conversation moved into the stock questions we were asking all ritual specialists, about what is prescribed for couples' violence and fighting. Like her colleagues in Umbanda and Quimbanda houses, she described a work done to reconnect the couple to one another *(se ligam)* and entreat the aid of Oxalá, the *orixá* ruling peace and harmony, using clear oil and other white foods, along with baths.

Reflecting on our exchange later, it struck me that perhaps Dona Alegrina had indirectly revealed to me how she had dealt with the "suffering" and "abuse," the words her children used, of her husband's polygyny. She had done a *redução,* made an interpretation, and elected to let love take its course. She had kept a firm grasp on her belief that on some level she, as a woman, was morally superior to a man; she grew to tolerate, and probably accept, a "male" compulsion to seek sex from multiple partners. In making this shift, she apparently salved her own suffering and found reserves of fortitude to maintain her position of power with her husband and in her household, and even increase it considerably after his death. Years later, Yancí suggested it was Iansã who moved to the front, guiding her mother in how to gamble with love and death.

I've never been told much more of the story, though. Yancí insists that polygynous households were not unusual in the area back in her parents' day and that her mother and the "co-wife" actually got along fine. Given Yancí's brother's and nephew's current propensities to have long-term unions with more than one woman, I believed it. I do know that in Dona Alegrina's husband's last years, many of which the *babalorixá* Pai Almiro spent blind, Dona Alegrina was the woman at Almiro Sr.'s side, for she outlived the *outra.* Whether Dona Alegrina had additional lovers, before or after she was widowed, I never heard.

Dona Alegrina's notion of her own triumph hinged, again, on her acceptance that human desire and impulse, as well as love's own free force, could not be controlled by abstract moral imperatives, such as those against adultery. Dona Alegrina's agentive love recalls what has been called the amoral or a-ethical ideology of those involved in Candomblé—the rejection of Judeo-Christian "good" and "bad," along with guilt—and the particular strain of individualism that marks the faith (Prandi 1991; Greenfield 1994). Mintz's (1974) observations of related forms of distinct individualism among Afro-Caribbeans run a similar course, suggesting that these forms derive from shared historical processes, most notably involving rapid cultural loss through enslavement and the forcible, accelerated, and improvised recreation of culture.

This brief encounter had afforded me further information with which to try to understand how Dona Alegrina could condone and participate in Jorginho's violence against Zizi. Dona Alegrina's problem with her daughter-in-law, according to Zizi, was that Zizi could not accept Jorginho having other women. Or, perhaps more precisely, Dona Alegrina could not accept Zizi getting so upset about this. Perhaps it was Zizi's agonizing against love's courses, losing her dignity, and seeming to cast herself even further into the role of victim that Dona Alegrina so disparaged. Did Dona Alegrina find fault with Zizi's inability, or unwillingness, to perceive the "truth" of Jorginho's desire for other women? Did Dona Alegrina see Zizi as lacking conviction about the ultimate "truth" of Zizi and Jorginho's love, thereby weakening it, or weakening herself? I wondered if what had won Dona Alegrina's condemnation for Zizi was Zizi's inability to perceive her own power and preserve it. Did Zizi only have to make a choice, to do a *redação,* and cease to suffer? Was this what led Dona Alegrina to *descontar*—to deduct or discount—from Zizi, to make her "pay in the same coin" *(pagar na mesma moeda)* that she herself had paid as a younger woman? The "coin," then, would comprise *abusos*—in Brazilian Portuguese, the word is often pluralized and refers both to harm and to inconsiderate impositions—writ large, so that the physical abuse in Zizi's past converted into the same currency as the psychological, emotional, and economic abuse Dona Alegrina suffered years before. Was allowing suffering to make oneself stronger at the crux of Dona Alegrina's female superiority, her own version of a *Iansã-ísmo baiano?*

The women of the Bomfim family, I began to perceive, plot out three quite different positions with regard to relative powerlessness (Zizi and the other daughters-in-law) and to relative authority and might (Yancí and Dona Alegrina, in distinct ways). Far from seeing Zizi's victimization against a backdrop of undifferentiated Brazilian women, all oppressed and subjugated by men, I was coming to see my *comadre* Zizi's subaltern position as equally produced by other women, principally Dona Alegrina. Dona Alegrina's position had shifted over her life course: she suffered as the victim as a young wife, and as aged widow exercised considerable power over others. Her wisdom and reconciliation in old age reminded me that she was a "mount" of Naná Bukuru (the "owner" of Dona Alegrina's "head"), ancient *ur*-mother of the saints; her passionate tenacity for holding out and winning the domestic battle invoke Iansã, one of two saints in her triangle that "stood behind." Like Lizabete, the Umbanda participant who was "of" Iemenjá but for whom Iansã had temporarily "come to the front" when her husband began to beat and abuse her, Alegrina's Iansã had moved up in crisis, whereas Naná Buruku resumed her lead later in life. Whatever the case, it appeared that ultimately the saints and spirits Dona Alegrina had enlisted to her aid had done right by her, for she now seemed *"normal,"* just fine.

Dona Alegrina and I were unable to pursue these conversations further. The next time I was in Bahia, she was ailing and secluded; she passed away two years later, right before *carnaval.*

YANCÍ'S YASMÍN

Yancí raised her only daughter, Ritinha, to be still more feisty than she was, if such were possible. These three generations of mothers and daughters, Dona Alegrina, Yancí, and Ritinha, were related by blood (consanguines); the latter are their mother's only daughters.[12] Their consanguinity seemed to be tied to their sovereign positions in their extended families; by this I mean that blood-relatedness held significance for them and was how they transmitted strong structural advantages and shared attitudes of insubordination, including what I have been calling Iansã-ísmo, through generations. This level of self-command, however, did not extend to the Bomfins's female in-laws (affines). The qualities and positioning that the grandmother-mother-and-daughter shared sharply contrasted those of Zizi and the other sisters-in-law. Zizi and the other wives of Yancí's brothers lived lives that Yancí deplored; she equally faulted her brothers for causing problems and her sisters-in-law for putting up with them.

Yancí drew upon on the marriages of her six brothers whenever she wanted to illustrate how bad married life could get. "Their behavior is horrible, with their women, every one of them. It's awful.

"I really don't know what makes them this way," she confessed, shaking her head. "I sit here watching. This brother that lives around the corner—Valdinho. When he got that girl she was a woman who was *formada.*" Here, *formada* (literally, "formed") meant she had finished high school, a prestigious distinction in this neighborhood. Yancí went on, "And Aldagisa was beautiful, with that long hair . . . But just look at the trash she is now, Sarah! A woman who doesn't work because he won't allow it, who doesn't go anywhere because he won't let her. She doesn't go to a party because he won't let her. And she disgraces herself in the cup," drinking like an alcoholic.

"Now, that Valdinho has women like the plague; he's got children everywhere that's a place in the world. He took after my father. . . . Aldagisa's husband has more than *fifteen* children!" I knew only four of these to be with Aldagisa.

Yancí then shared, not without irony, that she was considered the "black sheep of the family," and that she was not intimate with any of her sisters-in-law, who viewed her as wayward and dangerous. "I'm lost," she said, in mocking lament. The contrast between what a single businesswoman could do versus a "respectable" stay-at-home married woman was palpable. "They're married, Sarah, so in no time, I'll be having a bad influence on them. So, my brothers would want to bully me like they do with their wives—but not with me. With me the story is another one."

Because of her lack of tolerance for women who put up with controlling men, Yancí was not one to respect the adage that no one should *meter a colher* (get involved) in a fight between husband and wife. The question, she said, was whether a woman was willing to *tomar providência* (to take action) to remove herself from the situation. If a woman wanted to resist being controlled, Yancí would consider involving herself on the woman's behalf.

I had already been told of her multiple interventions on Zizi's behalf; it was only when Yancí became convinced that Zizi "did not want to help herself" that she adopted a condemning attitude. Then again, Yancí enlisted the aid of several local women to help Creuza, the mother of four who had been battered frequently and severely by her husband, make the final break from him. Unfortunately for Creuza, the price of her escape was leaving all four of her children behind, and now another woman has been their *mãe* for more than five years.

Yancí was careful to clarify that the interventions she would involve herself in, often in the name of the whole family and even of the entire community, were not always to help rescue a woman from battering by a man. As an example she told me why my next door neighbor, Diana, the nightclub singer whose story began this chapter, had moved out some weeks ago. She had left without warning in less than an hour after beginning packing; no one seemed to want to talk about her.

Yancí began by saying there was a long history of the family uniting to remove trouble-makers from the neighborhood. In Diana's case, they were certain that "there was going to be a death there. We felt there was going to be a bigger problem, so we sent her on her way."

Seeing that I was surprised, she asked, "Do you think she left because she wanted to? She left because we threw her out. You see, she was *amigada* [in an informal union] with a married man. The couple lives here, in the back. The woman, the wife, had already gone various times to attack Diana."

Remembering the scar on Diana's throat, I asked, "Is this the same one who . . . ?" I pointed to my own throat.

Yancí shook her head. "No, Sarah, this is another man, already! After she got better from the stabbing she got involved with another one—worse than the first one. Now, the woman swore she was going to kill Diana, so before this could happen, we sent her to the fires of hell [*p'ros infernos*]. Go live in the *infernos,* you're better off there, and leave us in peace here."

I now understood how Zizi had lost her "only friend in the world." For months after Diana had moved to a distant neighborhood, Zizi remained heartsick, and quite open with me about her loneliness. She said that she'd had no friends here before Diana moved to the Mungongo, and that the mistreatment she had received from everyone else had caused her to start to "lose her mind" *(perder o juízo),* but that Diana had treated her well and kept her sane.

My sympathy deepened sharply when Zizi told me that just as the scandal that would lead to Diana's eviction from the neighborhood was erupting, Diana had blamed Zizi and stopped speaking with her. Zizi had inadvertently passed on information about Diana's affair to an adult niece—Alegrina's granddaughter Sonia—whom Zizi assumed had already heard. Sonia, who had never gotten along well with Diana or Zizi and who several Mungongo residents saw as something of a malicious gossip, went straight to Diana with this news. Presumably she wanted to show Diana how disloyal her friend Zizi was. Zizi mourned that Diana never allowed her to present her case.

When I returned to the Alto do Mungongo for two months in 1995, Yancí and I grew still closer. She acted as something of a local "sponsor" for the focus group research I conducted, providing a house in which I could stay and hold the groups.[13] As I became increasingly impressed by this woman approaching her fiftieth year, I sought to better understand how she viewed herself, and how she maintained her position as a woman refusing victimhood in a social and economic climate where so many women found themselves trapped, subjugated, and dependent.

One day Yancí and I were talking about changes in gender roles in Brazil. She offered an insightful analysis of how things had begun to change for women, beginning in the 1960s. Back then, they were "not allowed" to wear shorts, low-cut blouses, or revealing clothes, or even to comb their hair into an attractive style. They did not see themselves as having any choice in the matter.

Yancí then added, "You know, Sarah, after the interviews you did with me and everybody back then, I got to thinking, and I arrived at a new analysis. Woman has conquered a lot of space [conquistou muito espaço] that used to be occupied by men. And women are more responsible, and they know better how to make do for themselves, selling this, sewing that, washing this."

As an example, she counted out for me all of the things her pregnant daughter Ritinha had managed to purchase (a refrigerator, a television, a bed, a phone, the crib, and much of the layette) through her work as a manicurist. She'd broken up with her partner, Danino, upon learning he'd had a vasectomy years earlier and withheld this information; Ritinha had tried to conceive for some time before finding out. She left Danino and quickly became pregnant by another man, with whom she never intended to cohabitate. Yancí concluded that Ritinha would provide an excellent life for her daughter. (All of the Bomfim women seemed to assume, without testing, that the baby would be a girl. It turned out they were right.)

"Now, in this time, what does Danino [Yancí referred to Ritinha's ex-] have to show for himself? If I could only *show* you, Sarah, how many men in this neighborhood are unemployed and lazy, while their women work! Now, do you know why so many of these men want to take it out on their women, by beating or bullying them? Envy. That's what I think: it's pure envy, because the woman shows herself to be stronger [ter mais força], and he doesn't believe in himself."

I saw her point, and in fact it jibed perfectly with our analysis that much conflict between women and men reflected women's gains and men's use of violence as a compensatory response to their failing power. Still, I asked how Yancí could reconcile her observation with the statistic that had appeared in the paper that morning: Brazilian women earn just forty-three *centavos* for every one *real* (the new currency, indexed to the dollar, introduced earlier that year) earned by men.[14] Yancí allowed that women might earn less for every hour they work, but argued that poor women, especially, worked so much more that they easily made up the difference. She felt that a major motivation for this female work ethic was women's awareness that they, in the final measure, were the ones who would ensure a life for their children: "*Negão não está ligado*" (The guy—more precisely, the big black guy—is not connected, doesn't care).

Yancí went on to share, in detail, her plans for beginning to save for her old age. First, she would divide her house, the vacant one where I was staying, into two. As a house with two bedrooms, a kitchen, and a sitting room (neighbors described it as a *"palácio"* in terms of the surrounding neighborhood), it was far too big and expensive for her to rent out as it was: "No one can afford to pay one hundred and fifty *reais,*" about $125.00 at the time, "which is what I would have to charge." But, divided in two, she could charge a hundred for each per month. Put a hundred of this away each month, and in ten months—she dramatically counted it out on her fingers—she would have arrived at the sum of a thousand *reais!* Yancí nodded at me, tapping her temple to indicate that the machinery within was always at work.

Alongside her economic enterprising, Yancí had developed her own, materialist critique of consumerist values and of people aspiring to ever-upward mobility. She commented on how, in a national society with such extreme differentials of wealth and class polarization as Brazil, the consumerist fetishism—Taussig's 1986 [1980] term, but effectively what she described—thrust incessantly upon Brazilians through television and other mass media could not avoid making the masses feel excluded, magnifying their sense of relative deprivation.[15] She often remarked that she viewed those who chased after status symbols, who were caught up in conspicuous consumption, as involved in a futile quest.

"My goal," she told me, "is to live well within *my* world. Within *my* world," she repeated. In practical terms, this meant that she refused to shop at the new *supermercado,* full of endless choices, that had sprung up across the *avenida* and threatened to put small-scale merchants at the local open-air market out of business. She said, "This place is a village *[aldeia]*, Sarah. My great *grandfather* was here! I never needed a supermarket here."

Yancí shunned the city's luxurious malls, as well as its chic neighborhoods. (She and I avoided revisiting the racist and classist way she'd been treated once, when she and Rei went to an apartment in Graça, an exclusive, "noble" neighborhood area, to pick up a box of gifts I had sent through someone arriving from the United States. Her fears that they would be treated as thieves for their dark-skinned, humbly dressed appearances were realized.) Possibly it was not only a penchant for tranquility and simplicity in values that underlay her resolution to "live well within her world"; it also reflected her awareness of, and some degree of reconciliation to, the limited possibilities for one born to her station in life in Brazil.

I took solace in the idea of Yancí, living well within her world. It offered hope that the relative autonomy and power of Afro-Bahian women that so intrigued me held some ultimate value for them, subjectively but also factually. Such an idea could always permit a false consciousness, underwriting woman's participation in their own oppression, or be a mere "weapon of the weak" (Scott 1985) protesting domination but not really disrupting it. Still, for Yancí, her mother, and her daughter, the belief in female superiority seemed to serve them as a genuine ideological resource, a form of sociocultural capital, aiding their survival and, at times, their success and prosperity.

With time, though, I faced the fact that the self-assured and satisfied way in which Yancí presented herself to me was far from being seamless or without inner conflict. She was not always as comfortable with her own identity as she might have me believe. She revealed this one night by introducing me to her "real" self, Dona Yasmín. I had wondered if this were her given or baptismal name because I'd heard it before—Yasmín—perhaps her mother had called her this, or Rei. But that evening Yasmín arrived, in the form of Yancí's alter-ego.

It was a Saturday night, and I arrived back at the Alto do Mungongo late. I was concerned, once again, to see that Yancí and Rei lacked patrons in the bar. This had been happening a lot lately. Men from the comparatively middle-class focus group that convened in the nearby housing development told me that they no longer frequented Yancí's bar like they used to, because of the persistent brawls that broke out—they mentioned at least one shooting—along with the "*grosseria*" (rudeness, coarseness) of Yancí herself.

Yancí shared her side: problems involving drugs had been brewing around a gang of men she called the local "*máfia*," and so she had simply called the police, and asked them to make periodic appearances at the bar. Her clientele felt betrayed, she thought, and that was why they'd stopped coming. Naturally, the longer the bar remained empty, the greater became Yancí's perplexity around financial matters.

Yancí's morose mood seemed to trigger her decision to invoke Yasmín. Six years ago, she explained, she had been obligated to abandon the high life she had sustained for twenty-two years. "I am known around this entire city. Everywhere I'd go, they would part the crowd to let me by. Aaaa! Princesa Yasmín! No one knows me as Yancí. They don't know who Yancí is." It was not just among the *povo* (the masses) that she circulated, no—it was among the "elite of the elite." They all recognized her, all knew her to be a person of quality (*gente fina*).

I asked what had changed. Why had she left off with the life of Princesa

Yasmín? She explained that as her mother's only daughter, she had no choice. Her mother was ailing and getting weaker. Who would take care of the house, and the *terreiro?* Although Yancí and all her brothers had had their "heads made" *(cabeças feitas)* in Candomblé as *filhos de santo* (daughters and sons of the Orixás), Yancí limited her involvement with the activities of the sect, and did not intend to pursue its more demanding obligations when her mother passed on. But meanwhile, who would look after things, with her mother sick? Her brothers? She snorted to show just how ridiculous she found such a proposition.

No, she had abandoned her existence as Yasmín six years ago for her mother's sake. But now, it was time to go back. Yancí began to rummage around in the space curtained off at the back of the bar where she slept. She produced a tangled mass of necklaces and bracelets, along with a box filled with rings and earrings. I had no idea of the elegance of who she truly was, she told me. She produced pictures for me to see how she "really" wore her hair, made up her face, and wore stockings with high heels. "I have always worn this *mannequin* (dress size)—a perfect 42! Even though I am older, I still have the body I had." She spoke of perfumes, of sipping expensive scotch, of going everywhere by car. "This old black woman you see, Sarah, these clothes I wear around here, it's just that I don't want to get all dirty." Yasmín was a woman who knew and understood quality, and the Yancí that I knew just a temporary lapse from long-standing glory.

Yancí told me of an encounter that morning that was obviously still bothering her. She had gone to the bank, where she bumped into a gentleman from her Yasmín days. "Ah, Dona Yasmín," he had said, pleased to see her. But at the same time, his eyes had flicked down, scanning the clothes Yancí wore, taking in the undone hair and nails. Perhaps he also took in the gauze bandage Yancí was wearing around her ankle, just like the ones her mother wore in increasingly wider swathes. Yancí's varicose veins were ulcerating again, only this time the wound never seemed to close. "All that is *ilusāso* (illusion)," Yancí said. "He sees a tired, poor old black woman. But I'm tired of *her.* Yasmín is coming back." She shooed away a fly that had landed on the now-uncovered wound, scratching at the skin surrounding it.

In the last days before my return to the United States, Yancí and I set about planning a huge bingo party, which I had promised all of the participants in the focus-group research—over fifty men and women and five researchers. At the end of each group, all participants had received two bingo cards (bingo bashes were all the rage in Salvador at the time). The bingo cards would serve as tickets for free drink and food at the party.[16] The bingo cards also positioned those who came and played bingo to win prizes, which included a large, portable tape player, a blender and other household appliances, a travel bag, and many smaller prizes.

Yancí was particularly excited about the party as a way to jump-start business at the bar again. It was to her advantage that I would supply the capital to stock her refrigerators' dwindling reserves of beer and soda too, much of which we hoped could also be sold to those without tickets and after the party was over. She also announced that the party would be the occasion of the much-anticipated return of Yasmín.

The party was a tremendous success. Attendance exceeded our expectations and many invisible boundaries in the neighborhood were crossed: strict Evangelicals came into Yancí's bar, which they normally wouldn't do, because it was also a *terreiro* of Candomblé, and therefore dangerous. Apparently, my *gringa* presence provided a temporary whitewash. Members of the Bomfim family who had not been speaking for months could be seen cavorting together that night. (Disaster was narrowly averted, I later learned, when both the wife and the mistress of Yancí's brother Raulino turned up, along with their respective children. The air must have been tense enough to shatter when the mistress's boy asked, "Where's my father?" in front of the wife. But the wife called to her oldest daughter, and said, "Marísia, I'd like to introduce you to your brother." Meanwhile, the phone was kept unplugged for the entire party so that none of Raulino's *other* women would call.)

After the grand prizes had been awarded and the party began to wind down (around 2 A.M.), my main research collaborators, Carlos and Meire, and I each took the microphone from the bingo master of ceremonies to express our gratitude to the community and the focus-group participants. I finished by thanking Yancí, the party's hostess and the local "sponsor" of my research, for providing the space in which the work could be carried out.

Yancí took her cue, and strode to the front to stand before the microphone, where she delivered a spirited addition. "I have proved to *everyone* here that I have *força* [strength], and that I can do whatever it is that I set out to do. People here don't want to recognize this or appreciate me. But you all *know* that it's true, and you've all *seen* what I've given this neighborhood. *I* am a woman of *força* [strength], *that many of you men would like to be!*"

Yancí was shouting now, indignant in her moment of vindication. She ended her speech with this crescendo, and abruptly stamped away. Later,

Carlos told me that he had heard the young men who were present snicker, saying that Yancí misspoke: Yancí may have the *força* that many a man would like to *have,* but of course she was not a *woman* that many men would like to *be:* No man would want to be a woman.

We cleaned up after the party, and the sun was dawning when Yancí, Rei, and I walked Meire and her partner Fátima to the bus stop and waited with them. As we walked wearily home, Yancí looked at me and said sadly, "Yasmín never arrived."

AGENCY, RESOURCES, AND SLAPS SUSPENDED

In this chapter I have tried, as much as possible, to let the mother/daughter/ in-law triangle of Dona Alegrina, Yancí, and Zizi unfold in their own voices. The three women, I have suggested, occupy strikingly different positionalities with respect to women's relationships to male violence. The central theme, of course, is how well women deal with Bahian men's inevitable philandering and polygyny, but behind these issues lie more important questions about how women deal with men's greater freedoms, privilege, and power. If they allow themselves to be dragged down by it, sacrificing their dignity and perhaps even being beaten in the course of the embattlement, they tip themselves toward victimization. Against this criterion Zizi most resembles a woman subordinated, victimized by abuse, and under others' control. Dona Alegrina suffered "abuse" as a younger woman, psychologically, economically, and verbally, but was able through her *redução* of the situation to cast herself as a slow, patient winner, letting love take its course. For her part, Yancí utterly defies any linkage between being a woman and submitting to victimization or oppression.

At the same time, I have tried to show that it is not quite this simple. The different roles that the Bomfim women take on are interrelated; each is implicated in the construction of the other. Moreover, none of the women are wholly subordinated *or* sovereign. Even Yancí reveals that, on some level, she has difficulty with the degree to which she is a captive of circumstances beyond her control—being the only daughter of a *mãe de santo* of an aging, family *terreiro* and navigating the generalized poverty, racism, and sexism as they manifest in Bahia. In compensation, she creates an alterego, Yasmín, who, more so even than Yancí, is the anti-victim supreme. And yet, Yasmín is such a heavily produced, labor-intensive personage to pull off that it is not always possible, in real life, for her to make an appearance.

Just as Yancí is not always able to set the course of her own life, Zizi has never been absolutely subjugated. The violence in her marriage was often instigated by her, in protest of Jorginho's behaviors with other women, and on several occasions she physically attacked Gabriela, who appeared to be becoming Jorginho's second wife. Cases like Zizi's remind us that there is less violence in societies and social contexts where women are rigidly socialized not to "talk back" or to question men. In refusing to meekly accept Jorginho's compulsion and prerogatives for "other" women, Zizi's shows herself to be resistant and rebellious, so much so that she wins her mother-in-law's wrath and complicity in Jorginho's physical attacks, aimed at keeping Zizi in line.

But Zizi's ultimate rejection of victimhood, her most decisive victories, involved her use of the Salvador's women's police station, the Delegacia da Mulher, to gain an edge at two critical moments. She never even had to step foot in the building.

The first turning point came following the final time she was actually battered by Jorginho, when she was pregnant with Almiro, in the very year the DM was created, 1987. He kicked her in the thighs repeatedly, the imprint and the gravel from his boot leaving a lasting impression; she escaped into the bush *(mato),* hiding for the afternoon. She finally went back home, her legs hugely swollen (the pregnancy was quite advanced), and began to make a compress for them. Jorginho entered and sneered, "Oh, here you are," preparing to beat her once again. Raulino, Almiro's older brother who would have been under ten at the time, tried to intervene: "Don't, *pai, mãe* is really sick."

That didn't stop Jorginho from coming. Zizi, holding up her hands expecting blows, blurted quickly, her voice panicked, "You touch me and I'm going straight to the Delegacia da Mulher! I'm not kidding so don't even try it!"

"You don't even know where it is," he snorted, derisively. But, astonishingly, he walked away.

"A few weeks later we were driving around and I pointed out to him where it was. 'How did you know that?' he asked me. 'I don't need anyone to teach me,'" Zizi told him.

Years later, when Zizi became my comadre and I her son's *madrinha* (godmother), she had succeeded in avoiding being truly battered by Jorginho again. Still, he would occasionally hit her, and she was getting sick of it.

One day Zizi ran to my house with an excited, and somehow also frightened, look on her face. She said she had seen a bite mark on Jorginho's shoulder and knew it must be from his other woman, Gabriela. She confronted him, and he swore the bite was from another man, that he'd been bitten in a barroom brawl. Zizi would not believe it and would not let the issue drop. When Jorginho raised his hand to hit her, however, she was ready: "I still know where that women's *delegacia* is"—for Zizi knew it had recently been relocated—"and if you touch me you will too!"

Jorginho's hand remained in the air, suspended. From what I've been told, it has never fallen on Zizi's body in violence since that moment. Zizi had managed to avert a slap meant for her face, with mere words—words that issued a threat Jorginho found plausible.

Zizi triumphantly added that she had spent the two days before this fight reading through the transcript of her interview with me. Many interviewees were impressed to have a twenty-page or so document, all in their own words, placed in their hands, especially those who were semi-literate or illiterate. Zizi told me that reading hers had made her think—leading to her once again using the Delegacia da Mulher as a threat.

RESOURCES AND RESISTANCE

Zizi may not have been positioned to draw on *Iansã-ísmo,* a cultural model of an indomitable woman, in the way her mother- and sister-in-law were able to do. Nonetheless, she was quite capable of availing herself of other resources—such as the specialized women's police protection—that had not been available during most of the time she had suffered at Jorginho's hand.

Focusing in this chapter on three women, Zizi, Yancí, and Alegrina, is not meant to suggest that any one of their experiences or profiles represent fundamental types of Bahian women. My material offers examples of mothers- and daughters-in-law who, unlike Alegrina and Zizi, bound together against husbands' violence, for example, where marriage was stronger than blood, and hence my objective is not to suggest that affines are always, already fundamentally more antagonistic than consanguines. Although for the Bomfins it is natural to turn to *orixá* imagery to help culturally contextualize their gendered conflicts, for the family across the little plaza, or another up a muddy *ladeira,* or the one down the avenue in the apartment complex, or the other by the sewage canal, it might be equally natural to ground a family's story in Catholicism, Espiritism, Evangelism, or non-religious icons, such as those from social movements. Bahians in Salvador are far too variable for the Bomfins to be representative in any fundamental sense.

The point of taking the Bomfim family as a focal point, then, serves to highlight the stark differences women can occupy within the same families, and how their interrelatedness constructs and magnifies these differences. These differential positions, in turn, shape how advantageously an individual woman can draw upon resources—ideological and cultural, such as proto-feminist Iansã-ísmo, or immediate and practical, such as the women's *delegacias.* In the final reckoning, regardless of the social or religious orientation of a given Bahian family, no woman negotiating conflict is an essential, a priori winner *or* loser, victor *or* victim. Rather, as in the case of Zizi, Yancí, and Alegrina, the lot of each woman would depend upon the resources available to her, and her calculation of her potential to succeed if she elects to use them.

TWO

When Cocks Can't Crow
Masculinity and Violence

Invocation for Ogun
Orixá of iron, blacksmiths and all who use that metal,
tied to sea depths, mud, and good deaths.

Ogun, who, having water in his house, bathes in blood. . . .
The pleasures of Ogun are combat and battle.
Ogun eats dog and drinks palm wine.
Ogun, the violent warrior.
The madman with muscles of steel. . . .
He kills the husband in the fire and the wife by the fireside.
He kills both the thief and the owner of the thing that was robbed.
He kills both the owner of the thing robbed and any who criticize his
   action. . . .

PIERRE VERGER
"Orixás da Bahia"

Ogun's Shame
Ogun . . . God of Warriors in Brazil.

. . . Oyá [Iansã] was the companion of Ogun before becoming the
wife of Shangô. Shangô liked to sit by the forge and watch Ogun
hammering the iron, and frequently cast a glance at Oyá. She also
looked furtively at Shangô. Shangô was very elegant, very elegant
indeed, affirms the storyteller. His imposing nature and his power
impressed Oyá, and one fine day she ran off with him. Ogun gave
chase, found the fugitives and brandished his magic staff. Oyá did
the same and they hit each other simultaneously.

Ogun never had a right to wear a crown. . . .

. . . The day he arrived, the people of the city were performing a
ceremony during which the people were forbidden to speak for any

reason. . . . No one had greeted him or answered his questions. Ogun, whose patience is short, was furious with the general silence, which he considered offensive. He broke the pots with his saber and soon, unable to contain his fury, began cutting off the heads of the people nearest him. . . . Ogun regretted his acts of violence and declared that he had lived long enough. He pointed his saber to the ground and disappeared into the earth, transforming himself into an Orishá.

PIERRE VERGER

Os Deuses Africanos no Candomblé da Bahia

RESEARCHERS OF GENDER-BASED PARTNER VIOLENCE frequently observe that the available literature and mass media sources on the subject are disproportionately informed by women's voices. By contrast, men's voices are comparatively absent. Why don't we hear more about violence in relationships from men's points of view?[1]

When asked, Bahian men related violence against women to decidedly masculine forms of insecurity, even where they may exert nearly total dominance. Just as Yancí and her mother's indomitability reminded me of Iansã and Naná Buruku and as Zizi's wounded wife- and motherhood invoked Yemanjá Assaba, so Zizi's husband Jorginho (and many of the other violent men I spoke with) reminded me of an "archetypal" Ogum—the *orixá* of warriors and the owner of Jorginho's head.[2] In Jorginho and other violent men who attacked and wounded that which they held most dear, there was much of Ogum, the insulted sovereign, so certain that he was entitled to better treatment, greater recognition, and more respect.

Efforts to discuss men's perspectives on violence can provoke accusations that doing so distracts us from attending to victims. Critics worry that overvaluing men's subjective viewpoints can prevent us from acknowledging the power structure that favors men's dominance or can serve as apologia for violent men. This chapter looks at Bahian men's views on partner violence, but from a vantage point informed by, and accountable to, feminist research and activist goals.

We begin again with the *família* Bomfim, expanding the portrayal. Where the previous chapter concentrated upon the mother/daughter/

in-law triangle of Bomfim women, now we turn to Jorginho, the son-brother-husband the three women hold in common. Our fieldwork afforded opportunities to listen to Jorginho account—or avoid accounting—for the violence in his history in diverse settings. We could draw upon conversations—and yes, gossip—garnered through participant observation, including those with Yancí and Zizi discussed in chapter 1. There were also formal interviews and informal, private conversations, many by phone, with Jorginho. Finally, we listened to Jorginho talking with other men in focus group exchanges. A focus group separate from Jorginho's included his nephew and one of his sons, Almiro's second-oldest brother. In this chapter I draw on all of these resources, but I focus selectively on these two groups' discussions in order to concentrate on the Bomfim men's voices.

A series of questions shape the chapter. Because my times in Brazil have covered the period in which assaulting a female partner became criminalized, I am interested in the effects criminalization may be having, both on general cultural tolerance for men's violence and on how individual men's relationship to that violence might be changing. How might such shifts be shaped by generation, ethnicity, class difference, regionality, and so on? I wonder what functions violence plays in the lives of Bahian men: do they use it to exert dominance, to uphold themselves as "successful" or "passable" men, or in response to feeling insecure as men? Although violence clearly can serve as an effective tactic for maintaining power and control, I will argue that it equally may signal a man's failure to control events or other people. Resorting to violence with a woman, Bahian men told us, was rarely the ideal or optimal strategy for the successful *macho*. Rather, the men who embody *machismo* most absolutely are able to present a credible *threat* of force, so credible that they don't have to actually employ it. By contrast, men who resort to interpersonal violence against women have shifted into a last-ditch, little-to-lose, damage-control mode; their use of desperate measures may reveal they already experience their masculinity as "thwarted" (Moore 1994) or "marginalized" (Connell 1995), and thus somehow as falling short of Brazilian gendered ideals.

Compensatory violence, or aggression as a response to a man feeling emasculated or somehow violated, forms the second concentration of the chapter. Men's focus-group conversations established female adultery as the "key scenario," the prototypical honor violation, the most obvious place where a man might conceivably be viewed as being reasonably provoked to violence. I interpret the model of male honor in which a man feels obligated to "wash his honor with blood" *(lavar a honra com sangue)* as one that necessarily extends the subjecthood of the man beyond himself onto the body of his *mulher* (which means "woman" unless preceded by "his," where it becomes synonymous with wife). Bahian men interact with a hegemonic model of masculinity that can mandate that they enact an expansionist, colonizing model of selfhood that is also intrinsically patriarchal; each man is expected to control and account for the actions of another person, his *mulher,* as though a woman's will and her body were appendages of her man's. The notion of male honor being violated arises from this notion of selfhood, allowing "honor" to shape conflicts far afield from female adultery. By tracing men's selfhoods through far more mundane and frequent causes of violent incidents, I show how the mere idea of a man's honor extending to his wife's behavior ultimately creates infinite practical senses in which men may feel their honor violated. The adultery scenario somehow insinuates itself into everyday instances where a real man *should* be able to control events; linked by expansionist selfhood, slippage from the key scenario into more mundane matters functions to legitimate his use of force with a female partner.

The chapter's final section considers my analysis against the backdrop of other scholarship on masculinity and gender-based violence. Drawing from a range of anthropological and historical accounts, I attempt to locate contemporary challenges to domineering forms of masculinity comparatively, arguing that they are interrelated through the combined forces that spell women's gains and men's losses.

Ultimately, I conclude, we must treat conflict and violence as distinct in order to unravel the relationship between them. This is critical from a feminist history perspective, particularly in view of the fact that women's movements emerge and progress, in part, by promoting critiques and activism that inherently foment conflict. But although many women actively promote conflict, they also seek to avoid losing out to men with stronger arms (physically) and upper hands (socially and politically), which becomes more likely when violence accompanies conflict. Can women seeking to improve their positions *as women* promote conflict while also refusing and preventing violence?

JORGINHO: DENY, MINIMIZE, HALF-ADMIT, BUT (ALMOST) NEVER HIT

The first of many conversations with Jorginho about his history with Zizi began on the same day Zizi and I talked, while the monkey chattered and

Zizi's work piled ever higher. Carlos, one of the project researchers, had approached Jorginho for an interview at the same time; he turned out to be a much more available interviewee than his wife and agreed to talk immediately. I returned to my house to find Carlos and Jorginho in the midst of an interview that would last over three hours. Carlos was following up from the survey he and Chico had done with Jorginho in Dona Alegrina's dining room, something we did when we had indication that there was some violent couple history. I looked in on their interview occasionally.[3]

Jorginho's energetic narrative appeared to be carefully calculated: he seemed to have decided beforehand what he would or would not discuss. In my presence especially, perhaps owing to what he assumed I'd been told by others, he seemed to muster up resolutions and repentances, declaring that it was time to make changes. This proclivity for redemptive declarations, possibly issued for my benefit, would later be further exacerbated when I became not only the local gringa researcher, but also his son's *madrinha* (godmother) and thus Jorginho's *comadre* (co-parent). At the time he spoke with Carlos, I would never have anticipated that this man, about whom I seemed to be learning more than any other man with a violent history, would eventually become my *compadre*.

Jorginho's narrative progressed from heavily idealized in the beginning toward an account more easily reconcilable with what others had reported by the end of his interview. For example, early on Jorginho reported that he and Zizi attended the local Catholic church every Sunday. As their close neighbor, I knew that this was not the case; later when Zizi and I attended the educational program for Almiro's baptism, it was clear neither had been to the nearby church for years, except for the annual street party for Iemenjá that followed the church Santa Ana's *lavagem* (washing; the way saints' days are celebrated locally).

Similarly, early on Jorginho explicitly denied that violence or even conflict had ever arisen between himself and Zizi, in sharp contradiction to Zizi's and others' reports. When Carlos asked whether disagreements arose in their relationship, Jorginho was categorical in his response: "I don't argue."

After a tense pause, Carlos persisted. "Are there fights *[brigas]?*"

"No, I don't fight. My law in this respect is very cut and dried *[seca]:* if it doesn't serve any purpose, I send the disagreement on its way *[se não serve, mando embora].*" Jorginho spoke loudly, with slow deliberation, punctuating by striking the table with his large palm. He added, "If I say to her, 'You're going to do this,' then, she's going to do it."

Later, Carlos posed several hypothetical questions about violence. Such questions were more than coy attempts to prompt disclosures that had thus far been avoided—we were genuinely interested in how people set limits for tolerating physical force, when they saw the use of force as legitimate and when not (allowing it to be considered "violence"), and if or when they expected family or neighbors to interfere. As with other respondents, Jorginho appeared more comfortable speaking in hypothetical terms, and in this way disclosed things he had thus far evaded. In the following exchange, for instance, Jorginho slipped from speaking conditionally to using the present indicative tense in a telling manner.

"If there were an argument in your home," Carlos asked, "and Zizi reached the point of slapping you, what would you do?"

"That never happened. If it were to happen, what could I do? I don't know. Because our reactions—man is of the moment. I could react back with another slap, I could not react at all, I could say nothing. Because, I don't know how—would I punch her? No, I can't do something like that."

"And do you think that someone from outside you two would try to help resolve the problem? Or help separate a fight?"

Jorginho shook his head. "I have few problems, and I'm the person who resolves my problems. The children just watch; they don't say anything."

"And your mother?" Carlos wondered.

"My mother doesn't say anything either. She sticks more to Zizi's side because she doesn't want anything to happen to Zizi. She gets crazy, like, 'Jorginho, what happened? What happened? Does Zizi need anything?' But she doesn't get worked up [não esquenta]." Jorginho's account has Dona Alegrina protecting Zizi, in apparent contradiction to Zizi's, but it is quite conceivable that the old woman had played both roles in different turns.

Later, Jorginho revealed himself to be accustomed enough to fights that he could schedule them around other, incompatible, activities: "All families have fights, but this is a passing thing. But at the moment one occurs, I let it be known that I'm not going to fight when it's noon: put my meal here, put it here, because it's time for me to eat. Afterward I continue with the noise, because fighting on an empty stomach . . ."

Eventually, Jorginho recounted the occasion that culminated in Zizi's spinal injury, although he omitted this detail. But he freely offered that he beat his children, who had disappointed him by their disinterest in school, by flunking grades, "not measuring up to my own efforts," and by the "illiteracy" of the three eldest, who "don't want anything from life." (Of Almiro's siblings, I had seen only Raulino read, and he was not proficient.) As a result, he "*partia para a ignorância*" (used to go off into ignorance), ignorance here being synonymous with aggressiveness. Zizi often interfered because, as Jorginho put it, "Their mother doesn't like them to be beaten, that's the main thing that convinced me to change *[me invocou]*."

Carlos asked, "She was the one that . . . ?"

"Yeah," Jorginho affirmed. "She was the one who intervened. Understand that I didn't want to lose my woman; I *don't* want to lose her. To arrange another is difficult."

"So when you started to beat your son Jorge, did you lose control?"

"I did," he admitted, "because I don't like to beat on anyone, but if you beat me I'll beat you back. So, I'm a very violent guy; that's why I stopped boxing, because I'm the kind of guy I knew was going to end up in the penitentiary. . . . As a result, I know how to fight, despite being a skinny man, a guy can punch me five or six times and not get me, and I throw him one and he's in pieces *[desmancho ele]*. If one day I were to give too strong a punch, I would kill him. Because you know, rage is very serious business. Our strength grows a lot, and we lose all sense *[noção]*."

Jorginho could admit to his own tendencies to react violently, and he could even allow for the situation that resulted in Zizi's injury: "If you beat me I'll beat you back"—even if it were inexplicably cloaked as a defensive response to the "assault" of his children's lack of scholastic achievement.

It seemed exceedingly important to Jorginho to create an image of himself as being/becoming a conscientious and thoughtful citizen, a caring and exemplary father, and especially, an attentive and considerate husband. Given that he knew what topic we were researching, and also what we were likely to hear from his wife and others in the neighborhood, this was not surprising. It would be difficult for such an interview to avoid throwing him into an attempt at image maintenance or damage control.

Jorginho described his penchant for other women as a vice, but one he had mastered. "Today I feel I myself to be recuperated, in this way—dedicating myself completely to Zizi and the family—I am recuperated. One person is addicted to drugs, another is a thief; for my part, I was addicted to women."

Throughout this addiction, however, Jorginho took some pride in having shielded Zizi from direct knowledge of his transgression.

"The one point in my favor—and also against me—was that I had the other women. In my favor was that I never went to Zizi and said, Zizi, I have a woman in the street."

To explain what he meant, Jorginho enacted a dialogue between himself and Zizi:

" 'You have one,' Zizi would say.

'No! I don't! You never saw me with a woman.'

'I saw you. It was you.'

'It was not. I have you, my dear [*filha*, daughter, girl]. What would I want with another woman? I don't need another woman. I need you, and no one else.'

"And so it went. This same thing all the time: there was nothing, nothing, nothing."

Jorginho's suggestion that were he to carry on with another woman, it was at least more considerate to conceal this from Zizi than permit her to learn about the affair, was again a view many Bahians, men and women alike, supported. Zizi herself corroborated the view that it was more respectful for her not to be told if her husband were having an affair. Anyone, but especially a woman, who would tell only wanted her unhappiness.

Jorginho reported that his sister Yancí and their mother Dona Alegrina were complicit in covering up Jorginho's other women. Jorginho remembered that to his face his female relatives would "say that I am wrong," otherwise they "kept applying hot towels" *(botando panos quentes),* protecting Zizi and attending to her figurative and literal bruises. Their collaborative dissimulation allowed Jorginho to sustain what he saw as far more important than his sexual fidelity: he could still make Zizi feel assured that she was the *número um*—number one—the most respected and most respectable woman in his life.

Carlos asked about how one should go about treating the *mulher de casa* (woman of the house); in responding, Jorginho somehow slipped into prescribing how she should treat him. "Because woman is very *melindrosa*," Jorginho explained, choosing a word meaning delicate, coy, and affected all at once. "You have to know how to understand woman.[4] At times she sees the man all overwhelmed *[abafado],* and says, what do I do to understand this man? A man gets upset because he doesn't have money to buy shoes, to buy things for the house. And the woman gets upset too. So, when she sees the man all worked up like that, she starts to caress him, to kiss him. . . ." Jorginho left implicit that the *homem de família*—the family man—is responsible for providing money and merits comfort and support in this charge.

Jorginho was unabashedly lucid about his double standard for male versus female infidelity. He attributed the difference to men's capacity to remain emotionally disconnected from sexual activity, where this was impossible for women. Jorginho made clear how uniquely unforgivable a violation women's adultery represented when Carlos asked whether serious conflicts, such as those leading to violence, could be overcome.

"It's possible, yes!" Jorginho affirmed without pausing, almost anxiously. "It's only impossible if it were a *very* serious thing. For example: the woman betrays the man. There's no way to overcome that. She no longer has any attraction to you."

"Now, why is that different?" Carlos probed, playing devil's advocate.

"Now this gets at the point," Jorginho responded, "that I don't know how to explain. I don't know if it's the vice of the flesh, if it's the physical attraction of the woman that is no more. I don't know. This I *can* tell you—and I have a lot of experience to be able to say this: a guy has a sexual experience with a woman, over in Pituba," he said, referring to an elite neighborhood not far away. "Then he returns home, and kisses and embraces the woman. And the other thing didn't happen, from my point of view.

"I don't know if everyone is like me. I've had various affairs in the street. The woman gets more agonized. If she has an affair in the street, you're going to discover it."

"Yes," I chimed in, "but that might just be because it's more acceptable for a man to have an affair. Other than that, it might not be that different."

Jorginho turned to me, to explain. "There are two women here, married women, whose husbands give them everything *[toda a assistência]*. Let's say that one of them got to liking another man and, because of her doubts *[por via das dúvidas]*, she leaves and goes somewhere in the city with him." Jorginho seamlessly changed voice, now speaking as the seducer of the married woman. "We have a very strong relationship sexual encounter between us. For me it didn't exist, nothing happened. But for the woman— the woman gets more attached to the man. It's very easy to hook up with a woman. She thinks that I'm going to give her the sea, the sky. She creates that fantasy. Everything I give her is bad, and she wants more."

Jorginho, who has stalwartly refused to let his wife hold a steady job outside of the home, sees the role of providing primary material support as properly falling to men. A male breadwinner commands the right to his wife's fidelity. The logic operates to keep him in control. By constraining a woman's ability to earn for herself, moreover, he also controls her access to respectability, which women who are financially dependent only gain through marriage. Jorginho said his reason for marrying Zizi, long after the older three children were born, was "because she deserved it." Zizi, too, expressed gratitude at her fortune in Jorginho's "gift."

The need for a man to provide was also critical to his relations with women in the *rua,* according to Jorginho. Like the woman at home, every woman in the street fantasized about all that a man could give her. For Jorginho, it was understood that their expectations were unrealistic, and inevitably he would come up short. The game, as he seemed to see it, was to keep getting back the maximum from women (fidelity, sex and affection, household and child-rearing services) based on what little—but never enough—he could give them.[5]

One of the hypothetical cases he offered of a woman betraying her husband was apparently a middle-class or wealthy woman. This was an image that Jorginho offered at three different points in the interview, showing himself aware that his sexual capital as a lover also merited material recompense.

Jorginho entered into such calculations in response to Carlos asking if he'd ever considered leaving Zizi.

"No, I never thought about getting separated from Zizi, because I'd never do that unless a '*barona*' [a baroness, or rich woman] appeared, who gave me all the status, a car, a house—but a *nice* house. Then I'd go live with Zizi afterward. Because I'd get rid of that one and return to live with Zizi later. The woman would have to pay a very high price, because everything I got I'd give to Zizi." Ultimately, Jorginho suggests, Zizi would be the beneficiary of him "peddling" sexual services for goods.

Such statements lend nuance to Jorginho's broader assertion that the woman "always wants more" from her lover or spouse. His conception of man-as-provider and woman-as-dependent appears fixed and naturalized. Yet he also shows this conception to vary by class: the wealthy or middle-class woman must "pay" the less wealthy man. The difference here is that the man, albeit in the prostitute-like position of gigolo for the well-heeled woman, nonetheless controls the situation as a result of all women's tendencies to get emotionally attached to the object of their sexual attractions.

"My home is completely different now," Jorginho reflected. "Because I'm forty-three years old, I have my woman who is thirty-three, already hardened [*calejada*], tired. . . . Now that I earn a reasonable income, I'm going to take everything I've gotten, in these thirty-three years, my compensation to her has arrived, in such a way that everything I do I have to do for her."

I asked, "And how did this change happen?"

Jorginho looked at me, then shook his head. "My change happened because I got tired. I'm tired of the street. I've already *namorei* [fooled around] a lot. I wanted to know what the street was all about. I wanted to know about other women. Everyone has the right to know. I wanted to know if they are different from my woman. . . . This I'll say and prove to any man: What all this difference gets you *[o que tem de diferente]* is I pay for a hamburger for her, go out with her, spend money, three or four thousand cruzeiros [over a hundred dollars at the time] sleep in the street. . . . You get home and find your woman with a frowning face, worried."

He looked up at both Carlos and me, placing his hands flat on the table to emphasize what he was about to say. "Now, my woman is seeing that I'm a different person. Because I'm not young any more."

"Do you think that she is going to recover from how she's suffered?" Carlos asked.

"She is, and do you know why she's going to recover, Sarah?" he responded, but turning toward me. "Because I'm going to do everything that she has always wanted. Only if God doesn't let me win back her trust, or if He doesn't give me permission."

Jorginho began to lay out his plan of action of how he would regain Zizi's trust and confidence. First, Jorginho would allow Zizi the vacation she had been wanting, to go back to her home town of São Felix and visit her family, especially her mother, who was ailing. Jorginho appeared aware that Zizi might have told us of the various times she had tried to leave him by going home to her mother, each of which had ended with Jorginho going to retrieve her and bring her back home, where she was needed (Zizi reported these reunions with an air of vindication, and of being touched by her husband taking the trouble to go after her). This time, Jorginho made clear, Zizi "could come back the day that *she* decides, when *she* wants to"; this would be his "first gift" of compensation.

But before Zizi departed, he would convene a *"papo formal"* (a formal talk) with the whole family in order to see whether he could "recuperate" the family, adding that what he was trying to do was like "trying to rescue something from the bottom of the sea."

Anticipating the upcoming holiday, he planned, "For this coming New Year, I'm going to call a family reunion. I, I who am the family head. I'm going to put some things on the table. What do you want from me? You have the chance to say what you want to. What do you think of me? What am I for you?

"From that point, you're going to do what I want you to." Jorginho left unacknowledged his sharp turn from asking for input to authoritarian control. "I don't want a conversation between father and children, all sentimental. I want a formal conversation."

I had come back into the room a few minutes earlier, having left them alone for most of the interview, and now I asked Jorginho what he wanted to get out of such a talk.

Jorginho looked at me, serious. "That my children take a different direction, that they go to school, to work, and not go toward drugs, robbery. . . . Because I am a guy that serves as an example. They are looking to me more these days. For many years, they've been looking and seeing   feeling—a person that was distant. But today, I do not have a woman in the street."

Jorginho rehearsed what he would say to his children. "*You* are going to make your bed when you get up. Not Zizi! She's not doing it. You are going to clean your room," Jorginho said, anticipating when the children would have a separate room; one had been in construction for some time. "Zizi is not going to wash this cup that you drank from. For this to happen, it's me that is going to give the example. I'm going to use the cup, wash it, and leave it upside down to dry."

"Have you done this before?" wondered Carlos.

"No, I've been waiting for the opportunity," he said, his excitement mounting. "It's already begun. It's starting as of now. Washing, sweeping . . ."

"When did this begin?" Carlos asked, trying to clarify.

"Right now. Now my woman is going away for a while, for this. Because, look, Carlos, the kids don't know how to buy food, cook, wash up—nothing! Zizi is not a servant. This is wrong. She's not being a mother of a family; she's being a servant. She is not paid a good enough salary by anyone in this house to be a servant.

"I want her to recuperate, drink milk, go to the beach or the pool if she wants, or make a work of culinary art. So that she can get back all the energy she has lost. Zizi works for six people!" Jorginho proclaimed, now indignant on her behalf.

At the close of their conversation, Carlos asked if Jorginho had "words to leave us with." Seizing the opportunity, Jorginho elaborated with fiery flourish and conviction upon his beliefs about how women should be treated.

"I am with my sights turned toward my family, especially toward my woman. I would say to other people, principally men, to stay focused on their wives. Because woman is not a forgotten being. She should be looked to. . . . I should arrive home from work and say, 'Let's go to the island tomorrow.' She'll say, 'We don't have enough money to travel.' And I'll say, 'It's enough. We'll just buy a little sandwich, but it's enough.' A kiss, an embrace, a *cheiro*." The last word meant "taking a whiff"; smelling a loved one is a common form of affection.

"Because any psychologist will agree with me: Ninety percent of the women out there lack love. . . . Making a child is something anyone can do. But give love?

"I don't know if you agree with me. You meet a girl today, and you put her in your car, and she's a goddess for you. Kiss, embrace, take her *[pega]*, grasp her *[agarra]*, hold her: it's so elegant *[estica]!* Why is it that at home you don't feel any more desire *[vontade]* to do this? I want to know, why? Why does all that end? There's no *casa* that can come and tell me they aren't this way. There are men who for days and days don't give their woman a kiss. All he talks about is money and expenses *[despesa]*. . . . Am I owing? He doesn't talk to her. Here's the check. . . . Let's go out walking hand in hand *[de mão dada]*, for people to see that you are my woman. Why doesn't this happen?"

Jorginho lamented that the news was full of crime and violence, but no one celebrated love. The prisons now employ psychologists, and "they're there just to rehabilitate *[recuperar]* those men. Do you know why they can't be recuperated, Sarah? Because they come and they say, 'Do it.' They say, 'You are a thief. You are a *marginal*.' He doesn't say please, he doesn't say, could you do something for us?" Jorginho shook his head. "No! He says: you are a *marginal*, you are disqualified." Jorginho paused, then anxiously added, "I've never gone through this, and I ask God that I never have to."

I was certain Jorginho didn't know that our next-door neighbor swore that he had apprehended Jorginho "*em flagrante*," robbing his house of a stereo, a television, and "everything else" he had. Worse, the man was family: he was Jorginho's brother Zumbi's father-in-law. Jorginho had more of a sense of how it felt to be viewed as a *marginal*, in the criminal sense the word holds in Brazil, than he let on.

Jorginho drew his soliloquy to a close: "Is love absent or is it not? Meanwhile, wherever your woman is circulating, there are people with their eyes on her. Talking with her, with a conversation a lot more interesting than mine. Because I'm not able *[não tenho condições]* to converse with her. But he is. All of the sudden she arrives at that point: of the woman betraying *[falseando]* the man. The man killed the woman, he stabbed her, he did it, and it happened. Because they are lacking something. They are lacking love."

Carlos and I both found Jorginho's vehemence heartrendingly ironic. He was not digressing when his narrative visited the penitentiary, in reference to the rehabilitation, or *recuperação,* of the prisoners. Only minutes before he had announced to us his own recent recuperation: "One person is addicted to drugs, another is a thief—and I was addicted to women." He explained how it is due to the inmate's continued marginalization—a marginalization to which there is reason to believe Jorginho indeed feels himself subject—that he may not find it worthwhile to reform. Despite his disavowals, despite his efforts to portray his life and his family as approximating some idealized, middle-class norm, Jorginho paints a portrait of a working poor, black male Bahian who has at least been suspected of a serious crime—other than beating his wife—because he knows this experience first-hand, "on the skin" *(na pele)*, as they say in Brazil.

BAPTIZING ALMIRO

In the years following this interview, I would repeatedly witness Jorginho's failure to put into practice his professed conversion to a life of fidelity and devotion to his first family. He has become a polygynist who now spends more of his time with family number two, perhaps because there are young children there and one is disabled.

Several years after the conversation between Jorginho and Carlos recounted above, I arrived in Brazil in the aftermath of a particularly bitter series of confrontations within the Bomfim family. Yancí's only daughter Ritinha, who was pregnant at the time, had apparently called the police against Jorginho and his sons for the fourth time that year. The *confusão*—confusion—erupted after Raulino, Almiro's older brother, and his new wife rented out the other half of Ritinha's house. Ritinha's ex-*companheiro* had rented the space to Raulino after he and Ritinha separated and constructed a wall dividing their house in two.

Meanwhile, Ritinha, Dona Alegrina's only daughter's only daughter, vowed she would not show the new great-granddaughter to Dona Alegrina when she was born, because the old woman had taken Jorginho's side in the altercation. Ritinha had begun pre-term labor, she felt, as a result of stress, which she attributed to Dona Alegrina willfully trying to hurt her pregnancy. Dona Alegrina growled under her breath, in my presence, "I have much hatred within" *(Tenho muito odeio dentro de mim)*. To be denied being able to greet her great-granddaughter, the fourth generation daughter, did strike most in the neighborhood as beyond the pale; the Bomfim women were locked in serious wrangling indeed.

For some time, no one in Jorginho's family had been permitted to speak to Yancí. Although Zizi maintained that Yancí had been the only one ever to defend her and that Zizi appreciated that, she acknowledged she didn't speak to her sister-in-law in order to avoid more *confusão*.

Jorginho had never left his other woman, Gabriela. He was reportedly paying for her English classes and also financing the rebuilding of her house, which had collapsed that year in the rains. Zizi recounted two confrontations between herself and Gabriela that came to physical blows: one in the Mungongo itself, and another outside Gabriela's own house in a distant neighborhood, where Zizi had chased her down.

The latter incident was precipitated, Zizi recalled for me, by "an anonymous phone call telling me where Gabriela lived." Who would do that? Zizi looked at me mysteriously, dragging on her cigarette, but did not elaborate. "I went there, and heard Jorginho's voice inside. I heard her calling him cowardly and weak [frouxo], trying to make him leave his family. Then, I was distracted, and Gabriela opened the door, and saw me there, hidden and listening. Jorginho ran away, and Gabriela came at me with a broom. I took the broom out of her hand, and we went at it."

While rolling around on the ground with Gabriela, Zizi broke open the skin on her back and hurt her arm. When they took her to the hospital, a cast was put on, but she sawed it off herself right away, so as not to appear the loser in the skirmish. I could understand why she felt she needed to save face: Zizi told me she knew that Gabriela even slept next door, at Dona Alegrina's, when Zizi was away for a few days, and that Jorginho had slept there with her. This cast in sad relief her promised "vacation" back home, the beginning of Jorginho making things up to her.

Zizi's former agonizing over Jorginho's philandering, however, now seemed alleviated, superceded by her determination not to let Ritinha's taunting get to her: "She said that about Gabriela sleeping here so that I would hear it, just to humiliate me."

Was Ritinha the one providing information? I remembered how Zizi and others told me that anyone who would tell a woman about her man's extramarital involvements was seen as wishing her ill.

"And," Zizi added indignantly, "Ritinha also thinks I'm dying of hunger, so when she passes by with a plate of food from Carla's restaurant, she wafts it under my nose. Whenever she gets something new for the baby, Sarah, she flaunts it to make me envious, since that baby of Josi's"—Zizi's retarded daughter's baby, whom Zizi was raising—"doesn't have anything. Do I care? I don't get caught up in it."

Little did I know that these would be the circumstances in which I'd be asked to take on my first mothering duties. Almiro, then nine, became my constant shadow those months in Bahia. In all this confusion, it was no wonder he seemed neglected. He was thin and weak, and his eyes had a worrisome yellow cast. When Zizi kept finding herself unable to take him to the doctor when she'd hoped to, I finally brought him, and he was diagnosed with hepatitis A. Luckily, he responded immediately to treatment. Still worse, Almiro had been out of school for the last eighteen months, even though Jorginho's bus company employer would subsidize the majority of reasonable private school tuition.

Almiro must have approached Zizi, who then talked with Jorginho, about me becoming his godmother. Toward the time that I was to leave, Almiro, Jorginho, Zizi, and I boarded a bus, on our way to the cathedral in the *cidade baixa* (lower city) to have the boy baptized.

Before this point in time, I do not think I had actively done anything to encourage the reformist zeal Jorginho seemed to experience in my presence. As a female, foreign ethnographer interested in his intimate history, I was quite invested in appearing nonjudgmental. This abruptly shifted when I became, in addition to anthropologist, Almiro's *madrinha* (godmother).

For the first time, I felt an obligation to tell Jorginho what I thought. I said something like, "I'm in no position to judge you, *compadre,* but I just can't understand how you could have let your bright, curious son sit out of school for the last year and a half. And when your employer would pay for it; you just couldn't get around to doing the paperwork?" He had no response—rare for a talker like Jorginho.

In our last conversation before I returned to the United States, I made a point of reminding Jorginho that I was writing about the research he had worked on with me; like all the folks in the Mungongo who asked, for example, I had told him that his own pseudonym was Jorginho. I reiterated advisements he had heard before: although I would change all the names of people, and even that of the neighborhood, it was nonetheless a book in which his story would appear. I said that I was glad that he and Zizi had "managed to end" the violence in their relationship. Since her threat to go to the police in 1994, Jorginho had not hit her. Still, I made clear I knew that there was a history there. Of course, I qualified, I had no way of knowing the facts as they occurred, only the stories people told.

Jorginho's response was unequivocal. "Sarah, I have never lied about anything that has happened. Some people will dissimulate, or avoid looking at the truth, but I have always assumed responsibility for my life. You wouldn't even have to protect my identity: You can use my name. I have nothing to hide.[6]

"You see, Sarah, right now I am needing to get rid of the *lado de lá* [the side over there; euphemistic for his parallel relationship]. Because, you see

Sarah, I've been distracted from my duties here. And it's time for me to make a life where Zizi and I can grow old together. You see, I'm building on to the house." As part of his yet-again rekindled resolve, Jorginho offered a listing of the home-oriented projects he was beginning, although the adjoining room and other projects from the past remained incomplete.

A few days later, before I left Brazil for the first time as Almiro's godmother, Zizi was happy to be able to offer me a cigarette; usually it was she who was asking for one of mine. The brand was Carlton, a more expensive brand than I and most economizers customarily bought. Zizi could hardly contain the overjoyed smile of gratification and pride at possessing her own pack in a neighborhood where many buy cigarettes singly. "You see?" she winked at me. "Jorginho is giving me things all the time now."

Almiro recovered from his illness and spent the next few years growing strikingly tall, his voice deepening more each time I heard it. A close Brazilian friend who had also grown fond of him assumed the role of surrogate godmother during my long absences, using money I sent down to pay for his tuition and school supplies at a modest private school in the neighborhood.

By the time of my next visit, Jorginho had lost his job as a bus driver; reportedly, he was accused of theft, and thus did not receive the full severance package he argued he was entitled to. His mistress Gabriela had progressed, it appeared to me, to occupy the *número um*—number one— woman position in Jorginho's life. He bounced between the two households, but it seemed he spent time with Zizi and Almiro only when there was an illness or death that required it, or when he had been thrown out by Gabriela. He had legally registered his children with Gabriela, and apparently there was a serious medical problem with the baby, because Zizi reported having found many expensive medical bills. Jorginho had never owned up to any of this to her face. Zizi generously said she wouldn't want a child in this situation to be abandoned by his father now, despite the fact that this divided the scarce family resources yet further. Already, even with Zizi working whenever she could, Jorginho and Zizi had not been able to assure their children lives that included adequate nutrition, education, and housing, not to mention clothing or recreation.

Even though it required a family crisis to find Jorginho staying for any length of time at Zizi's house, it seemed that crises were not infrequent. In the span of just one three-week visit in Bahia, we heard about three incidents involving violence. First, a drunk and drugged neighbor had been shooting a revolver off in the neighborhood. Jorginho says he had tried to persuade him to put the gun away, leading to the man to swear—and continuing to swear to police once taken custody—that when he got out of jail he would find and kill Jorginho and his kids. They seemed to take the threat seriously. Second, Zizi's sister's *comadre* (her child's godmother, and also her best friend) had been found in the undergrowth, three days dead, wearing only a bra and underwear and clearly having been raped. She had left a twelve-year-old orphan. Third, a pair of brothers, cousins of the Bomfim family, got into a fight after their mother died over an inheritance that even by the Bomfim family members was deemed to be of negligible value. One shot the other, and at last report had gone into hiding from police.

In other words, even as my then pre-school-aged daughter delighted in playing with her "brother" and "cousins," (who shared their ever-so-humble, grimy, and broken toys with her with heartrending generosity and delight), the adults in the family were often circled around a radio, listening to the police reports with worried brows, trying to find out whether the neighbor who had threatened them had been released from prison, or whether the fugitive cousin had been arrested. The feeling I had so often had of finding it difficult to stay focused on the specificity of gender-based partner violence amid the waves of so many other kinds was reinforced.

GROUPING AND FOCUSING: MEN TALK VIOLENCE

The conversations with Jorginho that I recount above unfolded during extremely rapid political and institutional change regarding responses to violence against women. How were Bahian men such as Jorginho, his family members, and neighbors reacting to efforts to criminalize domestic partner violence?

To ask whether cultural change followed in the wake of institutional change mattered, I believed, because ultimately, diminished cultural tolerance for violence would serve as a better preventative than would punishing assailants alone. The women's police stations were never intended to stand alone as the primary institutional response to high levels of domestic assault; legal, psychological, and socioeconomic assistance programs were widely seen as critical accompaniments to moving beyond palliative measures toward true prevention. Despite this awareness and some progress in this direction, for most Brazilians the punitive, criminally oriented police stations remained the sole response of which they were aware. I wished to understand the implications of this overreliance; in 1995 I returned, having analyzed my 1990 and 1992–94 material (Hautzinger 1997a, 1997b, 1997c), to share my conclusions with people in the Mungongo and adjoining neighborhoods and to invite their reactions.

Focus groups with survivors of assaults have been used to gain reliable information on domestic violence in the United States.[7] Focus groups with perpetrators, however, are particularly susceptible to such threats to validity as deception, social desirability issues, low levels of trust, face-politeness needs, and researcher bias (Albrecht, Johnson, and Walther 1993). It is critical, therefore, to stress that using focus groups in this study was not intended to produce reliable accounts or "hard" data about violent incidents. Neither were we exclusively interested in speaking to men with known or suspected histories of violence. Rather, in 1995 our primary goal was to ascertain shifting cultural tolerance for violence in response to criminalization; reflections from both observers of and participants in violence established the kind of normative discourse in which we were interested.[8]

Regardless of our commitment never to bring our previous knowledge about participants to bear upon the actual group discussion, our background information about the men enabled a deeper analysis than convening focus groups "cold" would have done. The transcript of the discussion from one of the men's groups, for example, reads as extremely normalized and progressive, full of received messages (from the media and Brazil's own nascent "politically correct" doctrines) about women and men having equal rights and negative regard for "those" misguided men who still harbored *machista* (the adjective derived from macho and machismo) beliefs. From the transcript alone, one would never have guessed that this group of four was composed of a man who had assaulted his wife continually for years and who had recently impregnated her while raping her; of a man who had just responded, in the women's police station, to charges lodged against him by his wife, who had recently left him; of a man who admitted to having assaulted his wife "because of a disagreement about food" (she later committed suicide, under circumstances that remained quite vague); and finally, a man who professed an idealized, egalitarian relationship with his wife, but whose sister (in a separate conversation) expressed the conviction that the couple had a violent history.[9] In this light, the group discussions became a comparative exercise in trying to understand the ways men's chosen self-narratives departed from others' accounts of their actions and then in speculating about men's decisions for self-presentation, including motives for dissimulating to maintain idealized images of themselves.

The six men's focus groups were roughly grouped by age: three groups included mostly younger men under thirty-five (average age twenty-four), whereas in the other three groups older men predominated (average age forty-six).[10] Jorginho and his family loomed large in the focus group conversations. How large I didn't realize, until I had written an analysis contrasting the dialogues in two groups in particular, only to later realize the strongest voices in each were Bonfim family men: Jorginho, in a group of older men, and Robi and Raulino, Yancí's only son and Jorginho and Zizi's middle son, in a group of younger men. The contrast between these two groups, in particular, sharply illustrated an apparent generational contrast. The content of the Bomfim men's contributions was representative of other men's input, and the general trends in generational differences were present across all six groups. With the combination of my depth of understanding their histories and their charisma and articulateness, however, the Bomfim voices stand out, thus justifying my focus on those two group's conversations here.

WASHING HONOR WITH BLOOD

The police-station research and individual neighborhood interviews made clear that the majority of severely violent domestic eruptions don't directly involve issues of female adultery or sexual jealousy as such. More common were power struggles around everyday, mundane issues: who gets home when, who does what work, how money is spent, how to discipline children. The fact, however, that nearly all of the focus-group discussions revolved around female-adultery and male-jealousy themes is significant. Female adultery supplied a critical key scenario, revealing the place where violence was viewed as most probable, as most readily defensible, and, from men's perspectives, as the situation in which it would be most *necessary* to avoid descending to the category of *corno* (cuckold). To be a *corno* was repeatedly contrasted with being a man: to be a *corno* is to be a nonman, to have one's masculinity neutralized.

What men's honor and female adultery tell us about the ideals surrounding being or failing to be a man helps reveal the models of power operative in the real, more mundane, everyday conflicts where violence more commonly flares up. Specifically, the "injury" wrought by female adultery to men is paralleled by cases where women nag men about being inadequate providers, partners, and fathers, and also where women protest men's extramarital affairs and unions, pointing out double standards and attempting to curtail activities men may see as part of their masculine "nature" and prerogatives. The more common, mundane counterpart of the *homem traído* (man betrayed by his woman's infidelity) is the *homem caseiro* (the "house man"), or more pejoratively still, the *pica doméstica* (domestic[ated] penis); neither are free enough from their women to "play" in the street, as men are entitled to do. As Gayatri Reddy has argued for India, the notion of honor (or respect, as she prefers to gloss the term *izzat*), can be overly "libidinized," where in fact it may involve multiple dimensions beyond sexuality. In this view, honor can function as the "currency through which [actors] craft their identities and negotiate their relative status," especially those related to gender difference and ambiguity (2005: 43).

Perhaps no other Latin American country shares Brazil's infamy for historical and cultural "codes" or "scripts" that virtually obligate men to "wash" their "honor with blood"—by killing wives, their consorts, or both—when subject to female adultery. In Brazil through the 1980s, such meanings could be understood as prescriptive cultural dramas that simply "happened," leading to astonishing numbers of men being absolved of wife-murder thanks to arguments supporting it as a legitimate defense of honor. Feminist groups scrutinizing court decisions, during the redemocratizing 1980s, created the first instances in which the legitimacy of such acquittals was questioned (Izumino 1998; Rohter 2001; Americas Watch 1991; Patai 1991; CEPIA 1993; Alvarez 1990).

One of the best literary illustrations of men's wash-honor-with-blood mandate can be found in Jorge Amado's novel *Gabriela: Clove and Cinnamon,* based in an earlier period, the 1920s, in the southern Bahian, cacao-driven city of Ilheus. Amado uses female adultery to echo the work's broader theme about custom versus modernity, old ways and new. Three examples of women who stray arise. First, Colonel Jesuíno, embodiment of traditional honor, met universal approval for discovering himself cuckolded and killing on the spot his wife, Dona Sinházinha, and her lover, the dentist Dr. Osmundo. Men praised him as "a real man, resolute, brave, honorable" (1962: 103), and when he was acquitted all agreed the verdict was inevitable and just, save the "modern" newcomer who questioned whether husbands who neglect their wives didn't get what they deserved.

In *Gabriela*'s second instance, the character Felismino was delighted to use his cuckoldry as an opportunity to rid himself of his insufferable wife. But his inability, or disinclination, to avenge himself with his wife's and her lover's blood—he felt the ultimate punishment for the man would be to saddle him with her persistent demands—led to Felismino's humiliation and ultimate departure from Ilheus. He lost clients, and some men even refused to shake hands with him.

At the novel's climax, the principal male protagonist was himself cuckolded by the lovely Gabriela, the sensual, mulatta *baiana* whose culinary abilities, as with other of Amado's female protagonists, serve as metaphor for her own deliciousness. Nacib was a popular bar owner, yet also something of an outsider as a "*turco*" (a generic term common in the period, which he objected to, as his parentage was Syrian). Gabriela slept with another man less from meaning Nacib any harm than from her irrepressibly sensual impulses, Amado suggests. Nacib, who loved Gabriela, ultimately refused the dilemma of having to sacrifice his own honor or kill her, rather negotiating a path between Colonel Jesuíno's and Felismino's extremes. He found a legal loophole allowing him to annul his marriage, thus erasing the stain on his honor and eventually allowing him to return to the woman he adored. "He had and had not been married; he had and had not been cuckolded; and so, in not killing his betrayers, he had and had not broken the unwritten law. In a sense, the cruel law had been outwitted ex post facto." All the same, everyone agreed that Gabriela "deserved to die," and that Nacib "was good; he only gave her a beating and put her out of the house" (1962: 372–373).

Compared to Nacib's day, the so-called "legitimate defense" of honor— and yes, it has, historically, referred specifically to men's honor (Borges 1992)—is losing its viability as a tactic through which to absolve wife-murdering Brazilian men. Men's impunity is slowly diminished through increasing criminalization. Nonetheless, in Brazil violence can still metaphorically "wash" honor, and it is still constitutive of meaning and value, holding undeniably positive connotations and values in the popular culture. Not only *can* a man use violence to "prove" that he is, in fact, a man, but ofttimes he may be seen as being *required* to call upon violence, particularly when his other options are few for succeeding in the high-maintenance, labor-intensive work of continuing to "be a man" (Buffon 1990; Lancaster 1992).

THE "BIG MACHOS CLUB"

Jorginho's focus group gathered just two days after I had passed Zizi, washing clothes but with her face more twisted than the cloth, obviously upset. She had just found out that Josi, the daughter whose three-month-old son she had undertaken to raise after Josi was found beating the infant, was pregnant again. Zizi's body keened over the sink in a sob as she told me. Perhaps because of this discovery, or perhaps in anticipation of the upcoming focus group he'd agreed to take part in, Jorginho was going through a *bom pai*—good father—phase, sleeping at Zizi's house and working again for the first time in a year on the new room's construction.

Jorginho's group of four men, with two in their late fifties, playfully nicknamed themselves the "*clube dos machões*" (big machos club) early on. They articulated the values of traditional *machista* entitlement plainly, spelling out what was involved with being a successful *mulherengo* (womanizer). Such a man, they said, had to "know how to err," to indulge in the vice of extra-marital sex with moderation, avoiding getting caught. Duty required that "you leave everything at home in a good way." The men contrasted the alternative: the *homem caseiro,* the domesticated man, who didn't "eat"—a common Brazilian metaphor for sex—"in the street." Jorginho proclaimed to his peers, "A man, when he turns *caseiro,* it just means he got tired. Because, really, there's no such thing. Can it be that one really exists? Not here, I don't think," Jorginho's eyes sought those of his neighbors' as he shook his head; his friends snorted their humored agreement.

Having established that a man bound by his wife's expectation of fidelity is in some ways less than a man, Jorginho and friends went on to eloquently qualify how a man's willingness to use violence revealed the strength of his masculinity. The conversation turned from men's adultery to female adultery, and two examples were offered. The first involved a case that occurred in the neighborhood, which was mentioned in several different focus groups. For the men in this group, the case exemplified negative or failed masculinity, for the cuckolded man in question was unable to act resolutely enough to prove his manhood.

Jorginho began the story, telling about how the neighbors were aware that the wife was sleeping with another man, but wouldn't tell the man because he was the type that consistently taunted other men, calling them "cuckolds" or "faggots." One day, the man came home to find the other man "on top of" his wife. The husband threw the other man out of the neighborhood at gunpoint.

Although one might expect that the betrayed husband proved himself capable of a "reaction," Jorginho later returned to the incident and made clear that whatever action the man had taken was inadequately resolute. Some men argued that the husband should have removed himself from the neighborhood altogether; others disagreed. But there was a consensus over his need to "do something" to preserve his name, his honor.

Mário, the group's oldest and most outspoken member, repeated, "Do *something.*" He turned from Jorginho to the others. "So he wouldn't have doubted his *own name!* Even a shout, he needed to give, but he didn't do anything: He was paralyzed." Mário lived in the Baixa da Vasco, an adjacent neighborhood, and didn't seem to know of this case beforehand.

Hélio, who also lived in the Baixa da Vasco, chimed in, shaking his head. "He lacked the *machismo!*" He clearly used the term in a positive sense. The men's ability to specify *what* the cuckold should have done, however, appeared frustrated by the rapid disappearance of "appropriate" options, particularly in the face of violence becoming an increasingly delegitimated response.

In contrast to this example of failed manhood, Mário shared another story, one that immediately captured the group's awe and admiration. In this instance, a betrayed man suspected foul play, and arranged to go home in the middle of the day, armed with a revolver that he made sure was visible when he entered the house. Sure enough, the other man was there, and scurried under the bed. The protagonist set about making himself some coffee at a leisurely pace, refusing his wife's nervous insistence that she make it for him. Mário says that the neighbors started to cluster around the front door, so the husband opened the door wide and called everyone in to the house: "Come see this beautiful painting that just got here."

Jorginho, Hélio, and Paulo interjected expressions of their admiration: "So he knows all about it, huh?" "What a head on his shoulders, with the guy right there!" and "*Rapaz!* This is a *man!*"

Mario, seeming to enjoy the suspense he had created, paused until the others were quiet. "With an audience gathered, the husband politely called the offending man out from under the bed.

"'Oh Fulano'"—Mario used the generic man's name to act it out— "'Please do the favor of coming out!' The guy said, very polite, 'But you, *senhor,* will kill me!'

"The husband responded, 'No, it's full of people here, full of witnesses. Do you think I'm going to kill you with everyone watching? You can leave, I'm not going to do anything to you.'"

All the men seemed to hold their breath, looking at Mario.

"'Now Fulana,'"—Mario again acted out the role, in a voice of determined calm—"'get yourself ready.'" It was clear from the context what he meant: ready to leave.

Jorginho asked, "The guy is still naked?"

"He is!" Mário nodded. "But the man said to his wife, 'Get your bundle ready, because you're going with him! And your punishment, my friend, is to take her. She is yours, and here will remain only my three children. Everything that's hers she can take.'

"'What?' The guy responded. 'That's it,' the man said. 'Either you're leaving and taking her, or you both stay here,' dead from being shot, it was clear he meant. 'You can choose. I'm waiting!' She was crying but went to get her bundle just the same."

The others gasped and whistled. "You have to say," Mario appealed to them, "there are few men that have a head like this man's. He wasn't flustered"—*abafado*—"no: he acted. He was not a coward, no. He did the right thing."

Jorginho was particularly beside himself with awe for the story's protagonist. "He didn't get overwhelmed. . . . He was no coward—he was macho, you know?" Jorginho continued, "He had two personalities, two or three personalities. Can you imagine? Because in my case—one thing we know for sure, man is of the moment. There are things a man does and then he can't even face what he's done, the irresponsibility of what he's done. You know? The guy shoots them and then he regrets it. . . . But what *this* man did, he went beyond his own imagination, beyond his own body, beyond his own size. He was *more* than a man!"

"He," Mario reiterated, with dramatic gravity, "acted like a *man*." He continued, "I'm already sixty-seven years old, and—like him—I've never been to the police station for any reason." Avoiding criminality, for both Mário and his hero, involved knowing how to keep proper distance from other men: "I don't knock on their doors nor they on mine," save for special holiday visits or the like.

Mário's hero's achievement, of being "more than a man," came through his *willingness* to use violence—everyone agreed that had the wife and consort not left right then, he would have killed them—and the credibility of his threat, while nonetheless showing restraint and being able to hold back from actually *needing* to use violence. Had he shot his wife and her lover, he would have been a man, but he became "more than a man," as Jorginho suggested, because he was able to listen to a cool-headed, reasonable voice and at the same time honor an "essential" male instinct to avenge himself. The balance he struck, where he maintained total control of both the situation and himself, proved him to be even more powerful than if he had resorted to violence, the last-ditch, desperate way to make a play for power.

The rest of this group's conversation that day covered as lively a range of topics as the other groups. Yet the Big Machos Club went further than most, outlining their own version of Marianismo, reflected in their consensus that women were unquestionably "smarter and stronger" than men, and that a woman could "dominate a man with a kiss." In fact, Jorginho and Hélio agreed, it was precisely *because* of women's resourcefulness and cunning that it was unwise to afford them too much freedom and power—such as allowing her to work away from home—if one wanted to hold on to them. Mário, Hélio, Jorginho, and Paulo all concurred that most women's interests in men were instrumental and doubted the sincerity or loyalty of women's love: "Patrimony; the man is the woman's patrimony and she has to be careful of him," Hélio put it, adding, "women don't have jealousy, they have caution." On the one hand, they agreed that a woman sexually betrayed by her husband should stay with him: "She should show her own prestige and value." Anyway, a "woman who knows how to captivate a man will never find him looking for another woman" in the first place. On the other hand, a man with any self-respect would never stay with a woman who was unfaithful to him.

"MY HONOR STAYS WHERE IT WAS!": CHANGING PERSPECTIVES ON MASCULINITY AND HONOR?

Although Jorginho's group, in its playful way, was comparatively outspoken about its self-declared, *machista* perspectives, I was impressed with how much all six of the men's groups seemed to hold in agreement, joking aside. Even the more *moderno* (holds both "young" and "nontraditional" senses) groups of men always included members who would denounce men whose wives' leashes were too long, whose wives could be found constantly "chatting in other people's doorways," or whose wives could seek recreation without husbandly vigilance; such men were characterized as "*acomodados*" or "*conformados.*" One man made the either/or options quite clear: "You have the *conformados,* and then you have the *perigosos* [dangerous men]." By conforming and accommodating to circumstances rather than dictating and directing them, by failing to pose a threat of being a force to be reckoned with, of credible, potential danger, such men suffered painful jokes and derision from their male peers. They were repeatedly referred to as "giving a big empty space *[vazão],*" or opportunity for being cuckolded. Being a *corno* also played into underlying homophobia: the man whose honor was destroyed when his wife was unfaithful figuratively "got screwed" by the other man, losing irreparably in a relentless hierarchy game. Such a transmutation, of course, rode on the premise that a properly controlled woman could be understood as an extension of her husband's honor, an appendage of his selfhood.

Younger men, however, sounded less willing to positively value violence, and one group sounded especially distinct in this regard. It comprised some of the youngest male participants (ages eighteen to thirty-four), three of whom had been raised in female-headed households. This group's most vocal member, not surprising given the strong personalities of the Bomfim family, was Robi, Yancí's son. Robi grew up without a father present, with the Bomfim principal surname unusually taken from his mother, but before that from his *babalorixá* grandfather, the first Almiro, Dona Alegrina's husband. The group's quietest and youngest member was Raulino, Jorginho's middle son, who had an artistic bent and so far was the only sibling who could read, but who also had a drinking and probably drug-using streak that worried me. Together with neighbors Pablo and Itamar, these cousins sat down with principal facilitators Carlos and Flávio, and me, doing my best wallflower imitation.

These young men discussed the same case Jorginho raised that had recently occurred in the neighborhood, where a young man had been "betrayed" by his wife but did not adequately wash his honor. Unlike the older group with Jorginho, the participants in this group maintained that in such a situation, they would not need to "react," or actively avenge their honor with violence.

Robi began by hypothetically placing himself in the betrayed man's place. "If she takes someone else, I accept it. . . . I'm still going to have high morale, you know why? Because *she's* doing something that everyone will always criticize, and I'm not. When the guys say, 'Ah, but your woman made you a *corno*,' I'll say, 'She did not make me a *corno*, no. Do you think *her* actions were correct? I'm going to continue with my head held high.'

"If this happened with me, I'd break up with her. I'd say, 'Go live your life with the person you're with.'" Robi turned methodically, one at a time, to the others as he spoke. "While the guys are there thinking about making fun of me, I'm going to go about living my life. Because of the *goza-ções*"—the jokes or mockeries—"do you think I'm going to grab her, beat her? Am I going to kill her? No: I want God to help her and not to abandon me. . . . Let her live her life and let the guys talk, make *gozações!* If they think that to show them that I'm the *mayoral"*—the boss, the greatest—"that I'm the big *machão,* that I'm going to beat or kill her—no way I'm going to do this! And do you know why?"

Robi paused, letting his rhetorical question hang in the air. The others waited. "That would have nothing to do with it; with me, or with what happened!" he finished persuasively.

Pablo nodded his agreement. "First, you're going to lose your freedom, so what's that going to resolve? You took away her life and also lose your freedom, and you can lose your life as well."

Robi opened his palm to Pablo, asking, "If it got to the point where I killed her and her family afterward, what's going to happen? Maybe not with me . . . but if he doesn't avenge himself with me, he'll get my brother, an aunt of mine, even my own mother, and then what? . . . I could stop, and analyze, and avoid all that, understand? . . . They can call me *corno,* and of course I'm going to be hurt by that, inside. But, I'm not going to show this to him," *him,* I took it, meaning a hypothetical heckler, "because he's there talking: 'Ah, man, aren't you going to *do* anything? What about your honor?' No. *My honor stays where it was!*"

Initially, I was struck by how sharply these young men's view of the case differed from that of the older men. In the position of a man sexually betrayed by his wife, the young men stressed the need to see their own sense of honor and self as separated from their female partners' behavior and subjectivity, whereas the older men insisted that the man's man control all circumstances around him calmly, issuing only the credible *threat* of violence. The shift, I reasoned, might result at least in part from the effects of recent criminalization: Robi and Pablo agreed about the risk of "losing liberty." They were equally concerned, however, with the threat of losing family members to local, vigilante acts of violence for revenge, typically played out between family members "stirring the brew" *(metendo a colher).*

Robi's assertion of an autonomous men's honor, which could not ride on a woman partner's actions, seemed a relatively new and precarious form of resistance to inculcated norms and scripts; this seemed evident in the very insistence with which such scripts insinuated themselves into Robi's thinking. The durable prescription encouraging Robi to "wash honor with blood" forced him to engage it, to reconcile it against a commitment to look within for his sense of honor to himself and his own behavior. His vehement claim that his honor "is" immune to the aspersions of his circle of male friends and neighbors—he even used the present tense, acting it out—he qualified by a rather exhaustively articulated strategy about how he "will" respond to them. Indeed, he identified the moment in which "the guys" were questioning his honor as precisely the juncture at which he might typically consider using physical violence.

A few weeks after this conversation, Robi took me to task for not following through with the conversation we had begun. Both he and Itamar had expressed interest in continuing the discussion in mixed-sex groups; I had been thrilled at their interest but realized I couldn't, in good conscience, spearhead doing so because I lacked approval from my home institution's board for the protection of human subjects. Robi's engagement in "this work," as he referred to it, electrified me; I pictured him, someday, as an emergent figure in the grassroots men's antiviolence movement.

But later, I began to wonder: did the case about which the two groups, older and younger, so sharply disagreed, possibly involve Robi himself? This might explain the urgency with which Robi desired to continue discussing male honor. It might also shed light on why Jorginho, the uncle at continual loggerheads with sister Yancí and her children, had gone to such lengths to disparage the cuckold: he who "doubted even his own name" was none other than the nephew Jorginho kept in the crosshairs. So believing had I become that the conversations being held were "third party" and "hypothetical," as indeed I had assured the Johns Hopkins University human subject review board I would make all attempts to keep them, that I had not realized that perhaps Robi sat defending himself, as a man and as an honorable person, before his peers. Did they agree with and support his views, as the transcript appeared to show, or were they instead just saying what was needed to help a neighbor save face?

Perhaps, even as recent criminalization dramatically undercut the rewards that violence-washing-honor could reap, the men who talked with us shared a fundamental feature with Amado's fictional characters of decades past. Perhaps Robi, like Amado's fictional Nacib, was refusing the kill-or-be-obliterated dichotomy, casting about for a loophole in order to forge a narrative that left his masculine selfhood intact. Where Nacib could tamper with legalities, Robi's generation faced a whole new legal and criminal playing field; thus, Robi turns to the terrain of subjecthood to salvage his being.

I returned to the transcripts and painstakingly analyzed them again; ultimately, I decided, the man who "doubted his own name" was probably not Robi. The impossibility of knowing for certain, however, was itself instructive. I was forcefully reminded of the fact that my material was limited to "stories about stories about stories," hardly less fictional, in some ways, than

Amado's novels. Was Robi's focus group's material worthy of a modest claim for a potential, nascent shift toward self-contained male, or had we "caught on tape" a man in the act of trying to narrate himself back toward honorability?

Either way, clearly what mattered was not so much "scripts" or "rules" about male honor, but rather how convincingly narratives of manliness could be told among men, and how well narratives were received by listeners. This seemed similarly evident in how the other stories the men's groups told departed from Amado's three examples, and the rules he claimed underlay them. Felismino, so disparaged by the men of Ilheus for merely ridding himself of an unwanted wife but failing to avenge his honor by violence, in point of fact acted quite similarly to the "hero" of the story Mário told Jorginho and the other men. Mário's hero's ability to brandish such a credible threat of violence may be the critical distinction. Surely of equal importance is the fact that a man would be more likely to be convicted for a criminal deed in the 1990s than Felismino in the 1920s, implying that the value attached to controlling events without violence was increasing.

One could argue that older and younger men's differences derive from their concerns with wholly different forms of honor. From among the five types famously elaborated by Julian Pitt-Rivers (1968), for example, one might reasonably conclude that the older men were concerned with public honor (which needs to be defended publicly) and personal honor (which needs to be washed with blood), whereas the young men shifted toward greater concern with moral honor (as demonstrated in the statement, "If she takes someone else, I accept it. . . . I'm still going to have a high morale.") My concern here, however, is to show how the young men's conception of honor sustains aspects of all three forms: the importance of peer acceptance of the new, nonmurderous logic continues to be as much about public and personal honor as it is about moral honor. The terms though which all these forms of honor can be preserved have shifted, though, in response to criminalization and declining cultural tolerance for washing honor with blood.[11]

THE DANGER OF "WOMEN TALKING IN OTHERS' DOORS"

Even as younger men grappled with ways of thinking of women partners as autonomous agents, they also expressed competing opinions that reflected entrenched and time-honored *machista* values. Three examples in which young men rejected viewing "their" women as equal and independent actors will illustrate: controlling women's tongues, subscribing to a zero-sum model of power, and romanticizing conflict and violence.

Nearly all the younger men were in consensus that in *brigas* (fights), intervention was appropriate to avoid a murder. However, they also shared a sense that some violence toward a woman might simply be part of keeping a woman, and specifically her wagging tongue, in line. Here again, the potential danger one risked by getting involved rarely tipped the balance in favor of interfering in a neighbor or relative's mere "alert" to his wife about how she should behave.

Pablo set the scene for a woman being reprimanded: "The woman's in the door of the house, and a pan is burning on the stove and she's in her '*ti-ti-ti*'"—her chatter or gossip, which Pablo illustrated with talking fingers—"'the soap opera yesterday . . . and *ti-ti-ti*.' Now, very well that *I* don't like violence, but there are people that, in this situation, would arrive with a hot head, and," he acted out with open hand—*clap*, "he lets go of a slap to her chest."

Carlos asked, "In this type of *briga,* should you get involved?"

"No," Pablo shook his head, "because he's just giving a reprimand"—a *chega*—"in order to alert her."

After a long spell of just listening, I volunteered that women I talked to, both casually and in the women's focus groups, frequently referred to feeling lonely, to feeling "prisoners of their homes." Carlos added that men's social lives were definitely more open and active than women's. The men assured me that there was no discrimination here, but that this worked in everyone's favor. Statements supporting women's freedom of movement and association were continually qualified: as long as her interactions with a neighbor were deemed a "healthy chat," with "someone of her own level" that wouldn't reveal compromising details about her life with her partner, or put rebellious ideas in her head; or, providing the "house were in order" before she left it. Often the language men chose to express their feelings around these decisions smacked of the benign sovereign, legitimately vested with the duty to oversee the welfare of his subordinates: "I would go so far as letting her go and visit an aunt" or "I prefer that she stays home, for her own good."

Unlike the older men, the younger men were anxious we not mistake their judgment on these matters for machismo: "It's not a question of the woman being a prisoner—it's to avoid problems!" a twenty-one year old man told us, adding after a moment's reflection, "Not for her, but for me. If you're my friend, and then, because of her, become my enemy. . . ."

Carlos asked if gossip among men could generate the same kinds of problems. They agreed that it couldn't; rather, a man's presence could prevent others from gossiping about his woman, whereas a woman would inevitably tell other women everything about her man. "Soon they know what we're eating at home and everything," said Robi, sparking off a round of laughter, due to the double meaning of "eating" as associated with sex.

Listening to these comments, one could almost forget that often these young men had been unemployed during periods when their female partners worked outside the home, and that women's greater participation in the informal economy often meant they provided more stable income over time, even if they earned less per hour (Palazinni 1995; Stolcke 1991; Safa 1995). The idealized division of space, with women in the home and men in the street, was so entrenched that it did not easily alter, even alongside the complexities of gender roles where both men and women work in the remunerated labor force. This is why so many of these men, despite their struggles with raising children in poverty, either attempted to prevent their wives from working outside the home or downplayed the fact that they did, presenting themselves as maintaining idealized house-and-street, male-and-female domains when this was far from reality.

Although shifts in individual younger men's "need" to employ violence to preserve honor may be in motion, then, often their characterizations of how power functions in relationships remained unchanged. Men (and many women), whether speaking in the police station interviews or in neighborhood interviews or focus groups, overwhelmingly subscribed to a one-up, one-down, zero-sum model of power. Indeed, informants explained the occurrence of domestic violence by saying that either the woman or the man "always needs to be on top," "doesn't want to be the one on the bottom," or "always wants to be in the right." Explicit in these accounts is that if one is right, the other is wrong; if one is on top, the other is on the bottom.

The facilitator Carlos noted to the focus groups with the younger men that the way they spoke about whether their wives should remain in their homes assumed that it was the man who would make the final decision; he asked if it were possible to have a balanced relationship, where no one was in charge or commanded the other. In response, the young men produced two lines of reasoning. First, women's efforts to escape from men's dominance were understood as, "Now the woman wants to dominate," and "The woman wants to be more than the man." This, in turn, was held as a violation of a seemingly natural order that passed "from generation to generation"; examples of why this was problematic included the presumption that if a man had to rely on a woman for clothing or food, she would "throw it in his face," whereas a man would never do this to a woman. Second, the men opined that deep down women neither wanted, nor were really capable, of dominance over *or* equality with men: "She herself won't allow" for a man not to take the lead, one man said; another pointed out that "She's got money, but she doesn't know what to do with it."

A third way younger men continued to view women as appendages of men concerned their romanticization of relationships, speaking of them as having their own destiny, agency, and agendas, often against the wishes or interests of wives. The best example came from Jorginho and Zizi's son Raulino, who of course we knew to have seen his mother beaten by his father throughout his early childhood, as well as to have endured his father's violence himself.

Carlos had asked about Raulino's view of the women's police *delegacia*. Raulino offered a "hypothetical" scenario, but one that closely mirrored the situation of his own parents. On the one hand, "Something in the relationship turns the two into enemies within the home," and the woman is "simply seeing that it can't work for them to stay together." She may try to leave many times, and "may even have to go to the police station, because he's just too much"; all the same they will stay together, because "that force still exists, that attracts one to the other." Raulino paused, thoughtful, then added, "Because if the police beat the man, they will still get back together. If the man beats the woman, they will still get back together. What they have cannot stop."

Like his mother, Zizi, Raulino clung to a kind of romanticism that dictated that the relationship must continue, and that a woman's efforts to leave an abusive marriage were overridden by a mystified and inevitable destiny ascribed to the relationship itself—against the woman's own decisions, interests, and safety. In the absence of models of women able to enact plans for their own protection, this romanticism—which includes violence—"explains" lives, like his mother's, where autonomous *female* subjecthood is hard for him to discern.

CRIMINALIZATION AND THE LIMITS OF CULTURAL CHANGE

The female-adultery, key scenario for wife beating and killing is linked to more mundane scenarios in one critical feature: in each, men saw actions performed by a woman as violating a man's honor. Honor, in this sense, refs to ways in which man's social relationships are also seen as extensions of his selfhood, and therefore as areas he should control. Thus, not only can a wife's adulterous behavior merit a violent response in defense of honor, but many other aspects of her behavior as well—her words, her movement, her appearance, her commitment to him. As Reddy writes, "The woman's body," and we would add behavior and public image, "becomes 'other,' the honor of which must be preserved and the dishonor avenged" (2005: 42). When her actions transgress "his" domains, notions of male honor help legitimate and perpetuate violence. Criminalization appears to be encouraging men to examine these boundaries, but because of the durability of an expansionist model of selfhood for Bahian masculinity, emergent models of what I've called autonomous masculine selfhood, such as that championed by Robi, remain fledgling and fragile.

These testimonies point up the acute limitations on shifts in men's attitudes relevant to issues surrounding cultural tolerance of violence. The older men's conversations revealed how violence is still very much positively associated with successful masculinity, albeit more with a "credible threat" of violence than its actual use. For the younger men, criminalization may be contributing to some rethinking of notions of men's honor toward a more autonomous, "decolonized" form, where, at least with regard to the spectre of female adultery, men might be less likely to treat a female partner as an extension of his sovereignty. It should be stressed, however, that this shift is reactive and defensive for these young men—a form of damage control. Moreover, one can expect the impact of criminalization to be especially profound for young, poor, underemployed Afro-Brazilian men of the social standing of the majority of those we interviewed. These are the very men most likely to "suffer"—or benefit from—the consequences of criminalization, because they fit the "profile," for police and the general public alike, of persons thought to be capable of criminal behavior.[12] Thus, to the degree that any "good" or "progress" might be associated with this response to criminalization, it is also problematic because of the way it is wrapped up with the discriminatory policing, confined to only some, and these among the most vulnerable, sectors of Brazilian society.

INCLUDING MEN'S PERSPECTIVES: APOLOGIA?

I opened this chapter with the observation that what we know about experiencing gender-based violence comes overwhelmingly from women. Women's accounts have largely been recorded through research conducted in the institutional trenches of battered women's movements—shelters, police stations, hospitals and so on—in diverse countries, and have often been applied expressly in the interest of advocating for women survivors of chronic battery. They have been used to exert pressure for improved criminalization in law, better policing, and provision of shelter and other services. That they overrepresent women and often omit men speaking in the first-person is not surprising. Methodological difficulties help explain the dearth of men's voices speaking subjectively about violent relationships with women: why would men participate in incriminating themselves, or in admitting behavior often seen as shameful, criminal, and bullying? Some charge, moreover, that efforts to include masculine perspectives in public discourse inevitably serve as apologia, excusing and tolerating men's violence, or distracting from the first-order business of aiding victims (Yllö 1993).

From the outset of my fieldwork in Brazil, I encountered cases that fit the battered woman model but also many others that simply did not. I grappled with an idea of what I then called "threatened masculinity,"[13] my best effort to characterize the many cases of violence I encountered that didn't seem adequately described by the male-abuser/female-victim dynamic that is pervasive in the literature, where men use violence to *secure* and *maintain* dominance over women. Rather, just as men could extend a notion of violated male honor into daily justifications for controlling their wives' tongues, movement, and clothing, men persistently linked using violence as a response to literally or figuratively being screwed over. The quintessential way for a man to get screwed over, interestingly, is for his wife to get sexually screwed by another man, rendering the husband a *corno* (cuckold).

The conversations recounted above explore how one phenomenon in Brazil, the criminalization of spousal assault, undermined the effectiveness of a tactic, violence, that historically had served men to gain or maintain control. Criminalization is, of course, but one of many shifts resulting from women's activism that together erode male dominance: others include women's rising earning power compared to men, declining ideological or religious currents underwriting male superiority, and the emergence of new social movements—especially those tied to feminism—that bolster women's opportunities, influence, and confidence. The remainder of this chapter surveys historical and ethnographic cases in which the cumulative effects of declining prerogatives for men, drawn from societies around the world, appear to have direct implications for men's use of violence. I then briefly present the divergent results that empirical and comparative research generate in testing the validity of a compensatory violence thesis, and attempt to explain why those results are so mixed.

While I invoke notions of men's "insecurity" as part of power shifts away from men toward women, my concern is not primarily a therapeutic one, focused on individualized feelings about male powerlessness such as impotence, identity crises, or senses of emasculation or failure per se. Nor is my suggestion that "masculinities in crisis" may have concrete implications for conflict and violence the same as excusing or apologizing for men's violence, assuming that men have fallen powerless, or saying that women somehow are gaining power *over* men. (Ultimately most men's senses of powerlessness originate, after all, in the power held over them by other men [Guttmann 1997.] Rather, I am interested in cases in which a decline in men's status and social control is concrete and observable. Women's gains are relevant in terms of catalyzing men's sense that their rightful prerogatives are being encroached upon. As Laura Miller (1997) points out in her study of men's resistance to women's gains in the U.S. Army, strategies that look a lot like James Scott's (1985) "weapons of the weak" are, in fact, often employed by the strong.

Why should the notion of "men's insecurity" initially strike oxymoronic chords? I think the answer is this: each time we focus on the insecurity of a privileged or dominant group, it smacks of apologia. If we express concern about the faltering might of the powerful, it suggests that we view their power as legitimate, and our concern is ultimately aimed at shoring it up.

As one Canadian critic of men's insecurity arguments put it: "Any man can use violence to acquire or maintain power over women and children. The 'insecurity' argument works as an instant excuse for sexist abusers. (The common-sense version goes: 'He hit/raped? Well, if he did, he must have felt insecure. . . . No secure man would hit/rape. He wouldn't be a real man if he did.') There are plenty of examples of men with all the power they can use and then some—including at least three [prominent Canadian officials]—abusing women. The key is (usually) being able to get away with this violence. Indeed, the more security one has, the easier that is."[14]

These are persuasive arguments. Indeed, why should we waste time worrying about men's "insecurity" in relationship to violence, when it is precisely their *security* that all too often allows them to get away with it?

The simplest response to that question comes in the form of another. If "insecurity" is a misguided theme for understanding male violence, why is it that the insecurity theme arises in so many different currents of contemporary research? What—beyond apologia—can we learn from such accounts?

The diversity of national and cultural settings that have produced analyses of violence as linked to men's insecurity is astonishing in breadth. As far away as Papua New Guinea, ethnographer Donald Tuzin chronicled the fallout from the abolition of the Tambaran, a long-standing, secret men's cult formed around a series of deceptive rituals that cemented men's domination. The influence of revivalist Christianity led reformist men to voluntarily disband the cult, a move which they "did not foresee . . . was also the death of masculinity" as it had been understood in local terms. Without the complex of myths and stories that sanctified men's superiority, Tuzin reported:

> Domestic relationships are increasingly raw and unbuffered. From both observed cases and the general impression gotten from living in Ilahita, it is clear that acts of violence by men against women—mostly against wives, but also against mothers—have greatly increased in frequency with the decline of the Tambaran. The reason is nearly always the same: with the Tambaran gone, wives no longer bend to their husband's will; indeed some wives, believing men are now powerless, attempt to dominate their husbands. What they find is that, with the Tambaran gone, husbands resort to their fists, which in the short term hurt far more than the rhetoric [of the cult] does. (1997: 177)

Strikingly similar accounts herald from Gabon, West Africa, where ethnographer James Fernandez studied the Fang ethnic group in the years following independence. Here, the reasons for apparent increases in wife-beating differed from the Papua New Guinean case in virtually every respect but one: contact with Western cultures was important in destabilizing men's considerable historical control of women in both cases. Traditionally, Fang women performed the vast majority of productive labor and were highly esteemed but, contradictorily, were assigned low status. Contact with the West brought women greater accessibility to divorce, more opportunities for economic independence, and greater appetite for newly available commodities. Whereas women's sexuality had been rigidly controlled by social mechanisms, these too began to break down, and men grew suspicious of amorous adventures and infidelities. Although in this extremely male supremacist society male dominance can hardly be said to have been toppled, the shifts I describe were destabilizing enough to increase violence: women "claimed they worked as hard has they ever had, but the men were striking them and insulting them more" (Fernandez 1982: 158).

Closer to (my) home, in New York City's East Harlem, ethnographer Philippe Bourgois traced the effects of changing masculinity for Puerto Rican, or Nuyorican, men. Here, deindustrialization was leaving young men, whose blue-collar fathers had found breadwinner wages and muscular identity in hard industry, with only "feminized" occupational opportunities. Most rejected entry-level office work, which they viewed as emasculation at less-than-living wages, and turned to drug dealing instead; Bourgois's work focuses on the crack trade. In this context, the "Spanish ideal" of large, male-dominated households unravels, and one glaring result is an increase in domestic violence and sexual abuse. Bourgois's account is replete with violence as an outcome of the Nuyorican crisis of patriarchy, as in the case of the man who, "as if by clockwork in the style of a failed macho, . . . would recover himself by beating up the nearest vulnerable female whose respect he no longer commanded" (1995: 301). The fact that most of these women eventually leave abusive men is no long-term solution, in Bourgois's view, in that they usually go on to unite with another equally insolvent and irresponsible man. "This process of serial household formation has spawned a street culture logic that partially exonerates fathers from the responsibility of maintaining progeny," Bourgois writes (1995: 315), thereby exacerbating the cycle of poverty and instability for the women and children involved.

Echoes of comparable dynamics resound throughout Latin America as well. Sandinista Nicaragua of the 1980s was a time when rhetoric about the non-macho "new man," devoted to family and community and eschewing violence, abounded. Here, ethnographer Roger Lancaster found that "violence comes up when women encroach on what men see as their domain" (1992: 39). Both legal impunity and cultural tolerance for men using violence to "discipline" wives were drastically diminished. And yet, the imperative for men to at least uphold a credible threat of violence and to dominate women was far more resistant to change, for according to Lancaster, "masculinity and femininity are interchangeable with domination and submission, aggressiveness and passivity" (1992: 41). Lancaster eloquently describes how already precarious masculinity under machismo is upset all the more by women's newly achieved rights and liberties: despite new sanctions against male-to-female violence, men seemed to "need" the masculinizing effect of violence all the more.

In Mexico City, participants in a group for men with violent histories shared with ethnographer Matthew Gutmann their use of "terms like *ninguneado* (nothinged), *minimizado* (slighted), *humillado* (humiliated), and *descontrolado* (out of control) to describe how their wives, mothers, and other women treated *them.*" Gutmann views arguments that suggest men use violence to displace their own anger and humiliation as ultimately serving "to release men from responsibility for their violent actions" (1996: 211). It is hard to ignore, however, the interpretations of his own informants: one man attributed violence in marriages to men not working, drinking, and not fulfilling their marital obligations. This sounds more like foiled machos resorting to violence as a desperate, compensatory measure than like dominant patriarchs maintaining power and control. Gutmann himself concludes, "one of the reasons the issue of jealousy is so recurrent a theme for these men, I think, is that many men feel they are losing control over their wives in general and over their wives' sexuality in particular. The have histories of employing violence to regain this patriarchal authority. For this reason, given what Giddens refers to as 'the waning of female complicity,' violent attacks on women may be on the rise" (Gutmann 1996: 213; see also Giddens 1991).

Writing about Chile, social historian Heidi Tinsman also links a rise in men's violence to concrete historical shifts. She compared patterns of domestic violence in two separate periods, during the agrarian reform under Allende's socialism from 1964–74, and during the conversion to export capitalism under Pinochet from 1973–88. During the first period, in which men especially benefited from new opportunities for economic gain and new social networks (because the reform was directed by and for men), the main pattern of violence served to "bolster an already existing male social and sexual privilege that was in many ways reinforced by the process of Agrarian Reform." By contrast, in the later period under military rule and export capitalism, "men used violence in reaction to a relatively greater social and sexual agency assumed by women" (1997: 266). Tinsman discerned these distinct patterns by analyzing what interviewees gave as the "reasons" for the fights. In the first period, when fights reflected men's efforts to maintain control, they were about male sexual jealousy (i.e., concern with women's dress, movement); women's opposition to male authority in the household; and women's objection to men's sexual liaisons. In the second period, women's proportionate earning power had significantly climbed, mostly through the fruit-packaging industry. Now, the violent incidents arose over different issues: men's authority in the household being generally challenged; men trying to control women's earnings; and men's jealousy over women's widened sexual opportunities. Men's insecurity in this period was made more acute still because of their frequent unemployment. In other words, writes Tinsman, "Female wage work and the changes it implied directly threatened men's sense of authority by undermining men's status as breadwinners and by weakening men's sexual control of women" (1997: 286). The shifting relation of power between husbands and wives resulted in a qualitatively different pattern of domestic violence.

These ethnographic examples of men using violence to compensate when their privileges and superior status were questioned hardly stand alone. Analysts of violence in North America (Faludi 1991, 1999), the Middle East (Naccache 1996; Majdalani 1996), and the Caribbean (Wilson 1973; Wade 1994; Ray 1998; Tafari-Ama 1998) report patterns in which violence is among the tactics men use to attempt to compensate for a perceived deficit in masculine control, confidence, sense of worth, and prerogatives.

Lest I give the impression that violence is an inevitable outcome of historically destabilized masculinity, it is worth mentioning that cases also exist in which male power is being challenged and encroached upon but contestatory patterns of violence do not result. To give one example, sociologist Diane Wolf's work on changing gender roles in Java would seem to supply all the conditions for men feeling their power to be eroded: greater employment and earning for women, easier access to divorce, all-female work groups developing. Although gendered conflict does indeed result, it does not appear to be accompanied by violence, probably because Javanese cultural values strongly inhibit violent responses, which are associated with a lack of self-control and loss of face (1992; also Berman 1999). Such standouts recall the multiple examples the ethnographic record provides in which interpersonal, gender-based violence is extremely rare or unknown, typically because it is strongly inhibited by nonviolent social values (Levinson 1989; Campbell 1999; Boulding 2000). Thus, the emergent dynamic of interest here is not inevitable, and relies upon a cultural foundation where violence is a conditioned response to conflict, supported by specific sets of cultural values.

The shifts in social power that result in destabilized masculinity that I have discussed here differ widely in origin: from abolishing male supremacist cults in New Guinea to colonial interference in Gabon; from deindustrialization in New York City to socialist revolution in Nicaragua; from the conversion to export agriculture in Chile to the criminalization of violence in redemocratizing Brazil. A nearly ubiquitous force is increasing earning power and economic autonomy for women, but this, too, does not apply everywhere. Perhaps the most meaningful generalization that applies here can be borrowed from R. W. Connell: "A gender order where men dominate women cannot avoid constituting men as an interest group concerned with defense, and women as an interest group concerned with change" (Connell 1995: 82; cf. Besson 1993). What I hope to have demonstrated is that, in some places and for some men, violence has become as much a part of men defending themselves against change as it has—and continues to be—used offensively by men to uphold the status quo.

CONCLUSION: REFORMING OGUM

For every Ogum or Jorginho in Bahia, for every man who feels disrespected to the point he does not "even know his own name" and responds by using violence against a woman partner, individual psychology and character clearly enter as factors. The approach taken here, however, assumes that the relationship between violence and masculinity has broader, cultural foundations as well. This chapter's focus on female adultery as a key scenario for culturally legitimated male violence becomes relevant to more common, mundane outbreaks because both rest on men's superior sense of entitlement: to enjoy gendered double standards, to circulate and socialize freely while restricting women partners, to expect the respect accorded patriarchs. As with many of the international cases considered above, successful masculinity in Brazil can be precarious, where a man must either dominate and prevail over others, or be demoted to nothing, to nobody. When social realities and historical shifts compound this precariousness, impinging upon men's expectations, patterns of compensatory or contestatory violence become more likely, even though these may not actually work to shore up men's power or control.

Invoking Ogum as a symbol of insecure-masculinity-grown-violent is provocative in several ways. First and foremost, Ogum is but one among multiple masculine *orixás,* so underscoring "his" violence does not essentialize a relationship between Bahian masculinity and violence but preserves a notion of masculinities as multiple. Recalling Matory's discussion contrasting patterns of gendered relationships around Ogun (Ogum) and (Sango) Xangô in the introduction, it bears remembering that Xangô archetypes can be equally violent with women; the difference is that Xangô's "sexually redolent" (1994: 7) violence does not lead to his failure as a husband wishing to control wives, but rather is part of his success. Thus, in archetypal terms, forceful men who have historically enjoyed Xangô-like success may increasingly find themselves cast as Ogum-like failures as male partners, and face women's abandonment as a result.

Second, despite Ogum's shortcomings, he is not rejected or expelled from the familial pantheon of *orixás,* but is still revered and valued, in large part for his decidedly masculine, bellicose qualities. This has value for the younger men of Robi's cohort, who struggle to retain their valuing of masculine strength and willingness take the warrior role, while loosening a grip on Ogum-like murderous rages that, in contemporary Brazil, are increasingly costly to all. Just as Ogum has adopted different faces according to different historical processes throughout the African Diaspora (Barnes 1989), so will Robi and other Bahian men be looking to reshape and reform Ogum (as well as Xangô), while preserving his variant of masculine spirit. The warrior-Ogum in Brazil, for example, offers equal potential for championing struggles for social justice as it does for fueling the cuckold's avenging rage.

Perhaps Bahians' reverence for the forceful Ogum, warts and all, offers a local way to quell uneasiness with discussing male violence in relation to insecurity or destabilized masculine power. This uneasiness results, I believe, from a series of presumed either/ors: if we weigh the significance of men's insecurity, we disregard that of women's; we are either working to aid women *or* men, and thus need to clarify our priorities; men's violence is either instrumental *or* expressive: if we identify how it serves men instrumentally, it nullifies any expressive elements.

I submit that these either/or dichotomies arise out of activist strategizing, which rightfully has often directed accompanying scholarship. In the activist's world, where extremely limited time, means, and other resources makes us lucky to accomplish anything, we have prioritized crisis intervention for women and punitive mechanisms for men. I am not the first to point out that too often this has kept our work in the realm of the palliative, as opposed to the preventive. Scholarship on male violence, including that on the significance of male insecurity, cannot hazard reproducing these either/or dichotomies. Research is one of the most fertile ways, I believe, that we can ultimately devise more effective and creative approaches to prevention.

To arrest cultural tolerance for men beating women, institutional responses must not be confined to punitive and other palliative measures. Not excusing men's violence is insufficient; it is necessary to enjoin and include men in formulating more comprehensive measures. To prevent violence before it occurs, the work Robi called for is essential: Brazilian men discussing with one another, and with women, the impossible dilemmas, none with good outcomes, of a man being seen as no-man-at-all, whether due to a partner's sexual betrayal or because he fails to control her conversations, movements, dress, and other behavior. Demonizing men as a group is not productive, since a majority of women lack the opportunity, leaving aside the desire, to live lives devoid of men's participation. Moreover, the activist rhetoric, "One who loves does not beat" *(Quem ama não bate),* notwithstanding, the men who beat women are very often the men women love, and vice versa.

However powerful men as a group in the Alto do Mungongo, or Bahia more generally, may be in relation to women, individual men—and especially these men—are not all-powerful in the world. In this sense, distinguishing between patriarchy in a macroscopic sense and individual men offers a critical tool for addressing specific forms of men's violence against women.

One part of the transformation must be women changing, through refusal; but until men change, too, women's changes may only increase contestatory violence, at least in the short term. To understand how men might change, we need to understand the specific social, cultural, and ideological pressures with which they contend. Clarifying the relationship of violence to social change and to the destabilization of men's roles and identities casts women's agency into relief, helping us see how rising confrontation between men and women fits into prospects for transformation, thus giving hope for the future.

THREE

Paths to a Women's Police Station

Perguntaram pra mim / Se ainda gosto dela
Respodi tenho ódio / E morro de amor por ela
Hoje estamos juntinhos / Amanhã nem te vejo
Separando e voltando / A gente segue andando / Entre tapas e beijos
Eu sou dela e ela é minha / E sempre queremos mais
Se me manda ir embora / Eu saio pra fora / E ela chama pra trás
Entre tapas e beijos / É ódio é desejo / É sonho é ternura
Um casal que se ama / Até mesmo na cama / Provoca loucuras
E assim vou vivendo / Sofrendo e querendo / Este amor doentio
Mas se volto pra ela / Meu mundo sem ela / Também é vazio

They asked me / If I still love her
I responded I hate her / And I'm dying of love for her
Today we're together / Tomorrow I don't even see you
Breaking up and getting back together / We keep going / Between
    slaps and kisses
I'm hers and she's mine / And we always want more
If she sends me away / I leave / And she calls back
Between slaps and kisses / It's hatred and desire / It's dreams and
    tenderness
A couple in love / Especially in bed / Provokes madness
And so I am living / Suffering and loving / This sick love
But if I go back to her / My world without her / Is also empty

"Entre tapas e beijos" [Between slaps and kisses],
Nilton Lamasa e Antonio Bueno

ZIZI NEVER PHYSICALLY STEPPED FOOT into one of Brazil's Women's Police Stations, yet she took advantage of their existence to defend herself by verbally invoking them as a threat. Jorginho was never summoned to account for his violence in a women's *delegacia,* yet knowing that he could be may have stopped his hand in the air, preventing the slap he had intended when he raised it.

Between 1985 and 2004, over four million women stepped past the line where Zizi stopped.[1] They made their way through the doors of Delegacias da Mulher (DMs) with the intention of "*tomando providência*" (taking providence). This may have meant filing a complaint and pressing charges, gathering information to explore options, or merely being able to state they had made the trip, lending more weight to threats to seek intervention. Their strategies were as varied as the situations these complainants confronted. For virtually all of them, however, resorting to police involvement constituted a drastic measure, one fueled by their high expectations for dramatic results: women expected to be protected by the specialized police, to find themselves less vulnerable to injury or death at violent partners' hands.

These complainants were not alone in holding great expectations for the world's first specialized, all-female police stations. When the first women's *delegacias* were created in the mid-1980s, the move was broadly hailed as the premiere victory of the Brazilian women's movement in criminalizing acts of male-to-female violence. The *delegacias'* all-female police staffs, presumably, would not ignore, minimize, or blame female complainants for the violence they wished to denounce in the way traditional police had so frequently been reported as doing; they would help neutralize the male-biased occupational culture of the police, which had made so many victims reluctant to seek protection or justice. Subsequent chapters explore when and how such goals have been accomplished. For now, we can state with certainty that with well over 300 DMs throughout the country, unprecedented official recording of gender-specific crimes against women has become possible, as have significantly increased (if still unsatisfactory) rates of prosecution and conviction for such offenses. Perhaps most important, DMs have sent a message that assaulting a partner is an intolerable crime, a stance that departs dramatically from historical acceptance of domestic violence.

In this book's prologue, I told of my encounter with a student who glorified DM policewomen as a fearsome, avenging group who battered men in retribution for their violence against women. Stories like his hint at the degree to which Brazil's all-women *delegacias* fire imaginations. Bahians and Brazilians elsewhere told me—in taxi-cabs, in *barraca* refreshment stands, on beaches—mythologizing stories about the women police. It was as though they served as a test case for women gaining an edge in timeless gender wars, or for a kind of police-and-state power that, when feminized, could be enacted for the good of newly democratized citizenry. This dynamic has undoubtedly fed not only the lofty expectations the DMs are subject to, but also the degree of disillusion that failure to fulfill such expectations can generate.

The next chapter, "Policing by and for Women," will delve into the institutional history behind Brazil's women's police stations. Before taking this broader view, the present chapter revolves around the question: What happens such that couples end up at a police station? I attempt to recreate for readers the path from relatively private, domestic space to the public exposure of the police station. Whereas Bahian complainants and accused found themselves playing out highly dramatic, intimate moments in this law enforcement context, such dramas shaped policewomen's workaday rhythms, somehow becoming ordinary. By introducing complainant and *delegadas'* (police chief/magistrates, feminine) voices and stories prior to the institutional history of the DMs, this chapter attempts to parallel the fieldwork experience my collaborators and I shared. No amount of anticipation or background research could prevent our sense of having somehow fallen from the sky into a setting that so concentrated intense conflict, tragedy, and violence that I doubt any of us would have said we ever felt prepared to face it.

But this chapter works its way there gradually. It begins, actually, with a brief glimpse of a folkloric event that most Bahians would witness in childhood: a folkdance that instructs about the conflict and violence "inherent" in marital unions. It stays with pre-*delegacia* settings, peering into the *casas* (homes) of women who become *delegacia* complainants, and asking about earlier stages of conflict. Long before women resort to police intervention—the ultimate *rua* (street/public space)—couples' troubles usually spilled into less distant and institutionalized *ruas,* in the form of involvement of neighbors and extended kin. Observing Bahians' precision when calculating the lines between "normal" versus intolerable violence, between appropriate versus unacceptable interventions, leads into a discussion of a Bahian ideology of non-intervention; women, men, family, neighbors, and police alike confront this ideology each time they decide that couple violence constitutes a collective, "public" concern meriting their involvement.

Four carefully chosen "crisis snapshots" from the DM follow, forming the body of the chapter. Each recounts a hearing where complainants confront their subpoenaed partners, the moment at which most *delegacia* processes come to a head. In addition to the couple and the *delegadas* (the police chief/magistrates who convene the hearings), often lawyers or other advocates, family or in-laws, and the occasional unrelated neighbor might be present. These cases present multiple contrasts; in particular I stress the complainants' diverse motivations and levels of power (or powerlessness), as well as the variable, at times idiosyncratic, approaches taken by *delegadas*.

In attempting to backtrack to the very beginnings of violent relationships, the next section draws directly from field notes; their present tense is preserved. The change of voice, into that-with-which-I-spoke-to-myself, creates a parallel: my own fieldworker's eye was akin to that of a child's, seeing something for the first time, before it became normalized.

DANÇA FOLCLÓRICA ON SÃO JOÃO

Saint John's day, which Bahians shorten to São João, is celebrated the twenty-fourth of June, marking the highlight of a cluster of late-June saint's days, collectively known as the *festas juninhas* (June festivals). The main holiday of the winter season, Bahia's São João commemorates the corn harvest. Traditionally, huge bonfires are built to draw the attention of the Saint. Daredevil youths make a show of jumping ever higher over the flames one by one, and close friends jump over hand in hand to become each other's *comadres* and *compadres* ("co-parents," or godparents of one another's children; the São João over-the-bonfire usage may simply mean "best friends"). A central element of São João is the *quadrilha* (square dance), and the most common version enacts a shotgun wedding scenario.

Tim and I were invited to a São João *forró*—a shindig, also the word for the polka-like dance step[2]—by Leila, one of Tim's private English students. She was upper-middle class but probably one of the wealthier members of her congregation, for the *forró* held at her Catholic church, Nossa Senhora da Ascenção, was relatively humble, especially for Pituba, one of Salvador's wealthier neighborhoods.

São João is a quintessentially interior, rural holiday, strongly associated with rural peasants. The families in Pituba are the children of urbanized parents, skilled sophisticates, playing for one day the farmers they are not. Tables are set up in the center of a big field, with families and friends mingling and milling about and countless children running around. There are bales of hay stacked against one side of the lot to form the backdrop for the stage, and loose hay is scattered all about on the ground. Above us, brightly colored streamers trace back and forth across the field. Everyone is dressed *caipira* —hick or bumpkin—drinking to the harvest. They don intentionally disheveled straw hats, have painted freckles on their cheeks, and blacken out a tooth or two, wearing huge and badly-sewn patches on their trousers held up by a course length of rope.

The smells fill the air of *abóbara* (pumpkin) and *milho* (corn)—there is corn absolutely everywhere, reminding me of a combination of Halloween and Thanksgiving in the United States. Little *barracas* (food stands) all around offer for sale boiled corn with margarine and salt, toasted corn, and popcorn with Parmesan cheese, caramel, or coconut. Perhaps best of all are the *canjica* (corn pudding), the *bolos de milho* (corn cakes), and *mingau de canjica* (sweet milk of corn), which may be spiked with *cachaça* (sugar rum). People keep buying servings of each of these seasonal delicacies and sharing them with us with great pride. "Try the *licor de genipapo* [fruit liqueur]!" "Eat some *amendoim* [salty peanuts boiled soft]!" "There's no *cuscus* [coconut pudding] like my mother's." We are pressed to try more cuts of roasted meat than I knew existed. We manage only to refuse the hot dogs (pronounced "hochie doaggies"), served Bahian-style with shredded beets, carrots, peppers, onions, and condiments, as these can be found any day on the street.

Soon the *quadrilha* square-dance starts, beginning with the central element, a dramatized shotgun wedding. There are some forty kids, from older adolescents all the way down to four-year-olds, making about twenty couples. Two of the couples are two girls, one in each dressed as a little boy.

The first couple, the bride and groom, lead the procession in. They are met by a priest, a chubbified (with pillows) mulatto, whose affected accent of the *interior* of Bahia is hilarious, and whose flatulence problem is forcefully amplified by use of the microphone.

The priest begins the ceremony while the father of the bride looks on suspiciously with gun in hand. The rite is interrupted by a very pregnant (very pillowed) teenage girl, who approaches the groom. She insists in a nagging, whiney voice that he has said he loved her and that he can't abandon her. The father of the bride brandishes his revolver under the groom's nose and at his temple. By the father's haste, we are given to understand that the bride is also pregnant, although this isn't physically obvious. The groom's inconvenienced, annoyed expression is more than matched by that of the priest, who quickly shuffles the bride's rival off into the wings.

The wedding ceremony begins again, this time a bit more rushed. But the groom is assailed once again, this time by a young guy in drag, again with pillows testifying to pregnancy. Now the bride's father loses all control, seeming ready to put an end to the groom entirely but also anxious to see the ceremony concluded quickly and irreversibly. When the cross-dressed claimant is violently pushed aside by the priest, the father quiets down immediately. All this time the bride, who is incidentally the only blondish creature on the floor, looks on with minimal discomfort, seeming far less bothered by her husband-to-be's philandering than by the possibility that her father would exterminate her catch. At last, the final vows are reeled off faster than an auctioneer's cant; the marriage is made and the *quadrilha* begins.

The band strikes up the bouncy *forró* beat, similar to a polka, with an accordion-like instrument leading. The caller takes the mike on the stage, talking over the music to guide and comment on the dance. The dancers take their places: two lines, boys and girls opposing. First, each girl walks alone down the row, briskly, nose in the air, actively ignoring the boy. He pursues her pleadingly, feverishly, yearning to catch her eye, earn a word, endear himself to her. Despite the fact that she keeps strutting to the end of the row, his persuasion seems to have worked: nearly all the girls crack a flattered smile at their partners as they reach the row's end. Their disinterest is but the invitation to *conquista* (conquest).

The next round, the roles are reversed, and the gals pursue the guys. With the very first couple, I am impressed by the fact that the girl's pleading for her love's attention is more physical than his: while the guys made lunges at ankles and the like, very few of these gestures actually seemed to constrain the girls' walking. But when the bride keeps hurling herself at the groom with full force, refusing to let him pass, the groom raises his hand against her. The caller encourages him, "*Bate nela! Bate nela!*" (Beat her! Beat her!) in a cheerful, all-in-good-fun tone. Many of the other girls' efforts are similarly more forceful than their partners.

Unlike the girl's, the guy's disinterest and annoyance do not seem feigned. She liked it when he threw himself at her, but she is clearly a nag and a nuisance, and I see no revealing "I'm really liking this" smiles cracked on the guys' lips. One imagines that right about now, at the beginning of their marriage, she is beginning to nag *(cobrar)* about the time he wants to spend in the *rua*.

Tension arising from men's lives "in the street" versus their lives at home would not be a new theme for the young wives and mothers whom the São

Figure 6. Boys congregate more frequently in public places, here at the Dique de Tororó, than do girls. Photo by Sarah Hautzinger.

João dance depicts. From the time they were young girls, they would have been accustomed to brothers, cousins, and other boys enjoying license to roam farther from home than they themselves or neighboring girls did. As the boys pictured at the dock by the Dique de Tororó in figure 6 illustrate, boys are strikingly more visible in relatively public urban spaces. The girls would likely have already grown accustomed to expectations that they confine themselves to domestic and neighborhood spaces and have their whereabouts known, perhaps socializing on *ladeiras* (steep walkways), as in figure 7, but always available to help mothers, aunts, or grandmothers and to mind younger children.

The problems with the husbands' fun in the street get worse. One by one, each guy staggers toward his partner, bottle in hand, stumblingly and sloppily sloshed. The girls' arms are folded, eyes in the air, unamused. He tries to put his hands on her and kiss her, and she pushes him away, disgusted. In response to the offense, the entire female line advances *en masse,* to deliver twenty-some synchronized slaps across the faces of the guys. In response the guys, now one by one, approach the girls remorsefully, hat in hands, looking down. The girls uniformly appear unconvinced and not

Figure 7. Girls visit closer to home on *ladeiras* (stairways) and *praçinhas* (small plazas). Photo by Sarah Hautzinger.

willing to reconcile. That is, until the magic moment when each guy delivers the kiss to each girl's cheek. Instantly, the girls smile in perfect synchrony. All is forgotten, and the girls sashay merrily down the aisle with their loves.

The trials and tribulations of marital relations having been demonstrated, the couples begin to promenade around the space in a line, then separating to whirl and turn together, dancing their polka-like *forró* steps into the night.

We saw another *forró quadrilha* after São João in a tiny neighborhood where I had lived in 1990, a unique combination of *favela* (slum) and middle-class houses.[3] The same theme of the role of violence in the tumultuous rounds of marriage was made plain here. The dancers in this one, however, were all very young children: the oldest were perhaps seven or eight, but most were three, four, or five. They were fairly bewildered by it all and needed a lot of guidance by the overseeing adults. The detail I most recall was the opening move, in which each couple of children approached one another and, one by one moving down the row, delivered mutual slaps. Many of them were so young that they had no idea what this was about; their mothers had to take their hands and guide them through the slap. The slaps of the youngest were so gently and vaguely intended that, were it not for having seen the theme more elaborated elsewhere, it might have been hard to figure out what was going on.

Doubtless these children will too soon come to grasp all too well what this is all about. Dance on, "*entre tapas e beijos,*" between slaps and kisses.

INFORMAL INTERVENTIONS: FAMILY AND FRIENDS

Fast-forward: the children have grown up, and the slaps and kisses are no longer play-acting, but have become chillingly real. What kinds of interventions precede women seeking out police involvement? The DM constitutes a relatively new path of recourse for assaulted women. By contrast, "informal" interventions by family and friends have always occurred to some extent; such personalized interventions, in fact, are the most accurate measure of cultural tolerance for, or rejection of, domestic violence. Not only can family members, friends, and neighbors intercede in *brigas,* my focus here, but so also can locally based organizations such as neighborhood associations, mother's clubs, churches, or *terreiros* of Candomblé.[4] Often, the DM is sought out only when the effectiveness of earlier interventions has been tested and failed.

Family members were the most frequent to intercede in *brigas.* It is interesting that in the interview sample, in-laws intervened in a son or brother's attack—and especially mother-in-laws and sister-in-laws—far more often than a woman's own parents intervened. Jose, a man summoned to the DM for being accused of beating his wife, was incensed that his mother—"*My own mother!*"—could take his wife's part, and suggested that it was only because of the "new conspiracy of women," presumably referring to the feminist movement against male-to-female violence, that such an outrage could occur. The marked frequency of interventions by in-laws, however, may simply stem from their being well positioned to do so: I observed a slight tendency toward virilocality (living with husbands' families) over uxorilocality (living with wives' families), although it is by no means a defined norm for urban families in Salvador.

Although a few cases of women's own parents intervening were seen, I was more struck by how often they failed to do so. Many parents of complainants appeared to be less concerned with their daughters' physical welfare than with protecting their daughters' marriages. Parents worried about the material stability of their grandchildren and of their daughters themselves, particularly where both women and children depended on the earnings of the husband and father; parents might cite this as sufficient rationale for encouraging a woman to stick it out with a violent man. Thus, the complainant Donalda was told by her mother to "do it"—to stay in the situation—"in order to live. To live!" even as Donalda grew increasingly fearful for exactly that—her life. The advice of Cida's parents was distressingly circumspect: "My mother never told me to separate. She always said that a husband and his woman *[marido e mulher]* is a very good thing, and that to raise three daughters alone is too much. My father said, 'Wait and see if things stay like this.'" Three other women said their parents simply stated, "He's the father of your children," suggesting this made taking any recourse, including leaving, inappropriate.

By far the most frequent kin group to intervene was made up of brothers (since the masculine plural, *irmãos,* is used for mixed gender groups, sisters might at times be included, but it was clear that brothers were particularly cast as important protectors). At the same time that Donalda's mother implored her to stay, for instance, her brother's adversarial relationship with Donalda's husband grew more and more strained, culminating in the brother "almost killing" the husband after he beat Donalda. Maria do Carmo's brother insisted that she go to the DM, saying that if she didn't that she would show she had no self-respect and "didn't even like" herself. Yet another complainant, Cilene, cited her brothers as the reason she held back from lodging a complaint for the eight years she endured battering from her husband: "When he'd give me a slap, I'd just stay quiet. Because of my family. If I'd arrived at their house and said he'd beaten me, my brothers would be out to get him, and that would just end up worse for everyone." Her brothers were also the reason behind her decision to finally press charges, however, for in the final altercation before Cilene arrived at the DM, her face was so bruised that "someone, either him"—her husband—"or one of my brothers, was going to end up dead. That's why I'm here."

Cilene's change in strategy here can be clarified by distinguishing between wife beating and wife battering. Wife battering refers to physical aggression that is "extraordinary, possibly resulting in severe injury, incapacity or even death" and that is usually seen as unacceptable behavior; wife beating, by contrast, involves "physical reprimand" which is culturally accepted and even expected, if not always tolerated (Brown 1999: 2). As long as Cilene herself deemed the violence tolerable, she found it more suitable to avoid allowing her brothers to become involved. When beating tipped over into battering—which, Cilene suggested, the tacit threat of her brothers' vengeance had until then prevented—she knew that intervention of some sort was imperative and opted to go to the police rather than see her brothers get into trouble with the law. Sibling support cannot be underestimated as a critical support for women, enabling them to project an attitude of indomitability and to resist falling into the role of victim. Some of the most resistant, least victimized women had involved brothers or sisters, who sided with them and tried to intercede on their behalf.

Children, tragically if not surprisingly, were frequently found intervening in conjugal battles. As was the case with sibling intervention, often it was only when offspring, as young as three years old in one instance, placed their bodies in the path of danger in order to protect their mothers that women were finally pushed to the point of invoking the more authoritarian involvement of police. Women expressed anguish over seeing their offspring's ambivalence and divided loyalties, along with other effects of witnessing violence: The five year-old daughter of one complainant had begun to stutter as a result, and the seven-year-old son of another had grown completely withdrawn, rarely speaking at all.

Of course, child abuse frequently entered the picture in related ways, as in the case of Cremilda, who sought to cover the "errors" of her children so they wouldn't be hit, preferring to "absorb the blows" herself. The politics around parenting could complicate marital relations in a host of other ways, including differences in parenting and disciplinary approaches, stepparents' treatment of children from earlier unions, and men's apparent jealousy for the attention that women focused on newborns. As conflict around any of these issues could precipitate outbreaks of violence, women's concern with children can be viewed as indirectly interventive as well: Although some women held off from leaving violent men for their children's benefit (economic and social), other women reported leaving men sooner than they might otherwise have done because they were concerned for their children's safety.

Neighbors often involved themselves in fights. Yancí spoke of her family practically issuing rulings on conflicts among residents of the Mungongo, to whom they were usually unrelated: "We threw him out of here," or "We helped her escape from him." In fact, one day when Yancí and I were talking about the first DM, when it was still in an old house in residential Nazaré (from 1986 to 1991), she recalled a time she had shepherded a gaggle of brawling neighbors there, and suddenly I flashed upon a vague memory of a similar circumstance during my first weeks of fieldwork. I looked back at my 1990 field notes, and shared with Yancí my details of the account, which she confirmed was the Mungongo group. I read what I'd written about her, as a "bossy kind of neighborhood manager, with no apparent direct connection to the conflict, yet somehow fashioning herself as the one in charge." She laughed, but rejoined that her family has always taken responsibility for what happened in the Mungongo, since it was "our community first."

Again, the level at which informal interventions are taking place represents a more telling barometer of cultural tolerance for domestic violence than do reports compiled in a police station. The many Bahians who shared with me convictions that intervention was appropriate and necessary may indicate that major shifts are already in effect; longitudinal data on this question would be invaluable. At the same time, so long as perpetrators of violence are protected by popular directives reinforcing the sacrosanctity of *brigas* between couples as "nobody's business," we should be cautious in declaring that any lasting change has occurred.

"STIR NOT THE BREW": THE IDEOLOGY OF NONINTERVENTION

Intervention is still strongly inhibited by the idea that what goes on between men and women is nobody's business. The dictum, "In a fight between husband and wife, don't dip your spoon" *(Em briga de marido e mulher, não se mete a colher)* summed up the common wisdom about getting involved in a couple's infighting. It means "don't stir the brew"; don't get involved, what goes on behind closed doors is nobody's business. Moreover, those who involved themselves will find that they pay a price. Men, women, and children repeated the saying often, and the saying's prediction that the interventionist's good intentions would not be appreciated proved frequently to be correct.

Dinerges, a man I met in the DM where he was responding to a summons involving his alleged assault of his wife, felt personally wronged by the involvement of neighbors and friends. He assiduously spelled out the logic that followed from the popular saying: "I think that no one should interfere"—*se meter*—"and that each one, the man and the woman, should look after their rights. Because if I meddle in a family *briga,* between husband and wife, what's going to happen? Tomorrow or the next day they're going to be getting along, and *I'm* on bad terms with them"—*eu saio a mal*—"understand? And also, I can enter into the fight and he'll say: 'If you butt in it's because you're interested in my woman, you are betraying me [*falseando*], committing adultery with my wife.' He could even attack me from behind, saying, 'If you are on her side you must have some motive.' All this is what I'm afraid of."

Dinerges appeared more concerned than most men about being suspected of having a sexual interest in the assailed woman were he to take her part. Such apprehensions among men did not appear to be as generalized as the expectation that "meddlers" would end up being ostracized by the reconciled couple, a concern men and women shared. Nonetheless, Dinerges's certainty that self-interested and sexual motives would be suspected was shared by many other men, revealing that women's significance as objects of sexual conquest overrode that of simply being neighbors, about whose safety and well-being one might be concerned. Such men clearly felt a greater sense of accountability to other men than to women in instances of clashing couples.

Dinerges was also concerned with his own interests if police became involved: "Now if I let them be, the police that come if he kills her or rapes her are *his* problem, not mine. . . . In my neighborhood there's a lot of this problem, but I don't meddle. I might see him filling her with slaps, but I won't say anything. The next day they are kissing each other, and I'm the guy's enemy."

Dinerges's last point is summed up in the oft-spoken phrase, "between slaps and kisses"—*entre tapas e beijos.* Because many Bahians argued that relationships needed *pimenta*—hot spice, in the form of jealousy and conflict—to stay interesting, at times they naturalized violence's role in romance, *expecting* vicissitudes, including violence, in intimate male-female relationships. Dinerges makes clear that slaps and kisses are two sides of the same coin; ignore this, hazard intervening, and you will pay the price.

None of the men who commented on the directive to not stir the brews of others' discord rejected it out of hand. But both men and women offered additional reasons for respecting the dictum. Jaldo, one of the men in police custody, was convinced that violence broke out between himself and his partner only because of the meddling of others. He echoed Dinerges's certainty that people want to "take advantage of an already-heated situation" to pursue their own interests, but added another theme about meddlers: most people who intervene in a couple's fighting are motivated by a more generalized sense of envy and spite. As an example, he used his sister-in-law who, "because her own relationship with her husband is not working out, began to feed the fire." Like Dinerges, Jaldo emphasizes suspect motives, disregarding the idea that interventionists may primarily wish to avert injury.

Among those who commented on the don't-meddle dictum were two women who were DM complainants who firmly supported the idea of never getting involved. One of these, named Heloísa, embraced the mind-your-own-business stance when discussing a fight that ended up in the *delegacia*. In this case, a female neighbor had tried to intervene, for in spite of the fact that Heloísa viewed the fight as strictly "between myself and my husband," the neighbor "thought it was a challenge to us women to be fighting with him." In other words, the woman acted through a sense of collective solidarity between women that Heloísa did not share.

The other woman, Socorro, was primarily concerned that the person intervening could get hurt: "That knife is likely to end up getting me *[pega em mim]*, for all I know. This already happened once, when my mother went to defend me and my daughter from my ex-husband, and she ended up getting beaten by him. Then I went back to him, and my mother said she would never again get involved. And she was right."

The logic of nonintervention was less clear-cut for another group of interviewees, all women, nearly all of whom had been subject to long-term violence. For these women, the micropolitical concerns of those who respected the logic were easily superseded by the real threats to life they had experienced firsthand. The certainty that intervention is necessary correlated strongly with women who felt they owed their own lives to others' involvement.

As Donalda expressed it, "I think you have to interfere, because with something like what he did with me—he would have killed me otherwise! He came out of the kitchen with a butcher's knife in his hand, and he was ready. If it weren't for the neighbor—she's not here giving a deposition because she's afraid of him, but she saw everything—if not for her, he'd have killed me. She got in there and gave me time to run."

I asked her, "If you witnessed a fight between your neighbors, would you have the courage to . . . ?"

"I'd telephone the police, first thing," she interrupted, showing no hesitation on the question.

Another pro-intervention woman, Katiana, made it clear that severe violence crossed over into something that went beyond the concerns of the couple alone. When asked what she thought of the don't-get-involved dictum, Katiana responded, "It's because of this that there is death from these fights, and that there is too much violence between men and women inside their houses. I think a person has to intervene, to take the lead [tomar frente]. It becomes something concerning everyone, it's not just between husband and wife, if someone is going to *die*."

Without a doubt, the commitment to intervene that this group of women felt came not only from their own debt to others who interceded, but also from the fact that, as women, they are less beholden to the code of inviolate household privacy. This code, after all, underwrites male impunity, expresses the authority of a male head-of-household, and constrains women more than men. In this sense, women's conviction that intervention is both appropriate and necessary—a feeling that appeared to be gaining support—reflects the same trend that the led to the creation of the DMs: the notion of a firm division between "house" and "street," between domestic and public spheres, is being called into question and progressively renegotiated.

The most revealing opinions regarding shifting concepts of domestic privacy were expressed by a third, intermediate group of female and male interviewees who felt intervention was appropriate at some times and not others, and went on to qualify what these conditions were.

Some thought that it was appropriate to interfere in *brigas,* but only to separate the parties and prevent serious injury or death. They made clear, however, that crisis intervention was the maximum intrusion acceptable. As one complainant put it, "To separate us is one thing, but to really resolve anything, it has to be between him and me alone. I don't want anyone telling me anything." Others, such as the complainant Rosimaria, specified that only those closely tied to the assailed woman should—and indeed were obligated to—intervene. "Should my sister, or my *prima* [female cousin], be fighting with her husband, even if I'm going to take a slap myself, I'll still intrude. Because it's my blood. I don't care"—*não quero saber*—"if it's a '*briga* between husband and wife,' and I'm not supposed to butt into the *brigas* of others. Now if it were a couple of strangers, of course, I'm not going to say anything. But my own sister? I'll go help her."

Another way to express Rosimaria's point is this: the extent to which one fits into someone else's life through bonds forged by *casa* relations, those of kinship and intimate friendship, determines one's right, and again, obligation, to intervene. Also, people of the *casa* are less likely to be figuratively thrown to the *rua,* outside the circle of intimacy, if they attempt intervention and the couple later reconciles.

The process of criminalization and delegitimization of male-to-female domestic violence under way in Brazil raises the question of whether new rationales for intervention are being constructed and whether new forms of relationships can serve as legitimate means for intervention beyond the "traditional" *casa*-based kin and intimate friendship networks. One incipient example of a conceivably "new" intervention is the woman who interceded on behalf of "us women" in the fight that Heloísa described; a similar "imagined community" (Anderson 1983; Steeves 1993) notion of women as a collectivity underlies the creation of the women's *delegacies,* after all. But Heloísa made quite clear that the intrusion was unwelcome and resented. Time will tell whether such alliances will gain greater legitimacy as intervening forces, and even eventually come to serve as deterrents in themselves, as well as whether kin and friends will come to feel an increasing obligation to intervene.

FOUR COMPLAINTS, FOUR AUDIÊNCIAS

An *audiência* is a semijudicial hearing convened by police; although "hearing" is the best English gloss, the notion that the *delegada* is "giving audience" is worth underlining. For only a *delegada,* a police chief or magistrate with legal training, can call an *audiência;* rank-and-file police officers technically cannot (in practice, however, I saw that backlogs create exceptions to this rule).[5] *Audiências* generally mark the second, and usually final, step in a DM process, following the registration of the initial complaint. The four cases presented below are chosen, from among dozens of *audiências* I observed while taking notes, for their contrasting features; none, however, is exceptional, and each shares themes with many other cases I heard played out in hearings, interviews, and waiting-room chatting.

The first two complaints, filed by Celeste and Judete, catch women in relatively downtrodden, victimized positions. In the latter two cases, complainants Janína and Joana pursue strategies as far more ambitious agents; their conflicts appear closer to genuine power struggles in which they are less victims than stake-holding contestants. Although distinguishing between levels of victimhood and agency is useful, it becomes clear that the victim-versus-contestant distinction does not neatly translate into whether the DM effectively helps complainants meet their objectives.

Celeste and Ediundo

Celeste and Ediundo are a lower-middle class couple; both have light brown skin and curly hair, suggesting mixtures of European, indigenous, and African ancestry. They would probably self-identify as "*morena*" or "*parda*" (both roughly meaning "brown"), although I do not ask.[6]

Doutora (Dr^a.) Márcia, a shift delegada who is subordinate to both the titular and assistant *delegadas,* presides. Celeste lodged complaints of *agressão física* (physical assault) and *ameaça de morte* (death threat); this is a repeat complaint for assault. Celeste has a lawyer accompanying her.

After Dr^a. Márcia calls the couple and the attorney into the bare office and offers them chairs, she invites Celeste to begin. Celeste explains that the couple has three children together and has suffered sixteen years of *brigas* (fights), in which she has repeatedly withstood beatings from Ediundo. Only recently, however, has he begun to threaten her life; this motivated the current complaint. She says she has left him many times, nineteen to be exact, but always returned.

Ediundo cuts in, interrupting Celeste, to counter that it is Celeste's own aggressiveness that sets him off. "She would leave and . . . I am nervous" (*nervoso,* beyond simply a nervous state, can connote a chronic condition or illness).[7] He offers no better examples of Celeste's "aggression" than that of her leaving the house when he wanted her there.

"Have you gotten any treatment for this?" Dr^a. Márcia inquires.

"He won't accept a treatment," Celeste complains. "I've done everything to get him to accept that he needs some, but it's no good."

Ediundo stretches out his hands dramatically, palms down and fingers spread. He waits a moment, looking into the *delegada*'s eyes, as if to prepare her for his own statement.

"My intention," he begins, "is not to separate. I plan to go on living with her. I don't have any other woman. I do everything I have to for the family. I may make threats, even death threats, but it's not to actually do it, it's to blow off steam *[desabafar]*."[8]

Ediundo then tries to describe his frustration at frequently coming home from work and not finding his wife at home, at not being able to count upon her to do her part.

Celeste's lawyer chimes in, "He doesn't even let her speak. He suffocates her! You know, Doutora"—to Drª. Márcia.—"that this is not my client's first complaint!"

Drª. Márcia's eyes scan the report of Celeste's complaint before her. She looks up and asks of Ediundo, "You said that you *hated* her . . . ?"

"Well, I also hate myself," Ediundo barks in a dry, confessional laugh. Returning to the prepared speech he was delivering before, he appealed, "I want to live with her but I also want her to treat me well, to treat me right. I want her to be a *mulher"*—both "woman" and "wife"—"to smile and keep the house light *[leve]*, and to do the things for me a *mulher* who cares does, with affection *[carinho]*."

Celeste speaks up, speaking softly and mournfully, but with finality. "I want to separate. Even though I like/love *[gosto]* him, unfortunately. I *can't* return to him. It's too much. I can't."

Drª. Márcia, seeing where this is going, now attempts a kind of intervention I have heard from her in other *audiências* apparently heading toward separation. "Let me share something with the two of you. I spent two years in the Delegacia for Toxics and Drugs, and in all that time, do you want to know how many of the kids I dealt with that were drug addicts [who] had parents that were not divorced? Just one. You can't imagine the terrible effect that divorce has on the children; it's very difficult to give them a structured life when the parents aren't together. Today it's fashionable for people to separate—one little thing happens and forget it. But you have to ask yourselves: Do you want your children to end up as drug addicts or homosexuals?"

Ediundo, seeing that Drª. Márcia's predisposition against separation could help his cause, continues to plead his case: "She's saying the problem here is all me, when I'm the one that doesn't want to separate. I'm not the only one creating problems."

Every time Celeste tries to get a word in, Ediundo, who is increasingly agitated, cuts her off. But then, he interrupts everyone, even the *delegada* Drª. Márcia. He begins making declarations in an ever more resolute, booming tone. "I swear to everyone here, our problems will end right *now*, as of this moment. And if things don't work out *[dar certo]*, then I give my word that we'll look toward a separation."

Celeste points out, under her breath, that they have already tried to work things out nineteen times. But she then adds, with a tone of concession, "I'll try to live with him again, if we can just move away from Pernambues"— their neighborhood—"there's just no way I could go back there."

Ediundo continues with his declaration. His voice rises to an even greater volume, and his gestures become more sweeping, abrupt, and nervous. He appears to be in a frantic attempt to take up the entire space of the small office in which we are gathered, to win the *delegada* and others present over to his perspective by sheer effort and by the force of his belief in himself.

"I give you my word, Doutora. The word of *man* [*palavra de homem; man's word*]. I am a man. And I am here accepting 100 percent of the responsibility, 100 percent of the blame." That this last admission is somewhat rhetorical is suggested by the fact that Ediundo continually qualifies: "*If* this is all my fault, then . . ."

"I swear, Doutora, that from this day forward I will treat her *na mão*"— literally "in the hand"; like "with kid gloves" in English—"the way she should be treated." Ediundo bangs his palm loudly on the desk before him, to punctuate. "And she, she also will treat me in the best way, the way I deserve to be treated." Again the palm slams loudly down.

Celeste is shaking her head slowly. "I still can't accept this. He needs to undergo a treatment for his problems, and then, then we'll see . . ."

Drª. Márcia hears Celeste, and regards Ediundo incredulously. His performance and his clear expectation that he can steamroll others appear suddenly to outweigh Drª. Márcia's misgivings about separation. She attempts to open a discussion of the immediate arrangements for their separation. But Ediundo is not through.

"I don't drink, Doutora. I don't party, and I don't have other women. We don't want for anything that we need at home. I am a good man for her. I have no intention of hurting her, of doing any damage to her at all. It is *she* who is betraying *me*! She's the one who is hurting *me*, destroying *me*."

Ediundo is now perspiring profusely, his voice working up to a higher pitch. His head whips from side to side, his eyes darting in disbelief from Drª. Márcia, to me, to Celeste's lawyer. "Why can't you see this?"

Drª. Márcia, Celeste, and the lawyer discuss living arrangements and child support until a more permanent agreement can be reached. Drª. Márcia entreats Ediundo to seek out some treatment for his nerves *(nervos)*, but his wall has gone up: so seemingly shocked is he at his inability to get through that he abruptly enters another state and acts sullen and dejected. Distanced and frosted over, he allows the *audiência* to be concluded without his participation.

The couple and the lawyer leave. Drª. Márcia turns to me and says, "I give her one month, and she'll be back with him."

Celeste's intolerable marriage, leading to her appeal to the police to protect her from life-threatening circumstances, illustrates a dominance-driven, long-term battering relationship of the sort that public awareness and specialist training campaigns have emphasized. Her resolve to end the relationship is fragile, easily in danger of being silenced and overridden, and therefore in need of support. For his part, Ediundo resists separation and is unwilling to relinquish the control he exercises over his wife, clearly believing this control to be his right. Furthermore, because he experiences her potential ability to reject him as so profoundly threatening, he equates their respective levels of power—"She is the one hurting *me,* destroying *me*"—refusing to recognize his dominant position or take responsibility for the violence he uses to maintain it.

Celeste and Ediundo's case underlines police officers' common difficulty: negotiating a solution between opposing objectives. Although police care about protecting women from harm and about punishing criminal acts of violence, many policewomen appear concerned with the association they believe exists between the breakdown of conjugal unions and families, on the one hand, and social disorder and conventionalized forms of criminality, on the other, as in Drª. Márcia's preoccupation with drug use and homosexuality. The tension between these two objectives leads to the apparent contradictions in Drª. Márcia's stance. It is significant that the position against conventional criminality and in defense of families is the one she is more accustomed to taking in her police work and more in keeping with what she considers to be police work.

Ediundo's behavior, body language, and language are more pronounced than those of many, yet his conviction that he can grasp the reins of a situation that appears to have long since left his control is not uncommon. He expects that he can invoke a version of male honor—in this case manifested in "giving his word," the "word of a man"—as a way to ensure his credibility before police, an oft-repeated cant for abusive men pleading their cases in the DM. Along with this are his assurances that he is complying with his role as husband-father: providing for the family, not philandering or carousing, and so on. His expectation that he will be able to muscle through his own solution to the impasse with his wife, and his incredulity at being (at least temporarily) overruled, betoken a denial characteristic of many batterers. Eduindo believes that his control over Celeste should effectively be total, and he therefore rejects her autonomous subjecthood. Like the *orixá* Ogum's violence, his is related to perceived intrusions into the respect, authority, and control to which he feels entitled.

Jandiara and Nilda were two other battered women I met in the DM who, like Celeste, spent years in perpetual fearfulness and saw police intervention as creating the possibility of escape; both were driven to desperate measures only when convinced their lives were at stake.

Jandiara had never officially married, but had lived with the father of her children for nineteen years. "*Oxente!*[9] He beat me so much I lived as a big bruise. I live suffering—so much suffering—because he drinks so much and lives to beat me. He's drawn my blood so many times, but I've suffered through. Because a woman who has children, at times, I don't know, she thinks of those kids and doesn't want to drop her husband." She now resolved to pursue the question in the courts and get him out of her life once and for all. Like Celeste, she had been ready for over a decade, after her husband had beaten her to the point of going into premature labor, resulting, she thought, in the baby being born with *nervosa*—nerves: "It's not normal, what this little boy has," she said, shaking her head. She thought that, with specialized police help, she could finally escape.

Nilda's story differs from Jandiara's only because her husband drank still more rum-like *cachaça*. After having her arm and then her nose broken, followed by having her cheek cut open, Nilda said, "I've come to the *delegacia* to ask for 'life insurance.' It's the second time I've come here. Before, I asked the *delegada* to tell him to leave me in peace. It's the only thing I want."

Celeste, Jandiara, and Nilda are battered women, women in the exact situation that most people think of when they think of the DMs, of shelters for women with secret locations, of intervention in overwhelmingly unidirectional, chronic, and life-threatening violence. For each of these three I met dozens of women in similar circumstances in the *delegacia*. There were others like them in the neighborhoods: Creuza, whom Yancí and others helped escape from the husband all were certain would kill her, even though escaping her husband meant abandoning her children; and Sandra or Estelita, who neighbors knew were regularly beaten, but whose husbands never allowed them to talk with us alone. Women in these situations share much with Zizi in the early years of her relationship with Jorginho, the battered girl for whom pubescence was retarded because of violence. What would a women's *delegacia* have meant for Zizi then? Would she have used it to prevent herself from descending to battered victim?

The DM's mission par excellence is to provide such endangered women with support. Nonetheless, Dr^a. Márcia almost missed her cues to intervene because of her commitment to preserving intact families and to fight social "*marginales*," as opposed to "good family men" like Ediundo. For women in long-term battering relationships like these, the absence of specialized shelters—Brazil counted seventy-two shelters in 2004, two in Bahia, but neither in the city of Salvador—is especially worrisome.[10] Too often, women like Celeste return home after lodging complaints at the women's *delegacia,* or go to other places they can be found, courting serious risk of being murdered.

Judete and Edilson

This *audiência* was conducted by the titular *delegada,* Doutora (Drª) Célia. The charge being brought involved death threats and "moral aggression," which in this case referred to stalking. Judete and Edilson are both around thirty years old; she works in a *barraca* (a street stand or kiosk) that he owns, placing them socioeconomically as working poor, but possibly meaning that Edilson, as an owner, earns a more substantial income. He is darker-skinned *(negro),* she lighter *(mulatta* or *parda).* They have two children together.

The hearing opens with Judete explaining that it had been nine years on Saturday that her own parents had separated, and that she went to visit her father to see how he was. Shortly before this visit, her "*colega*" (colleague; referring to the father of her children, Edilson, in very formal terms) arrived at home and threatened her with violence and her life. She states she is "*crente*" (which literally means "believer," but currently in Brazil denotes a born-again, Protestant Christian, usually of an Evangelical or Pentecostal persuasion), with the realistic expectation that it lends her respectability and credibility. Judete notes that Edilson, on the other hand, has always had many women on the side, and is always "*botando ela fora*" (which can mean either literally throwing her out of the house, or setting her aside for another woman), to the extent that their son is quite traumatized.

Judete told Edilson that she was also going to a girlfriend's house, on the way to her father's. He followed behind her, catching the same bus. "I stopped by my girlfriend's, with him following—something he'd already done various times. When I got there, she already knew everything, because I always tell her: I always said, 'Oh Rosimaria! He's following me again.' Then he comes up, and says he thought I was going straight to my father's house. He starts picking a fight, saying that he's going to kill me. Rosimaria saw a knife in Edilson's hand, and then Roberto's children—Roberto is a friend, another street-stand owner who was at Rosimaria's house—started to scream and cry. So I got out of there right away."

A few days later, a friend encouraged Judete to sit and talk with Edilson, in order to avoid getting killed. She tried, but again he pulled out a blade (a *peixeira,* a fishing knife) and threatened her life.

Drᵃ. Célia asks, "Did he go to the point of attacking you?"

"No, just threatened," Judete responds. "So, I went to my neighborhood *delegacia,* and they sent me to the DM."

Drᵃ. Célia then turns to Edilson, eliciting his side of the story.

After a pause, he begins with careful sobriety. "*Senhora,* for a long time now—for a *long* time—we've been fighting. I have a *barraca* that she was taking care of. One day recently, she shut the *barraca* at six in the evening, and we *never* close that early. She said that she was at her mother's house, but that's a lie!

"This woman says she's a Jehovah's Witness"—Edilson takes a deep breath and looks over at Judete skeptically. "But then, when I confronted her, she says she was at the *Bênça!*" This is a Tuesday-night celebration in the historical district, where generally various *Bandas Afros,* Afro-Brazilian bands, play in the streets; music and celebrations of this sort are usually spurned by *crentes* as hedonistic or demonic.

"And, that she was with some girlfriend that I don't even know!" Edilson continued. "Does this sound like a *crente* to you?

"The next day, she's asking me for money to buy medication for her father. She called me to bed, to give me a little affection to calm me down. She gave me a strong kiss, and then left the house, without any lipstick on. After she left, she puts on lipstick, and changes her shoes and clothes!"

Edilson admits to seeing all this while keeping himself concealed while she rode the bus and got off. Then, he says, he saw her meet another man, whom he had never seen before. She gave him an embrace, then went upstairs.

"This guy lived in an apartment on the third floor. So I went up and knocked on the door and asked for a cup of water. Then, I had to force the door open. And the lights were turned down—a low-life atmosphere. The guy who opened the door was Roberto, another *barraqueiro*"—kiosk operator—"that is no friend of mine. I went in looking for her, and found her behind a closed door. Roberto's screaming, 'But this is my house!' but I said to him, 'But the *woman* is mine!' I wanted to be sure of her infidelity. I found her in a darkened apartment. Who ever heard of a *crente* woman acting like this?"

Drᵃ. Célia addresses Judete, "Is this true?"

Judete responds firmly, "I have proof of everything I said." She makes no move to clarify the relationship between her friend, Rosimaria, and her alleged lover, Roberto, or why they were in the same place.

"I always believed in her, because she was always studying the Bible all day," bemoans Edilson, shaking his head and glaring at Judete accusingly.

"And what is the current state of your relationship?" inquires Drª. Célia.

"We're separated. She abandoned the home," says Edilson, not without self-pity.[11]

"I didn't abandon our home; I went to the police, and I never went back home because that was the advice I got. I'm not looking to get killed!"

Edilson focuses on Drª. Célia. "Senhora, I don't run with a knife on me, or a gun, despite the fact that I work in the *barraca* on Rua Chile, a dangerous place, and even though I'm not *crente*. . . . Now, when she lied, saying she wasn't going to use lipstick, and then puts it on after she left—"

Judete cuts in, "I'll go to the end of the earth to prove my innocence." Judete then makes it clear to the *delegada* that she desires to return home and to find a way of reconciling.

Drª. Célia asks Edilson, "Will you let her? *[Vai deixar?]*"

Edilson's resolute answer surprises all of us, given the possessiveness he has shown for Judete. "No. There's no way to work this out anymore." His voice drops, with finality. "But," he adds, "I'm not going to let go of my two children, either. I want to take care of them, so that they aren't hurt by our separating."

Judete is taken aback, distraught by the direction the hearing has suddenly taken. She tries a different approach: "If he saw me kissing another man, why didn't he come in then? Why did he wait? I have proof that he has another woman; I have her telephone number, even," she protests, beginning to dig through her purse.

"So you think he's trying to throw you out in order to move another woman into the house?" asks Drª. Célia.

"Yes. That's exactly how he is. He has a lot of women *na rua* [in the street]. He's been trying to get me out for some time."

"So," Drª. Célia turns to Edilson. "How are things going to work with her and the house?"

"Everyone in the neighborhood saw her mother come and fill a sack of her clothing. I already allowed them the chance to get her stuff."

"But Edilson," Drª. Célia cautions, "the house is both of yours. You can't prohibit her from entering and getting the rest of her things."

"I went hungry often for that house," chimes in Judete, affirming that she has no intention of losing both her man and her home without a fight.

Drª. Célia straightens the papers from the case, then announces that they must go through the justice system to define the ultimate division of property. She chastises Edilson for reportedly having lit a pile of Judete's clothing on fire (this was mentioned in the document for the initial registration of the complaint before Dr³. Célia). Judete is instructed to make a list of all that is missing from her wardrobe so that she could be compensated later. Dr³. Célia asks how Judete will support herself after the separation, and Judete points out that she cleaned houses before. The *audiência* ends somewhat vaguely, with Dr³. Célia admitting that without Edilson's cooperation, she has no authority to enforce any aspect of the division of property.

This *audiência* illustrates the kinds of discrepant stories with which *delegadas* must contend, something that occurred in countless hearings. Here, there is enough to raise suspicion that Judete was indeed stalked in the course of committing adultery against Edilson. Yet she seems quite confident that, given the chance, she could prove her innocence.

In such quasi-judicial hearings in the DM, when accounts diverge to this degree, a *delegada* has not the ability to put her hands on sufficient evidence to assess what, in fact, has happened. Dr³. Célia lacks sufficient detective power on her staff to investigate most cases. Of far greater importance is whether Judete being caught in the act of committing adultery should be the issue. Whether the charges she lodged against Edilson—being threatened and stalked—were valid, and whether Judete genuinely feared for her life, are arguably the only relevant questions. The *delegada* allows the "social considerations"—normative concerns about appropriate behavior—of the story to take precedence over the juridical considerations, in part because her ability to assess what has actually taken place is so limited. Instead, the couple's divergent agendas shape and influence the process, taking center stage. The moral character of the woman ends up being placed on trial, to a degree that overshadows the focus on establishing whether a crime has been committed.

In Judete and Edilson's case, entrenched cultural values operate to weigh a woman's adultery as a far more severe transgression than that of her male partner: little time is devoted to discussing Edilson's other women. Complainant, accused, and *delegada* all collude in reinscribing, and inadvertently reinforcing, this value. The reason for this is that here the illicit acts Edilson is accused of committing are, for him, directly related to Judete's alleged treachery. He expects that his actions will be seen as legitimate if his suspicions prove valid, so firmly embedded is the double sexual standard in historical Brazilian morality.

Absent the ability to punish Ediundo's alleged offenses, the couple's "social narratives" take on greater weight, as it is through these that the *delegada* accomplishes what inevitably becomes her fallback objective: to decide what is to be done or what the next step can be for a couple at an irreconcilable impasse.

Edilson's stalking of Judete, and his apparent obsession with her fidelity, may appear to be confusing, in light of her certainty that he ultimately wants to get her out of the house to make way for another woman. However, the preoccupation some Bahian men display in controlling not one but two or more women with whom they are involved ought not be underestimated.

Another complaint I followed is revealing around this issue. This one was filed by the "other woman," or the *mulher da rua* (the woman of the street), rather than by the wife. The complainant, a registered nurse, presented herself as a single woman. "But," she felt the need to add, "my neighbors respect me," thus contradicting the implied lack of respectability of her singleness. She came to the DM to file her fourth complaint against her lover for physical assault (she declined to include a complaint for rape, although she said that all of her neighbors could serve as witnesses). She also, however, needed to counterbalance the complaint he had filed against her in a different *delegacia* and to establish that she had acted in self-defense. She had "for the first time, reacted" *(reagiu)* to his violence. "I lost control, and broke a bottle on his face."

Although he had been stalking and "persecuting" the nurse, his *outra* (other woman), for five years, it seemed he was equally obsessed with controlling his wife. During a volatile confrontation between the two women, the wife told the nurse that she herself had lodged eight complaints against her husband in the DM. In both cases, the man's violence stemmed from his certainty that "his women" were betraying him sexually.

Cases like these highlight how men's extra-marital privileges play out and the particular dynamics that the womanizing man—the *mulherengo*—creates. As evidenced by Zizi, who started physical fights because she was enraged about Jorginho's other women and ended up getting punched hard, and who also physically attacked Gabriela, Jorginho's mistress turned number one, fights can arise not only because men and women are sexually jealous *(ciumentosos)* of one another, but also because women protest men's ability to get away with philandering. Women who attempt to even the score by pursuing extra-conjugal sex or romance, as Judete may have, find it doubled against their favor. Her adultery is seem as meriting Edilson's leaving her, even in the DM, whereas Edilson's adultery is simply how men behave. Zizi, as I understand it, never dared to betray Jorginho, but he is on record nevertheless stating that her betrayal could not be forgiven.

Janaína and Jorge

I began following this case when Janaína appeared in the DM after a fight with Jorge and filed a complaint of physical assault. A male-female police duo then picked up Jorge with the DM's one functioning police car, and an *audiência* was held immediately following.

Janaína is an extremely poor woman with three children. She lives in Boiadeiro, a neighborhood locally notorious for being a community of *palafitas,* houses on stilts that rise out of mud flats on the polluted inner shore of the city's bay.[12] The visual images of Boiadeiro epitomize abject poverty and the land shortages that lead to squatter settlements and shantytowns throughout Salvador's metropolitan area. The desperation accompanying this neighborhood's impoverishment is accentuated by the frequent stories circulating of toddlers and children killed or injured by falling off the rickety planks that connect the walkways of the "village on stilts." The young (not to mention inebriates and others with balance troubles) have been electrocuted when hitting live wires during falls, had their flesh pierced by the old, rotted stilts that stick up out of the mud like deadly stakes, or have simply drowned in the fetid, sewage-contaminated waters under their homes.

I would not need to know much about Boiadeiro to perceive the level of Janaína's indigence and misery, however. It is stamped on her face and carved into her body. Although the baby she nurses around the torn, soiled tank-top is three months old (she has two others, a two- and a three-year-old, in tow), her face still bears the darkest "pregnancy mask"—the dark pigment under the eyes and along the line of the cheekbones—that I have ever seen. These masks appear most frequently on women of predominantly indigenous descent, as Janaína looks to be, but are also associated with folic acid deficiencies during pregnancy. Whatever the cause, the mask framing her eyes heightens my impression that she is exhausted, malnourished, and deeply mournful about her life.

Janaína explains to the shift *delegada,* Dr^a. Aparecida, that the older two children with her are from her previous *marido* (husband, in this case by consensual union), who died. Her current *marido,* Jorge, is a jack-of-all-trades handyman who picks up work where possible *(biscateiro).* Jorge was living on the street when Janaína met him, and he drinks a lot. This morning, he beat her up—for the first time, she says, turning away and lifting up her shirt to reveal the deep red marks beginning to turn to bruises on her back, and looking back at us with injured eyes. He also threatened her with a broken bottle, saying he would kill her. To top it off, Jorge tied up the two-year-old daughter, a little girl. He was hurting her, and would not let Janaína get to her to untie the girl and get her away from him.

Dr².Aparecida is told all of this just before lunch. Dr². Aparecida instructs Janaína to wait until after lunch when Dr². Célia, the *delegada titular,* will return, because her authorization will be necessary to send a squad car out to apprehend Jorge. Janaína agrees, and settles down to wait. She and I continue to talk. I realize she must be hungry and will go without lunch as she awaits the *delegada,* so I bring some sandwiches from the snack bar for her and the kids to eat while we talk.

The main problem with Jorge, Janaína continues while ravenously attacking her sandwich, is that he is "prejudiced against" her taking care of the two children from her earlier union, children who aren't his. He interferes with her giving food to the infants, and if she feeds them first he complains and refuses to eat, saying she doesn't want to feed him. He also wants her to "give" the children away; when I ask to whom, she offers nothing specific but nods when I suggest an adoption agency or some such organization.[13] She says she wants to live alone, wants nothing more to do with men. When Jorge leaves she is so relieved—she begins singing, she feels relaxed.

Janaína declares that she never wanted to live with Jorge in the first place, but he managed to convince her. She is in public housing, in a dwelling given to her by the mayor's office (probably in the part of Boiadeiro where landfill replaced mud flat). Janaína almost was refused a place, she says, but she sobbed and refused to leave the housing office, throwing herself on their mercy, until the answer became, "Don't cry, *senhora,* we'll take care of you." She recounts this triumph righteously, appearing to feel her deservedness vindicated, and proud of herself for having the tenacity to demand justice of the powers that be. Dr². Aparecida later tells me that the arrangement is but temporary housing and bemoans Janaína's dependent attitude as a prime example of the effects of *assistêncialismo*—social welfare without emphasis on self-help or self-determination—on Brazil's underclass.

Janaína is worried that Jorge will have gone and taken everything in the house while she's here, and then escape, never to be found by police.

Although her relationship with her former husband was good, she's had nothing but bad experiences with men since. Ironically, her poverty already seems so inescapable that she assumes she will go on living on public assistance of some sort, so the economic issues of independent living don't seem to inhibit her resolve. She does not have a pension from her first husband, though, which in Brazil usually means he did not work *de carteira assinada* (literally "with a signed card"), or in a job in the formal economy paying contributions to social security.

Two hours later, the police have brought Jorge in. I sit in on an *audiência* conducted by Dr². Aparecida.

Jorge is young and baby-faced, wearing fairly ragged clothes and a battered baseball cap. Dr². Aparecida invites the couple to sit across from her before a steel utility desk and declares that each will speak separately and that she firmly upholds the rule of not letting them get into a back and forth. Asked what he does, Jorge responds, "I'm not going to lie to you, Doutora. I work in the trash and get most of my food this way. And I do whatever *biscate*"—odd jobs—"I can." Jorge shows Dr². Aparecida a huge, once-bloody scar on his forehead, which he says Janaína inflicted with a broken bottle, the same weapon she says she herself was threatened with by him. He shows another such scar on his shoulder. Later, Dr². Aparecida observes to me that this is the first time she's seen this, where the woman did more damage to the man than he to her. She also notes that this case was noteworthy in that Janaína made a complaint after the first time she was beaten.

Jorge says the present incident was precipitated by some missing money *(cruzeiros);* Janaína denied having taken it, but if not she, who could have? Jorge says Janaína is jealous and possessive of him and of his life, but her tense, protruding lips and urgent eye contact with me stubbornly deny this. He says she beats the kids for wetting the bed. Dr². Aparecida explains to Janaína that bedwetting is always a symptom of emotional trouble that beating will not resolve.

Jorge's criticisms continue: Janaína isn't equipped to raise children—she gives them the wrong food at the wrong time, and this is why he sometimes takes food away from them. The children don't know how to behave or be quiet when they have to be. Janaína defends herself, engaging Jorge: "Children will be children, you can't ask them to be responsible for their actions."

Jorge, determined to bring their stalemate to resolution, announces to all present, "Know what I'm gonna do? Go get my clothes and leave. I'll bring by baby milk"—by which he means powdered formula—"to the baby and be a father.[14] When she needs help I'll try to give it, and if I get sick she can help me."

I write an aside in my notes, to myself, "This is heartbreaking. He obviously loves the baby."

Janaína is not moved. "But I'm not going to care *[ligar]* anymore, I don't want/love *[querer]* him anymore."

Dr^a. Aparecida begins to draw the hearing to a close, as Jorge's declaration is as close to a resolution as she feels this couple will come for now. But first she takes the opportunity to chastise Janaína: "You've drawn serious blood from him, Janaína, and you yourself admit that he never has from you. Did you ever consider what trouble that could create for you when coming to a *delegacia?*" Janaína, never denying the accusation, replies that her motive was just to curse him *(xingar)*, that she was mad *(zangada)*. Dr^a. Aparecida also confronts Jorge about his drinking, which he swears he's working on. "I was drunk when all my documents were stolen," he adds, as if to acknowledge that this experience itself was sobering enough (in Brazil, all citizens must carry identification at all times).

When Dr^a. Aparecida turns the ledger in which she has recorded the hearing proceedings and offers a pen so each can sign, neither Jorge nor Janaína accepts. Both shamefacedly mumble that they don't know how to sign the document. Dr^a. Aparecida tsk-tsks and repeats to herself while shaking her head, "No one can sign . . ." Perhaps she acts out this disapproval so unmistakably for my benefit, even though it clearly humiliates them further. Later Dr^a. Aparecida said both had *problemas mentais* (mental problems), which severely curtailed what the DM could do for either.

Janaína and Jorge's troubles are not primarily characterized by Jorge using violence to dominate or control Janaína. Although Jorge is physically stronger, neither appears to be more powerful in the context of their relationship. In fact, given their shared destitution, the powerlessness of both is most striking. The violence in this relationship is episodic and mutual, as opposed to chronic and unidirectional. Jorge also appears to accept the separation—or at least not expect to have the means to reject it, suggesting that he does not assume it is within his right to continue to control Janaína's activities.

Of the cases so far discussed, Janaína and Jorge come closest to representing Bahia's underclass, often referred to as *marginais,* people living on the margins. As I discuss further in Chapter Five, *marginais* can also refer to "criminals," a meaning that police often problematically conflate with the impoverished, underclass sense. Although Dr^a. Aparecida does not appear to consider them part of the criminal element (aside from their interpersonal violence), her dismissive diagnosis that both suffer from "mental problems" also effectively places them in the margins of Bahian society and outside of what Dr³. Aparecida sees as being the jurisdiction of the DM. Jorge confirms his own illicit sense of self-identity when he says he won't lie to the *delegada* about the fact that he survives by picking through the trash. So without structure—*sem estrutura,* as the policewomen say—are the lives of such *marginais* that the DM is not equipped to help them. Policewomen view the obstacles as two-fold, both practical and what I will call "cultural." On the practical side, the residences of marginalized peoples are unstable, making the delivery of summons or tracking the history of such relationships complicated. Often police are unwilling to enter the kinds of neighborhoods in which Janaína and Jorge live because they perceive the physical danger to them as prohibitive and because other neighbors are automatically hostile to police and will never help them locate the persons they seek. Moreover, the lives of such persons are so precarious that police feel they cannot count upon a woman of this sort to follow through with a complaint and continue to appear on the appointed dates for hearings or follow-up investigation interviews.

Police such as Dr³. Aparecida see the violence that emerges in a relationship like that of Janaína and Jorge's as inherent to the couple's social and cultural identities. So embedded are violent impulses in people who dwell in the margins, police argue, that in most cases it is futile to attempt police intervention, much less prevention. Rather than attribute these perceived tendencies to chronic socioeconomic distress, many police tend to essentialize such characteristics to the marginalized poor as a breed, or strain, of people.

Dr³. Aparecida is no exception. After this hearing she had some time, and we chatted for quite a while. She began by deploring the state of humanity in general, and the population of Brazil in particular, as caught in a hopeless downward spiral. The population explosion in Brazil was responsible for most of the violence, she believed. People like Jorge and Janaína, people "without conditions," should never "be allowed" to have children in the first place. "How can they value human life when their own lives have never been validated?" She told me that her religion was Espiritismo, a religion founded on the teachings of the nineteenth-century Frenchman Allan Kardec and based around spirit mediumship, reincarnation, and a doctrine of an evolutionary hierarchy of souls. Jorge, she said, was a perfect example of the part of humanity that was "beyond recuperation." Dr³. Aparecida said that her *espiritista* beliefs helped her to accept that there was no hope for a huge percentage of Brazilians—about a third of the population, she estimated. As far as her personal spiritual development, she had concluded that there were those whose souls were evolving upward and those, like Jorge and Janaína, who were in a state of spiritual deterioration. Drª. Aparecida's beliefs provided her with a way to dismiss the violence that arises among Jorge and Janaína's "kind" as an inevitable result of their spiritual degeneracy rather than of their class position in a crisis-ridden Brazil.

Joana and Chico

Drª. Márcia, the shift delegada from the first case, once again presides. The complaint lodged was *agressão física* (physical assault); the accused, Chico, has brought an attorney to the hearing. Both Joana and Chico are respectably, if not affluently, dressed; with medium-dark skin tones, each might be seen by Bahians as either *pardo/a* or *negro/a,* depending on context.[15]

Joana begins, explaining that she and Chico have two children and have been separated since Christmas (it is now late January). Their current troubles started one night when Chico was heading off to a party being thrown by his brother and refused to let Joana get into the car to come with him. Shortly thereafter, in early November, Joana discovered that he was with another woman, and she assumes that this woman was at the party that night. Then, right before Christmas, Joana discovered that all the money that they had set aside for Christmas had disappeared. She was sure it had somehow gone to the other woman. When she confronted Chico, he gave her a punch *(porrada).*

Joana says she talks about all of this with her mother, explaining that "there are things that you can't discuss with either neighbors or friends." But confiding in her mother, she implies, has become a further point of conflict between herself and Chico.

Drª. Márcia, focusing on Joana, advises her that the problem is hers to resolve, that she will have to *sair* (which could mean either "leave" or "find a way out") with "dignity, self-love, and self-esteem." Then she notes, from the document with the registration of the complaint before her, that Joana works outside the home. "But with two children? How is she able to do this?"

Chico hastens to explain, appearing to feel accountable and somewhat ashamed, "It's that I work as a chauffeur. It doesn't pay well, so we always come up a little short at home."

"And what do you think it is that makes a family, sir?" Drª. Márcia asks Chico.

"To live well together, to get along." Chico replies. As if in effort to head off the lecture he knows Drª. Márcia is about to launch into, Chico cuts to the chase, denying having assaulted Joana. Drª. Márcia points out that the medical exam administered Joana after she lodged the complaint verified that she had been beaten, at which point Chico cries out, "But it was she who attacked me!"

"Ask him why this violence arose," Joana encouraged the *delegada*. But she went on without pausing, to explain that after the Christmas money disappeared, she learned that the little boy of the other woman had received a big, expensive dump truck for Christmas, while their own little boy had gotten a little, cheap matchbox car. Chico, she says, even said that he was going to raise—*criar*—the other child! "I'm a mother, Doutora, and I feel these things."

Chico threatens, getting more heated, "I'm not going to live with her if she keeps—"

Drª. Márcia cuts in, "You want her to stay at home, alone, acting like everything's just fine, when she knows and you know it's not?" Drª. Márcia repeats the same foreboding warning about the effect of divorce on children that she issued in the earlier hearing, complete with assurances that their children are likely to end up as addicts or homosexuals.

Joana interjects, returning to her own situation, "If I know he's with other women, am I going to just greet him '*kiss-kiss,*' and pretend nothing's going on? We can fight and everything, but if people sit down and talk, then we can get there. I abandoned my studies to marry this man, and my family didn't like him. We had a lot of obstacles! But I stuck by him."

Joana continues, defensively, saying, "There are people who can work *or* be a mother, but I'm just not that way." To add to her complaints, she tells of receiving a phone call from her husband's mistress saying that her baby was sick with a high fever and needed medicine, but she had no way to get any.

Here Drª. Márcia cuts in: by participating in such a conversation, she told Joana, "You're just encouraging your own fate. If he's not worth anything, then leave him." It's difficult to reconcile this with the plea Drª. Márcia has just made in favor of couples remaining together; she appears to be trying to call Joana's bluff.

If so, she succeeds: "Ah, but I don't have the courage," confesses Joana, shaking her head. "But he won't sit down to talk to me," she adds, raising her lamenting gaze to Chico, who looks away.

Her initial contact with the other woman, Joana recounts, occurred because a picture of Joana's son fell out of Chico's pocket when he was on the beach with his mistress. Before this, the other woman had no knowledge of Joana, but now she called her to talk and to let her know. But the woman's motives were probably not altogether altruistic: she also informed Joana that Chico talked constantly of marrying her.

Still, says Joana, "I dedicate myself so much to him, at times more than to my own children."

For Chico, this dedication appears smothering, especially insofar as she seems to feel her loyalty to him and the children gives her the right to monitor his movements. He says he can't stand her jealousy: "I can't even work or be away from the house without her feeling jealous!"

Joana protests, saying he misunderstands. "My jealousy is about your lack of affection [carinho] and your other woman, nothing more!" She begins showing Chico doctor's slips that she says are proof that the problem in her head was caused when he hit her. He looks on, professing disbelief, repeating that he doesn't know what she's talking about.

Looking Drª. Márcia directly in the eye, Joana lays it on the line. "It's not me that is here wanting to separate, Doutora. That's not why I'm here."

For the first time, Chico's lawyer speaks up. "Why don't you two sit down, and talk, and work this out." He appears to have concluded that his client is not in imminent danger of being punished for assaulting Joana, but neither is he making headway toward having his name cleared of the offenses.

"But it has to be him that is saying that to me. I'm not going to live with him with another woman at his other side." Joana shook her head while looking from Drª. Márcia to Chico's lawyer.

The lawyer entreats her, "Forget the past, senhora." To his client, Chico, he says nothing.

Chico keeps silent, for the most part, until the back-and-forth dialogue of the hearing dies down. When it is clear that the session is beginning to draw to a close, he calmly relates his position. "When I'm wanting to enjoy myself with her, her mother is always there alongside. I don't want anything anymore. I give up. I want a legal separation."

He says it flatly, with finality. Apparently Drª. Márcia, despite her efforts to champion the preservation of marriage, sees this. She summarily works out the informal terms by which the couple will live until the official separation hearing, to occur in the courthouse, not in a delegacia. He will provide child support for food until that time.

Joana appears completely desolate, barely containing the urge to sob. It is clear that the role she hoped the DM would play, in bringing the situation to a head and forcing Chico to make a choice in favor of his "real" family, has backfired.

Joana's complaint serves as another example of a situation in which violence arises as "contestation." Violence in Joana and Chico's relationship is episodic and recent rather than long-standing, and if Chico is to be believed—and Joana does not deny this—there has been some mutual violence as well. With his extra-marital union and desire to leave Joana, Chico definitely holds the upper hand; the most severe abuse Joana experiences is emotional. And yet she is far from defeated. Joana appears to have involved the DM less out of fear for her safety than to push Chico to do the right thing and return to her.

The role that jealousy and the *outra* (other woman) play in this case is ubiquitous in the DM, arising in numerous other hearings. Once again, now at Joana's behest, a hearing dwells at length upon whether adultery and betrayal, now the husband and father's, have occurred. This again distracts from the focus on whether a crime involving violence has been committed. Similarly, the "question to be resolved" in the hearing becomes, "What will become of this union?" and not, "Has a crime occurred, and if so, what measures should law enforcement officers take?"

Undercurrents to this theme recurred in multiple hearings: the sense of entitlement that men felt to wear "long leashes" and wander far; men's assertions that women's resulting jealousy was misplaced; men's belief that that women's expectations that men modify their behavior were unrealistic. Often men directed dialogue toward issues of freedom versus confinement, whereas women framed the question in terms of loyalty versus betrayal.

In the case of Joana and Chico, Drª. Márcia's messages about the deleterious effects of divorce on children, seen in the first hearing, repeat, as they generally did in her hearings whenever separation began to look imminent. Certain other *delegadas* and *comissárias* revealed themselves to be equally dedicated to the preservation of marriage. Just as Drª. Márcia's bent is shaped by her time policing drug trafficking and use, other *delegadas* or *comissárias* of this predisposition had particular beliefs that underwrote their convictions. Two *comissárias* were fundamentalist Baptists, for example, and their urgency to preserve marital bonds were communicated in religious terms.

At the same time, other *delegadas* and *comissárias* were comparatively open to separation as the most appropriate solution to unions in chronic conflict, especially where violence had recurred. Drª. Márcia herself turned out to be more open than she initially appeared to be. Recognizing the variability of stances that DM policewomen held, coupled with the degree of latitude they felt they had to tailor their approaches to personal values and convictions, helps us understand how wide-ranging can be the cultural messages and social effects in which a women's *delegacia* may become involved.

Between Drᵃ. Márcia, Joana, and Chico, it appeared that three different agendas were operating. Drᵃ. Márcia's first commitment was to defend the traditional family, hence her criticisms of Joana working. At the same time and in apparent contradiction, her commitment to what might be considered "traditional" stopped short of defending male freedom and female confinement. She argued that Joana should have the same freedoms as Chico and not be expected to await him, the loyal wife at home, as he is out gallivanting. In reaction to Drᵃ. Márcia's criticisms, Joana became defensive about being a working woman while also trying to be a successful wife and mother; she clearly felt vulnerable in the face of the implication that spreading herself thin was in part to blame for the troubles she and Chico were experiencing.

For her part, Joana hoped to use the hearing as a last-ditch effort to get her marriage back on track. Chico, by contrast, seemed concerned with clearing himself of accountability for his treatment of Joana and with creating sympathy for his own position, while escaping the marriage with minimal loss or future responsibility to his wife.

Shaped by these three discrepant agendas, the hearing becomes a negotiation among disparate values surrounding gender roles, marriage and its commitments, and freedoms versus responsibilities in intimate relationships; the rising criminality of domestic assault recedes into the background.

POLICE AS REPRISAL: WHEN AND WHY

The four cases reveal four distinct strategies: Celeste was a battered woman in the "classic" violence-against-women sense, trying to escape. Judete was stalked, and she "abandoned" the home fearing for her life; by the time of the hearing she hoped to reconcile but was unceremoniously dumped. Janaína injured Jorge more severely than he gave back, and she used the DM to rid herself of a partner even more destitute and marginalized than herself. Joana's strategy to use the DM to make Chico leave his mistress backfired, and she, too, was surprised to find herself separated at the end of the hearing.

Of these four cases, only Celeste was a full-fledged victim in the "battered woman" sense. Judete, Janaína, and Joana all expected to find the DM to be a supportive context through which they could "take providence." Like these three, many DM *clientes* held tactical notions of services the DM could provide; they involved the DM long before a situation became life-threatening. These were not women whose self-esteem had been ground into nonexistence by chronic abuse: rather, they resisted men's authoritarian efforts to take over their lives, or to exercise prerogatives they, as women, wives, and mothers, were denied.

Three further examples illustrating resistant, strategizing, and contesting women were Donalda, Rosimaria, and Olivia. Each of these women's histories included involved siblings—mostly brothers—who had intervened well before beating could develop into chronic battery.

After two incidents of aggression, Donalda was looking to end the relationship with her daughter's father, and was primarily concerned to secure financial support for her daughter and avoid committing murder herself: "Because if he does another thing like this with me, I'll kill him. I won't go back to the police. Without thinking of the consequences—I'll kill him." She used the DM to defend her daughter and herself against her own potential criminality.

Rosimaria also went to the DM early, after her husband beat her for the first time; she had been physically aggressive with him on many previous occasions. For Rosimaria, it was the greater force her husband wielded that made his behavior, and not her own, life-threatening and therefore criminal. "Yesterday was the first time he ever beat me. Look at my face, all swollen, bruised, and with these two black eyes. I was putting up my arm to protect myself, and he pushed me, and I can't even touch the place on my arm now. So I bit his finger, and he punched me in the face. He hit me in the face! When he did that, I said to myself, we aren't going to fight with a man, now are we? But, I did try to fight back *[descontei],* and he started hitting me all over my head and face.

"If I was a wimpy woman *[mulher pacata]* that liked to put up with violence, seeing him drink—my God on high—I'd be afraid, and run and hide. But no, I'm not going to do anything of the sort. If I have to confront him, I confront him: 'Because you're a *macho,* if you have to beat me, then beat me. But you'd better leave me lying on the floor. If you beat me so that I'm still standing, you'll regret it.''

Rosimaria saw her own violent ferocity as critical to women's freedom from violence: "If all women acted like this—seeking out their rights and saying no, no, no!—we would never see women who were beaten by men and accepted it." Her stance, then, cannot be understood as anti-violent, but expressly as against *men's* violence against women.

Olivia, finally, took care to make it known she was perfectly capable of defending herself, physically—and hurting her partner as well. She worked as a domestic servant, had spent time in prison, and waxed philosophical on why, in most cases, she chooses not to fight back. Not fighting back, she told me, "is not cowardice. I feel like you just shouldn't do it. Like yesterday, he threw a bottle at me and everything. I said, 'You're a man using a bottle on a woman? Setting her on fire? Well, I'm here with my club in my hand. Just waiting for you to give it to me.' But I'm not going to wait around for him to cut me all up. I'm gone. I think man is much more of a coward than woman."

For Olivia, the relationships between cowardice and violence were the opposite for women and men. She was brave because if needed, she would hit him; for him to hit a woman, however, epitomized spinelessness. If this implied that male and female violence were composed of utterly different stuff, she confirmed this view, repeating the saying "five slaps from a woman don't hurt." For her as for Rosimaria, the significance of a woman's violence was either symbolic or a last-ditch defense, but the differences between men and women (men's strength inflicts more damage) made woman-as-aggressor technically impossible.

In the late 1990s, the chief *delegada* and three policewomen of the (then-titled) Delegacia de Proteção à Mulher (DPM, Police Station for the Protection of Women) independently observed that complaints by non-victimized women like these were on the rise. That is to say, they were seeing more complaints of first-time male-to-female assault, or complaints about such aggressions that had occurred in but a few incidents. This trend appeared to correlate with a decline in complaints involving more serious domestic battery, along with a decline in domestic murder.[16] In contrast with the "classic," dominance model of violent relationships, which assumes escalation of violence and deterioration of power symmetry in relationships, these women have acted early, preventing violence from becoming chronic. In addition to its punitive, repressive function, Salvador's DM has made available another channel of recourse for women, which also has potential deterrent value. It is not surprising that women readily seek to take advantage of perceived opportunities the DM offers, not only to prevent dangerous situations from fomenting and exacting greater costs, but also to prevent widening asymmetry in their relationships, as men gain, and women lose, power. As the cases examined here make clear, the ways in which the DM can advocate for women are neither predictable nor consistent but are constrained by a host of factors.

DOMINATION VERSUS CONTESTATION

In a watershed work that helped jump-start scholarly discourse on violence against women in Brazil, Maria Amelia Azevedo wrote: "Violence presupposes oppression. It presupposes the dominion of interests between oppressors and oppressed and as such, hierarchical relations of dominance and subalternity. In this sense, violence against women can be understood as a 'necessary dimension of the domination of men over women,' and, therefore, as an exacerbation of an asymmetrical pattern of the social relationships of gender" (1987: 7).

This quote begs the question: If violence is necessary to secure male dominance, does not the "need" for violence also presuppose women's resistance to being subjugated? Would violence be necessary if men seeking to dominate women were not faced with women's noncompliance? Moreover, does violence always "work"? That is, does it always succeed in heightening gender asymmetry? Azevedo's view does not seem to take into account theories of hegemony, which hold that if one can succeed in getting a subjugated group to internalize the values of the dominant group, domination does not require force because the subjugated will willingly participate in their own oppression (Gramsci 1971). Such questions lead me to propose amending Azevedo's initial statement: violence presupposes the *intention* to oppress.

As with the international examples of contested masculinity and compensatory violence discussed in the previous chapter, the diverse dynamics encountered in the *delegacia* and neighborhoods pointed up for me that a one-size-fits-all approach to partner violence made no sense. As I observed marked variability in the cases I followed in these settings, I began to elaborate qualitative distinctions between two contrasting dynamics of violence, one whose outcome was maintaining male dominance, and another that reflected power struggles between men and women in which both were viable "contestants," if never on truly equal footing because of the influence of patriarchy as the broader context (see table 2).

The most important contrasts to be noted in table 2 involve the eclipsing of women's agency in dominance-driven dynamics versus the emergence of women as undeniable players in dynamics characterized by contestation. In cases of full-blown dominance, women may be so desensitized to their

TABLE 2

Domination vs. contestation dynamics in gender-based partner violence

	Domination	*Contestation*
Power Dynamic	Asymmetrical power	Power relatively balanced, or status inconsistent* (women more powerful)
	Dominance/submission	Conflicting goals and interests
	Abuser-ego centered	Conflicting views, needs, models
	Victim's esteem damaged	Agents asserting desires and needs
Violence	Chronic violence	Acute, sporadic, flashpoint
	Systematic, severe abuses	Less severe, with distinct *exceptions*, e.g., when woman tries to leave
	Unidirectional violence	Possibly mutual violence
Functions and Reflections	Maintaining patriarchal values	Resisting patriarchal values
	Maintain status quo	Social/gender change
	"Domination" (feminist) approaches	"Conflict" (also feminist) approaches

*Status inconsistency is discussed in note 18.

own needs and interests that they are literally unable to give them voice or to find ways for them to be heard if they can. Conversely, in cases marked by contestation the presence of men's and women's conflicting perspectives and interests is unquestionable. Manifestations of violence vary accordingly, probably because women who are relatively empowered (those involved in contestation dynamics) can refuse to allow themselves to fall into full-blown victim positions. Finally, the "functions and reflections" of the respective dynamics refer to how each is encouraged by broader societal circumstances, and in turn reflects these circumstances. In other words, where rapid change in gender roles operates in women's favor, as in the presence of influential women's movements, increasing contestatory dynamics would be both catalyzed by, and reflective of, those changes.

The intention in teasing out these contrasts is not, ultimately, to create a typology of violent relationships, or of victim-versus-contestant *types* of women, or of abuser-versus-compensator *types* of men. In foregrounding

Zizi's life trajectory, for example, my emphasis has been on broader cultural contexts and social circumstances and on a dynamic process whereby early in her life she more closely resembled a dominated victim, and later she was able to act more as a contestant, eliminating the violence in her relationship by availing herself of resources, such as the existence of the women's police station as a deterrent and the generally diminishing cultural tolerance for wife-beating. Similarly, men like Jorginho or his aspiring-to-autonomous-subjecthood nephew Robi are not most usefully painted as "abusers" or "browbeaten roosters," but as agents who must negotiate themselves amid changing circumstances, find new ways to perform or narrate themselves as men, and, in doing so, chance that such presentations may be rejected by their peers. Women angle to avoid being dominated; and providing them new resources, while simultaneously raising the costs of using violence for men, enables many to resist falling into, or even to climb out of, situations of profound victimization.

Virtually all cultural contexts, interpersonal dynamics, and individual experiences are more complex than any typology can fully capture, no matter how useful a heuristic it may be. These human complexities are indeed what prefigured the commitments to holism and relativism that anchor anthropology. That said, my goal in contrasting domination and contestatory violence is less for purposes of categorization than to underline the value of making distinctions and not lumping all gender-based partner violence together. Those concerned with policy formation or administrative challenges, including police in Brazil's DMs, cannot afford to be so quick to reject models that flesh out distinctions. Those working directly with victims of violence are best served by research that provides direction by being willing to provide meaningful, if imperfect and simplifying, generalizations *and* distinctions (cf. Campbell 2004).[17]

EMPIRICAL AND COMPARATIVE RESEARCH

After initially developing the above model, I later discovered other social scientists grappling with the same problem. The notion of (at least) two distinct patterns of gender-based partner violence has been corroborated by recent work in other areas, notably by sociologists in the United States employing hypothesis-testing paradigms.[18]

In the mid-1990s, sociologist Michael Johnson and colleagues offered a surprisingly simple solution to what had grown into an acrimonious academic standoff: rather than view groups of scholars as sharply disagreeing about the nature of family violence, Johnson argued that these groups might in fact not be looking at the same data (Johnson 1995; Johnson and Ferraro 2000; Johnson and Leone 2005).

On one side was the "family violence" or "sociological" approach, which drew primarily on surveys of large probability samples, using scales (most notably the Conflict Tactic Scale) to measure discrete violent acts and attempting to pinpoint causal relationships (Gelles and Loseke 1993; Dobash and Dobash 1992). The group's most significant claim was that women initiated and carried out physical assaults on their partners as often as men did, and that despite the lesser severity and consequence of women's aggression, it nonetheless constituted a serious social problem (Straus 1993: 67). Family violence scholars stressed that their samples were representative cross-sections of the public and less focused on pathological violence than those ministering to victims in the trenches; they were equally informed by men and women. In not assigning women roles as a priori victims by privileging violence against women as the topic of inquiry, family violence scholars claimed greater objectivity (Gelles and Loseke 1993). At the same time, they also strenuously defended that acknowledging women's violence need not mean ignoring the effects of patriarchal domination (Straus 1993).

Critics of this perspective included researchers with "feminist" or "violence against women" approaches. They charged that survey-and-scale research instruments were overly value-neutral, failing to capture complex behaviors, emotions, or social processes (Dobash and Dobash 1992: 276). Family violence approaches did not give appropriate weight, they argued, to how patriarchal structures underwrite tolerance for violence across many social contexts. Rather than privilege the family setting and study partner violence in connection with elder and child abuse, violence-against-women researchers studied gendered violence in workplace, public, and familial contexts, relating it to the same gender inequality that promoted sexual assault, harassment, and discrimination. They noted that men's established tendency to underreport and minimize the severity of violence explained the discordance between men and women's responses on surveys (Dobash and Dobash 1992: 278). Most problematically, critics of the family violence school argued that the use of a "neutral" scale instrument underplayed ways in which gender inequality shaped marriage and intimate heterosexual relationships, rendering it inadequate to address how male-to-female violence was reinforced by patriarchal domination and obscuring why male-to-female aggression was of fundamentally greater significance than that of female-to-male (Kurz 1993; Flynn 1990; Loseke 1989).

The pictures suggested by these two research currents were starkly contrasting. The violence-against-women analysts described profoundly asymmetrical power between men and women and saw violence as primarily male-to-female. The family violence researchers stressed both the surprising prevalence of family violence throughout the population and the mutuality of violence between men and women. The violence-against-women group presented models about cycles of violence, the inevitable escalation of violence, and traditional-patriarchal families in which violence was most likely to occur. The thrust was to illuminate the distinct and forceful ways violence reinforced women's oppression; even if women did often instigate violence, there was no counterpart "battered husband syndrome," as has been suggested (Steinmetz 1978).

Johnson argued that rather than viewing these as conflicting readings of the same data, in fact the two groups of researchers were focused on distinct phenomena, owing to the different contexts, methods, and samples of couples studied. He labeled one dynamic Common Couple Violence (CCV) and the other Patriarchal Terrorism (1995; also Macmillan and Gartner 1999), later revised to Intimate Terrorism (IT) (Johnson and Ferraro 2000). CCV was situational rather than chronic, marked by lower per-couple frequency, not as likely to involve severe violence or to escalate as IT, and finally, more likely to be mutual. Johnson and Leone (2005) further established nearly all of the violence in large survey samples to be CCV, therefore suggesting that this pattern had shaped the perspective of the family-violence scholars more than that of their violence-against-women counterparts.

Intimate Terrorism, by contrast, displayed all the characteristics violence-against-women researchers had described: perpetrated almost exclusively by men and marked by gender asymmetry in power, in this pattern violence was but one tool in an artillery used to achieve control and dominance. Intimate Terrorism cases evidenced greater frequency and severity of violence, were more likely to escalate over time, and were less likely to be mutual. Moreover, this pattern of violence correlated with batterer profiles of men embracing traditional and patriarchal models for masculinity and families (Johnson 1995; Johnson and Ferraro 2000; Johnson and Leone 2005).

Johnson's two types closely paralleled the contrasting domination and contestation dynamics I had distinguished. One way my perspective departed from Johnson's was that he tied a "feminist" approach to those focused on IT, because they were working in feminist-activist contexts tied to battered women's and feminist movements more generally. Just as some family violence scholars have objected to the notion that their work was not feminist (Straus 1993), I would extend the designation "feminist" to my own approach, precisely because my efforts to highlight women's "contestation" tie this phenomenon, in part, to the agitating influence of women's movements. Feminists, after all, encourage women to question male domination and to advocate for their own interests, inevitably fomenting conflict. For this reason, I prefer the violence-against-women label to that of "feminist," so that studies of CCV, or what I've been calling contestatory violence, are not precluded from being seen as feminist.

FROM "SLAPS AND KISSES" TO "NO!"

There *is* love in this chapter, but it is the played-at love of the child learning how to flirt while square dancing, or the heartbroken love of men and women losing love already tainted with violence. The dearth of romantic love means that I have failed to live up to the "kisses" portion of a chapter entitled "Between Slaps and Kisses." Suffice to say I found remarkably little romantic love, enacted lovingly, in the field site of the Delegacia da Mulher, and thus am resigned that the task of describing and interpreting love in Brazil must fall to the many others—musicians, poets, authors, and other artists—already dedicated to this enterprise.

Regarding ethnographic sources on the topic of love in Brazil in English, anthropologist L. A. Rebhun (1999) has contributed an invaluable volume entitled *The Heart Is Unknown Country*, focused on love in the interior market town of Caruaru, Pernambuco, another northeastern Brazilian state to the north of Bahia. Rebhun identifies distinct currents in the vocabulary of love *(amor)*, including *romance* (story); *amor verdadeiro* (true love, enduring love, modeled after parental love); *consideração* (companionate love and respect, a traditionally rural model of marriage); *paixão* (passion, mostly a masculine perspective); *sofrimento* ("suffering," mostly a women's perspective); and *loví* (American-influenced "*telenovela* love" emphasizing personal emotional experience and intimacy). Of particular interest for purposes of this work is Rebhun's insight into how love differs for women and men, rendering it ambiguous. "In an ambiguous economy," she writes, ". . . whether an emotional interaction is a gift or a commodity is both a highly charged moral question and a matter of point of view" (1999: 85). Because of the more constricted emotional and economic spaces in which women move, Rebhun views women as investing more in *amor*—as both sentiment and resource—than do men. She describes women's frequent feelings of abandonment, both economic and emotional, not only by partners or husbands but also by fathers and, ultimately, by sons. These dynamics help set the stage for why Brazilians perceived a need for an institution like the DMs, and why women seeking out police aid pursue objectives far more diverse than the simple criminalization of men's violence.

The description of the São João square dance at the beginning of the chapter painted a picture in which young children were instructed on how to expect and reproduce violence as part of "normal," intimate relationships between men and women. The task of the chapter has been to explore how and why this violence can move from being seen as a naturalized part of love—"between slaps and kisses"—to being deemed problematic and "violent," as an illegitimate use of force, at least by the women who lodge complaints in the DM.

This chapter has taken seriously some of the features the *quadrilha* dance foreshadowed. Just as the first slap in the dance comes from the women, in apparent response to the men exercising masculine prerogatives of drinking, gallivanting, and impregnating other women, so have similar currents about men's privileges emerged as prominent in the *audiência* hearings from the *delegacia,* clarifying that patriarchy provides the wider backdrop for conjugal power struggles. Paradoxically, even though in the *audiências* social considerations continually overshadowed questions of whether crimes had been committed, the DM was shown to perform inconsistently and unpredictably, both in protecting women from violence and in advocating for their social equality. Each case's outcome was highly particular, depending upon the proclivities of the police personnel, complainant women, accused men, and others assembled.

The chapter argues that the most conclusive significance to be drawn from studying the paths women take to the *delegacia* is that many of them arrive there not as downtrodden victims but as contestants for power and self-determination. They attempt to use newly available means to prevent themselves from falling into (greater) subjugation at the hands of male partners. Cultural intolerance for violence, like the DM police, represents another "resource" women can marshal to avoid falling victim. Is the link between "slaps" and "kisses" seen as "natural," or unacceptable? Is "stirring the brew" by intervening when violent *brigas* break out seen as nobody's business, or part of caring about women as family, community members, and fellow citizens?

The point of the distinction between victim and contestant is this: the more effective the reprisals and paths of recourse available to a woman, the greater become her opportunities and probabilities at avoiding full-blown victimization. At the same time, when a person lives in a dangerous and subordinated situation, acquiescence to domination can be difficult to distinguish from resistance, as the former can set the stage for the latter. Sidney Mintz made a similar observation about the seeming conformity of the slave woman on a plantation, who has pleased her master enough to rise to the relatively prestigious position of cook for his family in the big house.: Her apparent compliance in the face of her enslavement situates her, ultimately, to commit greater acts of rebellion, such as placing ground glass in the master's food come the hour of revolt (1971b: 321).

The choices facing a battered woman are not dissimilar. If she makes her revolt known before she can feel assured that it is a risk worth running, before safety appears within her grasp, she heightens her immediate danger. Many women appear, instead, to bide their time and strategize, gradually laying the foundation for escaping oppression and violence. In such a process, the DM can serve as a critical resource for "victims" who summon the courage, and seize the chance, to become resistant "contestants."

FOUR

Policing by and for Women

> We cannot lose sight of the fact that criminalization, even if
> ineffective, functions as threat, and as the symbolic power of
> the state to neutralize the power difference that is the basis of
> the variable forms of violence against women.
>
> CECÍLIA MACDOWELL SANTOS
> "Delegacias da Mulher: Percursos e Percalços"

BY WAY OF RELUCTANT confession, I admit to being on record stating that the Brazilian women's *delegacias* were the "world's first" specialized, all-women police stations (Hautzinger 1997a, 1997b, 1997c). So much more readily available has information become that later I could easily discover how wrong I was.

India, in 1973, saw the first All-Women Police Stations (AWPSs) installed in the southern states of Kerala and Tamil Nandu. Other states eventually followed: Madya Pradesh, Rajasthan, Jammu, and Kashmir (Sharma 2002). By 2003, Tamil Nandu state, long distinguished for being progressive regarding women, alone counted 188 AWPSs, one for each district; by 2005, all-female commandos and a thousand-woman battalion were inaugurated as well (Kandaswamy 2005).[1] Neighboring Pakistan began creating all-women police stations in 1994, claiming ten by 2004 and projecting an increase to fifty stations.[2] South Asian countries were recently joined by an African country, when a women's police station was installed in Nairobi, Kenya, in 2004; that same year, a woman-only motorbike squad emerged in South Africa.[3] Since 1993, the Philippines has installed "women's desks" in all police stations.[4] In the Americas, Brazil's women's *delegacias* also now have company: Colombia, Nicaragua, Peru, Ecuador, and Uruguay all have installed specialized stations.[5]

Brazil's experiment in progressive, gender-segregated law enforcement is clearly far from exclusive. India and Brazil can be accorded starring roles as pioneers: although Indians now look back on over thirty years of experience to Brazil's twenty, only in these two countries do women-only stations now number in the hundreds; moreover, each appears responsible for later offshoots in other countries in their respective regions.

It surprised me not to have known this about India, because through the early 1990s, as this research took shape, India often caught my attention. In grant proposals, I cited India as a good illustration of how institutional responses to violence needed to be tailored in ways informed by sociocultural features. The shelter systems successfully serving battered women elsewhere were not an initial fit in India, largely because an unattached woman fleeing a violent home is understood as socially "dead," therefore making the option of a refugee seeking secret shelter relatively unattractive. India's earliest shelters were deemed deeply problematic at best, and more often altogether failures. Instead, women's groups found activities that "outed" abusers, such as singing shaming songs in front of houses, more effective at protecting women from violence (McCoid and Desai 1989; Purushothaman 1998). In these sociocultural circumstances, the AWPSs played critical, interventionist roles on two interrelated fronts: against women citizens' intimidation before police on one side, and against profoundly masculinist police subcultures on the other.

From India to Brazil to their offshoots, women's police stations across the globe have shared certain concerns. Although I would reiterate that partner violence is far from culturally universal, in the uniformly complex, stratified societies that *have* created women-only police stations, the battery of women tops lists everywhere. Gender-based partner violence appears to trump the secondary staples for specialized police—rape and sexual harassment—in many if not most countries' experiences.

Considering this commonality, the degree to which all-women police forces diverge in gendered-crime specializations, beyond the ubiquitous woman-abuse and sexual-misconduct concerns, is equally remarkable: different societies vary wildly in their particulars. In Kerala, the need for women police was first felt in order to "arrest and disperse women demonstrators," presumably reflecting ethnic tensions and violence in the region, and "for keeping women prisoners in custody, [to] search them and [to] raid cat houses." Bride burnings, suicides, and dowry deaths are specializations for women's police throughout India; eve-teasing (harassment of girls) is a significant hazard in many places, but most notably in Delhi, where AWPSs famously focus on fighting it.[6] When a new AWPS was installed in Ranchi,

Jharkhand, where more than 700 women had lost their lives over a ten-year period after being called witches, witchcraft accusations quickly became a focus.[7] Indian and Pakistani realities alike have required AWPSs to focus on trafficking in girls and women, whereas, to my knowledge, this has not become a focus for Brazil's DMs, despite the many nongovernmental organizations (NGOs) in Brazil working on trafficking of *brasileiras* to Europe.[8]

In Nairobi, Kenya, the creation of a police station serving "women and children" followed a rape epidemic. Inspiration came from the success of the "crack unit," Spider, which grew legendary when two rapists were gunned down in the act of attempting to rape women undercover police officers.[9] The other African example, South Africa's all-women motorcycle squad, was created primarily with the goal "to empower women": specializing in protecting VIPs, the squad also concentrates on crime prevention, especially hijacking and robbery calls, for its motorcycles allow quicker response times in traffic. In the South African case, the focus is not gendered crimes, but the positive role models set by competent, all-women law enforcement.

Latin America's non-Brazilian examples in Peru, Ecuador, and Uruguay share specialization in "La Mujer e La Familia"—women and family—in line with materialist feminist analyses so influential in Latin America that definitively link gender inequality to women's productive and reproductive ties to family (Colombia's are simply "Familia" stations, but also concentrate on serving women). This emphasis is still more evident in Nicaragua, where the Comisarias de Mujer y la Niñez—Women and Childhood Commisariats—in 2000 stood at eighteen offices, where police recruits receive a six-month course in the academy on sexual inequality; "mainly for the edification of men," the program focuses on "the structure of poverty that results from discrimination against women and popular ignorance about family planning."[10]

As these divergences suggest, the rationales for creating women's police stations, and the functions they perform, correspond closely with particular national, regional, and local histories and sociocultural processes. This chapter deepens the account of one police station in one nation: Salvador's Delegacia da Mulher, in the broader context of a redemocratizing Brazil.[11] After portraying *conquistas*—successes—and challenges experienced in Bahia and Brazil, I develop the comparison to similar experiments elsewhere. I place the Bahian case study against a comparative backdrop in order to pursue fundamental questions. What advantages and disadvantages do sex segregation, specialization, and compartmentalization in law enforcement bring? Why have all-women police stations emerged in certain settings, notably in less-developed countries, when explicitly all-women organizations appear to be avoided in more-developed, postindustrial countries? I argue that many of the difficulties Brazil's DMs and other all-women police have encountered stem from the same feature—their sex-segregated nature—which is simultaneously their greatest asset. In Brazil, India, and other less-developed countries that have opted for women-only police, the advantages have outweighed the disadvantages, at least initially. In North America, Europe, and Australia, by contrast, where express sex segregation in law enforcement has not proved attractive, advantages have been seen as fewer and outweighed by disadvantages.

WOMEN'S POLICE STATIONS: A PRODUCT OF BRAZILIAN REDEMOCRATIZATION

The broader context for women's antiviolence activism in Brazil is second-wave feminism, which emerged as part of Brazil's political *abertura*—"opening," or political liberalization—beginning after 1975. Before that time, state repression precluded widespread feminist activism although, because women's organizing had been seen as less threatening by the military, women's groups were afforded greater freedoms than their counterparts in opposition political parties, trade unions, or human rights organizations. The resulting "head start" translated into women's groups' superior organization, as compared to that of other grassroots movements; feminists were more efficient and effective at "mobilizing the troops" as civilian reforms were gradually introduced in the late 1970s and early 1980s. The installation of the civilian New Brazilian Republic at the presidential level in 1985 provided a redemocratizing political climate in which feminism continued to thrive.[12]

Beginning in the late 1970s in Brazil, public protests broke out against a series of jury verdicts in which men who had murdered their wives were absolved. Among the most prominent domestic killings of women was the murder of Angela Diniz by playboy Raúl Doca Street. Street was first absolved in 1979 in a highly publicized trial that transformed him into something of a popular hero, but later he was sentenced to fifteen years on an appeal made possible only by organized protests by women's groups. Also in 1979, two wife-killings occurred within fifteen days of each other in the state of Minas Gerais. Feminist onlookers observed that both murders generated trials that revictimized women, which is to say they "transformed victims (women who sought to break away from deteriorating marital situations) into the accused (women whose behaviors had coerced their husbands into defending their honor)" (Sorj and Montero 1984; Albano 1985). When juries absolved or lessened the penalties for male suspects, defense strategies ranged from "defense of honor" to "violent emotion" (similar to temporary insanity in the United States) (Americas Watch 1991).[13] Such decisions fanned outrage, which erupted in angry protests, over male impunity in the Brazilian legal system.

Out of these protests evolved the first organized feminist activism around domestic violence in Brazil, bringing the issues of wife beating, battering, and killing to public view in a way never before seen.[14] The visibility of antiviolence as an issue was partially catalyzed by the emergence of a battered women's movement in Europe and the United States, as well as the return of women to Brazil from European nations after years of exile, where they had been influenced by second-wave feminism more generally.[15] Over time, feminist SOS-Mulher (SOS-Woman) groups formed in the major Brazilian cities, focused on providing psychological and social aid, as well as legal advocacy to female victims. Several of these early groups were based in São Paulo and Rio de Janeiro; the Centro de Defesa dos Direitos da Mulher in Belo Horizonte and SOS-Corpo in Recife were also prominent.[16]

In São Paulo, grassroots groups exerted influence in the Conselho Estadual da Condição Feminina (State Council on the Feminine Condition), which presented recommendations promoting *"atendimento integral"*— holistic services—to governor Franco Montoro. Montoro responded with the unprecedented idea of creating specialized police stations, staffed by women. Although focusing on police restricted the feminists' comprehensive vision to criminal aspects of gender-based violence, the proposal gained their wary support, and they shifted to concentrate on how to ensure that police would be adequately trained to carry out the work. São Paulo's Secretary of Public Security, Michel Temer, also favored the proposal, despite strong opposition on the part of some police *delegados;* in 1985 the first DM opened its doors, and "on the day after the inauguration there was a line of 500 women in the door of the *delegacia*" (Santos 2001: 4).

The rapid proliferation of DMs throughout the country—125 by 1993, 307 by 2001, 339 by 2004—means that the criminalistic *delegacias* quickly became, and to this day remain by far, Brazil's most extensive institutional response to male-to-female violence.[17] From the outset, the specialized stations signaled a critical shift from the kind of institutional responses that violence against women had thus far generated; previously, the organizations working on violence were autonomous, feminist, and grassroots in nature, whereas the police stations represented an example of what Alvarez calls "state institutionalized feminism," or "taking feminism into the state" (1990: 198–222) This shift occurred as part of Brazil's incremental return to civilian rule following twenty-three years of military authoritarianism.

The intention in creating law-enforcement environments controlled exclusively by women was to avoid the intimidation and discrimination experienced by female complainants in conventional, predominantly male police stations. Critics of police performance worldwide argued that the male-dominated police forces reflected the inherent biases of the patriarchal state they represented (Hanmer, Radford, and Stanko 1989). Women seeking police aid, they complained, were often subjected to a second round of abusive treatment by male police officers, who might inquire into a woman's morals, her "decency" or "honesty," or how well she fulfilled conventional models of wife-mother to assess whether she "deserved" to be treated aggressively. In short, male police minimized and naturalized the violence perpetrated against women by men.

It was expected that policewomen, armed with the state's authority, would take seriously complaints of sexual and domestic assault, along with other crimes specifically aimed at women. It was hoped female police would also feel greater identification and empathy for fellow women who fell victim to violence and avoid reproducing their victimization.

At the same time, the women's police station concept appealed to the ambitions of politicians and to constituencies of newly enfranchised voters. First, the idea was (still largely believed to be) a uniquely Brazilian invention, appealing to the national pride of a country chronically traumatized by its mixed international image.[18] (This aspect has sometimes backfired, however, as foreign reports have usually upheld the police stations as evidence of the barbarity of Brazilian *machismo,* rather than its gender progressiveness.) Second, the women's police stations offered a chance to give security forces—still freshly associated with human rights offenses and brutality against civilians—an image makeover as more humane and legitimate representatives of a just, civilian state. Finally, although just one women's *delegacia* was created in places like Salvador (São Paulo's metropolitan area counts twenty-one, with 150 in São Paulo state), the women's stations could be modeled around other specialized stations already in existence. In Salvador, one could find police stations specializing in robbery, burglary, drugs and toxics, and even "theft of antiquities." This was true in most states, where the bureaucratic structure for law enforcement was already compartmentalized into specialized precincts.[19] Preexisting compartmentalization meant that installing the women's police stations required minimal institutional jostling and yet promised high returns in terms of public favor.

The fact that the implementation of a DM was in many cases a relatively routine matter was overshadowed by the level of publicity and propaganda the new police stations generated. Pamphlets advertising the DMs acclaimed the special, trust-inspiring reception that awaited complainants and assured them of the vindication and justice awaiting them if only they could surmount their fear and shame to take action. As stated in a booklet published by the National Council for Women's Rights and intended for general distribution, the rationale for the DMs reads: "When victims of violence, women do not always have the courage to denounce their aggressor or seek out aid in traditional *delegacias* where they will be attended to, the majority of the time, by men."

The paragraph that follows extends the promises still further: "The *delegacias* for the defense of women have a special kind of service, provided exclusively by women: *delegadas* [police chief/lawyers], investigators, agents, clerks and social workers. This special service inspires *confiança* [trust/confidence] in women made victims of violence and helps eliminate the fear and shame that they generally feel."[20] Perhaps in an effort to keep the language accessible to all education levels, the simple use of "special" here seems to point more to special-*ness* than to special-*ization*. Indeed, many such materials were distributed before it was first ensured *how* attendants would be consistently prepared to offer this unique attention. This foresees what my and others' observations would later confirm: in many cases, what proved most "special" about the *delegacias'* handling of female victims was confined to the fact that both police staff and complainants are overwhelmingly—although not exclusively—female.[21] The policewomen working in the specialized stations are conventionally trained police, many of whom have no specialized training, vocation, or qualification for serving as specialized "women's police" apart from the fact that they are female officers.

Although parallel campaigns to address violence against women have been mounted in Brazil in the areas of public education, legal reform, and community development, none of these other efforts has had anywhere near the impact of the police stations. A notable exception, the high-profile and popular television drama series entitled *Delegacia da Mulher* or "women's police station," which ran for two seasons in the early 1990s, is nonetheless an outgrowth of the police stations. The show, ostensibly aimed at educating the public while entertaining them, featured dramatic scenes of policewomen who heavily empathized with the experiences of complainants (explained through police flashbacks to abuse scenes and sexual assaults they had themselves lived through, usually before becoming unassailable policewomen) and enjoyed unlimited time and resources to pursue each case that presented itself, thus reinforcing Brazilians' great expectations at what the *delegacias* could deliver. But, as will become clear, in actuality the ability of individual policewomen to identify with victims' plights, much less devote hours to the pursuit of justice in any single case, has been unexpectedly limited at best.

GREAT EXPECTATIONS: STATE MAKING AND FEMINIZATION'S SYMBOLIC FORCE

Part of the impression Brazilians were given of the women's police stations owed to the symbolic force of the feminization of the police: maternal overtones aided the transition from viewing the police as agents of a state warring against its civilian population to police as agents of a legitimate and representative state. As it happens, even the idea of segregating female police was not altogether new; when the Bahian police force first admitted women in 1956, they were assigned to a separate *polícia feminina,* whose history suggests that the creation of the DMs was not the first time law enforcement had served as a medium to propagate and politicize gender ideology. A measure approved in 1963 allowed female police to marry (no counterpart mention was found regarding male officers; Mattos 1979: 193–95). Dória, a police agent of fifteen years who entered the segregated *polícia feminina* in 1974 and later was among the original group of officers assigned to the DM, draws a likeness between past and present feminine specialization. Whereas today's DM staff focuses on other adult women, the *polícia feminina* worked primarily with children; Dória describes the DM role in aiding other women as like that of an "elder sister," whereas in the earlier *polícia feminina,* when the focus had been on children, it was like that of a "mother."[22]

Comparing how masculinity and femininity are played upon in diverse pieces of propaganda usefully indicates how expectations for the all-women police stations were generated. One bumper sticker and poster distributed by the Catholic Church comes to mind for its clarity of role designation: "*Peca a Mãe que o Filho Atende,*" which roughly parses "Ask the Mother (the

Virgin Mary) that the Son [Jesus Christ] Attends [to your need or cause]." Although not related to state or law enforcement per se, Brazil's pervasive Catholicism—variously reckoned between 70 and 90 percent—permits one to argue for a ubiquitous salience in the way gendered symbols are played upon. Individuals in distress rely on their personalized relationships with an accessible and sympathetic mother figure; through her, it is possible to gain the ear, and aid, of a more distant—yet significantly more powerful—male figure. Similarly, the women's police were representative of a receptive channel through which women could be represented to, and gain access to, the deliberative power of an otherwise distant, masculinist state.

Closer to the domain of law enforcement, the imagery of a protective, benign father figure caring for his children has explicitly been tied to state-civilian relationships. One poster pictured a military policeman (the branch most vividly associated with violent abuses) embracing a young boy and girl, the caption mentioning the concern and love of the *pai* (father/police officer) for his *filhos* (children/civilians). To any Brazilian cognizant of the rampant abuses of the *polícia militar,* the reformist intentions of such a message are apparent. Asking where women police fit into such a scheme, symbolically, points to further parallels: Policewomen are positioned in the interstice between the abusive, violent masculinity of law enforcement run amok, on the one hand, and the abusive, violent masculinity of the father figure in the home, on the other. In this sense, policewomen symbolize bringing police under civil rule and protecting a new civil society.

This interstitial and redressive femininity "assigned" DM policewomen inevitably interacts with more conventionalized Bahian currents of femininities. A major current in this regard constructs femininity as receptive—not necessarily passive, but as primarily acted upon by, and reacting to, the active behaviors of men. As an individual, *mulher* (woman) is much associated with vulnerability and often victimhood. The ubiquity of the symbolic relationship between femininity and vulnerability in Brazilian culture may partially explain the exceptional political force that the women's movement has attained. Because women are equally distributed across all Brazilian classes, regions, and ethnic groups, femininity may even represent a master or key form of subalternity, such that all other subaltern groups—indeed, vulnerability and "weakness" itself—are inevitably associated with feminization.

This association between femininity and the vulnerability of oppressed groups more generally is also part of the historical legacy of military authoritarianism. Both "women" and "citizenry" are historically downtrodden collectivities with nascent political viability, but whose welfare nonetheless hinges upon the existence of a benign state. The recent experience of oppression and tyranny in Brazil at the hands of a dictatorial, patriarchal state underlines a moment in which civilians and citizenry became symbolically "femininized" in senses connected to violation and victimhood. The admission of women *as women* into positions of newly democratic state authority parallels the admission of civil controls into the formerly totalitarian state.

When Brazil's relegitimizing state invests policewomen with newfound authority for specific, gender-defined reforms, potential meanings of woman-as-symbol multiply. Now, in addition to "vulnerable citizens," women can also connote enforcers, enactors, and beneficiaries of a legitimate, civilian state. To take a mundane example, when administrators argue that female officers are necessary for frisking or strip searching female suspects, it is expressly to avoid the improprieties and inevitable abuses resulting from men exercising inappropriate authority. The male commander of the Companhia de Polícia Feminina—the (military) Woman's Police Company—observed that the advent of female policing was the "fruit of the social, political and economic revolutions and evolutions";[23] in other words, its causes and meanings are so widespread that they betoken truly systemic shifts. Without the existence of a legitimate and moral state, *permitting* women to be vested with Weberian monopoly on legitimate force is unthinkable. In coercive right-is-might politics, the feminized weak arm always loses. Thus, at least in some ideal sense, policewomen's successful use of force symbolically epitomizes state legitimacy.

Brazilians associate women, including policewomen, with nonviolence or justified defensive violence; by contrast, men's violence, including policemen's, is more apt to be associated with aggression and illegitimacy (Boselli 2004; K. Silva n.d.; Calazans 2004). More accurately, authoritarian forms of masculine violence are increasingly subject to a process of delegitimation that parallels the criminalization of gender-based violence, set in motion by democratic, feminist-influenced reform. In such a context, a policewoman's violent behavior becomes symbolically charged, often problematically so, precisely because it is contradictory: it simultaneously suggests legitimate use, and abuse, of power. Machado and Noronha (2002) emphasize the ambivalent feelings that residents of a poor, marginalized neighborhood in Salvador feel toward police: the same group that is likely to unjustly brutalize innocent civilians because they "resemble" criminals in socioeconomic, racial, and situational terms is simultaneously viewed as the force guaranteeing their protection. This ambivalence is perhaps even more pronounced with policewomen, as expectations can be mirrored with bitter disillusion when female officers are abusive.

If viewed as fundamentally illegitimate, policewomen's violence can precipitate cries for reform and punishment of law-enforcement bodies. In one such case reported in a Salvador newspaper, a military policewoman identified only as "Sondre" allegedly arrested, assaulted, and tear-gassed a male citizen in an arbitrary manner.[24] Bahians are no strangers to police brutality: police were responsible for 20 percent of all homicides in the capital in 1977,[25] and in 1992 alone police murdered 700 persons.[26] In Sondre's case, the policewoman's gender was the only thing rendering a comparatively minor event newsworthy, as evidenced in the many mentions of her sex in the headline, that her use of a masculine uniform (female military police normally wear skirts) irked the civilian victim, and the Picasso-esque stylization of the policewoman's pursed lips in the accompanying cartoon-like graphic. As I shall relate in more detail shortly, the meanings attaching to policewomen's violence are altered by the essentialist expectation that a policewoman's primary purpose is to counteract male violence, be it police or domestic, and that it is her nonviolence or, ironically, her defensive and defensible, legitimate violence that permits this function.

The deployment of symbolic and instrumental uses of "femininity" was largely responsible for generating expectations about the DMs. Another piece behind these expectations, however, was the presumption that policewomen would actually become specialists, educated on issues surrounding violence against women and women's subjugation in society in general. This element may have been most important to feminists, who as a group were divided on the potential of the women's police stations—as well as other state institutionalized feminist organs, such as the women's councils—to actually further women's interests and better women's treatment within a patriarchal state.[27] Here the divisions among feminists tended to occur along partisan political lines. Feminists affiliated with the center-left party that moved into power with democratization (PMDB) argued that the state was not (or need not be) unwaveringly masculine or antifeminist, pointing out that the state under civilian rule—albeit bourgeois and male-dominated—was much more friendly to women's interests than the state under military authoritarianism.[28] Feminists who leaned further left (especially those affiliated with the PT, which in 2002 led a successful coalition behind Luis Inacio "Lula" da Silva for the presidency) warned that state-institutionalized feminism, rather than bringing women closer to their political and social objectives, could provide the means for the state to control and demobilize feminist activism (Alvarez 1989a, 1989b, 1990), as many argued had been the case for state-controlled unionism (Keck 1989).[29]

'CAINDO NO REAL' (REALITY STRIKES): EARLY SIGNS OF TROUBLE IN THE DMS

From the outset, Brazil's globally hailed women's police stations frequently met with highly critical reviews closer to home.[30] The comments of two *delegadas* (the magistrate–police chiefs who head the DMs) are revealing:

> Generally speaking, now that there's a women's police station, whenever a situation involves a woman, police in other stations just toss it our way. They send her to our station—it's enough for the victim of a crime to be a woman—even when they are much closer to the incident and could solve the problem better there. And they have a *responsibility* to take care of it there, if the woman goes there first. So you see, one problem we have now is that the women's police station keeps other police from doing their jobs.
>
> *Edilomar Angela Oliveira, Assistant Delegada*
> *(Police Chief), Salvador, Bahia*[31]

> I see the decade of the '90s as the decade of decadence of the DMs. . . . In truth, the DMs were discriminated against from the beginning. The first was created in 1985, when a larger number of women were approved as *delegadas* [in São Paulo]. At this moment discrimination began to emerge, because our male colleagues came to see the approval of these female *delegadas* as a loss of turf *[espaço]*.
> They call the *delegadas* social workers, with disrespect for social workers. They call the DMs confessionals, and the *delegadas* priests. . . . It ended up that the *delegadas* came to represent uselessness.
> The DMs are not the cause of the women police. They are the fruit of the women's movement. We were only the instruments placed at its disposal.
>
> *Drª. Suzana Mª Ferreira, Section Delegada*
> *(Police Chief), Monte Aprazível, São Paulo*[32]

One of the first obstacles to the fulfillment of the expectations for the DMs was that, in practice, whether policewomen actually received specialized education and training on violence against women was hit-or-miss. In several cases, the initial staff of a new DM did undergo training, often instigated and designed by feminist activists. More often, however, such training was absent or woefully inadequate; in Salvador's case, training was one afternoon of standard police academy lecture. And even when an initial DM staff underwent more thorough preparation, as occurred initially in São Paulo and Rio de Janeiro, such training tended to be one-time or erratic; in both early cases it was eventually removed from police academy curriculum as a result of funding cuts. Although many fruitful efforts to improve police knowledge about gender-based violence, provide specialist training to work in law-enforcement trenches, and share diverse municipal experiences have occurred since, consistent training of all women's *delegacia* personnel has yet to be realized (Boselli 2004; Soares 1999; L. Machado n.d.; K. Silva n.d.).[33]

Newer police in all police branches spoke of belonging to a new generation of "nonauthoritarian" police; Calazans identifies "old police" as tied to physical force and "traditional identification with the masculine figure," whereas "new police" are oriented around "intelligence, conflict resolution, innovation and teamwork" (2004: 3, 6). Some of the policewomen stationed in the DMs viewed the advent of the specialized stations as representative of this change and were enthusiastic about their unique role. Just as often, however, policewomen proved apprehensive about being assigned to the special stations: they felt subject to constraining "feminine" stereotypes and that they were doing a job more closely resembling social work than "real" policing. At one point in 1993, for example, it became policy for the few men on the DM staff to undertake all *diligências,* or the urgent calls for intervention that entailed leaving the station (two experienced female detectives continued in this capacity, however), whereas policewomen were charged with all *atendimento,* or in-house reception of complainants. Such gendered divisions of labor, policewomen feared, would limit their opportunities to prove they could perform across a range of duties, thus impeding their future careers.

Confusion arose around this issue in part because the mission of the DMs, from the beginning, was intended to provide social services alongside the punitive and repressive functions of law enforcement itself. Police agents themselves were never intended to act as counselors or advocates: advertisements for the DMs regularly mentioned the multidisciplinary staffs of social workers, psychologists, and lawyers that would be present. In many cases, efforts were made to supply such comprehensive services in the beginning but soon were devastated by the jealous economics of the notoriously underfunded state Secretariates of Public Security (SSPs) charged with administering the DMs. Given the chronic disquiet of the security ranks because of low salaries, it is not hard to imagine that all of the professionalized services that were supposed to accompany the DMs generated a great deal of tension within respective SSPs. Professionals providing ancillary services typically required more education than police themselves, and in consequence could command higher salaries. In the climate of funding shortages, the addition of other services to DMs could be seen as antagonistic to police officers' interests.

In the absence of ancillary services, police were often called upon to play roles as counselors, social workers, and, yes, simply "sisters" who would lend an ear to fellow women unburdening themselves. Although social work is the one secondary service most often present in the DMs, it is also the area in which a perceived inadequacy was most apparent: 60 percent of the nation's DMs lack social workers or psychologists on staff. At the same time, 94 percent of DMs reported that they offer "counseling," meaning in many cases police improvised this service (K. Silva n.d.: 14).

My observations in the DM in Salvador revealed that the presence of social workers was sporadic; budgetary cuts meant the service was missing from the DM as often as it was available. Although there was never more than one certified social worker on staff, occasionally the ranks swelled with interns from the local Universidade Católica—at these times someone "just to talk to" could be found with regularity. Often, however, police asked me to step in and play social worker (how different could that role be from those interviews I was always doing?) because that was what a complainant really needed, and the policewomen simply didn't have time. When social workers were available in the DM, they echoed police in bemoaning that what they could be expected to accomplish in such an atmosphere was woefully limited. A police station's repressive environment precluded in-depth therapy, so the most they could hope for was to make contacts and direct persons to longer-term resources elsewhere. With the constant reminders that they were not providing exactly what the public required, and at the same time segregated from many of the police functions they were trained to perform, it is not surprising that often policewomen felt their assignment to the DM detracted from their identity and status as police officers.

To the DM's leadership's and staff's credit, many personnel did attempt to meet complainants' needs, even in the absence of jurisdictional authority. DM hearings, interrogations, or investigations served many purposes seemingly far afield from simply gathering evidence to prove or disprove the occurrence of a crime.[34] Couples could be counseled against separation or divorce, cautioned about the negative effects on children, and advised to "disinvolve families and reconcile," to "learn how to listen to and respect one another," or even to "bring Jesus Christ and the spirit of love back into the marriage." (Not surprisingly, individual police agents or *delegadas* showed strong pro- or antiseparation tendencies in their advice, often depending upon personal beliefs.) The actual authority of a *delegada,* much less a police agent, to adjudicate division-of-goods or child-custody agreements was tenuous at best, and no such terms would be upheld in court. Nonetheless, *delegadas* reconciled themselves to providing the services the DM's "clients" most immediately required, realizing that for many, particularly couples from informal unions, access to such adjudication at more legitimate juridical levels was, for practical purposes, unattainable.

The emphasis of many of the women's police so often given to reconciliation meant that, overwhelmingly, violent assaults that could qualify as criminal were "undercriminalized." Frequently, however, the opposite occurred, in a phenomenon I call "hypercriminalization." The public expectation that the DMs would provide services, in addition to law enforcement, meant that many women arrived at the DMs seeking different routes, such as counseling or legal advice. When alternative services were lacking, women contending with conflictive unions were left with no options other than to pursue punitive police responses. For example, I witnessed men made to stand for long periods of time facing walls, or tossed into a cell for a few days "to think about it." The worst example I recall was an old, very dark-skinned and shabbily dressed man, whose wife had accused him of slapping her, who was told, as a malicious and careless joke by a police officer (in this case, male), that he was being charged with rape. The old man grew so nervous he urinated on the floor of the station, thus subjecting himself to further ridicule. This is the kind of problem arising when a repressive, law enforcement response—complete with racist and classist biases—is the only sort available to civilians experiencing domestic discord, particularly for those expecting other services and those who seek out intervention early, before a domestic situation becomes life-threatening or irreparable.

The first question a policewoman would ask a complainant who appeared at the DM was typically, "Why are you here?" Generally, the complainant would spill out a story, usually involving a crime against her. The policewoman might then clarify that it sounded to her like a crime may have been committed, and then ask, "What do you want us to do?" At times answers were explicit: "I want him to go to jail," "I want you to make sure he doesn't to this again," or "I want you to make sure he doesn't come near me." However, many complainants came to the DM without express intentions of pursuing punitive reprisals against the men with whom they were in conflict. This might be because complainants themselves were vague about what they wanted *police* to do, responding "I want him to stop," "I want someone to talk to him," or even "I want God to make him stop." Similarly, women often had specific ideas about what they expected from the DM, but it was questionable whether the DM was the appropriate place, or whether its officers possessed the authority, to meet women's wishes.

For every case in which extralegal, improvised punishments or adjudication were dispensed in the DM, another crime was duly registered, for which the state was responsible for pressing charges. At times such "criminalization" was premature, or unlikely to be the most appropriate response to a particular situation. For their part, however, policewomen held steadfast to work in the law-enforcement paradigm in which they had been trained.

Hypercriminalization helps explain why many women complainants desisted from "staying on top of" *(ficando em cima)* or pursuing a criminal complaint after they had initiated it, failing to return to the DM or follow through with their role in seeing a complaint prosecuted. Such failure may often have been consistent with a woman's original intention, when she was closer to wanting to give her partner a good scare than to wanting to see him behind bars. But women are also subjected to pressures from family and friends to drop charges. Belinha, a mother-in-law whose daughter-in-law reported being beaten by Belinha's son, her husband, lay in wait for her daughter-in-law to appear for an *audiência* in order to confront her. Meanwhile, she stated her case to the other waiting women, "My son is a good man *[homem certo]*, employed, who has never had another woman. . . . For her to file a complaint against him I take as a personal offense, a sign of her selfishness." Other waiting complainants tried to convince the mother-in-law that these were separate issues: it was still a crime if he'd hit her. "If your daughter-in-law only wanted to separate, she'd have found other channels," said one. "She had to have a greater motive to have done this." But Belinha could not be convinced. It wasn't that she denied the violence outright; she simply saw her son's behavior as more defensible than her daughter-in-law's, who betrayed the entire family by bringing police into a personal matter.

Along similar lines, Nora went to stop her daughter, Zilda, from pursuing a complaint against two of her sons, Zilda's brothers. Zilda received a blow to the forehead that cut to the bone, but even in the face of this evidence, Nora alleged that Zilda was continually "talking nonsense" *(besteira)* about the family. For Nora, to protect the family as a whole from the police was more urgent than protecting her daughter from her sons. One frustrated young complainant commented that if she had her life to do over, she would become a politician and pass a law so that mothers "would themselves be punished" for attempting to uphold their sons' impunity before charges of conjugal violence. "I think the mothers are worse than their sons when they defend them," she said.

The accusation of betraying the family to an "enemy," the police, is but one factor, amid socioeconomic dependence, threats of broken family ties, and so on, that lead women to abandon processes. This apparent vacillation on the part of complainants aggravates the cynicism and morale problems of police officers, who decry the weak-willed indecisiveness of their would-be plaintiffs. In some cases, officers used women's seeming turnaround to support the wisdom of the aphorism, discussed in chapter 3, "In fights between husband and wife, no one should stir the pot" *(Em briga de marido e mulher, ninguem se mete a colher)*. Whereas complainants might desist from following through because of disillusion with the DM itself, with their inability to receive counseling and legal services, or with the lack of a timely, efficient response on the DM's part, police tend to retreat to the same views of violence that they learned in their neighborhoods growing up: that men and women will wrangle, then kiss, make up, and make love, that violence is part of the spice that seasons blends of lust, jealousy, and love. Just as neighbors in chapter 3 imagined elaborate ways in which they could come out the worse if they committed to intervention, the policewomen feel "burned" *(queimado)* by women who abandon complaints; part of this is feeling trivialized as professionals by complainants, accused and other civilians, and by their police counterparts in other stations.

SALVADOR'S WOMEN'S POLICE STATION: AMBIGUOUS MISSION

My acquaintance with the women's police station in Salvador, Bahia, began in June 1990,[35] three years after the student on the street first mentioned the women's police to me. Although I had gone to one such station in Rio de Janeiro before arriving in Bahia, it had not prepared me for the level of activity I would discover at the DM in Salvador. I perched in the entryway of the old-house-cum-police-station, amidst some seventeen women and two men. Like myself, most of the others remained standing, as there were few places to sit. An assistant *delegada* periodically came into the waiting area to conduct triage, questioning those waiting—were they here to register an initial complaint, or to respond to a summons to an *audiência?*—and eventually directing them to the appropriate desk inside. Amid the complainants, respondents, and their companions could also be found accompanying lawyers and reporters on the crime beat. The occasional pair of military police brought in a recent arrestee. Many arriving at the *delegacia* might be ushered inside with comparatively little delay, ahead of the women waiting to file complaints who crowded the reception area. The waiting women might grumble "*gente fina*"—high-class people—to one another with resignation.

Early in my DM work, I would arrive and sit, for as long as possible, in the waiting area, talking with prospective complainants. The first day, armed with a letter of introduction from the local university, I sat for an hour before the police discovered I was not a typical complainant and immediately ushered me to the head *delegada's* office, ahead of women who had been there much longer. Later, when I was given free run to attend hearings and take interviews and was escorted to speak with prisoners, police never seemed to understand why I habitually planted myself in the waiting room when I arrived, chiding me loudly—and in front of women weary from hours of patient waiting—for not realizing I should come right in.

I would learn that long lines, and accompanying long waits, were a daily affair at this and other DMs throughout Brazil, thus proving that there was no lack of demand for this form of law enforcement. The majority of complaints—again, roughly 80 percent—involved some form of domestic violence, including beating, battery, stalking, and, very rarely, marital rape, registered variously as physical aggression, moral aggression, or death threats (see table 3). Other forms of complaints included statutory rape, rape, abduction, or sexual coercion *(atentado violento ao pudor);* both statutes, as written, refer to acts committed toward "libidinous" ends, defamation, and illegal use of arms. Surprising to me, cases involving civil wrongs like sexual harassment or sexual discrimination in places of employment were relatively rare: the specialization of Salvador's DMs ended up being squarely in the area of interpersonal, gender-based crimes against women, involving coercion or violence.

TABLE 3
Types of complaints registered and percentages of crimes
investigated and delivered to the judiciary system
Special Police Station Attending to Women (DEAM),[a] *Salvador, Bahia, 1987–2005*

Crime Registered	1987–1990	1991–1995	1996–2000	2001–2005
Rape	90	108	76	53
Moral aggression[b]	—	—	805	506
Threats (death)	1,665	2,302	2,094	2,515
Aggravated assault (with bodily injury)	1,094	1,723	1,585	2,282
Physical assault (no bodily injury)	3,364	4,417	4,631	3,215
Other[c]	2,208	713	562	195
Total registered (felonies/ *ocorrências/queixas*)	8,421	9,263	9,753	8,766
Investigations for the Judiciary				
Investigations opened	152	97	53	39
Investigations closed, submitted to courts	146	99	50	39
Percentage investigated, submitted to courts	1.73%	1.07%	0.52%	0.44%
Cases expedited to Jecrims—opened	—	—	379	914
Cases expedited to Jecrims—closed	—	—	335	909
Percentage expedited to Jecrims	—	—	3.43%	10.3%

SOURCE: Statistics provided by the DEAM, Salvador.

[a] The station now named the Special Police Station Attending to Women (DEAM, Delegacia Especial de Atendimento à Mulher) was called the Police Station for the Protection to Women (DPM, Delegacia de Proteção à Mulher) when it opened in October 1986.

[b] Moral aggression includes humiliations, controlling movement, and nonmortal threats. This category was not separately reported at the DEAM until 1996.

[c] Includes "*sedução*" (sex with a minor), sexual molestation, and sexual harassment. From 1990 forward, statutory rape allegations were processed by the Delegacia de Menores (Police Station for Minors), another specialized station. Until 1989, "other" included attempted rape allegations, after which these were registered as aggravated or physical assault.

During the fourth National Convention for Delegadas of Women's Police Stations held in 1993, the working definition used for the kinds of violence encompassed by the DMs' jurisdiction read as follows: "An action that causes injury, be it physical, psychological, symbolic or sexual, to the integrity of the victim." The open-endedness of such a definition begs the question of why mention of gender and gender inequality is absent. This appears to stem from awkward efforts of a state organ not to appear biased in favor of women or predisposed against men. Of course, for an institution expressly established to redress patterns of violence shaped by gender, the contradictions generated by the mandate to advocate for women, but at the same time not *favor* women, created inevitable tangles.

In legal terms, a further series of ambiguities obscures the jurisdiction and function of the DMs. The Brazilian penal code currently in force was drafted in 1940 and amended in 1998. An altogether new penal code drafted in 1984 was never approved but nonetheless serves as officially "suggestive," leading to a complex "hybridism." "Praiseworthy the democratic debate, condemnable *[censurável]* the delay," is how one legal critic sums up the resulting confusion (Cunha 1989: 128). To compound matters, the federal constitution of 1988, once ratified, in theory overrides the Brazilian penal code of 1940. But the constitution is a document written primarily to articulate citizen rights: for example, Article 263 Section 7 reads, "The State ensures assistance to the family and to any of its members by creating mechanisms to prevent violence in family relations." Unlike a penal code, it is not a detailed criminological document guiding law enforcement and dispensation of punishment. Between these discrepant, and somewhat competing, versions of "the law" in Brazil, challenging issues of interpretation can arise. Judges, legislators, and activists can take quite different views on the same questions.

One of the greatest liabilities resulting from this lack of clarity is laid bare when grave criminal offenses such as criminal assault and battery, which in theory obligate the state to prosecute regardless of victim participation in pressing charges *(ações públicas incondicionadas)*, so frequently fall by the wayside. Meanwhile, punishments for crimes constructed by terms considered obsolete by most criminologists, legal critics, and police alike can still be enforced. Virtually all of the offenses of the latter type, however, are crimes that require the victim to press charges.[36] Most of these crimes fall under the rubric formerly known as "crimes against custom," meaning that societal sensibilities as a whole were believed to have been offended, rather than an individual person. A violated girl or woman's honor reflects most importantly, in this version, upon her father, brothers, husband, and so on. However, the 1988 constitution and subsequent court decisions reinterpreting the 1940 penal code stipulate that it is first the violation of the rape victim (female or male) that is needful of redress, and that a revised penal code should reclassify such offenses as "crimes against a person." These crimes are at times still referred to as crimes against honor.

Sedução (statutory rape, literally "seduction") was the primary kind of case I encountered in which the DMs can be obligated to reinforce paternalistic notions of womanhood. In the penal code *sedução* is defined as, "Seducing a virgin woman, less than 18 and more than 14 years old, and having carnal relations with her, taking advantage of her inexperience or justified confidence. Penalty—confinement, 2 to 4 years" (Cunha 1989: 139). Most commonly, the parent (typically the mother) of the "offended" girl would file the complaint, using the threat of penalty as a way to force the male party to marry the daughter. In one such case the young couple in question, Mario and Josi, stated their commitment to their relationship and their mutual intention to marry. Each independently asserted, however, that to force them to marry now (she was sixteen, he seventeen) would disqualify them for finishing school and, in his case, getting his career in real estate off the ground, ultimately hurting their chances for making it together. The presiding *delegada,* who felt obligated to represent Josi's mother's interests against her better judgment and her personal sympathy with the couple, ordered that a marriage arrangement must be worked out within six months, or the mother could return to the DM and have Mario arrested. At the *audiência's* close, Mario dared to respond with a speech critical of the DM's predisposition to treat all men as criminals. He was in part responding to being forced to stand, looking at a wall, for forty-five minutes when he arrived for the *audiência;* he was the only accused man I ever heard question why he had to do this.

Following this *audiência,* the *delegada* confessed that she felt embarrassed and conflicted by the "ridiculous" role she was forced to play in representing a law she saw as obsolete. "How could anyone argue that the girl [Josi] was not consenting, that she was taken advantage of, despite what her mother said?" On *sedução,* legal critic Roberto Salles Cunha asks whether it is reasonable to admit such a "crime" today, when it is "rare to find an inexperienced young woman of 16 years?" He adds, "The new rights obtained by women, providing them with different circumstances, have the effect of impairing 'old rights'" (1989: 140).

The language included in the penal code for other, less commonly registered offenses—that is, fraudulent inducement of carnal relations, sexual molestation (without age connotations), sexual molestation of a minor, and sexual kidnapping—is replete with anachronistic notions of the kind of women deserving of state protection. Various requirements for a woman to qualify as the victim of such crimes include being a virgin, and being a *mulher decente*—decent woman—who "has modesty, a minimum of 'decency,' [and] conforms to customs in the opinion of her teachers *[doutrinadores]*" (Cunha 1989: 133–142).

Despite interpretations of law rendering these concepts obsolete, DM *delegadas* understandably do not feel justified in denying these "rights" to citizens so long as the statutes remain in force. Demands that DMs devote resources to upholding laws many—and feminists in particular—view as anachronistic detracted from the ability of DMs to pursue punishment for other offenses, especially physical assault and battery.

Beyond such anachronistic legal dramas, a range of miscellaneous complaints seemingly unrelated to the DMs' specialization siphoned off staffs' time and resources. A fight between two female neighbors would end up at the doors of the DM, or a married couple who had been threatened by a male neighbor. Sometimes women directed such nonrelated complaints to the DM on their own, figuring that because they were women, it was the best forum in which to be heard. More problematically, at times police from other precincts would send women to the DM for complaints, such as theft, wholly irrelevant to the DM's gender-based violence focus. A station specialized in crimes specific to women should not, in theory, ever have relieved police in other stations of the duty to register complaints of domestic violence or other gendered crimes, should a complainant prefer to denounce a crime in her nonspecialized neighborhood precinct. In other words, the existence of the DMs and their specialized law enforcement services could obstruct women's access to general police aid that presumably should be available to all citizens, and in this way could ironically constitute an additional form of discrimination.

INSTITUTIONAL GHETTOIZING: BACKLOG AND OVERLOAD

The great demand for services from the specialized police stations has paradoxically led to some of their greatest difficulties. A comparison (see table 4) of the number of cases processed to the number of personnel in Salvador's DM and other police stations, both specialized and conventional, statistically demonstrates the DM's inadequate staffing. Since 1986,

TABLE 4

Police staffing in relation to caseload

Three specialized[a] and two neighborhood precincts,[b] 1992 vs. 2002, Salvador, Bahia

Police Activities	DEAM Special Attention to Women		DTE[c] Drugs and Toxics		DRFR Prevention of Theft[d]		1° Precinct Barris		6° Precinct Brotas	
	1992	2002	1992	2002	1992	2002	1992	2002	1992	2002
Delegados/las	6	6	4	5	7	7	5	6	5	5
Agentes de policía	38	46	32	65	130	130	46	51	56	56
Total policías	44	52	36	70	137	137	51	57	61	61
Total cases registered[e]	7,247	9,107	1,026	931	15,304	13,632	5,368	13,441	6,801	8,719
Investigations opened	86	31	132	473	167	275	5,368	627	130	382
Investigations concluded, sent to courts	99	38	129	484	154	272	86	513	158	156
Number of cases per police officer	154	175	25	13	112	95	105	236	111	143

SOURCE: Data provided by the listed stations or through the Centro de Documentação e Estatística Policial (CEDEP).

[a] Specialized stations were selected that had high caseloads, most closely comparable to those of the DEAM (one other "crimes against persons" specialized precinct, one economic crimes precinct).

[b] Neighborhood precincts were selected from the higher end of the mid-range of caseloads (omitting the highest), again because these were most closely comparable to those of the DEAM.

[c] In 1992, 70 percent of the activities of the DTE (drugs and toxics) involved repression of traffic in marijuana; by 2002 crack cocaine cases constituted the majority of DTE registrations.

[d] In 1992 prevention of theft was divided into two stations, one for the prevention of roubos (robberies), and the other furtos (burglaries). The 1992 figures present the combined cases and personnel of both stations; by 2002 they had been merged.

[e] The number of ocorrências, felonies, and other complaints constitute "total cases." For 2002, where possible (DEAM, DTE) I use statistics obtained directly from the delegacias; for the other stations figures were obtained through CEDEP.

when the DM in Salvador opened, complaints registered typically totaled between seven thousand and ten thousand per year. By comparison, the DM had fewer staff members per complaint processed than nearly all conventional precincts and other specialized precincts alike. Dividing the number of police officers in a *delegacia* by *ocorrências* (roughly "felonies")[37] and *queixas* (roughly "misdemeanors")[38] yields an average number of offenses registered and processed per officer: for the year 1992 (chosen because it appeared to be a typical year) the DM processed 184 offenses per staff member, compared to an average of 87 complaints processed per staff member in all other stations surveyed. The number of felonies processed per staff member in the DM was 40, compared to an overall average of 27 for other stations.[39] Table 4 compares the situation in the DM in 1992 to a more limited selection from the same stations in 2002. Although certain improvements are evident, notably the addition of four social workers, the staff member *occorrência* ratio rose from 154 to 175. The inadequate number of personnel was compounded, too, by inadequate material resources: physical space, basic clerical materials such as paper, pens, and files. Police-specific tools such as guns and police cars were also in chronic shortage. These shortages were present at DMs nationwide: K. Silva reports that 33 percent of DMs lacked firearms altogether, 21 percent lacked telephone lines, 19 percent had no police vehicles, and 74 percent were unable to collect ballistic evidence (n.d.: 19).

Complaints in DMs nationally continue to rise precipitously, appearing quickly to supersaturate as many designated *delegacias* as are made available. In one year's time (1996) in São Paulo, for example, 65,812 complaints were filed; this number rose to 86,684 in 1997. In Rio de Janeiro, with a total of eight DMs, complaints rose steadily, totaling 30,540 in 1994, 34,344 in 1995, 38,045 in 1996, 43,590 in 1997, and 49,279 in just the first semester (through July) of 1998.[40]

That numbers increase at this rate in Brazil's southeastern states, where 60 percent of DMs are located, can only mean that violence is increasing in epidemic proportions; that reporting of violence is increasing; or that some combination of both is in operation. Although calculating the relationship between incidence and reporting is notoriously difficult, I would observe that contestatory violence patterns could indeed be rising along with rapid change in gender roles, and so these figures need not exclusively denote sharp increases in dominance-based, asymmetrical violence. At any rate, such increases for Rio de Janeiro and São Paulo suggest that even in relatively well-equipped settings, the supply of specialized policing has not begun to meet demand, thus necessarily creating overburdened and under-resourced police units. The effects of overload can be expected to be especially dire in places such as Bahia, where awareness of the women's *delegacias*, and anxiousness to use police services, is high, but DMs are far and few between.[41]

This inadequacy in human and material resources contributed to diverse problems:

The need for extensive complainant contact time, and an accompanying high volume of paperwork needing processing, compounded the desk-bound nature of DM work, relative to other assignments, for most police-women. Even when alerted to a violent incident at the time it was occurring, disposing adequately armed personnel and transportation to intervene was often impracticable.[42]

The DM's backlog eroded the efficiency of these in-house activities as well. The woman who finally summoned the courage—or desperation—to file a criminal report was told that the next step would be to summon the alleged perpetrator for a semijudicial *audiência* with the police-chief/magistrate *delegadas*. Frequently, however, the next opening for such an *audiência* was as far as six, or even eight, weeks away. Even then, if the woman did not return to the DM to "*ficar em cima*" or stay on top of the process, chances were that the summons might never be delivered to the accused.

The most worrisome factor about scheduling *audiências* so far out was that once a women takes decisive action to escape a life-endangering relationship, she enters into a high-alert period, where she is most vulnerable; the probability of homicide escalates when women seek to separate. Therefore, waiting six to eight weeks significantly prolongs this vulnerable period. More disturbing still was the practice observed where women were given the summons themselves for delivery to the perpetrator. Police defended the practice by claiming that women were instructed to enjoin a local civil or military police agent to deliver the document, but the mere fact that women in violent situations went home with the summons on their persons posed an alarming risk, particularly should an abuser discover the paper and react explosively.

For those complaints for which the DM succeeded in convening an *audiência*, most processes ended there. Despite limited actual authority, the *delegadas* often chastised the accused—along with the complainant, when applicable—for his purported crimes (the veracity of which often were simply assumed), warned him about the criminal nature of his actions, and attempted to broker agreements between partners, including attempts to reconcile the couple and avoid future conflicts or to set the preliminary terms for a separation, child custody and support, and future contact. Sometimes police would order a man to stand for hours, facing the wall, or hold him in a jail cell for a day, figuring that the impromptu, informal punishments geared toward shaming—facing walls, time in cells, enduring mockery—were justified by the dead-ends of most complaints, as police calculated that these would be the only a presumed offender would ever receive. Such measures compensated for the fact that the jurisdictional force of the *delegada*'s authority in these hearings was actually quite limited; police tried to put teeth into what would probably be the accused's only contact with punitive state power.

In any given year, the percentage of reported cases that were formally investigated and sent to the court system pending prosecution was rarely higher than 2 percent in Bahia; the national figure for 1999 was just 6 percent (K. Silva n.d.: 26).[43] Of these, a still much smaller percentage resulted in prosecution and conviction. Not surprising, the offenses formally prosecuted and punished have tended to be only of the most serious, demonstrable sort: primarily battery causing grave injury, and occasionally rape when reliable witnesses were available. In this light, the degree to which "lesser" offenses such as illegal constraint, threats, destruction of documents, or calumny are being criminalized in Brazil has relied upon informal mechanisms. Brazil's version of a fast-track court for domestic violence and other crimes considered less "potentially offensive," the "Jecrims" system (discussed below), has made the first significant dent in the numbers of halted processes, achieving over 10 percent judicial resolution.

Many policewomen were overwhelmed by the workload. Some felt traumatized and desensitized by hearing one *audiência* account of violence and abuse after another. As a result, they may have felt impotent to effectively intervene, punish, or prevent offenses. Initial educational preparation along with ongoing training and regular contact with professionals involved in gender-based violence have fortified policewomen's resolve and sense of purpose, when and where such measures have occurred. In the overwhelming majority of cases, however, such preparation and support have been lacking; their absence only exacerbates policewomen's alienation and resentment.

In sum, all these factors have severely undercut the efficacy of the DMs' role in criminalizing violence against women—particularly those acts involving violent assault—at least insofar as criminalization can be measured in concrete, punitive terms. But women still come to the stations in droves. The fairest evaluation of the DMs, therefore, should not be confined to such measurable outcomes alone. That the DMs could be vastly more effective than they are does not change the fact that they are still the single most important means by which violent crimes against women are increasingly being criminalized, to an unprecedented degree, in Brazil. Many would argue that the most powerful deterrent effect of the DMs comes not through measuring rates of conviction so much as through the message that their mere existence sends to the Brazilian population: violent assaults against women are crimes that will not be tolerated.

However, the chronic overextension and backlog in the DMs have gradually become part of their image, which in turn erodes the force of their image as a deterrent. I was told in 1987 that men in Salvador thought twice about hitting their women, owing to a team of fearsome, avenging viragoes who sought out male bullies and exacted justice by returning the beatings tenfold. Even men who suspected that the DMs represented a predisposed, unfair female bias seemed to delight in the images of ruthless female power, even when that power came in the form of police brutality.

As time went on, however, and more people had direct contact with the DM or knew someone who had, awareness of the realities of a struggling institution mired in bureaucratic overload spread. Many women I interviewed underlined their levels of desperation when seeking out the DM by pointing out that friends and neighbors had made clear that they "would get nowhere" through the specialized women's police. Some of the more forthcoming men that I interviewed who had faced complaints through the DM, particularly those contacted in their neighborhoods and away from the police station, made clear that they felt less subject to DM-generated punishments than they once had: knowing of complaints for which arrests were never made or hearings never convened contradicted their initial sense of vanishing impunity. By the time the DM had been open for five years, I was more likely to be told about the impotent hand-slapping its *delegadas* meted out than of the formidability and ruthlessness of its "Amazonian" heroines.

RESPONSES AND ADJUSTMENTS

The late 1990s saw developments intended to mitigate problems of inefficacy and low institutional status in the DMs, again with the state of São Paulo leading the charge. In 1996 a federal law was passed allowing domestic homicides to be investigated through DMs, the previous prohibition of which had always been seen as a slight by DM policewomen and feminists. Also in 1996, infanticide and abortion—a crime in Brazil—were shifted to DM jurisdiction. Finally, in São Paulo and some other states, the DMs had their jurisdiction extended when crimes against children and adolescents were added (Santos 2001: 3–4).

In 1995, the "Jecrims"—short for Juizados Especiais Criminais, or Special Criminal Judgeships—were created as a means "to substitute repressive penalties for alternatives (monetary compensation, community service and conciliation) in the case of 'penal infractions of less potential offense'" (Santos 2001: 3) that would normally receive sentences of less than one year in detention. In such cases, it was deemed that a full police investigation could be substituted for a simplified inquiry, culminating in a legal judgment. A major effect of the Jecrims was to relieve the DMs of playing the quasi-juridical and extra-legal roles described earlier. The Jecrims quickly ended up processing the "greater portion" of the complaints registered in São Paulo's DMs; the two largest categories of complaints, "light" bodily lesions (25 percent) and criminal threats (20 percent), qualified for the Jecrim fast track (Santos 2001: 3).

Anthropologists Guita Debert and Adriana Pitiscelli call the effect of the Jecrims upon the DMs "radical," feeding men's impunity by taking away much of the "pressure power" from the DMs and putting it into the hands of judges, the majority of whom are men with no specialization in gender violence. Jecrim judges overemphasize reconciling couples (Santos 2001: 3) and impose irrelevant penalties: "Often a husband aggressor has to give a food basket for some charitable institution, something which does not fail to be quite humiliating for the woman," Debert reported.[44] In short, the Jecrims display defects similar to those of the early DMs, where lack of education about gender-based violence impeded their attending to women-citizen's rights.

A *delegada* in Salvador acknowledged that the Jecrims allowed her to reach resolutions on cases that previously caused backlog; even if the penalties were light, at least the dead-ends of uncompleted investigations were alleviated. But the other side of the story concerned her. Showing researcher Pitiscelli a file with impressive photo images of victimized women, the *delegada* commented, "'The problem is the law, which says that this is *light* bodily harm.' It being impossible to work for thirty days, or losing an organ or something like that, the case is treated as a light bodily assault."[45] Jecrims have provided better follow-through for the DMs (see table 3), but at the cost of criminalization "with teeth."

Disappointment with the Jecrims' weakening effect on the DMs generated, in feminist and some police quarters, redoubled commitment to the
notion of a special, all-women police avenue for processing crimes involving gender-based violence. In 1997, São Paulo's police superintendent
(Delegado Geral) issued an edict, for the first time, that the DMs "should
be staffed, preferentially, with civil police of the female sex, principally for
the exercise of functions related to attending the public" (Santos 2001: 3).
In the essay reporting this, Santos further comments, "Be that as it may, it
is common to have [male] detectives integrated into, and leading, teams in
delegacias da mulher in the capital, including attending the public telephone
lines. The *delegadas* don't complain about the masculine presence; to the
contrary, they consider them necessary for the best fulfillment of their
functions" (Santos 2001: 3). By 2006, Investigation Chief Tânia Mendonça
informed me that such codification of all-female staffing was rapidly unrav-
eling, and the utility of men working in DMs was widely acknowledged
and, in some cases, legitimized in written policy.

These tussles make apparent that sex-segregation in the DMs grew no less
controversial over the years. When Delegada Titular Célia Miranda
returned, in 1993, from the national convention of *delegadas* of DMs, she
reported that ambivalence about the utility of sex segregation was far from
resolved. Reports abounded, from *delegadas* in multiple states, of ever-
increasing numbers of men appearing at the *delegacias,* imploring the *delegadas,* "If you don't do something to make my wife stop hitting me, I'm
going to end up hitting her back, and that would be a crime!" As a result,
many *delegadas* had come to feel their work could be more effectively
accomplished if the stations converted from "women's" police stations to
police stations specialized in domestic violence.

In 2003, a report from Rio de Janeiro described a 100 percent increase
in men seeking help for aggression from wives, from 108 in 2001 to 259 in
2002. Delegada Catarina Noble underlined mutual violence emerging out
of complaints initiated by women; also, "In many cases men usually engage
in verbal abuse, and women respond with physical violence."[46] The most
recent round in this area has been the assertion of *travestis* (transsexuals or
transvestites) and other woman-identified transgendered victims of violence that they deserve protection from the DMs; generally, the DMs have
so far resisted such an accommodation, as most police view it as undermining the notion that violence against women is a gender-patterned syndrome requiring similarly gendered response (Tânia Mendonça, personal
communication).

The notion of protection from domestic violence being unavailable to men has long made some women police uncomfortable, as it violates their commitment to impartial attendance to all citizens, even as they acknowledge that male-to-female violence constitutes the preponderance of couple violence. Along similar lines, *delegadas'* concerns are often about expediency, which may favor utilizing male police to efficiently execute tasks over what many police view as an abstract, and ideological, commitment to "women's space" within state law enforcement.

In August 2006, Brazilian President Lula Ignacio da Silva signed into law bill number 11.340, which for the first time afforded protection for victims of partner violence of any sex, including same-sex couples. The law is commonly known as the "Maria da Penha" law, after a woman who was shot, electrocuted, and rendered paraplegic by her university professor husband. He was finally sentenced nine years after the attempted murder of his wife but served only two years of an eight-year sentence, thus making Maria da Penha's case an alarming reminder of persistent impunity for abusers. Most significantly, the law retracts the Jecrims' authority to mete out light punishments in cases of physical abuse, mandating judges to follow the criminal code as a guide to sentencing.[47] This project has generated controversy in Brazilian feminist circles: praised by most for toughening up penalties, it has also been criticized for relying exclusively on criminalization and not developing alternative, preventive programming for less extreme cases (Heleieth Saffiotti, personal communication).

PARALLEL CHALLENGES IN INDIA AND BEYOND

The obstacles that have undercut the effectiveness of Brazil's DMs are echoed in similar experiences elsewhere in the developing world. In nearly every instance, the demand for specialized police responses to gendered violence has so exceeded expectations, and so surpassed the institutional capacity to process complaints, that many of the problems—overloaded, understaffed, and underresourced stations, as well as insufficiently trained personnel—should be understood as resulting at least in part from overwhelming, unanticipated need.

Once again, India's relatively long history provides the most fruitful basis of comparison. Many have hailed the Indian experiment as a success based upon the high degree of response alone, especially in view of what was initially a "low level of awareness" of gender-based forms of violence as prosecutable crimes, and the availability of specialized police assistance (Sharma

1994, 2002). India's All Women Police Stations (AWPSs) have been criticized as weak owing to the inexperience and lack of confidence of women police officers; it has never been easy to factor out how gender bias contributed to these perspectives. In any case, time in the trenches and public recognition of the value of their work has raised competence and confidence levels.

Increasing numbers of more experienced women police have not necessarily had felicitous effects on women's careers or standing in the Indian force as a whole. Nationwide, women constituted just 2.09 percent of the entire police force in 2003, thirty years after the first AWPS was created, and general conditions for women on the force did not inspire confidence.[48] Kerala police constable N. A. Vinaya, the "first policewoman who proved to be a crusader for gender parity" and who "insisted on wearing a pathloon and shirt tucked inside rather than a sari, which was disturbing for her seniors,"[49] was summarily dismissed from service in June 2003 after participating in a protest against discrimination against women police athletes.[50] In September of the same year, Mumbai's first woman senior inspector of a police station, Anita Chavan, was transferred to a crime cell "with no branch to report to."[51] A study comparing two cohorts of Indian women police, those serving in AWPSs and those placed in regular battalions, found considerable dissatisfaction in both cohorts, attributed to women's low status positions in Indian society overall (Natarajan 2001). This suggests that the AWPSs have not necessarily provided breakthrough opportunities for Indian women police officers' careers.

As in Brazil, periodic reports appear of men claiming mistreatment by police in Indian AWPSs. Some such reports tied AWPSs to "quack-court" practices, participating in illegal debt collection and arbitration;[52] these may not be particular to AWPSs, but the fact that women police participate in corruption, against public preconceptions, has called attention. Other grievances are distinctly more gendered. A 2004 petitioner to the Madras High Court lodged a complaint concerning "gender discrimination," alleging that he and his parents had been "abused in the filthiest language" and "subjected to mental harassment"; a police inspector reportedly slapped the accused's father, forced him to sign documents relinquishing funds and property, and "forced the pet[itioner] to perform fellatio on her, while the other women police watched and cheered."[53] And just as Brazilian men have decried the unavailability of state protection from partner "mistreatment" to which they themselves fall victim, Indian AWPSs have had to "turn away men who queue outside to complain about their wives." An inspector stated, "We are not encouraging men to lodge their complaints here since the station has been opened specifically to hear the grievances of harassed women whose numbers have grown alarmingly." No cases of women beating up men were recorded; men's complaints included wives' irrational expenditures, and men being force to do "household chores such as washing and cooking."[54] Most remarkable, perhaps, in such somewhat sensationalistic media reports is that those claiming to be "battered husbands" connect their abusive *wives* with *policewomen* they find abusive, thus bolstering their condemnation of "unjust harassment and use of illegal force" by feminized arms of the state.

As in Brazil, the low percentages of police investigations completed and delivered to court systems concern observers of women's police stations in India and beyond. The thrill of logging record numbers of complaints annually, at times even doubling police registrations in single years, has translated into dizzying bureaucratic and administrative challenges for police. Sharma (2002: 2) reports that 55 percent of the 4,923 complaints received at Women's Crime Cell of the Delhi Police in 1988 were left unfiled, and only 14 percent were "recommended for action." Citing cases of individual AWPSs where numbers of cases being filed declined,[55] she objects to police explanations that these could reflect "police settling disputes amicably" because reports of dowry deaths, rape, and molestation are not reconcilable, and therefore case numbers should not be declining.

Observers of Pakistan's Women's Police Stations lament that the initiative has fallen on hard times. By 2003, nine years after the creation of the first specialized station, that facility was reported to be "in shambles," lacking properly trained staff, a holding cell, and a single police car. "The idea to establish a women's police station exclusively for women to make the process of reporting for women easier has turned out to be a fond dream," a report by Lawyers for Human Rights and Legal Aid concluded. Critics of the stations' performance advocated establishing separate cells for women police in all stations, attributing the substandard processing by the special stations to their institutional isolation.[56]

Indian critics have also arrived at the conclusion that maintaining separate women's police stations has become more of a hindrance than an advantage. Sharma concludes, along with her counterpart Pakistani analysts, that women police with gendered-violence specializations should be distributed across the police force, forming "a separate cadre till Assistant Sub-Inspector level beyond which they should integrate in the general police force."[57] This recommendation, in conjunction with admonishments to ensure "special attitudinal training" and equal promotion for women who do specialize, seems carefully constructed to recognize women's roles in criminalizing and policing crimes of gender-based violence, while ameliorating the obstacles and stigmas that full-scale segregation poses for policewomen's advancement.

GENDER-SEGREGATION REVISITED: THE TRIPLE-GENDER COCKTAIL

Three distinct forms of gender difference run through the experiences of women's police stations: policing exclusively available to women citizens; policing by exclusively women police officers; and specialization in gender-based violence, alongside structural compartmentalization of police organizations to permit such concentration. Each of these forms connects in unique ways to the general issue of advantages and disadvantages of gender segregation and specialization.

First, nearly ubiquitously, is the notion of law-enforcement service directed exclusively at the woman citizenry, in recognition of women's preponderance as victims in gender-based violence, and of women's greater vulnerability to men's violence than men's to women's. This vulnerability is reinforced by various forms of oppression that women experience in diverse societies, compounding their heightened susceptibility to having their status and rights undermined by violence. The advantages of targeting women citizens come through acknowledging gender inequality as foundational, thereby permitting specialized police response to pinpoint gender-based patterns of aggression. As we have seen, however, a small minority of men has decried their exclusion from state protection from assaults by women; greater numbers have complained that police responses constructed a priori as pro-women are automatically anti-men. Substituting male-biased policing with a form viewed as female-biased may not constitute a long-term solution, some *delegadas* argue, particularly insofar as gender-segregated services may bolster perceptions of men versus women citizens' interests as intrinsically opposed and irreconcilable.

Second, specifying that women officers should ideally staff specialized police stations has offered the ostensible advantages of creating a more welcoming environment for inhibited citizenry, drawing upon policewomen's greater ability to identify with and advocate for women complainants, and presenting greater opportunities for women in police careers. The symbolic capital gained by this empowering form of state feminization has also contributed to what Santos calls the construction of a "citizenship of gender" in Brazil, a citizenship that "recognizes the social, hierarchical positions in function of sex and promotes an equality of rights, including the right to have rights and the right to have access justice through law" *(acesso à justice)* (Santos 2001). Meanwhile, male police officers' helpful and, for police insiders, largely unobjectionable presence potentially calls into question whether women-only staffing is crucial. However, the intriguing implications of a feminized workplace in a macho profession have so stimulated national and international dialogue on policing men's violence that the resultant discourse alone may be counted a tremendous boon.

Structurally speaking, the advent of a "women's track" through a police career has not proved, on balance, to be more beneficial than impeding. Although the upcoming chapter focuses on police careers from police officers' own perspectives and adds to this discussion, here we may observe that the DM has at times led to a ghettoization of training and experience; the more adapted officers became to a DM context, the more they diverged from "mainstream" police experiences, thus losing mobility potential. Meanwhile, conventional police in neighborhood-based districts have gotten off the hook, being exempted from both training and the astonishing workload that promises of police response could generate.

Third, a notable aspect of the DM phenomenon, along with India's AWPSs and other women's police, has been compartmentalization within police organizations, permitting specialization in diverse forms of gender based violence. The fact is, an astonishing response has been witnessed in every place that has specified partner and other forms of gender-based violence as criminal and has publicized the availability of relevant *specialized police services.* What remains in question is how critical becomes the role of such specialization being provided by women (or *to* only biological women). Of particular note is the lack of gender segregation in police organization in some of the world's most developed, "Western" regions—Australia, North America, and Europe—even where specialization in gender-based violence has emerged.

Australia implemented police units specializing in domestic violence in parts of the country through the 1990s; their experiences underlined the advantages of specialization for providing adequately trained personnel (Clarke 2003) but also were cautionary regarding the hazards of allowing such units to become too isolated and undersupported by broader police hierarchies (Werken 2002). In the United States, where police commissions have approved police units specialized in domestic violence, domestic violence offenses recorded by the police department generally have doubled. Similar increases in prosecutions have followed, however, only when specialization was continued at the level of the district attorneys' offices.[58] Some Canadian jurisdictions have specialized domestic violence units, typically associated with specialized courts or, less effectively for prosecutions, crisis-response teams geared around victim support. Such units in Canada and the United States were largely products of the Domestic Violence Council (originally called the San Diego Domestic Violence Task Force), formed in 1989 and now comprising over 40 agencies. These varied experiences suggest that institutional designation alone was insufficient: only with the introduction of training did the number of reported incidents rise, almost 60 percent in just one year.[59] Specialization appears to be more critical than sex segregation in latest developments, although both versions—institutional designation with and without sex segregation—show recent growth. In Europe, Spain by 2001 had begun creating "women's care units" in police stations as part of a sweeping reform.[60] More common has been to emphasize global retraining for male and female police alike: Austria holds the distinction of providing in-depth training on domestic violence for all police since 1985;[61] other countries have followed, with Armenia and Estonia recently joining the ranks.[62]

What is striking in all these instances is the absence of a stated priority given to women police staffing special units, either exclusively or even preferentially. Although women police officers make significant contributions, and in some cases surely predominate, for the most part postindustrial liberal democracies have chosen to avoid nominal gender separation of police staff.

For Brazil, India, and other developing nations that have opted to conjoin all three features of gender-specialized policing of domestic violence—serving women citizens, staffing with women police, and institutional compartmentalization—the triple cocktail has proved more attractive than daunting. The high-profile, triply feminized Brazilian *delegacia* project has been effective at unmasking the male bias of the state in underwriting male impunity. Praise and credit are due the DMs and their international counterparts for bringing the magnitude of the problem of gender-based violence to light. The Brazilian DMs have made criminalization a reality to a greater degree to date than seen in any other Latin American country. Given the ghettoization effects discussed above, however, which span issues of workload, stigma, isolation, and undercriminalization alongside quasi-legal hypercriminalization, it appears that the most enduring benefits of the triple-gender cocktail stem from its symbolic force, including the ability of women like Zizi to invoke the DMs' existence as a deterrent to violence.

It is fair to ask, why bother? Why continue to "make politics" that play upon the feminization of police, when it would be arguably more expedient to "ungender" the police stations, and the related politics around gendered violence altogether, as so many of the *delegadas* desire?

Failed expectations for Brazil's DMs can be consistently tied to problematic essentialist premises, or to the notion that women and men embody essences that are intrinsically distinct. Given the urgency to address gender-based violence, and the vast need for intervention the *delegacia* project has uncovered, it is frustrating to note the erroneous preconceptions and oversights in the way the police stations have been deployed, for these have dramatically undermined the DMs' ability to fulfill their potential. Anti-essentialist feminist theory offers a useful perspective for understanding why this is the case.

First, the presumption that policewomen would provide a different kind of policing—one more reflective of democratic, rule-of-law governance than the brutality and repression Brazilians still strongly associate with the paramilitary organizations under military dictatorship—has been true only insofar as specialized training about violence and gender dynamics has been provided. Positive examples in this respect number in the minority. The compelling public image of a feminized police response to gendered violence—whether in the form of "kinder gentler" or "beat the crap out of abusive men" models—itself appears significant in lowering cultural tolerance for spousal assault in Brazil. But this effect operates on an impressionistic, symbolic level and is often contradicted by the ineffective manner (if the 6 percent prosecution rate can be taken as a measure) in which so many of the all-female stations in reality operate.

Second, expectations that the agenda of grassroots feminism could be carried within an organ of a patriarchal state have generally been disappointed, with the exception of the few instances when individual *delegadas* led their stations to collaborate extensively with women's groups. The incompatibility of the police/feminist match, discussed more in the following chapter, has been underestimated.

Third, hopes that somehow policewomen could promote a nonviolent model of domestic relationships in the context of a repressive and often authoritarian state institution were similarly overly optimistic. The specialized, sex-segregated environment generated its own problems, such as seeming to reinforce the notion that men's and women's interests were so distinct as to be irreconcilable.

In sum, the central contradiction hampering the women's *delegacias* was the essentialist assumption that the "female" element in policewomen's identity would naturally take precedence over the "police" element. The specialized climate in which female solidarity was supposed to thrive was left to chance.

Anti-essentialist theory, which stresses the disjunctures between different groups of women (such as police versus complainants, but emphasizing cleavages by class, ethnicity, race, and so on) is useful for understanding where the women's *delegacias* have fallen short. It is less instructive, however, from the standpoint of the feminist activist. Anti-essentialism does not explain how Brazil's specialized women's police stations came to exist in the first place or why the triply gendered approach was so effective in intervening in patriarchal bias, nor does it provide guidance to those who must ask, "Where do we go from here?" Concern with ameliorating the effects of violence against women inevitably throws one back to constructing, to some extent, women as a social group with at least some common interests. Feminist activists, it seems, cannot afford to dispense altogether with the notion of "women" as a unified—albeit imperfectly unified—category.

Feminist philosopher Diane Fuss (1989) observed that when essentialism is successfully avoided around one category of difference, it inevitably resurfaces around another: some element of essentialism, she argues, is inescapable. She points to the contradiction between the anti-essentialist currents that crosscut much feminist thought and the simultaneous fascination, and concern, with *difference* that enlivens feminism. In sharp contrast to poststructuralists who would deny any connection between gender and biological sex, Fuss can be read as challenging feminists to take the risk of essentialism, in the sense of recognizing and strategically deploying essentialism's force as a political tool for liberatory—and *not exclusively oppressive*—ends. Similarly, bell hooks (1994) points out the difficulties in definitively separating essentialism from an "authority of experience" that women, or any social group, collectively share.

Indeed, it is such a form of essentialism "writ small" that has allowed women to create "imagined communities" of women that can cross-cut boundaries of class, ethnicity, and nationality and devise reforms and institutional innovations—like the DMs in Brazil—to redress injuries commonly, though not exclusively or uniformly, shared by women. Essentialism writ small need not be absolute or devoid of anti-essentialist, deconstructive elements that take seriously the divisions between women by class, race, and so on. But we might pause before rejecting any and every analysis or initiative that presumes that many women have shared interests on topics like violence, before dismissing this as crude essentialism. In so doing, we preserve one of the most critical tools for uniting women for political ends: that there is some common ground and basis for women's collective struggle, even if individual women experience, describe, and "imagine" these differently.

The early essentialism surrounding the creation of Brazil's women's police stations was effective at unmasking the male bias of the state and its role in underwriting men's impunity. The inability to correct the problems simultaneously caused by essentialist biases, I would argue, stems from the *delegacia* project's inability to move beyond an essentialist model. By limiting the power of the institutionalized feminist law enforcement to sex segregation alone, the Brazilian project has been impeded from transitioning into something like an imagined communities model. Anti-essentialist critiques, the domain of feminist scholars, are in themselves of little use in capitalizing upon the headway gained by the creation of Brazil's *delegacias:* ultimately, they point up the divergence between policewomen and feminist activists, and then are stalled. By contrast, the imagined and approximate commonality Anderson (1983) perceived as underlying the psycho-political unity of nations has direct parallels to the nonessential ways women can be conceived of, and conceive of themselves, as diverse yet still sharing common interests. Mohanty (1991) views the imagined communities model put to the service of feminist politics as a way of mobilizing the political—not biological, cultural, regional, or national—basis for forming coalitions (Steeves 1993). If the commonalities among policewomen, battered women, and feminist activists in postauthoritarian Brazil were not so complex and imperfect, it would not be necessary to "imagine" the community of female citizenry, as its basis would be clear.

Political scientist Paulo Sérgio Pinheiro admonishes, "[T]he election of civilian governments does not necessarily mean that that state institutions will operate democratically." He laments the fact that Brazil's "second transition," meaning a period in which democratic practices would be institutionalized at all levels of the state, is still so hampered by the legacies of the authoritarian past that it has yet to occur. These legacies underwrite what he calls "the 'microdespotisms' of daily life, manifested as racism, sexism and elitism" (1996: 20; also O'Donnell 1993).

Whatever their failings, the women's *delegacias* represent important symbolic and political terrain for waging battles against the patriarchal, authoritarian legacies Pinheiro describes. The entrenched police *machismo* and oppositionalism that women's police stations were *supposed* to miraculously resolve continue to pose critical impediments to meaningful democratization. Gender has been the primary medium that has allowed Brazilians to "imagine" the women's police stations as a truly distinct state-institutional space, and in turn, to imagine a society in which paramilitary police truly advocate in favor of its most dominated and oppressed citizenry. Although sex segregation alone has proved insufficient to create a truly reformist space inside patriarchal states in both Brazil and India, imperfect essentialist premises have nonetheless provided an opportunity for more critically minded perspectives, influenced by feminism, to be heard. Those same approximating premises have created opportunities to build heterogeneous and sophisticated "imagined communities" of women, grounded in the areas—such as generalized vulnerability to male violence—where diverse women's interests converge. As Leila Linhares (in CEPIA 1993: 53) observes, in the minority of cases where DM police actually *have* received specialized training, where the gender politics went beyond essentialist pigeon-holing that produced resentful complainants, accused men, and policewomen, the women's police stations represent the most genuinely specialized civil police stations in Brazil. Imagining a women's police station that truly *is* distinct and specialized, that serves as a vehicle to build coalitions between women with divergent histories and social locations, is but one example of the kind of work that moves Brazil in the direction of becoming an increasingly democratic society under an increasingly legitimate state.

FIVE

Reluctant Champions

Policewomen or Women Police?

They call the DMs confessionals, and the *delegadas* priests. . . .
It ended up that the *delegadas* came to represent uselessness.

DRª. SUZANA Mª FERREIRA
Section Delegada (Police Chief), Monte Aprazível, São Paulo

. . . the power of these queens and mothers is more attractive
than coercive. Like male priests, they provide healing, shelter,
and entertainment. To a far greater extent than most male priests,
these well-connected priestesses can also arrange . . . protection
for their followers.

J. LORAND MATORY
Black Atlantic Religion: Tradition, Transnationalism,
and Matriarchy in the Afro-Brazilian Candomblé

POLICEWOMEN IN THE DM in Salvador repeatedly shared with me their
belief that "a police officer does not have a sex." When such statements are
made in a context where police specialization is explicitly based upon the
gender of individual police officers, the ironic and contradictory implications cannot fail to ensnare an ethnographer's attention. What meanings,
in fact, does the "women" part of "policewomen" assigned to a DM hold?
Where the previous chapter's analysis rested at political and institutional
levels, concentrating on police as a corporate group, in this chapter I privilege individual police officer's voices, and policewomen's personal and
career perspectives take the foreground.

Beginning with a more detailed history of women in Brazilian policing,
the chapter proceeds to flesh out police subculture in relation to an ideol-

ogy of marginality, referred to in earlier chapters. Ethnographic scenes follow, which demonstrate police complicity in revictimizing complainants and show how police violence, in particular, becomes gendered in the DM context. A discussion of the DM's politicization of police careers leads into an analysis of gender identity and ideology for policewomen, with particular attention to their relationships to feminists and feminist thought. Because the DM project was a feminist brainchild that was eventually plopped onto the shoulders of police who just happened to be women, I argue that a strange bedfellow phenomenon has developed among policewomen, women complainants, and feminist activists. The constraining effects of these incompatibilities cannot be explained solely by their disparate social positioning but requires an understanding of gender ideology that constructs femininity and feminism as antagonistic.

WOMEN IN BRAZILIAN POLICING

As a profession whose ranks, until relatively recently, were formed exclusively by men (Neto 1992; Mattos 1979), it should not surprise us that characteristics of police occupational subculture bear important commonalities with those of hegemonic Brazilian masculinity more generally (Connell 1995; Buffon 1990). Of particular interest for my purpose is that police share the obligation, at times, to brandish a credible threat of violence in order to be seen as effective, successful, and indeed honorable (Pinheiro 1996: 19). The parallel to the credible-force mandate to which Bahian men in general are subject, as is for Bomfim men such as Jorginho and Robi in chapter 2, testifies to the tenacious masculinization of police occupational subcultures.

Policewomen are far from exempt from this imperative to masculinization and may be even more beholden to it. Just as sociolinguist Bonnie McElhinny found Pittsburgh, Pennsylvania, policewomen employing an "economy of affect" paralleling emotionally flat masculine speech patterns, applied linguist Ana Cristina Ostermann found Brazilian DM policewomen employing similar accommodations. Ostermann compared DM policewomen's discursive strategies (2003a) and pronoun use (2003b) to that of feminist crisis intervention center workers in pseudonymed "Cidade do Sudeste" (Southeast City). She found DM policewomen using "distancing, authoritative, and many times even dehumanizing responses (if any)" (2003b: 374), whereas the feminist center's staff's strategies were nonjudgmental, cooperative, and intimate, thus effectively affiliating themselves far more closely with victims, as fellow women, than policewomen were willing to do.

The value of masculinized speech patterns for policewomen finds a parallel in their use of force. Police proving themselves by posing credible threats of force is critical; indeed, the burden may well weigh more heavily on policewomen, whose ability to effectively use the force seen as necessary for carrying out their jobs is continually questioned by their male peers. Calazans's study of military policewomen in Rio Grande do Sul finds violence to be the critical, necessary component for successful "*policização*" ("policization"; 2004: 7), an idea echoed in work on civil police in the DMs. Of the many contradictory aspects of Salvador's policewomen that I detected, this one most confounded their ability to be effective champions for antiviolence and for women who were made victims of male violence. Policewomen's imperative to use violence or threats of violence to gain power and control directly paralleled the logic of batterers' own use of violence, and stood in stark conflict with an antiviolence stance that construes physical force as illegitimate.

This strong identification policewomen felt *as police,* or as potentially violent, somewhat masculinized workers, complicated their ability to identify, or as Ostermann prefers, "to affiliate" (2003a, 2003b) with the female victims they attended. Although the feminists, policymakers, and elected officials responsible for implementing the women's *delegacias* anticipated that policewomen would provide a more sympathetic, sensitive reception for victimized women, in practice this often backfired. Policewomen's internalized, *machista* values (the adjective associated with *macho* and *machismo*) often contributed to their blaming female complainants, whether for precipitating abuse or tolerating it. *Machismo* refers to attitudes and behaviors surrounding Latin versions of male supremacism; important aspects of *machismo* include an acceptance of might-makes-right hierarchical logic, positive value given to virile and strong-arm versions of masculinity, and an association of femininity with emasculation, weakness, and impotence (Barker and Loewenstein 1997; Lancaster 1992; Guttmann 1996; Parker 1991; Nolasco 1993).

Policewomen, mostly of lower-middle or working-class origins themselves, tended to advocate individualistic, pulling-up-by-bootstrap solutions for complainants. They frequently seemed resistant to recognizing that, to a large degree, the apparent helplessness and vulnerability of many of the female complainants they served was rooted in poverty, routinized sexism, and limited options, rather than in an inability or unwillingness to stand up to a bullying partner. Instead of perceiving that for many complainants, arriving at the point of seeking out police was in fact a critical turning point involving women's rejection of victimhood and availing themselves of a newly created resource, often policewomen's *machista* notions of strength registered such appeals as weakness.

Some policewomen showed genuine zeal at bringing the rule of law to bear on violent couples; others, however resented being assigned to disentangling interpersonal conflicts—some pejoratively called it "social work," and made clear they preferred more conventional police work involving "real" crime. The DMs are depreciated within the institutional police hierarchy, where they are called "dry"—*seca—delegacias,* police stations that stay "on paper" because they don't carry out "grand raids or pursuits, actions associated with masculinity, with the public and with force" (Boselli 2004). The DMs are associated with being "a woman's place" *(lugar de mulher)* and even the "kitchen of the police"—*a cozinha da policia*—"where women gather to cry over their sorrows" (Izumino 1998; Boselli 2004). Policewomen as a whole felt constrained by the contradiction of their assignment, in which impartial arbiters of the law were simultaneously expected to advocate for women, as women. Ironically, the frustrations policewomen felt were often deflected onto the female complainants, compounding the tendency of policewomen to see complainants as weak and helpless victims with whom they could not afford to identify. The fact that most police were generally lighter-skinned, not *as* poor, and better educated than most complainants exacerbated this lack of identification through internalized racism and classism.

Policewomen clearly saw themselves as discriminated against, as women, in their police careers—they could cite endless accounts of male counterparts who "didn't think they could handle the tougher cases" and so on. However, most were leery of integrating perspectives, such as feminism, that might link the discrimination they themselves experienced on the job to that felt by women they saw as weak and victimized. The fact that Brazilian feminism is strongly associated with middle-class professionals and intellectuals, and frequently with leftist politics, was also not lost on policewomen, and this reinforced their wariness of the feminists with whom they came in contact. The word for activist in Brazilian Portuguese is *militante,* and indeed anyone who chose to label herself as feminist *was* considered militant. Policewomen, I have explained, were already careful to minimize how being a woman might be seen as affecting their police work. Thus, policewomen at the *delegacias* forged bridges with feminist activists with difficulty, and incompletely, particularly in the earliest years of DM implementation. Many feminist *militantes* came to look upon the *delega-*

cia project with disillusion and disappointment, asking if they ought not just "call a state a state" and let go of hopes that a patriarchal state apparatus could incorporate a grassroots movement intent upon radical social change (Alvarez 1990: 246).

POLICE SUBCULTURE AND THE IDEOLOGY OF MARGINALITY

Policewomen, along with police officers in general, are acculturated into a comparatively isolated occupational subculture, based upon a mentality marked by oppositionalism (Muir 1977; Mattos 1979; Neto 1992; McElhinny 1994). Significant numbers of police, in fact, grow up in police or military families; thus the far-reaching occupational subcultural separation has intergenerational aspects (Chevigny 1995). Police officers, women and men alike, display greater acceptance than their civilian counterparts of the necessity of frequent official violence, even as the democratizing Brazilian state struggles to achieve a monopoly on legitimate use of force (Huggins, Haritos-Fatouros, and Zimbardo 2002; Chevigny 1995). In the Southern Cone countries of South America, police and militaries have gradually shifted away from the military authoritarian mode of opposing the "subversives"—first actual militants, then eventually leftist activists, intellectuals, and students—of the 1960s, 1970s, and 1980s (Alves 1985; Stepan 1988). Under the new democracies, police focus has turned to the fast-growing legions of marginalized poor produced by sweeping neoliberal reforms (Pinheiro 1996; Perry, 2000).[1] The degree of arbitrary police violence directed against the poor may in some cases have increased with democratization; as police "project another war . . . against ordinary delinquency" (E. R. Zaffaroni, quoted in Chevigny 1995), the line blurs between combating delinquency and criminalizing poverty, thus heightening civilian ambivalence about police (Machado and Noronha 2002). Through the transition from authoritarian to democratic rule, police attitudes remain consistent in viewing social order as dependent upon forceful police repression.

The degree to which DM policewomen identify with and participate in creating a police subculture grounded in an anti-*marginal* mission was not sufficiently anticipated or accounted for by policymakers, politicians, and administrators in the creation of the special women's stations. That is, police were accustomed to seeing their work as focused on traditional criminal and subversive elements hailing from the margins of society and were not always comfortable with sanctioning the conventional and otherwise law-abiding citizens that could be perpetrators of spousal assault. This is key to understanding ways in which the DMs were prevented from wholly embracing a "counter-cultural" mission—that is, to the extent that mission contradicts central aspects of *police* subculture. By extending the law's declaration of criminality into domestic spaces and against patriarchal authoritarianism, the DM policewomen were positioned to confront a kind of offender who did not fit into the profile of marginality their training was designed to oppose.

Police subscription to an ideology of marginality was evident daily in Salvador's DM. Most often, this belief emerged because the unique nature of the DM's assignment distanced police from dealing with typical criminal suspects, or those readily identified as *marginais*. In one instance, a *delegada* complained of having been demonized by the media for not having allowed reporters to be present at a hearing of a man accused of attempted murder. Her reasoning was that the man "was not a *marginal*" (by which she meant he had no police record, other than that of repeatedly assaulting his wife) and therefore ought not be subject to the kind of police reporting typical of Bahian newspapers, which are often marked by a tone of "guilty because accused." The *delegada* was put in a difficult position. She attempted to respect the nature of domestic conflict between conjugal members, as distinct from the criminal activities with which police normally contend, as perhaps deserving greater privacy and sensitivity. In so doing, however, she qualified and diminished the extent to which such offenses are viewed and treated as crimes like any other.

The same definitional difficulty emerged repeatedly in *audiências* (hearings) when men were called to account for accusations of violent assaults, threats, and so on. Continual refrains heard from men were: "But I work, every day, I provide everything for the home. I am no *marginal!*"; "I've never been inside a police station in my entire life!"; and "I'm a family man, a hard-working man! *[pai de família, homem trabalhador].*" Figure 8 captures an indignant man explaining himself to police, who listen with dubious expressions, unconvinced. Frequently, in such exchanges, it would seem two completely disconnected conversations were taking place as the police *agente* (officer) or *delegada* tried to ascertain whether or not the criminal act of which the man had been accused took place.

Têlma, a *comissária* (the only position authorized to conduct *audiências* other than *delegadas*), asked an accused man, "But if all were well at home, the police would never enter into the picture in the first place. I'm trying to determine if you hit her, if you broke the door down, if you broke the refrigerator, as she says. Are you saying none of this occurred?"

Figure 8. Salvador's DEAM Delegada Titular Isabel
Alice questioning an alleged wife-beater. Photo by Sarah
Hautzinger.

"Her mother never leaves me anything to eat, and I'm the one that sustains the [her] whole family!" he responded, quite agitated. "Those people do nothing to sustain themselves, and I have my own sick parents to look after."

The two were talking past one another on one level, yet the assertions of the accused man were not wholly misplaced. Têlma had already stressed to the man that the things of which he had been accused were criminal acts, and that he "needed to be more conscious of this." But later she made clear that she would take no further measures to see the man prosecuted, some-what vindicating him by concluding the hearing with the advice that the two separate, adding that "a couple only fights when both want to," and that they (or the female complainant) "shouldn't bring problems to the *delegacia* that have other solutions: talk, communicate, yes; but curse one another *[xingar]*, fight, no."

Here, Têlma the police officer struggles with contradictory understandings of what her role, as a representative of the state via the DM, ought to be. As was seen earlier, she wrestles with what practical role she can play in view of conflicting stories, limited evidence, and even more limited police power to investigate and, most important, how to deal with a man who may have committed a criminal act but who is not the criminal-*marginal* that all of her training prepares her to confront. The result is a compromise in the degree to which conjugal assault is criminalized and a reinforcement of the notion that the factors that qualify a man as a provider, husband, and father also *dis*qualify him from the status of criminal-*marginal*.

If police reveal themselves to be conflicted about criminalizing individuals they perceive as non-*marginals*, the reverse is true when a man with a police record is also accused of assaulting a female partner. Cristina recounts her experience of filing a complaint at the DM:

> When I first arrived here, I was afraid, you know? I went up to the young woman [the police officer], and she asked me what was going on. My face was all swollen up, and she asked what it was and I said my husband had attacked me. She asked me, "Do you know what you are doing, filing a complaint?" And I said, yes, I know, and I even said, you know, he's not exactly a *flor que se cheire* [all good; lit. "a flower that smells good"] himself—he's got a police record for various things. Then she goes, "So, he's a *vagabundo*, he's a *marginal*!" and I say, that's right. And then I was no longer afraid, I continued to talk and I wasn't going to break down. . . . He can leave at any time, but I'm not going to leave Salvador because of him. I'm going to show I'm not afraid of him.

The shift in this account, from when Cristina is unsure of gaining police support for her complaint to the tone of confidence with which she ends, turns on the policewoman's recognition that the accused could already be considered a *marginal* on other grounds. Note, too, the cautionary air with which the policewoman began, as if attempting to suggest to Cristina the precariousness of her charges based on the allegation of assault alone, despite the clear physical evidence. In this case, the accused was arrested shortly after the complaint was filed. My impression from conducting frequent between-the-bars interviews with men in the DM holding cells was that men who were arrested for assaulting female partners invariably already had criminal records for other offenses. Conversely, I witnessed countless cases in which women reported being beaten and evidenced clear injury but no arrests took place, presumably because of a lack of other character-damning criminal histories, and the best the complainant could hope for was that her assailant be chastised in an *audiência*.

REVICTIMIZATION PERPETUATED BY POLICEWOMEN

A corollary to the difficulties police have in fitting violent men into their *marginal* profile of criminality comes in the ways this dynamic can contribute to the revictimization of female complainants. When police perceive that female complainants themselves originate from sectors of the population they identify as marginal, they frequently direct considerable attention to pointing out to the women how the improper or immoral lives they lead set them up for the abuses they experience.

One early afternoon, a *diligência* (an arrest made on the street) arrived in the DM, brought in by a military policeman (PM). A couple had been fighting in the street: she was seventeen, of a color Bahians might call "*mulata clara*"—light-skinned, nonwhite—and he was twenty, *negro*—darker skinned or "black." They lived in Maciel, a slum in the historical district noted for prostitution and drug trafficking activities (Espinheira 1971, 1984) but were picked up "*lá em cima*"—up above—close to Campo Grande, the city's central plaza, close to the DM. The military policeman said in a loud voice that she seemed "*viciada*"—like a drug addict. Her complexion was very bad. I asked him how he could tell.

"Experience," he responded.

"But there must be something concrete," I probed.

"Look at her stance," he said, "at her arrogance." She did stand with her chest puffed out, very nervous and angry, with her hand on hip. However, I did not see signs of being high or strung out.

Then, she started to crumble and cry; seeming very self-conscious about what she heard being said about her. Railda, a policewoman on duty, brought her into the kitchen to talk. Then another woman in the room suddenly burst into loud sobs. All the while, the PM, a sergeant, talked in a loud voice about how he argued with his wife, but never laid a hand on her. He said if he were to start in with his left hand, well, his right hand was "too loose." He touched his gun with the right hand: who knew what he'd do? All this was by way of reprimand to the young man who has been put to stand facing the corner.

"What a shame"—*vergonha*—said the PM, "a man beating a woman—men should beat on other men!"

The young man denied ever beating her: he was supposed to take her to the dentist and she arrived late, because—he said—she was with another man. They were taken to an *audiência* with the *delegada* Imperatriz. She asked whether the young woman wanted him put in jail, and she responded that she didn't, that he wouldn't beat her anymore. Imperatriz told her that what happened once could happen again, but the girl shook her head, adding, "It was my fault." Imperatriz looked at me: you see, Sarah?

Imperatriz asked the girl, "Do you like [love: *gosta*][2] him?"

She responded, "Very much."

"I think you're a fool," Imperatriz cut in. "Because you don't like yourself. You have to give yourself value. Take care of your body. Of your skin." The young woman looked down, ashamed, crying again.

Imperatriz asked, "Have you ever worked as a prostitute *[fez vida]*?"

"No," the girl responded.

Imperatriz persisted, "Have you ever lived with anyone who has?"

"No, but I live next door to one," says the girl.

Imperatriz then asked the accused to tell his story. "But I don't know if she was really with this girlfriend," he began. "She started to curse me in the street, and I gave her a few slaps."

"Do you want to be a father?" Imperatriz intoned. "Are you going to treat your woman like a child? Because you took the right of a father, to be corrective."

He shook his head: "Wait a minute . . ."

"Wait a minute, nothing," the *delegada* interjected. "Just for this, you're going to spend some time in the cell. I didn't tell you to speak."

"I'll stay quiet, then," he responded, lowering his eyes.

"You should have before," she countered. "Not only because this is the DM, but because this is a police station, plain and simple."

This incident is far from clear-cut: the ways in which the girl's character was "put on trial," by accusing her of being a drug addict, of inviting or deserving abuse because of low self-esteem, and by suggesting that she might work as a prostitute, were all intended to help her, to jolt her out of a life "in the margins" that, from the perspective of police, contributed to or created the situation in which she found herself. At the same time, this event was interpenetrated by other messages, implying the girl's situation was of her own making and preventable if she only valued herself more. Self-regard may have entered in, as when the girl insists on taking responsibility for the incident. But the backdrop for the treatment given to both her and her partner originated in police knowing where they lived, along with their appearance—poor and Afro-Brazilian. The resulting conclusion is that, as presumed *marginais,* they had more in common than that which separated them as complainant and accused: their predisposition to marginality, against which police ought to attempt to intervene, overrides her ability to be seen as an appropriate recipient of DM protection.

I witnessed other events in which the revictimization of female complainants was more overt, revealing the extent to which many policewomen internalized and reproduced sexist or *machista* values. Although in theory all mediation in the DM was premised on the notion that, whatever a woman does, it is "never an excuse for [male] violence," and that couples "must find other ways to resolve their problems [apart from] physical aggression,"[3] on several occasions police appeared to blame women for provoking abuse. One policewoman was heard to say, "Well, if I were your husband, and we hadn't had sex for a year and I walked by a cafe and saw you there drinking beer with another man, well, what would you expect?" Police advice about how to avoid violence often revealed conservative conceptions of gender roles: "It's a woman's duty to feed a hungry husband!" when the husband's hunger turned nasty or, "It's a question of courtesy and manners that you tell him where you're going when you leave the house"; only afterward was it affirmed that, yes, he too should tell his wife where he was going—and the woman had to ask the policewoman if this was not also so. The advice given by two DM veterans summed up the irony of women's situation with striking self-awareness: "Our so-called domestic duties must be done in order to avoid a variety of problems," and "Rights? Forget your rights: you have to learn how to play the game."

In an *audiência* between a troubled couple and a DM social worker, the wife sobbed throughout, vehemently insisting that she wanted a separation after "three years of nothing but suffering," while the husband continually asserted his competence as a provider for the family in a level, calm voice. In this case, despite the female complainant's repeated insistence that she wanted a separation, the social worker said to the woman, "I think that you are too wound up *[muito nervosa]* to make a decision today," and arranged another appointment for the following week. After the couple left, the social worker explained to me that "they would return to announce that they had decided to stay together." She was sure of what the outcome would be and saw little point in complicating the situation.

In these examples, the ways in which a police ideology of marginality becomes bound up with gender bias become clearer. If the mission of police is to battle against the criminal-*marginal,* it is the interests of the breadwinning, family-oriented father-husband, "*pai de família,*" that police champion in that fight. For police, the *pai de família* and the *marginal,* both archetypically male, were mutually exclusive types, with women as either appendages or irrelevant figures caught in between. Despite their sex, the occupational gender roles of policewomen protect the *pai de família* over the *marginal,* thereby creating tensions and ambiguities.

A final corollary resulting from the police ideology of marginality is that police at times refuse to serve female complainants who fall too far into the margins, away from the mainstream. Any one in a series of disqualifiers could be used as a reason for police failing to register complaints by women: "She has a mental problem," "She was drunk," "She had no documents," or simply, "I just know she'll never come back" to follow up on the complaint. Frequently policewomen equated a perceived level of destitution with making it logistically impossible for complainants, or police themselves, to follow up. Police wondered how a woman without shoes and wearing tattered clothes, who lived in the city's impoverished outlying area (*periferia*)—even though she made it to the center of town to file a complaint once—stood much chance of showing up for a hearing in four weeks, at a specific time on a specific day. If she had no identification document and could not sign her own name, how could she "have the conditions" (*ter condições*) to stay on top of all that was involved in pressing charges? Finally, there were some neighborhoods so gang-ridden and violent that police felt they could only enter at their own peril: if a woman lived in one of these, police were not about to guarantee that a summons to a hearing would be delivered by police. In such instances, if DM police agreed to register the complaint at all, they might resort to giving the woman the summons to deliver herself, thus creating obvious risks for someone who already felt endangered by a domestic threat. Police argued that they intended her to pass on the summons to a local police officer, either civil or military, for delivery, but this did not mitigate the original problem, that the complaint arose from social spaces where police were not to be found (Machado and Noronha 2002). I learned of two incidents in which a man finding a summons on his partner's person precipitated a new round of violence.

One morning in the earliest phase of DM research, I arrived in the *delegacia* at 8:00 A.M., just in time for the changing of the guard. Each platoon of six agents and one platoon *delegada* worked twenty-four hour shifts every four days.[4] These four platoons were supplemented by the daily personnel, who worked business hours (eight to six with a two-hour lunch usually taken in-house) during the five weekdays.[5] On this particular morning, the departing platoon was that of the agent Madalena, who had first been introduced to me by the nickname *"bate homem,"* or *"*manbeater.*"*

Madalena was not the only agent introduced by a name other than her given one. In exploring the novelty of the still tongue-tied gringa who began to frequent the DM relentlessly, police took great delight in introducing their colleagues as "horse," "cow," "corrugated tin," and "crab louse." They got even more chuckles at watching my brow furrow in efforts to figure out the deep-seated meanings behind the names. It fit into a stream of playfulness that peeked through the tension of the workday; the same impulse might trigger an ad hoc soccer match played with a brass bullet on the concrete floor or a lengthy examination of my sandals—inquiries into where I bought them, for how much, and how they might be found for sale in Brazil—all while a complainant groaned beside me as the bandage on her head seeped blood. The persistence with which some police maintained a police-centric atmosphere, resisting succumbing to the somber atmosphere that their specialization imposed, often made me uncomfortable. Idle chit-chat and gossip between police cut into the performance of their duties too frequently and casually, it seemed to me. Often a policewomen would be perusing the wares offered by a peddler or a fellow officer, telling of a first date the night before, or trying food someone had brought and exchanging recipes while long lines of women, some of them seriously injured, crammed into the waiting room and overflowed into hallways and out of doors. Complainants often appeared dejected, their heads patiently bowed, waiting to remind police when asked, "Now, where were we?" Those policewomen who seemed to want to give complainants primacy seemed uncomfortable doing so, as if police-centrism were an unwritten code, and often compromised by negotiating a balance of attention between their police colleagues and complainants.

This dynamic reflected, I believe, intra-police solidarity and collective police alienation from non-police, which was related in large part to frustration about the poor remuneration they receive. Many police could not survive on police salaries alone and generated other income by holding down second jobs (e.g., a grocery clerk, a furniture salesclerk), selling prepared foodstuffs, cosmetics, and natural products on their own, or renting out rooms or personal automobiles by the hour. Police themselves admitted that, in concert, the heavy workloads and meager salaries severely undercut their incentives to provide female complainants with the kind of "special service" expected of them. Undoubtedly, burnout from working in the DM trenches and perhaps even some posttraumatic stress were additional factors. As a DM officer told Ostermann, "Many of us quit. We don't have the aptitude for this. . . . The work demands too much from us. We're not prepared for this" (2003a: 479).

When I told Madalena that her coworkers instructed me to call her *bate homem,* she laughed. I, too, chuckled nervously. We both paused, and then I asked if it were true. She again gave an amused grunt and said, "Only when they deserve it."

Of the police I met in Salvador, Madalena was among the most philosophical about her work, or at least the most anxious to expound her views to me. She was outspoken in her criticism, at times of her coworkers, but more often of DM administration and of political interference in the civil police through its administering body, the Secretary of Public Security. It was Madalena who articulated the difference between authority and power inside the DM structure. She would often "mistakenly" call her platoon's team *chefe* (chief)—a police agent like herself, typically without the university training in law of *delegadas*—the platoon "*delegada.*" When I asked about this, she explained that the *chefe* was really "the one who commands [us]." This was one of several ways in which she protested the inexperience of (some) *delegadas* in police matters and highlighted the class and education differentials between *delegadas* and police agents.

Madalena, with less than three years on the force, identified strongly with the "new police" generation, having joined with the arrival of democratization. She spoke of the police who served in the authoritarian era (at that time still the majority in the DM) as "yes women" who too often "look the other way" when they should speak out. Still, she retained hope that her work could be "on a philanthropic level" despite profound disillusionment with her experience on the force to date.

On this particular morning, I inquired how things had gone during the night. Madalena responded "pow pow pow pow pow," slapping index finger against middle finger in that singularly Latin gesture which inadequately translates as "hot stuff." Seeing that the exact meaning of her performance escaped me, she explained, "*A gente bate em homem*," or "We beat [up] a man."

Late in the night, she told me, a couple was brought in by military police. The man had hit the woman over the head with a hammer, probably fracturing the skull. The two were given immediate, separate *audiências* during which each party related her or his side of the incident. He was held in one of two DM cells while his wife told her account, then taken out to recount his own. On the way back to the cell, Madalena and two other agents delivered blows with what sounded like deliberate calculation: "We only hit him here, here, and here," she said, indicating her abdomen, back and thighs. "But not where it will leave marks that show," she pointed to her face and arms.

Madalena was reluctant to tell me exactly what time this occurred; suddenly she seemed concerned that I would say something. The platoon *delegada* heard what was going on, Madalena said, but turned a deaf ear. It would be problematic were the *delegada titular*—the head—to get wind of this. "She doesn't like it when we do it. But we do," Madalena confided.

Contrasting her sudden caution was an unmistakable element of pride, of righteousness; with the risks involved in telling me about it, there is little other explanation. Pride similarly steered Madalena's account of sneaking up alongside a cell where a different incarcerated man was bellowing, "Whores! You have no right to keep me here. . . . You're not police, you're a bunch of whores!" The man's hands protruded through the bars; when Madalena brought a shovel crashing down, she cut them to the bone.

What grounds Madalena's pride? The ability to use violence against a person caught in a heinous act, in order to avenge that act? The ability to use violence to protect her personal honor, as a policewoman, when it is slighted? Or are acts of police brutality rites of affirmation for all officers, underwriting their authority and public honor, especially where strict rule of law constricts them (Pitt-Rivers 1968; Huggins, Haritos-Fatouros, and Zimbardo 2002)? Are such rites even more salient for female police, who must doubly prove themselves sufficiently virilescent to carry out police duties (Martin 1989; McElhinny 1994, 2005; Calazans 2004; Ostermann 2003a, 2003b)?

Then again, some policewomen may identify with the victim's hammer-cracked skull. Perhaps like most women, despite their identities as selectively masculinized workers, they have experienced feelings of powerlessness as members of the "weaker sex." Is this situation unique in that policewomen, as police in a police station, are in a singularly advantageous posi-tion to exact eye-for-eye retribution for male violence?

The answers to these questions are no doubt far from unitary: surely ele-ments of each explanation play in to greater or lesser degrees. Although I cannot supply definitive answers, I can relay what policewomen told me.

An emphatic and essential caveat to any discussion about police violence in the DM was that one would be hard pressed to find a police precinct in Salvador where there was no police brutality. For the nature of work in the *seca* (dry) DM, it is reasonable to assert that there was no more (per case registered), and probably considerably less, police brutality than in other police stations.[6] But for most of the Bahians with whom I spoke, the issue was not police brutality. Again, the rumors of policewomen's violence directed against accused men at the DM were notable first for being per-petrated by women, and only secondarily, if at all, as police brutalizing civilians.

THE GENDER OF (POLICE) VIOLENCE

The tendency to see DM policewomen's violence first as women's vengeance, and only second as police brutality, suggests that in Brazilian culture police violence itself becomes gendered and that police violence per-petrated by women in the DM is viewed differently from police violence in general. For many, female police are women first and police second. As such, the issue of how Bahians view men's violence and women's violence as differing merits attention.

An event that struck me as curious at the time is useful here. Vânia, an officer with whom I had a warm rapport, was finishing filling out a ques-tionnaire I had given her. The last words she wrote were, "The goal is that women validate themselves, and *always say no to violence*" (emphasis hers). She looked up from her writing and exclaimed, "Sarah! I forgot something I wanted to show you! It's about a heroine"—*heroína*—"for all women!" She rummaged through her bag, producing a newspaper clipping about a woman who had knifed her husband to death in his sleep, terminating years of physical abuse at his hand. If Vânia's perspective suggests that violence has differing legitimacies in different contexts—specifically that defensive violence (often female) is condoned where offensive violence (usually male) is always to be said "no" to—I want to suggest that this gendered distinc-tion carries over into police violence.

When policewomen were asked in interviews about the DM's ruffian public image, most were understandably anxious to downplay it. Police indicated that this image is propagated in two places: among men of the lower classes who always feel antagonized by police (here two informants specifically said that the strong-arm image was a useful tool), and among civilian women themselves who want to play up the threatening image of DM police as their protectors.

The desire to deemphasize the thug-like image, however, is qualified by responses to a different question put to police: "Is 'hard treatment' [*tratamento duro;* implies physical force] necessary in some cases? When? What is the effect?" All police felt it was necessary, and a few mentioned that in severe cases (e.g., rape), some "greater punishment" was called for. The main theme that arose in these responses, however, was the question of respect, mentioned by nearly every policewoman interviewed. Policewomen felt they needed strong-arm tactics to instill respect and command authority. One informant said, "When complainants and accused encounter a more rigid treatment, they ask, 'Isn't this the *delegacia* of *women?*'" A level of flexibility, sympathy, and tenderness quite different from the typical police station was expected.

Historian Laurel Ulrich's distinctions between types of violence are useful in digesting the various perspectives on violence expounded above. She calls authoritative violence that which is "employed by a superior to enforce obedience by an inferior" (1980: 186). Police use of violence to garner respect and exact compliance falls under this heading. Since female police express heightened concerns about their authority, this type of violence may be of special importance for them. Ulrich terms defensive violence that which "involve[s] direct action against a perceived trespass" (1980: 186). Battered civilian women using violence as retaliation and police using brutality to apply "greater punishment" for grave offenses are both of this type, although one involves the direct reaction of the woman offended and the other the indirect defense of the wronged civilian by state authorities.

Images of police violence, and actual police violence, are produced through negotiation between civilians and police. The two things gained by police violence—respect for the law and its enforcers, and an eye-for-an-eye form of justice—benefit police and civilians alike. At the same time, one could class much of the violence explored above under Ulrich's third type: antisocial violence. She defines antisocial violence as "[signaling] the aggressor's alienation from the community" (1980: 187). As state agents and women, policewomen are able to incorporate elements of their defensive, righteous violence into a blend with both authoritarian and antisocial violence. Gender helps immunize this blend from being seen as illegitimate or abusive.

CAREER POLITICS AND POLITICIZED CAREERS

Ironically, policewomen's resistance to DM specialization in gendered crimes appeared more acute in states such as Bahia, where the female presence in the police force was already relatively strong, exceeding national norms, before the DMs were instituted (Mattos 1979). In most of the country, women's representation in civil police forces was minimal, and the creation of the DMs was seen as a way of bolstering women's participation. In Bahia, by contrast, the creation of the women's police stations did not represent a prying open of police academy doors for women as it did elsewhere. By 2005 this effect had grown: of the 64 police stations functioning in Bahia, 28 stations (43.75 percent) were led by female chiefs (*delegadas titulares*); all five of the delegacias specialized in "crimes against a person" were headed by women. By comparison, in São Paulo, women *delegadas* went from just fifteen, statewide, in 1985 to an impressive 388 by 1999. However, this number still only represented 12.5 percent of the state's total *delegados/as* (of 3,102 total; K. Silva n.d.: 3–4); the percentage of women head chiefs (*delegadas titulares*) is likely to be far lower. In short, because of women's head start in Bahia, recruits *already* expected rich and varied opportunities, causing them to be more likely to see assignments in women's delegacias as hindrances to police careers.[7]

Because the DMs were integrated into the wider police bureaucracy, routine transfers were common—in fact, administrative policy held as a general rule that regular rotations helped prevent police corruption by ensuring that no individuals become too embedded in a niche—thus making it difficult to ensure that once a station had a well-prepared leadership and staff that this could be maintained without repeated and consistent trainings. As such, the effectiveness in leadership of any single DM tended to rely overly on what Max Weber (1958 [1919]) called charismatic authority[8] on the part of the *delegada titular,* or head police chief-magistrate of the DM. Over the fifteen-year period that I have closely followed activities in Salvador's DM, I have watched the efficiency and effectiveness of the station's functions (as measured by percentages of complaints investigated and delivered to the courts for prosecution, along with other factors observed) vary according to the competence and commitment of the woman at the helm, more than any other factor. Often her abilities varied independently of the politics and policies of respective gubernatorial administrations that placed her in charge, thus defying the expectations of feminists, who anticipated DM leadership to be more sympathetic to women's issues from governors they viewed as more progressive.

In 1988, Salvador's DM's *delegada titular* was Iracema Silva de Santos. Iracema[9] was popular with DM staff and Bahian feminists alike, for she was known as an "action-oriented" *(atuante) delegada,* specifically dedicated to the project of the DM and an inspiring and supportive leader. Although not a feminist herself ("I am feminine, but I defend some feminist causes," she was once quoted as saying),[10] she had good connections with the women's movement and sponsored workshops with feminists and DM staff.

As the 1989 presidential campaign gathered momentum, Bahian Governor Waldir Pires, the leftist politician who had appointed Iracema, relinquished his post as governor midterm to run for the vice presidency on presidential candidate Ulysses Guimarães's ticket (the bid would prove unsuccessful, and Fernando Collor de Mello was inaugurated in 1990). For the rest of Pires's term, the lieutenant governor Nilo Coelho, who belonged to a less progressive, rightist party associated with the military era, assumed the governorship. Shortly after this shift, Iracema Silva de Santos was removed from her post in the DM and promoted to a more bureaucratic duty in the office of the Secretary of Public Security. This transfer was viewed as a political move, disappointing DM police and angering local feminists. One such feminist remarked that her removal constituted "a coup" within the DM, implying that Iracema's successor, the former second-in-command at the DM, had achieved her ascendance through personal connections. In any event, Iracema's successor, who led the DM during my initial fieldwork in 1990, was viewed as less effective and less popular by both DM staff and Bahian feminists.[11] Over the period that I was able to monitor DM activities, it was under her tenure that I witnessed the most disturbing police-civilian interactions and that the rate of complaint investigation sunk to its lowest level.

When I returned to Bahia in 1992, Antonio Carlos Magalhães had been elected governor. Commonly called simply "ACM," he had served as governor during the military era and, like Nilo Coelho, was viewed as a right-wing, authoritarian politician, even among his sizable Bahian following. Several of his supporters whom I interviewed cited the refrain *"ele roba, mais faz"* (he robs, but gets things done) in somewhat cynical recognition of the fact that ACM's reputation for clientelistic corruption went hand in hand with his reputation for accomplishment, particularly with large public-work projects. ACM was testing the waters for a presidential run in 1994, but apparently desisted when national surveys reported him as the public figure most associated with corruption, behind only disgraced former President Collor and his chief aid responsible for embezzlement, Paulo Fárias.

ACM's assumption of the reins of state government evoked pessimistic forecasts about the fate of the DM. Indeed, the initial changes suggested that the institutional support for the women's police station, already verging on inadequate, would be further undermined. First, the location of the station was changed from a freestanding building in a protected residential neighborhood to a police complex lodging five other stations along a busy thoroughfare. The first locale was actually a large, converted house, providing an appropriately "domestic" feel for a woman's police station, which the policewomen generally favored. At the same time, others thought the change in location aided in their work being respected and recognized by the police at the adjacent *delegacias,* who could not fail to notice how the traffic in people at the DM far outweighed that at any of the other stations. In other changes, the *delegadas assistentes* (assistant police chief-magistrates), who had previously serviced the DM alone, were now floaters, available to all the *delegacias* in the complex, and the social worker who had coordinated social work interns from the university had left the DM, leaving that service suspended. (Table 4 in the previous chapter indicates further changes by 2002.)

The negative implications of these changes, however, were offset by ACM's appointment of a new *delegada titular* in early 1992, Célia Miranda. Although Célia was sophisticated enough to know she could answer a newspaper reporter's "feminism or femininity?" question "both," and professed a strong personal commitment to women's rights, her lack of historical activism within explicitly feminist groups, along with her having been appointed by ACM, led feminists to anticipate that she would be insensitive to concerns and objectives of the women's movement and unwilling to collaborate.

GRINGA INTERLOCUTORS

Frequently, to my eye, it appeared that when there were miscommunications and misunderstandings, they had more to do with political cliquishness on one side, and the lack of organization in the women's movement on the other, than substantive ideological issues surrounding gender politics. Two examples come particularly to mind, both of which occurred during Célia Miranda's leadership of the DM. In each case, I and another Salvador-based foreign researcher of male-to-female violence with whom I often worked (Canadian Sherry Blackburn, a social worker) ended up shouldering intermediary roles, in the absence of other—preferably Brazilian—persons with ongoing communication both with the DM and the network of Salvador's women's movement groups.

In both years in which Sherry and I participated in the organization of celebrations for March 8, International Women's Day, the DM set up a booth and actually ran the shift from the city's central plaza where the celebration was being held. Since the DM was just down the street, female complainants were sent to the plaza to register their denunciations amid the revelry, an arrangement that most North Americans would probably find unacceptable but which Bahians received with ease. *Delegadas* and police agents took to the stage to deliver brief discourses about their work, and were delighted to be able to do so, despite the fact that such "heaviness" in a festival atmosphere clearly did chafe against Bahian sensibilities, as the crowd quickly grew restless and began to dissipate. Policewomen later complained that had Sherry or I not happened to invite their participation, they never would have even known of or been included in the day's activities. As it was, Célia Miranda and her staff seized upon the invitation enthusiastically. Police read the near-oversight as intentionally exclusionary, whereas in my view it resulted from disorganization and, again, a habitus of partisan cliquishness in the women's movement, where predominantly leftist, feminist women do not regularly associate with centrist, rightist, or apolitical women. Worth mentioning is that the DM was not the only women's group to read the movement's disorganization as actively exclusionary: this exclusion was a chronic problem in the medium-size city where the number of regularly active feminist participants was consistently insufficient for fulfilling the objectives established by ambitious leaders.

The second example was potentially more volatile. In the period from February through May 1993, conversations about Salvador's DM in meetings of the newly established City Council's Commission for Women's Rights (CDMCM—*Comissão dos Direitos da Mulher da Câmera Municipal*) became increasingly heated. Feminists and other community activists in attendance repeated accounts of women receiving poor treatment by the DM's police: their complaints were not taken seriously or given due process; the police joked around with one another and seemed distracted; the new location in the complex was cold and dehumanizing, and so forth. Sherry and I attended the meetings to represent the women's studies department (NEIM) that sponsored us at the federal university (UFBa). Although neither of us disagreed that any of the problems these accounts pointed to were of concern, as the only persons present at the meetings who spent extensive time in the DM, we worried that the individual policewomen staffing the DM were clearly being blamed for the problems. Instead, we saw many of the organizational, processual, and moral-based problems at the DM as originating at the administrative level, within the Secretariat of Public Security, which would not or could not provide adequate resources, both material and human, for the DM to function effectively. When the strategy to launch a surprise visit to the DM, in the company of members of the press, was clearly gaining consensus, and the spirit of the visit was unmistakably one of attack, Sherry and I decided to attempt a benign intervention; the decision was difficult, as we were acutely aware of our unusual, insider-outsider positions. We were insiders insofar as we were the sole feminist activists at that time that had daily presences in the DM, and yet would to some extent always be outsiders by virtue of our nationalities, which cast the appropriateness of such involvement into question. We prepared material discussing the origins of overload and backlog of the DM (expounded in the previous chapter), the disadvantageous policy changes, and the lack of ongoing training for its personnel. We entreated our fellow activists to consider shifting the visit from surprise to announced, without accompanying media, and to consider the notion that long-term interests might be better served if our objectives involved information gathering and bridge building, rather than attack and blame-laying.

In the end, our pleas were heard, and although tough questions were still put to Célia Miranda and other DM officials, the visiting activists were persuaded that more than anything else, the DM could benefit from advocacy from the women's movement, rather than antagonism from it. Following the Commission's visit to the DM, the same group instigated a series of meetings with Secretariat of Public Security administrators. Immediately significant changes were announced, most notably the restoration of assistant *delegadas* for exclusive service to the DM, rather than all five delegacias in the complex, and it was promised further improvements would be looked into.[12]

With time, feminists found that expectations that Célia Miranda's DM would be difficult to collaborate with were unfounded, and the DM moved into one of its most productive phases under her leadership. Célia embraced a rather apolitical stance vis-à-vis her law enforcement practices, and the conservative politics of the gubernatorial administration under which she served influenced little about her administrative style, other than affording her more stability to regularize practices at the station. Soon Miranda was commonly invited to speak and participate in other activities organized by the women's movement, such as the panel discussions and brainstorming workshops annually held in honor of November 25, the International Day for Combating Violence against Women. Célia eventually moved from the DM to head program development at the Bahian Police Academy, a development that boded well for improved preparation to work with gender-based violence for all graduates.

GENDER IDENTITY AND IDEOLOGY: "THE POLICE DON'T HAVE A SEX"

With a clearer portrait of some of the practical obstacles faced by DM police in realizing the mission with which they are charged, it is worthwhile now to return to examine more analytically the way policewomen in the DM think about themselves, as police, as women, and as political beings.[13]

One of the interview questions put to DM police agents was, "Do you remember any time in which you were discriminated against as a woman?" The vast majority answered with a simple "no." The few exceptions, however, listed several ways in which they experienced discrimination as women: not being allowed by male partners to go out on the weekends, being "scolded" for drinking alcohol, and not having a fair say in household finances, to name a few.

The follow-up question was, "Have you ever experienced discrimination in the course of your police career?" Here, every single informant answered in the affirmative. Their responses were most forthcoming: "Male colleagues avoid going on patrol with us—they think it puts them in danger"; "They think we 'get involved' with the men who come to the *delegacia*." Policewomen complained of getting taken off cases—"She's a woman"— because they are not thought to be qualified, and of being subjected to a host of other slurs: "They think we're too fragile"; "They think we're all lesbians."

The contrast here raises questions about how these police view the individuals they attend to in the endless stream of female victims of male violence. To the extent they viewed male-to-female violence as a form of oppression of women, they largely saw themselves as invulnerable to the same potential abuse. Most appeared not to see milder abuses—inequality in household decision-making, or double standards in the right of one conjugal partner to control or constrain the behavior of another, for example—as connected to the causes of male-to-female violence. In other words, many policewomen viewed themselves as categorically different *kinds* of women from those who find themselves subjected to chronic abuse; this is particularly interesting in light of reports of elevated family violence in military and law enforcement families. Either police were not familiar with analyses that related different aspects of women's oppression, or they rejected them on the basis of their elevation of "women" as the primary dimension of analysis over more individualistic perspectives. Moreover, where policewomen may have seen as inevitable the routinized, occupational discrimination they experienced as female police, they simultaneously saw themselves as individual women with sufficient strength and self-determination to avoid victimization in intimate, interpersonal relationships.

Another question asked of police was, "Generally speaking, how would you differentiate male and female police?" Answers here were more varied. Some said flat out that there was no difference. Others said that the only difference involved physical strength, so that, for example, women were less effective in apprehending thieves. A strong third line argued that what women lacked in brawn they made up in brains: "Women have to work harder to not be a joke *(brincadeira),* have to study more, be more vigilant." Similarly, "Here we have women with such good heads [on their shoulders] they have more aptitude for responding to emergencies." Some went further along this line, arguing that women "have a certain treatment, a certain knack *(jeito),* in resolving more malleable things," or, "There is a difference in the behavior of policewomen, in specific problems involving a woman. Male police treat her like trash . . . with insensitivity. They treat her like a criminal." (This last comment came from Mônica, a policewoman particularly disgruntled with the limiting effects of her assignment in the DM upon her career. Thus, dislike of the DM assignment did not preclude sympathetic treatment per se.)

Responses to these questions show that DM police possess keen perceptions about how their gender affects their careers. Many of the comments would seem to contradict, however, a theoretical maxim I heard often enough in conversation to suspect it was part of their police academy training: "*A polícia não tem sexo,*" or, police do not have a sex.

It is notable that the most impassioned defense of this claim came from a platoon *delegada.* In the DM police hierarchy, de facto socioeconomic and racial[14] stratification means *delegadas* are usually of middle-class origins, whereas agents tend to come from the lower-middle and working classes[15] and the majority do not attend university. The preparation to be a *delegado/delegada* involves a college education in law and then a brief follow-up course in the police academy; as a result, when first assuming command of a *delegacia,* most have little actual police experience commensurate with that of police agents, and they may never experience as much discrimination as agents. Hence, in practice, they are less likely to have "genderless ideal" undermined than their subordinates.[16]

That aside, why are police so ready to disavow their identities as women—in theory—in the police occupational sphere, the very sphere where they freely acknowledge that they are subject to discrimination on the basis of these same gender issues? The short answer is obvious: if being a woman is a liability for police, then renounce it or selectively downplay it. In theory.

But more can be said on this point. Remember the weighty majority of police that claimed never to have experienced sex discrimination *apart from* their police careers. Perhaps these women identify with "femininity" selectively, each striking her own "bargain with patriarchy" (Kandiyoti 1988); if being police renders femininity a liability in the work sphere, female police may guard their "social" femininity all the more closely.

Clues to this quandary may lie in policewomen's feelings about the relationship between femininity and feminism. It is almost a truism to say that "woman" and "femininity" are socially constructed, performed categories. Less common, however, is to underline that feminism, too, is a particularistic, variable phenomenon. Judith Butler was thinking along these lines when she indicted the "presumed universality and unity of the subject of feminism" and called for "[a] time to entertain a radical critique that seeks to free feminist theory from the necessity of having to construct a single or abiding ground which is invariably contested by those identity positions or anti-identity positions that it invariably excludes" (1990: 4–5).

Butler's performative conception of gender helps explain how many DM policewomen could indicate that, for them, femininity and feminism were mutually exclusive. Policewomen may be no different in this sense from most Brazilians, or most Latin or North Americans, for that matter. As police, however, their femininity was particularly "at risk," creating the possibility that feminist identification could feel doubly threatening to them: a proper woman may resist the crude, "bull-dykish" stereotypes surrounding policewomen, but a *feminist* policewomen, two-steps removed from lady-likeness, is a ball-basher for sure.

Curious to probe this issue, I included on the police questionnaire the following questions: "What do you think about feminism? Do you position yourself as a feminist"? Of the twenty-six police responding to the questionnaire, only one DM staffer identified herself as a feminist outright; it is probably not coincidental that this was a platoon *delegada* of upper-middle-class origin.[17] Four women spoke positively about feminism without identifying themselves one way or the other: each attributed gains in women's rights to feminist activism, one said feminism was crucial in confronting female-directed violence, and another called for heightened feminist activity.

The women disclaiming feminism formed the solid majority at fifteen (six left the question blank or said they had no formed views). The answers of this bunch, which included two *delegadas,* were the most interesting. They divided into three fairly even categories: those who simply said they were not feminists; those who juxtaposed femininity with feminism; and those who critiqued feminism (a few juxtaposed femininity with feminism *and* critiqued feminism).

The policewomen juxtaposing femininity with feminism all gave versions of the "I'm feminine, not feminist" axiom. This group's answers hearken back to former DM *delegada titular* Iracema's statement, "I'm feminine, but I defend some feminist causes"; several articulated support for "women's causes" while rejecting feminism itself.

This mutual exclusivity was elaborated to a greater extent by the women critiquing feminism. Several lines of thought stood out. Some women said they were not feminist because "today's women have already won a new position and [so] we don't need to be feminist. For this reason, I am against feminism." Or, "It's not necessary for us to be feminist to fight for freedom . . . growth, studies, participation, liberty." Other policewomen repudiated feminism simply because they were not "against men." In conversation, it became clear that this line of thought was linked to their positive valuation of the objectivity and impartiality so critical to police work. Conversely, feminists were seen as people who had relinquished the ability to be objective.

A third line included specific comments about feminists. All agreed: "They are awfully *[muito]* radical." One informant later expounded her views.

> Here in Bahia, you have a lot of women very concerned with "orienting" other women. . . . But I never heard of a movement of men *[um movimento machista]* with men orienting other men![18] You have to take this

into account. When women start defending feminist causes, they often are well-situated in life, and what happens is they are able to set people *thinking*. Here in Bahia, to be a feminist is a thing of great importance . . . [she gives examples of how feminists receive a lot of publicity]. With this, many end up being extremely radical. I think that when a woman wants to be feminist, it's because she does not have conditions to be feminine.

The comments of an agent we met earlier, Vânia, were particularly revealing. She spoke most positively about feminism but said she was not a feminist. I asked her why. She said, "I still haven't felt called to become one" *(ainda não me tocou de ser)*. I asked what it would mean if she did. She said it would mean becoming involved in organized group activity, and dedicating herself to "taking the woman's side" in all situations. I asked if she felt this would lessen her objectivity. She responded, "To the contrary, I think it would expand it." She went on to say that feminists are people who "do research, who investigate and assess situations."

What do Vânia's comments reveal about police conceptions of feminism? If feminists are researchers, it means they are likely to be journalists, lawyers, social workers, social scientists, and students, much like the feminist woman (me) to whom Vânia was speaking. Ergo, feminists are most probably well educated and middle class. Relatively speaking, Vânia was among the policewomen most open to the notion of feminism, and yet I read her sense of "not being called" as not being of the right sort, of the right class or educational attainment. Most critically, Brazilians see feminism as an activity (or set of activities), not a stance, viewpoint, or belief. If they equate feminism with political activism, the fact that every single policewoman surveyed disavowed involvement in party politics—some quite vehemently—becomes most relevant.

In closing this section, it should be stressed that these survey questions were posed in the mid-1990s; as will become clear below, significant shifts in Salvador's DM institutional culture may well mean that police officers working in the DM currently would answer differently.

HEGEMONIC GENDER IDEOLOGIES, FEMININITY, AND FEMINISM

Up to this point, I have been discussing femininity and feminism as contrasting gender identities from the subjective vantage point of DM policewomen. Because I object to the idea that the two are inherently opposed or incompatible, I must ask the question as to how they might come to be viewed as such. Such an inquiry can benefit by considering the relationship between feminism and the state in the wider political context; I propose a theory of standardized femininity as a hegemonic gender ideology used—though rarely consciously—as a way of isolating and disabling feminism.

When persons threatened by the purported goals of feminism desire to create negative images of feminists, one of the most common tactics employed to do so is to construe femininity and feminism as mutually exclusive, antagonistic ways of being. It is far more common to find a Brazilian woman who dares to declare herself sympathetic to feminism almost frantically asserting her claims to femininity, and to brandish overt iconic trappings of femininity in order to do so, than to encounter a feminist-sympathetic woman who renounces the basics of Brazilian femininity. By way of illustration, the stationery designed for the national commission of female *delegadas* sported a succulent pair of generously lipsticked, shapely lips to accompany its logo, and the woman's police station television series also had its title written out in lipstick in the beginning. Lipstick served as a symbolic means to feminize and counterbalance the disturbing, oxymoronic meanings arising around female policing, or female strong-arm power. If the masculinizing implications of strong-arm state power as wielded by women were troublesome, it somehow helped to paint them a curvaceously sexy, screaming hot pink.

Policewomen's occupationally masculinized identities destabilized their individual identities such that rectifying personal femininity became critical. The trappings of standardized femininity could be effectively deployed to compensate. When policewomen refuse to see the occupational discrimination they experience as women as in any way connected with the battering of the women to whom they attend, they betray inadvertent participation in a hegemonic ideology, or in "the inscription of consent into various forms of coercion, through which subordinate groups accept their subordination" (Verdery 1991: 10). In other words, if policewomen see themselves as vulnerable to some forms of sexism but invulnerable to others, this suggests that they are less likely to see woman-battering as deriving from a set of societal values, and more likely to individualize the circumstances of a battered woman. A powerful mechanism that inhibits police from linking different forms of anti-woman practices is the widespread subscription to a standardized, hegemonic ideology of femininity.

Gender is the primary organizing principle in the DM's specialization. A discussion of hegemony in the DM, then, departs from Gramscian models in placing gender—before class—as the primary conceptual category. Here, it is important to acknowledge the power that shared, and frequently naturalistic, assumptions about "womanhood," "femininity," and "female-female affinity" have in consolidating common ground among Brazilians with regard to gender-related issues such as violence against women. In fact, this essentialist foundation was critical, perhaps even indispensable, in consolidating a political foundation and allowing the creation of the DMs in the first place. And despite their differences, policewomen and feminists probably share more than they differ in their views on domestic violence, most notably in their corroboration of the view that violence is never an acceptable way to "resolve" domestic differences.

Political scientist Sonia Alvarez draws upon a distinction made by Maxine Molyneux regarding "strategic" versus "practical" gender interests. Citing Molyneux, she defines strategic interests as those "derived . . . deductively, i.e. from the analysis of women's subordination and from the formulation of an alternative, more satisfactory set of arrangements to those that exist" (1990: 23). Practical interests, however, are "given inductively and arise from the concrete conditions of women's positioning by virtue of their gender within the division of labor. In contrast to strategic gender interests, these are formulated by the women themselves who are within these positions rather than through external interventions. Practical interests are usually in response to an immediate perceived need, and they do not generally entail a strategic goal such as women's emancipation or gender equality" (1990: 25).

My portrayal of the DM suggests that the specialized delegacias were created by feminists with strategic interests in mind, but largely carried out by policewomen enacting practical gender interests. This would seem to be consistent with Alvarez's own employment of the terms when she writes, "[W]omen's organizations that seek to advance *strategic* gender interests are conceptualized as *feminist*," and "Women's groups . . . which advance *practical* gender interests are conceptualized as *feminine* organizations" (1990: 25; also Molyneux 1985).

In general, feminist and police activities do configure, respectively, along these lines. I would argue, however, that it is not constructive automatically to equate "strategic" with feminist and "practical" with feminine. Such equations overlook the fact that there are people—a minority, albeit growing—

with strategic perspectives in the DM, and that actions are carried out there with strategic intent. Since the bearers of these "gender progressive" lines themselves often eschew feminism (here the former *delegada titular* Iracema is again a case in point), to suggest that they are *really* feminist people or feminist actions ignores the fact that Brazilian feminism is a specific historical movement, associated more with participation than with belief. Brazilian feminism has a particular history that, problematically, has involved strong (middle) class associations (Alvarez 1990: 25). It may not be realistic to await a mass conversion of Salvador's policewomen to feminism per se. Nonetheless, "strategic" or "gender progressive" perspectives do exist in the DM and can be supported by the women's movement to positive result.

This is where hegemony enters the picture. Despite the problems Brazilian feminism has with de facto class exclusiveness, a pluralistic feminism currently offers the most broadly based, articulated, and "strategic" potential to combat women's oppression. As the policewoman Vânia acknowledged, such a perspective offers much of potential value for those working in the democratizing state's "women's institutions." A task for analysts, then, is to work to understand the mechanisms that constrain or altogether preclude the incorporation of feminist perspectives in some places, among some groups of people.

Standardized hegemonic femininity acts conservatively, resisting radical alteration of gender relations. In this sense, it in fact is incompatible with an "*assumida,*" an assumed feminist stance. The construction and deployment of standardized hegemonic femininity is not the exclusive domain of women; in fact, one could argue that such currents of femininity are more often directed by those—male and female alike—who have the most to lose from counter-hegemonic forms of femininity, such as those that incorporate feminist perspectives and identifications. Efforts of the military in the 1960s and 1970s to deploy conservative women as mothers and daughters protecting the status quo are a case in point. Of course, as nearly any Brazilian feminist will insist, femininities are altogether possible and practicable that are neither inherently conservative, hegemonically complicit, nor preclusive to feminism. We might read policewomen's power-painted-pink as apologetic in one moment, but in another it might act as a re-appropriation of the force of femininity for non-hegemonic ends. Such "reappropriation" of femininity's symbolic force away from hegemonic interests threatens destabilization—away from a femininity that serves primarily as a complement to hegemonic masculinity (Connell 1995), or as Hearn (2004) prefers, to a hegemony of men themselves.

In the most recent period in Bahia (1998–2005), former state governor Antonio Carlos Magalhães has retained great influence in Bahian politics, currently as one of Bahia's national senators, and managing to get elected two of his protégés, César Borges (1999–2002) and Paulo Souto (1995–1998, reelected in 2002 and currently in office) to the governorship. All are members of the PFL (Partido do Frente Liberal), a center-right party. This partisan continuity has allowed the DM's successor delegada titular, Isabel Alice Jesus de Pinho, a stable foundation within the state government, from which she has ably led the DM since 1996.

Doutora Isabel Alice is a tall, formidable woman (it is Dr^a. Isabel who interrogates the accused man in figure 8) who can also come across as approachable and good-humored. Isabel's presence appears to have galvanized esprit de corps, possibly because she has become much closer to a core of key personnel; she and Chief of Investigations Tânia Mendonça, who began at the DM at its inception, form a particularly effective team. Over the course of her tenure, Isabel's tenacious commitment to forging ties with women's movement activists and activities has eroded their political differences, as well as shored up her own identification with her work as feminist. This process has been aided, in turn, by the consolidation of feminist, civil society representation within state organs, for during Isabel's direction of the DM both the state and municipal councils on women's rights have moved from mere formalities on paper to active and influential bodies.[19]

These circumstances allowed Isabel to spearhead an expansion and relocation of the DM to a larger, autonomous site in Engenho Velho de Brotas, a sprawling, diverse residential neighborhood still centrally located. The new station, pictured in figure 9, is completely computerized; boasts a roomy waiting room with television; relatively private stalls for filing complaints; a two-way mirror for anonymous line-ups; a library with archives; a small auditorium for speakers, seminars, and performances; and finally, ample office space for social work consultations, hearings, and administrative and clerical needs. Isabel and Tânia proudly shared that in 2006 Salvador's DM was referred to as the *modelo nacional* (national model) at police conventions. This accomplishment resulted only through their and others' painstakingly work toward its building. The first wrangle came from Bahia's first female chief of police (Delegada Chefe Katia de Alves, legendary for her strong-arm leadership style in the vicinity near the Alto do Mungongo

Figure 9. The new DEAM facility in Salvador, inaugurated in 2004, is widely viewed as a model for the rest of Brazil. Photo by Sarah Hautzinger.

before being promoted). Doutora Isabel had to convince Kátia that looking at the DM as a low-priority station because it didn't yield "*resultados*" (results)—in terms of apprehending prisoners—was wrongheaded. Given proper facilities and staffing, the Delegacia da Mulher, Isabel argued, offered potential to "protect and serve" preventively, in a way that couldn't be registered by numbers of detainees.

After securing approval and funding for the new building, Doutora Isabel and DM police traveled after work hours from the multi-*delegacia* complex in Barris to the new site, working with construction workers to alter blueprints for better functioning. With the inauguration of the new station in 2004, the DM began a period that comes closer to fulfilling its promise than any time since its creation. Shortly thereafter, the delegacia instituted Disque-Denúncia (Dial-Denounce), a statewide, twenty-four-hour hotline for violence against women reports staffed at the Salvador station. Salvador's women's police enjoy measurable strides forward; a proliferation of other organizations lends diffuse support. By 2006 I found a functioning referral center (Centro de Atendimento à Mulher Loreta

Valadares) and shelter accommodating seventy-five women and their families (Casa Mulher Cidadão, Citizen Women's House, in a separate, secret location).[20] A growing number of state organs and NGOs were serving women seeking free legal aid, women victims of sexual violence, Brazilian women trafficked to Europe, women with AIDS, women with perinatal needs, or women wanting to organize in the poor, outlying *periferia*.

These multidirectional developments mark an undeniable boon for the DM project in Bahia, and yet as of 2005, Delegada Titular Isabel was far from satisfied. Having emerged from brokering an entire preventive policing vision to the state's public security administration, Isabel now looked to greater involvement and leadership from the women's movement with an impatience reminiscent, to my ear, of the way women's movement activists once spoke of the policewomen. Her plan for adjusting the way the DM attends to the public was three-pronged: to disseminate information about human rights and how to enact them; to promote more public-education discussions about violence and to reinforce the value of denouncing it; and to partner much more actively with the women's movement, using the theater and library in the *delegacia* in particular to share information, train police and other service providers, and strategize further institutional responses. She voiced frustration with the women's movement: with the notable exception of Sílvia de Aquino (2001; also a scholar Núcleo de Estudos Interdisciplinares sobre a Mulher at UFBa, my Bahian affiliation), she felt the ball was in feminists' collective court, and *militantes* (activists) just weren't stepping up.

In mid-2006, the announcement that an additional eight Delegacias da Mulher would be installed in the metropolitan area was taken as a vindication of what police had long claimed that meeting the civilian need for DM services actually required. As this work goes to press, a proposal is on the table to convert Salvador's new DM to a *departmento,* inclusive of the *delegacia* but also coordinating the four state-wide DMs already in existence and the anticipated metro-area additions. Attaining department status would be likely to facilitate Isabel's goal of creating a public space affording bridge-building and partnership with the women's movement, which after all tends to be composed of students and researchers working in a professionalized vein of feminism.

To sum up, the Delegacias da Mulher operate squarely within conventional police hierarchies and are subject to the variable competence, charisma, and commitments of the women who lead them, the whims of elected officials, and the vicissitudes of historical moments. Nationwide, with few exceptions, the early DMs received little "special" organizational treatment (that is, there was little attempt, or opportunity, to recruit interested police who specifically chose the assignment, or to avoid rotating such police to other delegacias). The specific climate in which female solidarity was supposed to thrive was left to serendipity: much depended upon the personalities involved, and particularly that of the *delegada titular*. In Salvador, the difference between effective leaders like Iracema, Célia, and especially Isabel on the one hand, and incompetent leadership on the other, may indeed suggest a structure overly reliant upon charismatic authority. However, with the passage of twenty years, policewomen have cultured their own, distinct involvement with and ownership of the *delegacia* project, thereby creating an atmosphere that in many respects *is* uniquely specialized and supportive to women.

ENGENDERING OR UNGENDERING THE POLICE?

Feminist scholarship in the 1990s significantly increased scholars' attentiveness to how lines of affiliation and identification drawn by gender are cross-cut and qualified by such social distinctions as class, race, and occupation. Since 1990, when I began this investigation, I have looked to feminist thought to guide my interpretations of Brazil's gendered policing experiment with mixed and often contradictory results. At that time, feminist anthropological work on gender (like that in many other fields) was primarily concerned with anti-essentialist goals. This meant that rather than treating all women's experiences as arising out of some common feminine "essence," or assuming that women constituted some unitary female "sex-class" (Moore 1988: 198), scholars sought to contextualize the variability of women's experiences. Similarly, they described the immense crosscultural differences in ways such categories as women and men were constructed, as well as multiple transgender categories outside or between women-men binaries (e.g., di Leonardo 1991; Collier and Yanagisako 1987; Yanagisako and Delaney 1995; Strathern 1988; Nanda 1990).

Work arising out of these trends tended in two general directions. Some authors abandoned the idea of "women" as a legitimate framework for analysis, whereas others continued to treat women as an adequate foundation for a unified feminist method. At worst, the former trend undermined any basis for feminist analysis or politics, and the latter trend often did not sufficiently address ways in which differences other than gender weighed in. I hope here to have avoided both these failings and contributed to the growing body of scholarship that successfully finds the middle ground—asserting that women can share experiences and struggles across class, ethnic, and occupational lines, but demonstrating how, when, and whether this occurs ethnographically, rather than assuming it.

This chapter has reviewed the specific circumstances that initially constrained the incorporation of feminism and femininity into a combined ideology that could most effectively aid Brazilian police in combating violence against women. These can be summed up as, first, an assumption of female-female affinity that many policewomen felt that ultimately worked against their career goals and, by association, their ability to attend to women in need of police services. Second, the propagation of a gender ideology in which femininity and feminism are represented as mutually exclusive, thereby making it especially problematic for policewomen (whose femininity is already seen as partially "compromised" by their occupation) to be receptive to feminist perspectives.

The "engendering" of the police has been celebrated as a way of intervening in a police subculture unreceptive to women's perspectives or interests, as in the title to Cecilia MacDowell Santos's (2004) article, "En-gendering the Police: Women's Police Stations and Feminism in São Paulo."[21] "Engendering" in such contexts has generally meant acknowledging that police organizations have never been gender neutral, and unmasking the degree to which police power must be gendered masculine in order to be effective or legitimate.

Significantly, however, many policewomen have rejected the engendering of their work and occupational identities. One way to understand their rejection is this: engendering specialized police work, without transforming the way that power and politics are already gendered masculine in Brazilian society, makes individual policewomen come out the losers. This sort of dynamic is what Peterson and Runyan have in mind when they advocate "ungendering power and politics":

The gendered division of power constructs power and politics as definitively masculine. It presupposes a definition of power as "power over," like Robert Dahl's classic definition of power as the ability of A to get B to do something that B would not otherwise do. So defined, power emphasizes control of materials, especially military resources, and a willingness to use them to enforce one's preferences. But this narrow definition obscures how other dimensions of social reality—moral commitments, ethnic allegiances, and sociopolitical ideologies—shape how power works and who is empowered. It is also masculinist to the extent that it presupposes male-as-norm constructions of strength, competition, aggression and coercion and because it focuses on power understood only in terms of the public sphere activities that are dominated by men. (1994: 40)

In terms of practical gender interests, they suggest, power can be ungendered by increasing the number of women in power, varying available paths to power, and valuing women's experiences as dimensions for leadership. In terms of strategic gender interests, they call for a "transform[ation] in the masculinist definition of power, expanding it from 'power-over' to 'power-to' or empowerment. This involves denaturalizing, deglorifying, and delegitimizing coercive power as it is exercised at all levels—from interpersonal, domestic politics to international, world politics. It also involves undermining gendered dichotomies that identify masculinity, power, leadership, and autonomy with public sphere politics and femininity, passivity, care-taking and dependence with an apolitical private sphere" (1994: 41).

One could argue that the differences between "engendering" versus "ungendering" power are merely semantic, but I would counter that for the individual policewomen speaking in this chapter that they are not. These policewomen's assignments were engendered before power in policing had been ungendered, despite what they had been told. As a result, they often felt they came out holding the short sticks, more disempowered than empowered. Only when police, over time, were able to take ownership of the DM project, and recognize the strategic returns in partnering with civil society and feminist activists in particular, did they begin to produce a version of "engendered" policing that served both their own stated goals and those of the women seeking their help.

"Engendering" versus "ungendering" police work need not be an either/or proposition, and indeed each process can ideally amplify the other; perhaps engendering (as in the creation of the DMs) is an important first step toward gradual ungendering (incorporating more women throughout the force and men in gender-specialized policing). What individual policewomen's voices make clear is this: no universal women's interests exist such that each and every individual woman representative of state power can be expected to champion, or to benefit from, gender policy reforms. As Mtintso (2003) commented, women's particular positioning must be weighed "beyond false sisterhood and rhetoric. . . . Seeing patriarchy as universal and amenable to simplistic solutions derails the agenda of transformation," and it is full-scale gender transformation that needs to be kept in sight.

Conclusion and Epilogue

RUTH LANDES'S TRANSNATIONAL feminist designation of Salvador da Bahia as "The City of Women" had mixed effects. On the one hand, she misrepresented evidence of men's centrality in a way that contributed to their marginalization; on the other, she valorized a local, Bahian form of feminized power, which today continues to represent significant symbolic, cultural, and occasionally social and political capital. I have argued, in parallel, that such forms of capital can serve as important resources for Bahian women as they navigate, and articulate their resistance to, violence and domination.

It is fair, therefore, to ask about the implications of this book's transnational feminist strategy of valorizing Bahian women's agency, and in specific cases, their escape and autonomy from men's control. Even as the impact of men's physical aggression and domination remain central, I've also made much of women's indomitability, and especially those who opt in diverse ways for separation and divorce from men. I have suggested that organized manifestations of women revolting from, and being revolted by, men's dominance and violence hold mythological proportions and invoke the "rival gendered outcomes" (Matory 1994: 25) represented by "women of Ogum," who separate from men, and "women of Xangô," who are legitimized through wifeliness, thus concurring with J. Lorand Matory's (1994: 240) expectation that these historical Oyo-Yoruban dynamics of separation versus wifeliness hold resonance for gender in contemporary Bahia. Whether in female-chauvinist lines of women kin like Yancí's, or in separate women police expected to make over cultural pockets inside the Brazilian state apparatus, women's escape and autonomy from rule by men has guided my effort to tie together two very different field sites, within the same City of Women.

INVERSION IN BRAZILIAN CULTURE: TROPE OR RUSE?

Salvador's many indomitable women citizens and its champions-of-women police, both of which appear to invert conventional Brazilian gender hierarchies, may draw interest for the same reason that other cultural instances of inversion have been so much of interest to students of Brazilian culture. Carnaval is the first and preeminent example: the common people become the powerful (in Salvador the festival is kicked off by the city mayor literally handing the symbolic "keys to the city" to Rei Momo, a buffoonish clown), and the profane is imbued with the sacred (flirting and adultery, drinking, drug use, and other illicit or prohibited behaviors are celebrated). One analyst extols the rejection of a unitary erotic version in Carnaval; "Nothing is ever quite what it appears to be" (Parker 1991: 164), and another focuses on the "anything goes" *(vale tudo)* aspects of Carnaval, arguing that it offers a reprieve from the suffocating weight of authoritarian logic and prescribed social norms (Linger 1992, 1993). Carnaval, in this vision, offers opportunities to defy officialdom and, potentially, to ignite rebellion.

Second, the logic of possession in Candomblé further illustrates how inversion may blur fixed differences and hierarchies, here with highly gendered meanings. Being possessed or "mounted" by an *orixá*, like being penetrated in sex, is inherently feminizing; one is by definition an *iaô*, a wife, of the saints, even if the *orixá* is female and the human "horse" male. Males who "receive saint" are structured into a ceremonially wifely role, feminized in a way that is both powerful and prestigious within Candomblé worlds, though this can operate independently of their secular sexuality or gender identity (Johnson 2002: 44; Matory 2005: 234). At the same time, a masculine *orixá* possessing a woman temporarily bestows masculinity upon her, and this masculinization may have more enduring effects within a *família de santo* (the Candomblé family), for a woman "of" Ogum, Xangô, or other powerful masculine *orixás* would in all probability be a powerful person in her community.

A third area where inversion has been valued for expressing liberatory and

subversive potential involves *travestis,* cross-dressing or transgendered biological males who perform feminized identities in speech, dress, and bodily modifications such as silicone injections. Most work as prostitutes, and
are, in theory, paid for allowing themselves to be penetrated, hence being
doubly feminized. However, most *travestis* reject surgical sex changes,
retaining their penises and saying they are vital to their livelihoods, as cus-
tomers frequently request to be penetrated (Oliveira 1994; Silva 1993;
Cornwall 1994; Kulick 1998).

The point to be taken from these illustrations is that Brazilians, and the
understandings of their culture as expounded by Brazilianist scholars,
betray keen interest in inversions of oppositional binaries. Brazilian culture
practices, and understandings about them, can also appear essentialist, and
as subscribing to the structuralist presumptions about the existence of
"things" like masculinity and femininity, house and street, sacred and profane; composed of genuinely distinct essences, they are understood, in
some sense, to be "out there," as ontological facts. That said, inversion
dynamics present individual actors with ways to subvert being bound to
binary, essentialist prisons in strictly dichotomous ways. Rather, actors can
draw on multiple gender binaries for high-risk "deep play" (Geertz 1973:
432–33), between and across gender and other binaries, recombining elements and avoiding being pigeon-holed.

Probably no scholar is more closely identified with attention to binary
arrangements and inversions in Brazilian culture than Roberto DaMatta.
His writings on social interaction, focused around the question "Do you
know to whom you are speaking?" *(Você sabe com quem está falando?)* (1991:
189), show how that question functions to put each in his or her place. It
invokes the code of persons, in which one is only humanized if one is
known personally to others. In the code of persons, identity is always
enmeshed and relational, and is associated with cultural values such as
complementarity, respect, honor, and hierarchical privilege. Contrasting
this value set is the code of individuals, based upon egalitarianism, rule of
impartial law, anonymity, and competition. The code of persons tolerates
ascribed inequality and evades the law through personalism and patronage;
at the same time, one's placement in a social context is unique, personal,
and imbued with human relatedness. Patronage and *dando jeitos* (string-
pulling; Barbosa 1995)[1] are the means through which the roughest edges are
sanded away and the starkest aspects of inequality are softened. The code
of individuals, by contrast, is less notable for on-the-ground human maneu-
vers through which actors better their lots or for the systemic imperatives

that codify equality: in a system that is impartial and just, asking for a *jeit-inho* is asking for favoritism and tantamount to corruption. Because an operative code of individuals requires a legitimate state and ubiquitous rule of law, a code of individuals, arguably, has remained largely unrealized in Brazil, even as authoritarian rule gave way to democratic rule. For DaMatta, Brazil's "double code" comprises two distinct logics existing in dialogic tension (1991: 189). The women's police stations spell a clear departure here, as they manifest a conscious, feminist upholding of a redemocratized version of the code of individuals. At the same time, the pulls policewomen experienced to fight *marginais* but not-family-men "persons," as well as to integrate as familiar (masculinized) police officers into the hierarchy, demonstrate the legacy of the code of persons.

At their best, DaMatta's interpretations go beyond dichotomous contrasts, however. He draws heavily on Louis Dumont's notions of encompassment, in which "one social group or idea includes its opposite at a higher level" (Hess and DaMatta 1995: 11). DaMatta offers the example of another of Bahian novelist Jorge Amado's (1969) characters, the *baiana* Dona Flor.[2] Dona Flor, who rivaled Gabriela in culinary and sexual sensuality, refused to choose between the ghost of her deceased husband Vadinho (representative of tradition, disorder, and "street spirit") and her new husband Teodoro (representative of modernity, order, clarity, and correctness). For DaMatta, Dona Flor becomes "the incarnation not of conflict (which would force her to choose individualistically between one and the other) but the relation itself. . . . Dona Flor says that the relation among different formal systems is possible, revealing mysteries unknown to Western sociology. . . . [This] allows for the possibility of encompassment by the relation and not by the forces in conflict" (DaMatta 1995: 283). In this way, DaMatta lays out his version of an ambiguous, quintessentially Brazilian both-and option, interestingly engraved upon the life of a woman whose preferred lover, her first husband Vadinho, was known to beat her. It is through such uses of encompassment that DaMatta claims to move beyond conservative analyses that reify binaries, and instead arrive at multiplicity, mediations, play, and ambiguity.

DaMatta's use of encompassment is directly relevant to United States–Brazil ethnographic discourses, because he specifically casts the United States as Teodoro, or as synonymous with the "modern," egalitarian, rational element. Brazil, in turn, is lusty, impulsive Vadinho on the one hand, but also Brazil is Dona Flor, encompassing the traditional and modern, meditating between the two and arriving at an ambiguity that DaMatta celebrates. Dona Flor as Brazil, as double code and both-and, "tempts us with the possibility of legitimating ambiguity" and "recuperates everything that the history of the West since Luther has rejected with force, energy and brutality". (1995: 283).

DaMatta's celebratory tone is matched in volume by his irritation at North Americans' inability to grasp what they perceive as the out-of-placeness, the "apparently prelogical untidiness" of such things as liberal ideas coexisting alongside systems of patronage or favoritism. He writes: "In the United States . . . the presence of two contradictory ideas presupposes a homogeneous setting wherein conflictive coexistence is its own 'natural' resolution. But in Brazil and in the rest of Latin America contradiction merely engenders inflamed speeches in public and lively sessions of anecdotes at home" (1995: 275). DaMatta's problem with an incapacity to switch between contrasting ideologies and codes is that it allows conflict to be the endpoint; instead, he strives to move beyond "a sociology of interests and individuals when in fact we live in societies where they coexist with friends, relatives, *compadres,* and *jeitinhos* [little string-pulls]" (1995: 284; also DaMatta 1991 and 1982). In theoretical terms, this impulse is functionalist: the desire to explain how Brazilians manage to get along and, ideally, to help them to get along still better.

In sum, DaMatta can be read as forwarding ambiguity—that mediated, encompassed result of the dialectical tension of Brazil's double code—as Brazil's root metaphor. For him, this ambiguity humanizes, providing room for maneuvering, play, and recombinant elements.[3]

"MYTHS THAT BRAZILIANS ENJOY TELLING ONE ANOTHER ABOUT THEMSELVES"

In his book on *travestis* in Salvador, Don Kulick notes that the three examples of inversion presented above are often related to one another in analyses of Brazilian society: the "gendered inversion [of *travestis*] is usually tied to other instances of inversion, such as men dressing up in female clothes during Carnaval, the male homosexual component in the Afro-Brazilian religion candomblé, and the androgynous personae of several of Brazil's most famous singers and songwriters. The conclusion is often that Brazilian society continually undermines and transcends its dour Roman Catholic patriarchal inheritance with displays and tolerance of behavior and persons that directly challenge that inheritance" (1998: 9). Although Kulick allows that "travestis could productively be analyzed as instances of a larger phenomenon of inversion," he rejects the focus on inversion for understanding the travestis themselves. "In my view, the focus on inversion is a ruse—it is part of an elaborate myth that Brazilians enjoy telling one another about themselves, in an attempt to convince themselves and others that they are more liberated, tolerant and hip than they really are" (1998: 9).

Travestis seem to risk a great deal in order to "perfect" femininity: they modify their bodies in ways that can cause physical illness (through injecting contaminated silicone), become permanent objects of social stigma, and are perpetually vulnerable to violent attacks. They are generally not willing to go so far, however, as to risk Carnaval frolicking. Along with others, Kulick details ways in which Carnaval is anything but liberating for the *travestis* themselves, who do not participate because they find themselves "extremely vulnerable to harassment and violence" (1998: 37).

Similarly, while Carnaval may liberate expressions of *femininity,* Nancy Scheper-Hughes observes that most of these expressions remain the prerogatives of cross-dressing (just for Carnaval), straight men; the poor *women* she worked with could not afford the time, energy, or resources to "play" Carnaval, calling it "nonsense" and "entertainment for men and children" (1992: 495). Along similar lines, Daniel Linger (1992), despite elaborating the "anything goes" ideology of Carnaval, takes still greater pains to detail how readily events could spill over into nonritualized, destructive, violent *brigas,* in the aftermath of which the big shots, the privileged, still called the shots. Yancí, Zizi, and other women in the Mungongo see Carnaval as an important time to make money, often triggering post-Carnaval health crises from overwork.

Finally, Dolores Shapiro (1995) joins the questioning about how liberatory the interpenetrations involved in Candomblé, the third area of inversion discussed, are for those most marginalized in society. She found that although whiter and more middle-class clients may cede superior force to the *trabalhos* (spells) of blacker, poorer Candomblé practitioners in their most dire hour of need, this did not have the commensurate effect of elevating the social status or power of these religious specialists.

In this light, are the Yancí's in the City of Women, and DM policewomen as avenging viragoes, just more myths Brazilians (and transnational feminist scholars) enjoy telling one another about themselves?

As with the discussion of Marianismo and "Iansā-ísmo" in chapter 1, it is fair to ask whether the ideologies about both DM policewomen and poor Afro-Bahian women as powerful actors are merely false consciousness. Do they delude women and prevent them from confronting the reality of their oppression? Or do they constitute real reserves of and for power, enabling them to overcome subordination?

This work does not arrive at a simple yes-or-no conclusion to this question but rejects a wholesale false-consciousness reading and affirms that self-concepts regarding agency, women's power, and the unacceptability of men's coercive violence indeed pose significant resources. Illustrating women deploying such resources helps avoid overdetermined portrayals about the intransigence, or uniform absoluteness, of Brazilian patriarchy. Individual actors such as Yancí, or Madalena the "Manbeater" policewoman, are border-crossers, and there is much "bargaining with patriarchy" gender-play that goes into their gendered self-productions. That said, beyond the individual level, the tenacity of the gender-specialization principle of social organization behind the Delegacia da Mulher project departs significantly from DaMatta's notion of encompassment. In the DMs, contradictions are *not* harmonized and it is conflict, *not* relationship, that typically becomes the endpoint. For confronting gender-based violence in Brazil, it appears that *jeitinhos* [little string-pulls] and reconciliations are not enough. Rather, Brazilians working against gendered violence appear committed for the long haul to a path where tangible gendered conflicts of interest on the interpersonal, microscopic level are reflected, in a structural and stabilized fashion, at the macroscopic level of state organization, through preserving the gender separation and specialization. The convictions gained through two decades of experience suggest that these explicitly oppositional, and even radicalizing, elements are essential for the mass-scale intervention, begun in 1985, to continue well into the twenty-first century.

THE DELEGACIAS DA MULHER AND THE GENDERING OF CITIZENSHIP

The Delegacia da Mulher project began, in the minds of its inventors, as one plank in a bridge toward a major social transformation. Two decades and many obstacles and missteps later, the project finds critical sources of fortification. Internally, policewomen grow increasingly identified with and committed to the project. Externally, DM police cultivate stronger relationships with a burgeoning network of cognate state organs, women's movement groups, and NGOs responding to gender-based violence.

This pivotal inroad has been made possible, I have argued, because gender relations in Brazil are changing with a rapidity that amounts to massive social upheaval, potentially constituting a reorganization across a single social distinction unprecedented in Brazilian history. Shifting gender organization of labor, household authority distribution, and individual senses of entitlement and empowerment catalyze new patterns of conflict, some more constructive and some more destructive. This work has called contestatory violence those patterns in which power struggle characterizes a relationship's violence more accurately than does patriarchal domination, and suggested that such dynamics appear to be on the rise. Multiple currents and high levels of gendered violence select for the "success" of institutions such as the DMs (successful in the sense of demand far outstripping expectations) precisely because they ratify a form of Brazilian citizenship that is not neutral, but rather always gendered, classed, and raced.

In Brazil, liberal statecraft produced the constitutional embryo of individualism and citizens rights that are necessary preconditions for the fulfillment of feminist goals. The DMs, however, represent a necessary departure from the neutral citizen model of classical liberalism. I say "necessary" because, in patriarchal societies, citizenship and state in fact cannot be neutrally conceived. "Neutrality" defaults, as feminist theorist Catherine MacKinnon puts it, to a "male" state, "in the feminist sense: the law sees and treats women the way men see and treat women" (1989: 161–162). MacKinnon continues, "The liberal state coercively and authoritatively reconstitutes the social order in the interests of men as a gender—through its legitimating norms, forms, relation to society, and substantive policies" (1989: 162). The DMs, by contrast, embody feminists' convictions about women's ability, and need, to build tailored, semiseparatist state subcultures within a broader liberal framework, a notably more radical notion. The DMs thus demonstrate how state organs can receive important "training" from social movements, partisan politics, and NGOs, any of which may insinuate radical elements, including separatist strategies (Alvarez 1998; Berkovitz 1999; Ramirez, Soysal, and Shanahan 1997). Ideally, a progressive democratic state draws from both liberal and radical elements, each in turn reinforcing the other, enabling meaningful progress in arresting gender-based violence.

My assertion that the DMs are path-breaking for Brazil is corroborated by the spate of similar state institutions being created in their wake: police stations attending exclusively to children and youth are now present throughout the country, and São Paulo and Rio de Janeiro have maintained police stations specialized in racial crimes since 1993 and 1995, respectively. In Bahia, the *movimento negro* (black movement) has thus far succeeded in obtaining a new *promotoria* (state prosecutor's office) dedicated to investigating racial crimes but continues to clamor for a specialized *delegacia,* as well as for representation focused on racial crimes within the Public Ministry.[4]

Much of my previous writing on the DMs disparaged the project's first decade plus as woefully flawed. Gladly, I can conclude *Violence in the City of Women* on a more optimistic note, reporting back commendable, steady progress in this newly reborn democracy's bold antiviolence experiment. Although not quite the Amazonian heroes fostered in the Brazilian imaginary, the DMs may rightly provide Brazilians with solace and encouragement, a silver lining behind the disillusioning dark clouds of multiple corruption scandals spanning all five democratically elected presidential administrations since 1985, and the ravages neoliberal reforms have dealt to democratic development, the extension of rule of law, and social services for Brazilians more generally.

That DMs are coming closer to fulfilling their original promise augurs well, surely, for their ultimate potential as key collaborators in radical gender transformation. And yet, social transformation in Brazil has historically been a difficult proposition. Smooth transitions, from colony to empire to republic to its developing, urbanizing present, without revolutions or civil war, have tended to leave the distribution of power by class, color, and gender intact as Brazil has moved from one historical period to the next, particularly in the northeast region. On a cultural level, the emergence of women as a citizen's constituency with strong voice, demands, and influence represents as significant a social and cultural shift as any in Brazilian history. Democratization and globalization, as simultaneous forces shaping Brazilian social movements, have allowed critical connections to develop between women's rights and human rights on the one hand, and newly wrought citizen's rights on the other. When the Delegacias da Mulher brandish their newest slogan, "You can be the Spoon," in response to the old adage, "In fights between husband and wife, don't dip your spoon," a wholly different version of citizenship is being articulated, with significance and potential utility far beyond gender politics. For once, being merely an "*indivíduo*"—and individual Brazilian citizen—is upheld as being deserving of protection, even in the absence of personalistic ties.

SALVADOR'S DELEGACIA DA MULHER: A FINAL SCENE

The most recent *audiência* (hearing) I listened in on at the Delegacia da Mulher in Salvador was in 2005, and it was presided over by none other than Chief of Investigations Tânia Mendonça, Doutora Isabel Alice's right-hand woman at the DM (and pictured in the doorway in figure 8).

The complainant filed charges after the fourth time she was beaten by her partner. Tânia began addressing the complainant.

"So, he's your father, is he?" The complainant demurred, shaking her head no.

"Ah—then, you're his property," Tânia continued, nodding rhetorically.

Tânia, at ease in the silence following this question, now turned to the young man. "So, how *was* it that you became her father?" To his stony non-response, she continued, "Oh—do you have a memory problem? Explain it to me, because at times I don't understand these things clearly." Tânia's got her "Lieutenant Colombo" routine down pat, where she feigns thick-headedness like the detective of American television fame.

After an uncomfortable pause, he grudgingly offered, "It's just that, she passed in front of my house with another man, knowing that I still like her, and drinking . . ."

To Tânia's skeptical pursed lips and lowered brow, he adds, "At times we [*a gente*] do something stupid; we only think afterward."

Tânia has turned to face the computer, beginning to fill in the hearing's record. The man resolves, "It's not going to happen again. This time was bad enough."

Tânia assures him that his penalty this time—possible public service and a contribution of a *cesta básica* (food staples basket), as the case is being expedited on to the Jecrim system—will be nothing compared to what he'll face if he comes back to the DM. Jail time would be a given, she warned.

Viewing a resolution in sight, the man presses his perspective. "But I do think she should behave herself better, as a mother."

"Fine," Tânia replies without missing a beat. "But one error doesn't excuse another. *Your* error was a *crime*."

"But doesn't she have to feed them right? Isn't that part of the agreement?"

"That may be," Tânia parried. "But we're not here questioning her maternal performance, but *your* behavior. The thing that gets me is, you did this—you beat her!—just to *dar satisfação* [account for yourself] to your friends. But *they* aren't there beating their wives, that I know of. What I know is *you* are sitting here because *you* did. The jail cells are downstairs, ready for you, if you want to try it again."

Completing the forms on the computer, Tânia admonishes the man when he can't tell her his (CPF) identity number from memory. "You don't know your identity number? *Puxa,* I know all mine—my CPF, my address, phone, insurance numbers. . . . That's kind of sad that you don't, don't you think?"

A look of slow satisfaction has spread across the complainant's face. She appears to feel that this session will accomplish what she needs, to put him in his place and remove her from physical danger. Although aspects of her respectability and decency as a woman and mother had indeed been questioned in the DM, they were only raised by her estranged partner; specialized police never once recognized or legitimized them as relevant to the criminal transgression at hand.

Tânia, a DM veteran of nearly twenty years, has been hearing *audiências* with this impregnable level of focus and clarity for quite some time. It's taken two decades, however, for exchanges like this one to become representative of the quality of police work performed at the Salvador DM in general. Tânia is both a reflection of, and a powerful agent in creating, a DM that has come full circle. With most of her colleagues, she has come to embrace the DM mission as one chosen, and no longer one imposed from without. She tells me of visiting and speaking at various groups' gatherings, and betrays special intrigue when catching me up on a wrangle about whether transgendered individuals (mostly male-to-female *travestis*) should receive services at the DM. Tânia concludes that—although she's still thinking about it—remaining clear on who constitutes a "woman" in Brazil needs to remain clearly defined, and failing to do so blurs the DMs' mission. At the same time, she is pleased to report that the validity of male police working in the DM is now being officialized, and that recent documents underline this as a boon rather than a deficit, a notion she has always supported. In other words, on the issue of there being citizens gendered "women" in very particular ways that merit the DM's services, Tânia voices stalwart commitment to sustaining a more radical, *en*gendered women-complainants-only platform. But regarding who can assist in delivering specialized professional law enforcement, she embraces a more liberal, *un*gendering stance, which entails not "letting male police off the hook," or suggesting that, properly trained, they are any less equipped to play valuable roles in DMs than their female counterparts. That said, none of the long-timer policewomen at the DM in Salvador would countenance male leadership of the station.

Far from the civil servant once surrounded by colleagues who resented the yokes plopped onto their shoulders, Tânia and the team she leads are on board, proud of accomplishments, ambitious about new goals, and enduringly, energizingly outraged about men's violence against women. She will continue to be a part of pioneering new areas of preventive policing, charting the terrain through which women and other disadvantaged social groups can demand that their specific vulnerabilities be recognized and rights be defended through enacted democratic citizenship and rule of law.

ALMIRO AND THE BOMFIM FAMILY

The phone in Colorado Springs would ring, someone would pick it up, and it would disconnect. Then it would ring again, and Almiro would say, "*Minha madrinha*" (my godmother).

"Almiro?" I'd exclaim.

He would give me a number, and I'd call it right back. Or sometimes, he didn't have any time on a prepaid calling card to say anything, so I would call whichever public pay phone number had last worked and hope he'd answer.

These calls are sliced through with the precarious infrastructure that engulfs my godson's life. Literally, the exchanges I share below often consisted of my having to call back six, eight, or ten times because the connection would "fall" *(cair)* every two minutes, like clockwork.

The phone calls tend to occur at crisis points. In 2001, Almiro tells me Jorginho shows up during a heat wave and tries to take the fan to his other family's house. They try to stop him and he gets so mad he breaks the fan so no one else can use it.

"He's no father to me," Almiro curses. "He's dead to me."

He is so distraught and demoralized, I give in to impulse, and tell him what I've been working on. "I'm going to find a way to bring you to the United States to live with us for a year. It's complicated, but I've been working on it a bit every day, and I am going to find a way." I don't want to raise his hopes falsely, but I'm determined. He needs some time in a different situation.

By the time Almiro calls back just after his birthday in November 2001, alas, things have changed. I feel obligated to tell him, "Since what happened on September eleventh, my *filho*, I don't know. My progress at getting you a visa has stalled, and I'm not sure how it will work, now." I don't tell him that every door now seems to have slammed firmly shut and then been locked.

Over the next three years, the family shares with me plans to use money I've sent to generate income, only to repeatedly face crises that interfere: the need to post bail and pay a lawyer when Almiro's brother Raulino ends up in jail, accused of theft; the money for an industrial sewing machine that Zizi and Yancí would use to work together being appropriated by Yancí without explanation from her. Once, Almiro works himself into near tears of "*vergonha*" (shame) at having to come back to me yet again, saying that things have gone awry with money I've sent, and his plans to for creating steady income have been dashed. "I want you, *senhora,* to come here and see what I've built and be proud of me. But instead I'm ashamed." I correct him: I am proud of him. Period.

Almiro is sixteen years old when he calls me in 2003. He immediately tells me he has some very good news; I can hear the smile on his lips. He announces to me he is *casado,* "married" in the informal-union sense most common in the Mungongo. He puts his *esposa* (wife), Glória, on the phone. Her voice is pitched high, and just tinged with shyness; she sounds very formal and polite, calling me *senhora.* She is fifteen years old.

A short few months later, though, Almiro says he is leaving his relationship with Glória, getting out *(saindo).* The problem? She hits him.

"She's very aggressive, my *madrinha.* The only time I use force with her is when I'm trying to get her off of me *[tirar ela].* This can't be. So, I'm slowly breaking up with her."

Just two days after this conversation, Almiro tells me that he was picked up by the police right after we'd spoken on the phone. He was at the phone booth, finishing talking when they pulled up; they waited and picked him up after we'd hung up.

He was taken to the *delegacia* in his neighborhood and roughed up for three hours, derided as a *bicha* (faggot) until the police gave up, deciding maybe he really wasn't involved in anything. Now back home, he is extremely bruised and sore. "They just assume anyone who lives in the Mungongo is a *marginal,*" he complains bitterly, his voice tight through gritted teeth.

It is 2005 when Almiro picks up the pay phone where he's been waiting for me to call. His voice sounds hollow, shocked.

"Jorge is dead," he tells me. "My brother. Jorge. Dead. He's dead."

Just hours before, Almiro watched his brother Jorge get shot in the head. "He was just lying there, *madrinha,* and the pool of blood—" his voice catches.

The guy who shot him fled, but the police came. Almiro, Raulino, and Jorginho had to hide for hours because, "they'll just beat on anyone they can find; they don't care about the truth of what happened."

That's all the story I can gather, except I ask and am told the murderer's name. I know there's more to it, and later will understand more, but now it's abundantly clear no one wants to explain the whole affair.

Zizi gets on the phone, and after apologizing for having no choice, asks for help with her oldest son's burial costs. I promise to do what I can.

Ten days later, Zizi answers the phone. I ask if they got the money and if everything had worked out with the burial, and Zizi demurs vaguely. "Well, there are still a few things . . ."

She tells me they are leaving the neighborhood. Jorge's murderer has been issuing death threats to the family, and they need to get out. She is taking Almiro and the two grandchildren she's raising to go to her family in São Felix. I think of the five generations of Bomfims who lived out their lives in the Mungongo before Almiro, persisting there through decades of struggle, only now to be ousted now by a form of violence I cannot fully grasp.

"Yes, we're leaving." Zizi continued. "As soon as we can resolve a few matters."

There is a long pause, and then she abruptly hands the phone to Jorginho, which surprises me. I don't talk with him that often anymore, and he is rarely in the Mungongo.

He begins with a very formal and elaborate thank you for my willingness to help them when they were in need. I respond, "*O compadre,* please don't thank me. I only wish I could do more."

Maybe the phone was disconnected, but it almost sounded as though it were suddenly hung up, clacking in the receiver. I wonder whether Zizi and Jorginho were working up to asking for more money, and gave up when I implied I had done what I could.

Still in 2005, just a few months before I am to travel to Bahia, the phone rings twice, stops, then rings again and stops. I call back, and Almiro picks up the phone, sounding more content than I've heard him sound for a while. His mother had gone to her family in São Felix, and he had been living for a time with his father and second wife Gabriela, at her house. I can't imagine what that would have been like for him. But now, he'd joined his mother in São Felix. "It helps her; I am calming for her." I arrange to visit them there during my upcoming trip.

And now, he tells me, he would like to share some good news. Again I heard that smile on his lips. "Glória is pregnant, *madrinha*. I'm going to be a father. And you're going to be a god-grandmother," he said, laughing at his own word play. "She's seven months along. And you have to be the one to name the child."

I pick Almiro up on the street in June 2005 the morning after I arrive in Brazil. He is a tall young man now, bashful and apologetic about the silver rings in both earlobes, until I say I think they look good. We pick up a seven-months pregnant Glória and drive to São Felix to spend the *festas juninhas* (June festivals), which will be punctuated by the roar of endless homemade fireworks *(espadas)* made from soda bottles. They terrorize the children, whom I huddle with inside the houses; the next day on the street, I will see bandages covering several adults' burned legs and arms.

In the afternoon I see deep marks from scratches, now almost healed, on Almiro's cheek. "It was Glória who did this to me, *madrinha,* three months ago," he confided. "I was ashamed to go out because it was clear that my woman was attacking me *[me agredindo]."* Almiro assures me, though, that he's making his best effort with Glória, what with the baby on the way.

Back in the city of Salvador the following week, I discover that Glória's father does not speak with Almiro and he's not welcome at their house. Almiro had tried to intervene in Glória's father beating up her mother, and thus became a *persona non grata* at his in-laws' home. Their immanent parenthood and my visit together seem to constitute an exception to this, though, as I was invited with Almiro to Glória's home and introduced to her mother. Her father entered shortly thereafter, and though everyone ignored him, I said hello and he nodded in response.

A few hours later, I sat slightly behind Glória's father as he reclined on the couch and petted and played with a kitten on his stomach. He may have been conscious of me watching: a moment to show his gentle side to the foreigner and long-time family friend. But eventually, the play turned rough. The kitten batted at Glória's father's hand, claws out. He grasped the small whiskered face with one hand and delivered an audible, sharp slap to it with the other. Glória's father held the face firm as he leveled an authoritative index finger and stared into its eyes. Know your place, kitten.

A year later, in 2006, I return to Bahia with my family, excited to meet Glória and Almiro's child, my "god-granddaughter," whom they have named Hannah. (I'd begged off naming her, saying that was a decision for her parents, but secretly wish they had chosen a less foreign, more Brazilian name.) She is all chubbiness and crinkled smiles; Glória is an attentive mother and Almiro a doting father. Still, Glória laments, Almiro is not around as much as she thought her child's father would be; he stays days on end with his deceased brother Jorge's widow in another neighborhood. I wonder to myself if he's continuing the tradition into a third Bomfim generation of sustaining parallel unions with more than one woman.

Zizi tells me of her plan to remove her remaining children and grand-children from the city once and for all, to "follow a straight path and make an honest living with the sweat of our own brows." But Almiro wants to stay in the neighborhood while he's finishing school and doing a job-training program, and to run a little bar out of the house in the Mungongo, to support Hannah. Zizi asks me to talk to Glória about her extravagant tastes in clothing for herself and the baby; "She rips Almiro apart [*xinga ele tudo*] if there's something he can't buy for them." I worry about Almiro staying in the neighborhood, especially with the implication that the drug dealing has gotten so out of hand that it's no longer safe.

If Almiro's family comes up in conversation, Yancí and Ritinha aver that they don't "wish to speak ill of anyone, so it's better not to say anything." After many rounds of this, one day I mention Almiro and his plan for the bar, and Ritinha looks me square in the eye. "I've always liked Almiro," she says. "More than the rest of his family. But, Sarah—you *do* know what he *does* for a living, don't you?" My fears that Almiro has gotten swept into drug dealing are confirmed. At least he's thought not to be using. I now better understand Glória's taste for expensive clothing, and Zizi's determination to set an "honest" course for the family.

In April 2007, a phone call from Zizi relates the most stunning, devastating news yet. Raulino, Almiro's only living brother, is in jail for murdering his girlfriend. Back in São Felix, where Zizi, Raulino, and the grandchildren are living, Raulino had been involved with a woman whose family disapproved of the relationship. Raulino himself was reportedly trying to end it, as the woman could be very aggressive, but she clung on determinedly. One day, three of her male relatives took him and not only beat him, but also tortured him and raped him with a broom handle. Raulino, who had not been "right in the head" since seeing his brother shot dead two years before, came home with his neck slashed, bleeding profusely, and passed out. He began muttering to himself and repeating to Zizi, "*Mamãe, I'm a man—a man!*" along with his intentions to kill himself. Raulino believes his girlfriend put her relatives up to this (she denied it). He refused to see her when she appeared daily at Zizi's door. One day she insisted and refused to leave, and he went to the door. Zizi heard them talking in hushed voices; then Raulino said he'd be right back, and left with the girlfriend. They never returned.

The next day, the girlfriend's father appeared at dawn, asking if they'd seen his daughter. Upon learning they hadn't, he broke into sobs, saying, "Then, it's true." A young woman's body had been found by the river. A short while later, Raulino was found huddled under a bridge thirty meters over the riverbed, trying to jump. His entire body was covered with knife cuts, apparently from a knife she'd had with her. No one knows yet what happened—it even could have been self-defense. He was taken into custody immediately. A lawyer friend of a friend of mine has offered legal counsel, as the family hopes to pursue an insanity defense. Zizi says, "Life in an insane asylum might be as bad as a prison, but I'm praying not."

Bringing Almiro's family's story up-to-date touches upon a dizzying array of violence: from the international terrorism that kept him from a god-mother's refuge, to the struggles of poverty, to police violence, homophobia, and the criminalization of the poor—it does not stop. Through a semi-vigilante murder of a brother, through death threats to a family, to a new father's face scratched by a new mother, to a father-in-law beating his wife and a son-in-law intervening, to a brother arrested for murder, it continues. Smells from firecrackers that burn skin and sounds of kittens getting slapped just add sensory seasoning.

Almiro, at the end of this story, has become the scratched-and-slapped husband not yet twenty years old, the son-in-law intervening, the drug dealer trying to clothe and feed his daughter and mourning two brothers' lots, all while attending school and work training. His mother used the threat of Salvador's Delegacia da Mulher to prevent his father's hand from falling upon her, and the physical violence between his parents apparently ceased. Meanwhile, other violences gather and press in at his flanks. So far, they are not of his authorship but are assaults he experiences, in complex layers of directness and indirectness, from others.

In the face of this spectrum of violence, some question whether the specialized and even exclusive focus on male-to-female violence as prevails in the DMs is warranted. I disagree, but will point up how the multifarious aggressions a family like Almiro's experience require that all tailored institutional responses be underwritten by shared coherent, comprehensive antiviolence values, practices, and visions. Consensus is widespread that concentrated attention must turn to youth education and services instilling explicitly nonviolent values and practices, and to ameliorating the sharp inequalities that form a backdrop of structural violence in Brazil.

The story of the Bomfim family is probably not typical in any statistically "average" sense, and the many other Bahians' stories in this volume reveal how they are singular in many senses. I tell it at length in this book because I find it so illustrative of a strikingly varied cast of characters. Between the assorted roles they play, family members are found authoring, negotiating, repudiating, intervening in, and deterring, and—not least—plain refusing violence. Their tale struck me as being worth telling in part for Yancí's, and her mother and daughter's, semiseparatist attitudes, grounded in an articulation of Afro-Bahian female superiority. Of course, the stories of Zizi, the injured and victimized wife turned someone-not-to-lay-a-hand-on, and of Jorginho, the once-violent, always passionate self-reformist and irrepressible "wife-maker," ground this inquiry in the poignancies and complexities that any account of couple conflict and violence deserve. Most important, these stories show how the very *idea* of the existence of a DM could be enough to tip events toward a woman's physical integrity.

Zizi, like her mother-in-law Dona Alegrina before her, begins marriage as a wife much younger than her husband. Eventually each will suffer her husband's violence, along with competitive parallel unions with second wives. Until the points when, through widowhood or abandonment, each finds herself leading an extended household flush with grandchildren, they appear contemporary echoes of Sangô-era women, their social beings meaningfully defined through wifeliness. By the end of this story, each finds herself largely consigned to matrifocal networks, less by defiant preference as in Yancí's case, than because widowhood and abandonment are directions Bahian wives and mother's lives can take by default.

There are limits, naturally, to the usefulness of this work's allusions to references to a simplified set of *orixás* as diversified gender archetypes, or gendered dynamics (or "ages") revolving around specific *orixá* complexes. Successive ages in early modern Yoruba-land (present-day Nigeria) are different historical animals than simultaneous, contrasting gendered dynamics in Salvador da Bahia, Brazil, as twentieth becomes twenty-first century. The locations are, in fact, so removed in space and time that what is remarkable is that there is any enduring, related language through which to strike analogies at all. Their significance in this rumination springs from their vivid demonstration of how varied, creative, and historically and culturally embedded the resources are that individual actors call upon to explain and direct their own plights in the face of violence.

VIOLENCE COMES HOME

In drawing this book to a close, I am nagged by lingering concerns about my own potential to do violence, as an author. As this book goes to press, the account of the Delegacia da Mulher in Salvador ends auspiciously. Yet the broader picture for Brazil, for millions of families like my godson

Almiro's, remains disturbing. Relaying updates, in as detailed a form as my professional ethics allow, is difficult—would that I could omit that Almiro has fallen into drug trafficking. I worry that it would be too easy to read this work as a characterization of Brazil, of Bahia, of the Alto do Mungongo, as perniciously violent places. This problem, about how to focus fieldwork on violence without creating pathologizing depictions—"exploit[ing] our hosts' hospitality by exposing a dark side of their culture" (Counts 1999: xviii), and creating bad impressions about good people—has long hindered ethnographers studying the topic. Anthropologists have endeavored, for multiple reasons, to portray "'their' villages in a favorable light" (Brown 1999: 5). Centering selectively on violence makes it difficult to do so.

It is probably obvious that I could write an ethnography about almost any city in the United States, or Brazil, that would rival the disturbing effects of this account of Salvador, Bahia. Denver, Colorado, for example, where I was born and raised, has the distinction of being the metropolitan-area home of the Columbine school massacre in 1999; of gang-related violence generating such historical highlights as "the summer of violence" in 1992; riots between Ku Klux Klan protesters and civil rights opponents; and, riots between Columbus Day commemorators and Native American objectors in multiple recent years. Last week when I opened the *Denver Post,* there was a heartbreaking story of a man who, after a violent altercation with his wife, took away his five-year-old son and shot and killed him before turning the gun on himself in suicide,[5] and this week the papers are abuzz with the arrest of a new suspect in the killing of six-year-old JonBenét Ramsey in 1996. Colorado in recent years is disturbingly close to an image as collegiate rape capital, USA, as scandals have erupted over the handling of female co-eds' allegations at University of Colorado at Boulder, and the Air Force Academy. And finally, Colorado shares the same deeply worrisome problems with gender-based violence seen throughout the United States, on par statistically (to the extent we can know) with Brazilian levels.

The gender-based violence of concern here, then, is by no means uniquely Bahian, although most anthropologists would concur that particular patterns and manifestations take on distinctive, local forms. My attention to local contexts, and to Afro-Bahian cultural currents, are intended as explicitly cultural arguments, with significance across Bahian society that is not bound by ethnicity, class, or race.

This book responds to the potential hazards of pathologizing in several ways. A performative emphasis keeps the focus on individuals, as agents and receptors of interpersonal violence, and care is taken that they may, to the extent possible in a book that I author, speak for themselves. Although analyses of gender-based violence must weigh heavily the greater power of men as a group in society, doing so does not mean automatically according this determinative value at interpersonal levels. Listening to individual actors' subjective experiences and perceptions requires that we factor in individual men's senses of vulnerability and powerlessness, even against a patriarchal backdrop that may privilege their sex as a group. Therefore, men's use of violence not only as a means of domination, but also as compensation for a failure to exert dominance, gets equal billing in this account.

Similarly, I have emphasized women's agency in relation to violence alongside—albeit at times in very different patterns from—their victimhood. We have met individual women who are themselves violent instigators, women who leave immediately, and also those who stay when subject to men's physical force. In Yancí and her blood female kin, we encounter women who condemn other women for putting up with men's violence, saying they are worse than the men because women are superior, and more is expected. Meanwhile, in her own extended family, Yancí counts on more than five fingers the sisters-in-law whom her brothers either behave aggressively toward or who share husbands between second homes with *outras,* the second wives in long-term, parallel unions. Thus, the Bomfim family offers a striking configuration of contrasting positions, in this case organized by gendered blood (consanguine) versus marriage (affinal) relationships.

The stories of the Bomfim women and many other *baianas* that unfold on these pages contradict macro-level, stereotypical notions of Latin American machos on the one hand and thoroughly subjectified, victimized Latinas on the other. On a broader level of social organization, once understood as a credit to feminist initiative rather than a response to unusually high levels of male violence, Brazil's Delegacias da Mulher demonstrate that the frontiers of feminist transformation projects are as pioneering—and as radical in potential—in Brazil as anywhere in the world. As criminalization is bolstered by other, more comprehensive and preventive measures that lead Brazilians away from resorting to violence, hopes of Brazilian feminists that their culture could one day be counted among Boulding's (2000) "Cultures of Peace" may yet be realized.

NOTES

INTRODUCTION

Epigraphs: Matthew Gutmann, "Trafficking in Men: The Anthropology of Masculinity," *Annual Review of Anthropology* 26 (1997): 385–409; Heleieth Iara Bongiovani Saffioti, *Gênero, patriarcado, violência* (São Paulo: Editora Fundação Perseu Abramo, 2004).

1. To provide some sense of the rate of installation of women's police stations, here are counts as reported over the years: Sara Nelson in 1993 (personal communication) put the figure at 125. By 1995, 156 police stations were reported ("Delegacia," *Bahia Hoje,* August 24, 1995). Harazim (1998) put the figure at 260, Santos (2001) at 304, K. C. Silva (n.d. [2002?]) at 307, and Boselli (2004) at "somewhere near 400." Many of the stations are actually substations hosted inside other stations, rather than complete and autonomous stations.

2. *Delegacia,* in Brazil, simply means "police station," but for simplicity I use *delegacia(s)* to refer to the specialized women's police stations when context allows. The simple acronym I use, DMs, for Delegacias da Mulher is actually used in such states as Minas Gerais, Matto Grosso do Sul, Maranhão, and Acre. The actual name used for the station in Salvador, Bahia, is DEAM, or Delegacia Especial de Atendimento à Mulher (Special Police Station Attending to Women). Before 2002, it was called the called the Delegacia de Proteção à Mulher (DPM, Police Station for the Protection of Women). Changing to DEAM responded to a national effort to make the names more uniform, and currently eleven of Brazil's twenty-six states use DEAM. Earlier, Ferreira and Izumino (n.d.) argued, apparently unpursuasively, for using DPDM (Delegacia de Polícia de Defesa da Mulher) as a general term. Despite DEAM winning out, even

the significance of DEAM varies between states: in Rio de Janeiro, DEAM abbreviates Delegacia Especializada no Atendimento da Mulher. In São Paulo the stations remain Delegacias de Defesa da Mulher (DDMs), whereas in Pernambuco and Rio Grande do Norte the same acronym, DDMs, formerly meant Delegacia dos Direitos da Mulher.

3. The day care centers established were largely privatized, ironically, by the centrist Partido do Movimento Democrático Brasileiro (PMDB) party early into democratization. The family-planning emphasis remained focused on avoiding high-risk pregnancies; abortion remains illegal except to save the life of mother or in the case of sexual assault (Marques-Pereira and Raes 2005: 78).

4. Birth control and condoms for disease protection were liberalized, while protecting women's rights to fertility also became important, as coercive sterilizations of women came to light. Abortion, then and now, remains limited to pregnancies resulting from rape, to save the life of the mother, or in the presence of fetal abnormalities. Extra-legal women's groups, such as the Coletivo do Ventro Livre in São Paulo, have been known to furnish women with pharmaceutical abortificients.

5. 2004—Ano da Mulher—Senado Federal. http://www.senado.gov.br/anodamulher/relatorio/diagnostic_2.asp [accessed July 14, 2006].

6. Epigraph: Erik Mueggler, *The Age of Wild Ghosts* (Berkeley: University of California Press, 2001).

7. Residents use the two names *Salvador* and *Bahia* interchangeably to refer to Salvador da Bahia. In this work both refer to the city, unless I specify that I mean Bahia state.

Epigraph: Ruth Landes, *The City of Women* (Albuquerque: University of New Mexico Press, 1994 [1947]).

8. Brazilians writing on the DMs include Grossi 1991; Neto 1992; Gregori 1993; Calazans 2004; and Santos 2001, 2004; these studies are examples of excellent São Paulo–based research on the DMs and violence against women.

9. Epigraph: Teresa P. R Caldeira, *City of Walls: Crime, Segregation, and Citizenship in São Paulo* (Berkeley: University of California Press, 2000).

10. See Kulick (1998: 247, n. 20) for a contradiction to the assumption that *travestis* actively participate in Candomblé; it may be that many sellers of *acarajé* are not actually active either.

11. I use the word *favela* because it is becoming known to international readerships; however, although known to Bahians, it is associated with Rio de Janeiro and is not considered a respectful way to refer to a humbler neighborhood. *Morro* (hill), *periferia* (periphery), *subúrbio* (suburb), and even *guêto* (ghetto) are more likely to be used, depending on the community's location.

12. Hence, Teresa Caldeira titled her ethnography of São Paulo *City of Walls*. The image of a wall is used here particularly as an image of demarcated social space. It should not be taken as a description of physical spatial separation

between classes, however: Brazil is rightfully noted as a place where mansion and shantytown can be caught in the same photograph frame more often than in most of the world (see photo).

13. See Paoli (1982), Quintas (1986), Caldeira (2001), and Goldstein (2003) on the relationship between criminality and marginality. Perlman (1976; see also 2006) and Woortmann (1987) discuss the debate on whether marginality is a viable analytic category, a debate that turns on disagreement about "subjective marginality."

14. O'Donnell's (1993) zones include an intermediate between blue and brown—green, with high territorial state penetration but low functional influence—not discussed here. See also Goldstein's discussion on degrees of state penetration, rule of law, and "disjunctive democracy" (2003: 198–199).

15. Caramuru, as the Tupinambás who met the French survivor of the shipwreck dubbed him, did indeed marry an indigenous woman, the legendary Catarina Paraguaçu, in France, in 1528. He was thought to have produced children both with her and other native women (Porto Filho 1991: 25). It is likely that Zumbi incorporated some details from this story, or learned it from others, into his own version. Alternatively, it is possible that a later shipwreck occurred, but I have found no record of this.

16. See Matory (2005: 109–110, 227–228, 230, 242) for discussions of subnations of Jeje, and for how through "anagonization"—the "juggernaut expansion of Nagô influence" (2005: 31)—a house historically Jeje might today consider itself more Nagô or Quêtu (2005: 225–226).

17. I was more than curious about whether Almiro's speech was a ritualized lect specific to Candomblé, or a living language, perhaps a creolized Quêtu/ Portuguese. Yancí and others insisted he was as likely to say "get me some milk" in "Africano," or comment on something that had just happened as he was to sing or incant, thus favoring the latter possibility.

18. In broaching the connections among economic hardship, poverty, and violence, I do not wish to suggest that the insecurities and instabilities generated are exclusive to the poor. A ubiquitous insecurity exists for Brazilians of all classes and ethnic backgrounds, deriving directly from Brazil's ongoing economic crisis. In some senses, the situation of the Brazilian middle class could be understood as even more unstable, or subject to dramatic and unforeseeable change, than that of the Brazilian poor, because the middle class has more to lose. Nonetheless, the crisis of the poor is certainly more existential, immediate, and desperate.

19. "Gendered variations in paid employment" refers to 1983–1998 (Noronha 2004).

20. Salvador is second-highest in Brazilian municipalities for female-headed households (following Porto Alegre in the South). See http://www.ibge.gov.br/ home/estatistica/populacao/perfildamulher/perfilmulheres.pdf.

21. The least felicitous literature along these lines, however, cautions against celebrating the relative independence and command of women, pointing out that Afro-Latin and Afro-Caribbean matrifocality rests upon a particular version of crises in masculinity seen throughout the developing world that are ultimately destabilizing for all concerned (e.g., Stolcke 1991; Machado and Noronha 2002).

22. The notion of Brazil as a racial democracy was first popularized by Columbia-trained anthropologist Gilberto Freyre (1946). During the military era between 1964 and 1985, racial democracy was embraced as official state doctrine, thereby effectively preventing wide-scale confrontation with racism.

23. Epigraph: Allen Feldman, *Formations of Violence: The Narrative of the Body and Political Terror in Northern Ireland* (Chicago: University of Chicago Press, 1991).

24. The sixteen societies Levinson records are Fox, Iroquois, Papago, Ona, Siriono, Pemon, Toba, Javanese, Ifugao, Trobriands, Bushmen, Andamans, Central Thai, Kurd, L. Bedoin, and Lapps (1989: 103).

25. Feminists have suggested that Napoleon Chagnon's portrayal of primal male violence among the Yanomami may be based on inaccurate projections and may reflect more about Western men's grappling with gendered power struggles than anything about the Yanomami. See Sharon W. Tiffany and Kathleen J. Adams, "Feminists Re-reading the Amazon: Anthropological Adventures into the Realm of Sex and Violence," Working Paper no. 253 (East Lansing, MI: Women and International Development Program, 1995), available at http://www.wid.msu .edu/resources/papers/subject/ed.htm. A recent scandal, in which journalist Patrick Tierney alleged that anthropologist Napoleon Chagnon and human-genetic epidemiologist James Neel intentionally started or abetted a measles epidemic as part of a eugenics experiment, may also call into question portrayals of Yanomami violence. However, the American Anthropological Association fully repudiated the accusations in 2003. See "Referendum on Darkness in El Dorado & Danger to Immunization Campaign," http://www.anth.ucsb.edu/ discus/html/messages/62/63.html?970367732.

26. Here I am in effect arguing that a subculture of violence theory is a necessary component of understanding where and why violence does or does not manifest. See also Straus (1983); Malone, Tyree, and O'Leary (1989); and Bowker (1993).

27. The phrase is used by domestic violence researcher Jeff Fagan, *New York Times,* March 31, 1997: A12.

28. See also Goldstein 2003, Bourgois 1995 for critical reappraisals of Oscar Lewis' culture of poverty notion.

29. A critical caveat on national statistics: these can vary considerably within a single nation; for example, in Uttar Pradesh, India, the percentage of men who said they beat their wives varied from 18 percent in Naintal District to 45 per-

cent in Banda (Heise, Ellsberg, and Gottemoeller 1999: 7). Similarly, ethnic groups within single nations may diverge widely from national averages: where one study documents the rate of women in Papua New Guinean villages ever assaulted by a partner at 67 percent (Heise, Ellsberg, and Gottemoeller 1999: 7), another reports that among the Wape people of Papua New Guinea, domestic violence is virtually absent (Levinson 1989; Mitchell 1999). The United Nations (2000) national studies in ten countries narrows the 10–50 percent estimate, revising it to between 17 and 38 percent of women having been physically assaulted by an intimate partner.

30. "Protocolo: Considerações e orientações para atendimento à mulher em situação de violência na rede pública de saúde." *Jornal da Rede Feminista de Saúde*—n° 19—Novembro 1999. See http://www.redesaude.org.br/jornal/html/body_jr19-encarte.html [accessed February 20, 2005].

31. Seven of the PAHO sites were also in Latin America (Salvador, Brazil; Rio de Janeiro, Brazil; Cali, Colombia; Caracas, Venezuela; San José, Costa Rica; San Salvador, El Salvador; Santiago, Chile); the other two were Madrid, Spain, and Houston/Austin, Texas.

32. Men's positive responses were 9.5 percent (compared to an average of 4.8 percent); women's positive responses were 10.2 percent (compared to an average of 5.5 percent); Salvador's averages for beating with an object were also higher than average but were second to Cali, Colombia (Pan American Health Organization [PAHO] 1999: 348, 353).

33. Men's and women's approval differs by 7.7 percentage points. The average discrepancy here was just 0.18 percent, due to the fact that in five of the nine samples *women's rate of approval was higher than that of men!* (This included Rio de Janeiro, although at just 0.9 percent.) In fact, the distant second greatest discrepancy between men's and women's approval of wife beating for female adultery was reported for San Salvador, El Salvador, where 4 percent more women than men thought adulterous women deserved to be beaten (PAHO 1999: 350, 355; see also Heise, Ellsberg, and Gottemoeller 1999).

34. Other areas in which Salvador displayed prominent distinctions in the PAHO sample included women's markedly greater tendency to notify police when they were beaten ("*golpeada*"; 45.7 percent of incidents versus 33.5 percent average; Rio de Janeiro reporting rates were just 10.7 percent). Men's rates followed a similar pattern but were lower in general.

35. Members of the family I call Bomfim, along with many of those I interviewed, advocated for the use of their real names in this ethnography. Scheper-Hughes (1992) avoids pseudonyms with a similar, northeastern Brazilian population, arguing that her informants were already all too anonymous. Although I am sympathetic to that stance, the book's focus on violence required strict assurances to be given the Human Subject Review Board of The Johns Hopkins University, so I adhere to pseudonym use.

36. I sought out the *jogo dos buzios,* along with the project's other researchers, to see what different mediums would tell us about ourselves and our lives, as well as what should be done in cases of severe domestic strife: usually the prescriptions involved baths and offerings for Oxalá, who is paramount in *orixá* religions and gifted with powers of "suggestion" and "realization" (Verger 1993: 259).

37. Just 8.9 percent of all Brazilians claimed Candomblé or Umbanda as their primary religious affiliation in the 2000 census; these figures would probably be significantly higher for Salvador (neither regional nor municipal statistics were reported). See Censo Demográfico—2000: Características Gerais da População: Resultados da Amostra. http://www.ibge.gov.br/home/estatistica/populacao/censo2000/populacao/censo2000_populacao.pdf [accessed June 10, 2005]. Many who participate in *orixá* religions, however, would probably still claim Catholicism as a primary identification; only recently have more politicized adherents viewed a conflict between these shared identifications, for example see Ilé Axé Opô Afonjá (1999).

38. Resource theory specifically predicts that ongoing violence occurs more often when rewards of using violence outweigh the costs (McCall and Shields 1986; Anderson 1997); in its predictive guise, it can be indistinguishable from exchange theory.

Campbell's review of resource theory disputes its predictive value, citing multiple examples where increasing economic independence for women and decreasing economic importance of men has led to decreased or stable levels of domestic violence (1999: 238). Again, it appears that whether or not negative sanctions exist or are instituted fundamentally affects the occurrence of violence. The fact that women often have used their increasing power to create negative sanctions seems itself not to have been studied cross-culturally. Although Campbell dismisses the predictive power of resource theory, she adds that "it may be explanatory at the individual level," noting several case studies in which "wives were beaten more frequently because they, as individuals, challenged the male role" (1999: 239).

39. Levinson finds that the most important factor in keeping down the costs for men of using violence is women's economic dependency (1989: 83). Regarding the "benefits" that using violence bestows on one's masculinity, Levinson did not find a correlation between hypermasculinity and wife abuse, but he did find that in societies in which men were more likely to settle disputes among themselves violently, wife beating also occurred more frequently. At the same time, men resorting to violence to affirm their masculinity may not come across as hypermasculine, because a perceived "deficit" in their masculine image may be what violent men seek to redress in the first place.

40. To expand on ecological theory's causes according to levels of analysis: on the individual level, Heise (1998) found just two factors to be influential for men: witnessing domestic violence as a child and experiencing physical or sexual

abuse as a child. On the family and community level (which Heise calls the "microsystem"), norms promoting male dominance in decision making and control of wealth come into focus. At the societal level (Heise's "exosystem"), social organizational factors such as isolation of women and the family take on significance. Unemployment and low socioeconomic status are also stressed, but the sensitivity to context intended in the ecological method is apparent when Heise qualifies that what is relevant "may not be lack of income, but rather some other variable that accompanies the experience of living in poverty, such as crowding or hopelessness, that is significant" (1998: 274). Although factors such as relative deprivation—the subjective perception of oneself as unfairly disadvantaged—or destabilized men's status are not addressed directly, they could be fruitfully incorporated. Finally, at the global (Heise's "macrosystem") level, cultural norms and beliefs operate: most notably patriarchy, manhood that is linked to dominance or toughness, and male entitlement to control women.

41. Feminist analysts disagree on whether patriarchal social organization should be viewed as the exclusive—or merely the primary—influence on wife-beating or battering as routinized social syndromes (Okum 1986: 98). Feminists have focused on how laws and social norms can justify and legitimate male use of violence against female partners, and also explained why discrimination against and revictimization have frequently impeded women from being able to use laws effectively to protect themselves (Merry 1994).

Feminist theory predicts that lower female status leads to higher rates of violence against women—and meets with mixed results when tested. While there is broad agreement that socioeconomic inequality between men and women is an important predictor of levels of violence, it is also clear that female status is multifaceted, and some factors weigh more heavily than others. Levinson (1989) concludes that the most meaningful macroscopic theoretical paradigm for predicting wife beating is an economically based sexual inequality model. His sexual inequality model incorporates exchange theory by focusing upon sanctions. Levinson writes:

> The results indicate that those factors that predict wife beating also predict the
> delayed use of interventions . . . and the absence of intervention. It seems clear
> that battered wives will have less chance of receiving outside help in societies in
> which they have little economic power, in societies in which the husbands rule
> the home, in societies in which they will have difficulty obtaining a divorce,
> and in societies in which disputes tend to be settled violently. This pattern
> of findings suggest that tertiary interventions [those directed at helping the
> assaulted wife], in and of themselves, have little impact on controlling or
> preventing family violence at either the community or societal level. Rather,
> it seems that tertiary interventions are linked to low rates of wife-beating be-
> cause both the low rates and the interventions are part of a general pattern of
> male-female equality and nonviolent conflict resolution (1989: 101).

Caveats that Campbell suggests for feminist theory include that sexual inequality tends to be more predictive of severe male-to-female violence (battery) than of less grave forms (beating); and that norms of male ownership or tight control of female kin can in some cases prevent battery. Finally, similar levels of wife-beating in distinct societies may occur for different reasons: "Aboriginal men beat women because they are angry whereas Ecuadorian men beat their wives to establish dominance" (1999: 237). Campbell ends by encouraging more attention to cultural context through ethnographic research on the problem.

ONE. WOMANLY WEBS

Epigraph: Pierre Verger, "Orixás da Bahia," in *Os Deuses Africanos no Candomblé da Bahia* (Salvador: Bigraf, 1993).

1. My use of *matriarch*—singular—here departs from the strictest technical, anthropological sense, where the *arch* root refers to governance and *matriarch* would indicate a female leader in formal public and political life. Nonetheless, Dona Alegrina's prominent role is not confined to her family but extends to her *terreiro* of Candomblé and the neighborhood, thus in some sense containing public dimensions.

2. North Americans familiar with other parts of Latin America may be surprised to find that the word *gringo* can have more innocuous, less politically charged, and at times even friendly connotations in many parts of Brazil. This is generally more true among the less formally educated classes, and less true as class and education levels, as well as degree of leftist orientation, increase. I frequently used the word as a way to recognize my outsider status and present it for discussion, as well as to diffuse tension.

3. Especially in Minas Gerais and Rio Grand do Sul; Walkiria Brown, personal communication.

4. The *cruzado* replaced the *cruzeiro* as the basic unit of Brazilian currency in 1986. Subsequent years saw transitions to the *cruzado novo* (new cruzado) and then the *cruzeiro novo,* until the *real* was introduced in 1995.

5. Epigraph: Verger, "Orixás da Bahia," in *Os Deuses Africanos no Candomblé da Bahia.*

6. Epigraph: M. S. Omari-Tunkara, *Manipulating the Sacred: Yorùbá Art, Ritual, and Resistance in Brazilian Candomblé* (Detroit: Wayne State University Press, 2005).

7. This Bahian folk theory closely parallels what social scientists have called the female masochism theory of domestic violence, for which little empirical support has been found (Okum 1986: 72–82; cf. Loseke 1989). As with the focus on adultery and male honor in chapter 3, the significance of such a theory here relates more to its salience as a story that people tell than to its reliable explanatory value.

8. This usage of *gostar,* to like, is interesting in that it can be used inter-

changeably with "to do"; to say someone likes to do something is the same as saying they do something. People would say, for example, "The person that likes to work doesn't go hungry." The implied ethic is highly individualistic, suggesting that any individual who finds herself in an oppressive situation has the power to change it. Moreover, if she does not change it, she can be viewed by others as complicit in its continuance—of *gostando*—liking it. Such convictions about free will merit notice in a society with a recent legacy of slavery and military authoritarianism, along with severe socioeconomic hardship, class polarization, and rampant sexual, racial, and class discrimination.

9. Carlos and Chico dictated this conversation to me immediately following. The quotations are not direct, however, as are quotations from recorded interviews.

10. This was a genuine request; I was advising a research project with three psychology students from the Federal University, where we actively sought out figures from Candomblé, Umbanda, Catholicism, and Protestant faiths to pursue this line of the research.

11. Slave, saints, and *orixás* are all different spirits believed capable of possessing (or simply harrassing) a person in Candomblé. A "slave" (along with *índios,* which Dona Alegria does not mention) refers to the spirit of someone deceased. The distinction Dona Alegria seems to make between saints and *orixás* is interesting, as these are typically used as synonyms for Candomblé deities. At the same time, there are many indications that Dona Alegria's Candomblé differed from documented practices in other Quêtu *terreiros.*

12. I don't know about Dona Alegrina's family of origin, but I have no reason to think she was an only daughter.

13. Yancí refused to accept any rent from me at this time. Instead, I managed to reciprocate through more personalized means, such as insisting that I would prefer to give her two hundred dollars, rather than lend it, once when she had requested.

14. This figure was shortly thereafter revised to 54 *centavos* to the *real;* see the Introduction, n. 5.

15. Simpson (1993) tells the story of TV Global, Brazil's preeminent network, through a stinging, beautifully crafted critique of Xuxa, the blond playboy bunny/Captain Kangaroo princess of children's television. See also Kottak (1992).

16. It was necessary to regulate this somewhat; without regulation, I knew, literally hundreds of people I had never seen before would have flocked to Yancí's bar. This way, the party could be open to all, but food and drink for those who had helped with the research was assured.

TWO. WHEN COCKS CAN'T CROW

Epigraphs: Pierre Verger, "Orixás da Bahia," in *Os Deuses Africanos no Candomblé da Bahia* (Salvador: Bigraf, 1993). The name is written *Ogun* in English and Spanish, *Ogum* in Portuguese.

1. Portions of this chapter appeared, in different forms: "Here the Cock Does Not Crow, for He Is Not the Lord of the Land: Machismo, Insecurity, and Male Violence in Brazil," in *Cultural Shaping of Violence,* ed. M. Anderson. (West Lafayette, Indiana: Purdue University Press, 2004); "Researching Men's Violence: Personal Reflections on Ethnographic Data." *Men and Masculinities,* 2003, 6(1): 93–106; "The Crowing of the Rooster: Violence and Masculinity in Northeast Brazil," in *Partners in Change: Working with Men to End Gender-based Violence.* (Santo Domingo, Dominican Republic: United Nations/INSTRAW, 2002), 31–51.

2. Ogum takes on different meanings in different locales throughout the Americas where the African Diaspora is prominent; not everywhere, then, is Ogum primarily associated with warriors (Barnes 1989). Johnson (2002: 67, 172–73) chides those who invoke *orixás* as archetypes as bastardizing Candomblé, against which I can offer no protest. My own "invocation" here follows literary and analytical interests, but again makes no claims to relevance for actual Candomblé practice.

3. In general we kept interviews one-on-one, with men interviewing men and women interviewing women—but sometimes I would join the men's interviews for five- to ten-minute stretches, as having heard some interviews in person helped my grasp of the transcript later. By this time a small room next to the room that was our home had opened up, affording the project a small but separate space. Two others worked with me during this phase: Carlos Ferreira Danon and Rosimeire (Meire) Gonçalves Silva. Both had already graduated from Universidade Federal da Bahia in sociology and were mature and competent colleagues in the neighborhood phase of the research.

4. I maintain this singular usage of "woman" in much of my translation, although it reads awkwardly in English. The monolithic and unitary implications bear, in my mind, significance that ought not be translated out.

5. Ira Lowenthal (1989) explains Haitian men's need to give to women materially in order to gain sexual access, making clear this bears no relationship to prostitution. Some of the contributing historical factors regarding African antecedents and influences of slavery are similar for Bahia.

6. Many informants encouraged me to use their real names; again, I am precluded from doing so because of previous agreements with Institutional Review Boards protecting human subjects.

7. For example, the Centers for Disease Control and Prevention in the United States used focus groups in the "Risk and Protective Factor Focus Group Study"; see http://cdc.gov/ncipc/dvp/fivpt [accessed November 1, 2005].

8. We convened six groups of men and five of women; unfortunately space does not allow me to present material from the women's groups here. Focus group participants were recruited from the three adjacent communities studied;

Meire, Carlos, Flávio, and I facilitated. Two of these communities were predominantly of working poor, the third was mostly lower-middle class. Nearly half of the focus group participants had been interviewed in the previous stage of the research. In each group, at least one participant was known to have had some conjugal history involving violence. However, we assured participants that, unlike in previous interviews, in the focus groups we did not wish to delve deeply into their personal experiences (nor would we disclose anything we had been told) but rather to better understand the results from the earlier research.

Group size ranged from three to eight people, and the duration of groups ran from about an hour and a half to over three hours. Although my (a woman's) presence surely affected the dialogue in the men's groups to a certain extent—often participants would excuse themselves before referring to something sexually explicit, or say they couldn't repeat some profanity with me present—the discussions were so productive even with me there (and maybe men sought to explain themselves even more because of my presence) that the loss that my final analysis would have sustained had I relied solely on transcriptions and my collaborators' reports outweighed what might have been gained had I absented myself.

9. Focus group no. 5, held September 13, 1995.

10. For the younger men's groups n = 12; for the older men's groups n = 16. Group no. 2 was convened September 4, 1995; group no. 7 met September 20, 1995.

11. I am indebted to an anonymous University of California Press reader for raising this issue.

12. I am not able to explore focus group conversations with middle-class men at length here, but the same response to criminalization was not evident; see also chapter 5 and Caldeira (2001) and Machado and Noronha (2002) for further discussion of police and general attitudes surrounding "marginality" in relation to criminality.

13. "Threatened" masculinity (or thwarted, marginalized, or counterhegemonic) has somewhat less appeal to me now as a concept because I believe we need to exert ourselves to think not in terms of reified abstractions, but in terms of men (or masculinized women or transgendered people where appropriate). This is what Jeff Hearn (2004) had in mind when he titled a recent article "From Hegemonic Masculinity to the Hegemony of Men." Along similar lines, I have tried to avoid using "male" and "female" as adjectives in favor of "men's" and "women's," to get away from biologically sexed bodies as actors. It is interesting that avoiding this altogether is extremely difficult, and the former adjectives do appear in this text.

14. Comment by "Martin," profem-l@cairo.anu.au (online discussion group) [accessed August 11, 2000].

Epigraph: "Entre Tapas e Beijos" is a popular song performed in highly varied versions by a diversity of artists. The version quoted and translated here is that of Nilton Lamasa and Antônio Bueno, available at "MPB Cifrantiga," http://cifrantiga3.blogspot.com/2006_05_28_cifrantiga3_archive.html [accessed December 27, 2006].

1. I arrive at this conservative estimate by extrapolating from a single-year country total of 326,000 complaints filed for 1999 by the Conselho Nacional dos Direitos da Mulher (http://www.ibam.org.br/viomulher/notnoticias.htm) [accessed December 8, 2005]. Estimating that from 1995 to 2005 an annual average of 300,000 (lower in the beginning of the period, higher toward the end due to growing number of Women's Police Stations) applies for a total of three million, I added one million for the 1985–95 period.

2. The astounding definition given for *forró,* in the well-respected Michaelis Portuguese-to-English Dictionary (compiled and published in Brazil), is "A nigger's ball" (Wimmer 1961).

3. Bahians would want me to mention the countless *quadrilhas,* much of it high-quality folkloric performance, at the Arraiá da Capitá, the large state fair. All of these were focused much more on dance performance and choreography than on reenacting the classic folk tale, with endless themes and scenarios. All except one departed altogether from the shotgun wedding theme, and although I could make out little of the spoken parts of that one, I didn't see any of the ritualized conflict written in. Of course, many of the pieces played upon gender roles for their drama: most fascinating to me, and more dance-theater than any of the others I saw, was one in which the Devil/*Exu* (Candomblé trickster with a naughty streak; guardian of the crossroads) was defeated, in turn, by Oxalá (Candomblé *orixá* syncretistically linked to Jesus Christ) and the Virgin Mary.

4. In a separate research project I worked on with four Universidade Federal da Bahia psychology students, entitled "I Want God to Make Him Stop" (aided by a Charlotte Newcombe Fellowship), we specifically looked at religious communities' different ways of responding to cases of domestic violence within their congregations. The communities included Catholicism, Pentecostalism, Evangelism, Jehovah's Witnesses, Espiritismo, Umbanda, Quimbanda, and Candomblé .

5. The sole exception to *delegadas'* exclusive authority to convene *audiências* in the Delegacia da Mulher (DM) were *comissárias,* police with some juridical training but far less than *delegadas* receive; they could legally preside at certain kinds of *audiências.*

6. In our interviews, we did ask individuals to classify themselves racially, or literally, "by color." We also had interviewers classify the same individuals, and spent a good deal of time discussing photographs and known subjects among ourselves until we had a reasonable sense, at least, of the cues each of us looked

for. Such discussions, far from underlining any clear-cut criteria or categories, tended rather to underline how contextual, contentious, variable, and subjective such classifications were; this appropriately parallels the invalidation of racial categories holding any scientific or objective status in anthropology as a whole, as well as the Brazilian social reality, where individuals can self-identify with more than one distinct racial category, depending upon the context (see Fontaine 1985; Hanchard 1994; Hasenbalg and Silva 1999; Twine 1998).

7. Scheper-Hughes 1992 has a chapter elaborating the extensive cultural meanings associated with being *nervoso* in Brazil, particularly those associated with hunger and anxiety over basic survival issues.

8. Confer with Linger 1992 for a thorough discussion of the concept of the *desabafo,* the purge or blowing off of steam. He relates it both to *carnaval* and to the purgative mechanisms that violence plays in *brigas* between men.

9. *Oxente* is a singularly Bahian expletive; not profane, it acts as "shoot" or "jeez."

10. The 2004 shelter count is from http://copodeleite.rits.org.br/apc-aa-patricia galvao/home/Casas-abrigos.doc [accessed July 20, 2006]. By 2005, a working shelter in Salvador seemed close; a pilot had been tried, but it ended up being riddled with problems, so the shelter stopped taking women and started over. It reopened in early 2006.

11. A point of confusion exists between popular understanding of the law in Brazil and its *de jure* state: the accusation of *abandono do lar* leveled in this hearing is, in actuality, not a crime, despite the fact that I observed it being registered as such in many DPDMs and other *delegacias* nationwide (Salvador was not one, however). Most often such complaints were lodged against women who separated from male partners. The confusion is with Article 244 of the penal code, which refers to Material Abandonment, or the failure to offer assistance to a spouse, minor, or infirm relative (Cunha 1989: 149).

12. Boiadeiro is a neighborhood with which I will later become well acquainted, when I consider living and researching there for the second, community study phase of this research.

13. For poor parents to "give" away their children is not unusual; children go to relatives, childless couples, or women desirous of children, or are given to financially better-off families, who raise the children as *filhos de criação* (literally, "brought up children" or—usually unofficially—adopted children; see Twine 1998). In the last instance, children are often treated quite differently from the family's biological children; frequently their position appears indistinct from that of an indentured servant, in the sense that they are unremunerated, into adulthood. Even less fortunate "given" children can end up living on the street—close to our house in Salvador, in fact, was an underground "colony" of dozens of street children in a vacated series of tunnels.

14. Scheper-Hughes (1992) worked elsewhere in northeast Brazil, in a slum

outside Recife, Pernambuco not unlike that where Jorge and Janaína reside. She identified the father's delivery of formula to the residence of the mother and infant as a poignant (because it interfered with breastfeeding) gesture, whereby fathers assumed paternity in social settings where most unions were informal.

15. *Negro* signifies the masculine and *negra* the feminine form, respectively.

16. I have no statistics to support this claim; however, the DPDM's Delegada Titular Célia Miranda, upon returning from a national convention of DPDM *delegadas* in 1993, reported that a consensus among veteran *delegadas* of DPDMs emerged to this effect (Célia Miranda, personal communication, 1993).

17. Campbell (2004) makes a similar argument against one-size-fits-all assessments. She looked at women seeking medical assistance in hospitals for violence-related injuries and how their levels of risk (of death) might be assessed to decide about treatment, advocate getting women into shelters, and so on. This is a concrete example of where understanding of distinctions in violent dynamics could have an applied dimension.

18. A second vein of research relevant to my dominance/contestation proposition is status inconsistency, or more specifically, the backlash thesis. Both are variants of resource theory, discussed briefly in the introduction, which is based on the notion that the more resources one controls outside the family, the less likely one is to resort to violence to maintain control. Status inconsistency holds that in societies where norms prescribe male superiority and dominance and a female partner commands greater-than-normal resources, the female partner may be more subject to violence. The backlash hypothesis predicts that when women take on nontraditional roles, some men might feel threatened and use violence to try to resubjugate women (Avakame 1999). Since these two ways of framing the question amount, for my purposes, to the same thing, I will address them together.

Research supporting status inconsistency and backlash hypotheses is virtually always qualified as to where it can be usefully applied. In short, this dynamic appears to be particularly evident during periods of rapid social change in which male control of or access to resources is rapidly eroding, and it consistently occurs in conjunction with cultural values that mandate men be in control, be primary breadwinners, and dominate women and children, and where violence has historically possessed some "positive" masculinizing cultural value (Handwerker 1998; Okum 1986: 90; Levinson 1989: 15; Avakame 1999; Stanko 1985).

Detractors of status inconsistency theory have objected that it does not account for counterexamples, where more equal power relations between genders appear tied to less violence. Campbell's review of status inequality theory, for example, disputes its predictive value, citing multiple examples where increasing economic independence for women and decreasing economic importance of men have led to decreased or stable levels of domestic violence (i.e., Indo-Fijians, !Kung and Iran; Campbell 1999: 271). Similarly, (Levinson 1989) rejects the notion that greater equality leads to higher levels of violence, demonstrating instead that women's gains in employment and income generation reduce violence when social relationships support equality. His model fails to consider how social relationships may be shaped by subcultural social circumstances.

Most critics, in other words, dismiss status inconsistency because it cannot be equally applied to all cases and thus lacks predictive value, instead of noting for which kinds of cases it does help explain violent patterns. Most of the cases I have looked at involve subcultural groups that are socially marginalized, and it is indeed among such groups that quantitative and comparative researchers have found the strongest support for the status-consistency/backlash thesis. Although Campbell dismisses the predictive power of resource theory, she adds that "it may be explanatory at the individual level," citing instances in ethnographic literature in which wives "were beaten more frequently because they, as individuals, challenged the male role" (1999: 271). One groundbreaking sociological study of Canadian spousal abuse data arrived at the conclusion, not unlike what I have been arguing, that the entire issue can be clarified if one ceases to treat all spousal violence as part of the same phenomenon. Ross MacMillan and Rosemary Gartner concentrate on the symbolic importance of husbands' and wives' employment, rather than concentrating on earnings as economic resources. They found increases in violence to be especially acute when women were employed and men unemployed. In such cases, what they call "endemic" interpersonal conflict can grow more acute, arriving at the level of systematic abuse, which they associate with "unemployed men married to women who work outside the home [using] coercive tactics in an effort to reinstate their dominance" (1999: 956).

If violence does, in fact, serve as a last-ditch resource for power, then in contexts in which the cultural value of violence is associated with masculinity and male power, the use of violence may be integral to counterbalancing "traditional" masculine roles being disallowed, questioned, or threatened. At the same time, this may be a short-term, transitional effect. When societal sanctions against violence and sanctuary to victims are instituted, equality can take root and masculinity can restabilize.

FOUR. POLICING BY AND FOR WOMEN

Epigraph: Cecilia MacDowell Santos, "Delegacias da Mulher: Percursos e Percalços," in Rede Social de Justiça e Direitos Humanos, "Relatório de Direitos Humanos no Brasil 2001" (São Paulo: Rede Social de Justiça e Direitos Humanos e Global Exchange, 2001), 163–171.

1. "All Women Police Stations Working in India." Oherald.com, May 27, 2003. http://www.sameshield.com/news/awps.html [accessed March 10, 2005].

2. "First Women Police Station in Shambles." Pakistan Press International Information Services Limited, December 22, 2003; "Govt. to Increase Number

of Women Police Stations," Pakistan Press International Information Services Limited, January 27, 2004.

3. The women's police station in Nairobi's was reported in *Africa News,* October 2, 2004. South Africa's women-only motorbike squad was reported in "Joburg's All-Women Bike Squad, Lucky Sindane." http://www.southafrica.info/women/women-bikesquad.htm, August 2, 2004.

4. "Domestic Violence." http://www.malostratos.com/contenido/biblioteca/articulos/domesticviolence.htm, January 8, 1998 [accessed May 31, 2005].

5. Santos (2001) reported that thirteen Latin American countries had women's (usually "and children's") stations; I report only those I can confirm independently.

On Colombia, see "Encuestra Nacional de Demografía y Salud, Ch. XI: Violencia Domestica," (Bogatá, Colombia: Profamilia, 1995), http://www.measured hs.com/pubs/pdf/FR65/11Capitulo11.pdf [accessed November 15, 2004]. For Nicaragua, see "A Lesson from Nicaragua's Quiet Revolution," *Asahi Evening News* Opinion section, December 24, 2000, http://www.unfpa.org/focus/nicaragua/asahi.htm [accessed March 20, 2005], and "El Instituto Nicaragüense de la Mujer, destaca el trabajo en pro del adelanto de las mujeres," Bolsa de Mujeres #68. http://www.grupoese.com.ni/2000/bolsademujeres/ed48/inim48 .htm [accessed August 24, 2006]. For Peru, see "Datos e Estatísticos/Peru." http:// www.isis.cl/temas/vi/dicenque.htm [accessed May 31, 2005]. For Uruguay, see "Unidades." www.policia.gub.uy/UNIDADES/UNIDADES [accessed August 24, 2006]. For Ecuador, see http://edufuturo.com/imageBDE/EF/30772.comisarias .pdf and http://www.cladem.org/espanol/regionales/Violenciadegenero/Proyecto/foronacionalecu.asp.

6. "Investigative Techniques of Specialised Police Stations—All Women Police Stations (India)." www.wjin.net/Pubs/2304.pdf [accessed March 1, 2005]; a fuller version is available in Sharma (n.d.).

7. "Jharkand Moots Women-Only Police Stations." Indo-Asian News Service, October 20, 2004 [accessed January 2, 2007].

8. "All Women Police Stations Working in India." Oherald.com, May 27, 2003. http://www.sameshield.com/news/awps.html [accessed March 10, 2005]; "Govt. to Increase Number of Women Police Stations," Pakistan Press International Information Services Limited, Jan. 27, 2004. For more on trafficking of Brazilian women and the NGO response, see CHAME 1998.

9. "Police Step Up Hunt for Rapists." http://www.awcfs.org/contentcreation/noviolence/noviolence2.html [accessed March 20, 2005].

10. See http://www.unfpa.org/focus/nicaragua/asahi.htm; see also Lancaster (1992) on the emergence of the "new man" ideal, committed to gender equality and anti-violence, from the Sandanista Revolution.

11. Salvador's station is actually now called the DEAM, for Delegacia Especial de Atendimento à Mulher. For more on *delegacia* titles, see the Introduction, n. 2.

12. The women's police stations, or DMs, are but one of the most prominent products of the opportunities afforded feminist activists during the return to civilian rule. On feminism in Brazil, see Sardenberg and Costa 1994; Alvarez 1989a, 1989b, 1990; Saffiotti 1976, 1987; Jaquette 1989; Hahner 1990.

13. For an in-depth analysis of legal decisions and defense strategies in male-to-female violence cases, see Ardaillon and Debert 1987. Among the most significant works in related areas, by category, are the following. On battering and domestic murder see Blay 2003; Grossi 1991; Azevedo 1985; Corrêa 1983. Chauí et al. 1984 is a collection of feminist anthropological essays on the topic; Feiguin et al. 1987 is a compilation and analysis of victim/accused profiles in São Paulo *delegacias*. Silva 1992, Nelson 1996, K. Silva n.d., L. Machado n.d., and Santos 2001, 2004 analyze the experience of the DMs.

14. But see Besse (1989) on a movement to address family violence in Brazil in the 1920s. The concerns here were more in keeping with social control—controlling and "rationalizing"—of the family as a whole, rather than with women specifically.

15. Feminist activists were often self-exiled for their own safety but in some cases had no choice. Many also had affiliations with oppositional groups whose "subversive" nature left them vulnerable to military authorities.

16. See Sorj and Montero 1984; Alvarez 1989a, 1989b, 1990; Patai 1988; Saffiotti 1994; and Gregori 1993.

17. Silva (n.d.: 8–10); she also specifies that 73 percent of the DMs were created between 1986 and 1996, possibly suggesting a slowing rate of implementation.

18. In the Fourth World Conference on Women, held in Beijing, China, in 1995, Brazil "was considered the champion of violence against women," owing to the high levels of denunciations registered (Santos 2001: 4).

19. São Paulo has even inaugurated a police station for crimes related to racism, and the southern state of Rio Grande do Sul is in the process of instituting an Itinerant Anti-Racism Police Station (Delegacia Itinerante Anti-Racismo—DIAR); these are the closest cousins to the women's stations to date (http://www.interlegis.gov.br/comunidade/20040818093125/20050224102916/view) [accessed March 1, 2005]. Rio Grande do Sul has also pioneered a court system for "special crimes," including gender-based violence; Azevedo's (2001) analysis of these courts suggests that they move away from adjudication and toward mediation in forms productive of instilling democratic citizenship.

20. From the National Council for Women's Rights booklet entitled *"Guia de Defesa das Mulheres Contra a Violência."*

21. Many of the *delegacias* nationwide do have male police on staff, either because not enough female police have skills such as driving, because female-male pairs are thought to be more effective for tasks such as delivering summons to homes, or because administrators do not subscribe to the belief that women are more appropriately assigned to this specialized work. However, according to the

philosophy by which the *delegacias* were originally conceived, all police staff should be women.

22. Separate women's ranks have been instituted in the Brazilian navy and air force, with "fields of actuation compatible with their abilities," which include directing traffic, helping children and elderly, and publishing a military women's magazine (*A Tarde,* September 6, 1993).

23. "A homenagem às mulheres cadetes," *A Tarde,* March 3, 1993.

24. "Policial feminina agride homem e será processada," *A Tarde,* October 28, 1993.

25. Reported by researcher Eduardo Paes Machado. http://www.policeuseof force.org/Merida2001.pdf [accessed December 27, 2006]. Police violence in Brazil is most grave in Rio de Janeiro: in 2003 1,195 police "executions" of favela residents were reported (http://www.listin.com.do/antes/octubre04/221004/cuerpos/mundiales/mun5.htm) [accessed March 19, 2005].

26. "Policiais da Bahia mataram 700 pessoas somente em 92," *Tribuna da Bahia* August 7, 1993.

27. The women's councils, also begun in São Paulo and subsequently instituted throughout the country, typically form part of state or municipal governments and generally were organized through secretaries of justice. By 2003, twenty-one state councils and ninety-one municipal councils were operating, with imminent plans to create an additional three state and four municipal councils. The National Council for Women's Rights (CNDM), which had been embraced and repudiated by groups of the women's movement at various turns since its creation in the 1980s (Jurema 2001), has been restructured under Ignacio Lula da Silva's leftist government. A redoubled effort to install more state and municipal councils results, and in 2002–3 the CNDM received frequent solicitations for assistance from state and municipal governments and women's groups.

28. The Partido do Movimento Democrático Brasileiro (PMDB), or the Brazilian Democratic Movement Party, evolved out of the MDB, which was the "official" (state-approved) opposition party under military rule, and thus was subject to criticisms of collaborationism from parties from further left that evolved out of the "true" opposition.

29. The Partido dos Trabalhadores (PT), or Worker's Party, was the most important leftist party to emerge out of democratization. "Lula" (Luís Inácio Lula da Silva) became the first PT candidate to be elected to the Brazilian presidency in 2002.

30. *Caindo no real* translates literally as "falling into the real."

31. This and all following translations are my own, unless otherwise noted.

32. Drª. Suzana Mª Ferreira was a speaker at the Seminário Nacional: Violência contra a Mulher, São Paulo, May 30–31, 1994.

33. L. Machado (n.d.) credits DMs in the state of Minas Gerais as exceeding

national norms regarding consistent training, including sensitivity training, for police.

34. A *delgada* in São Paulo expressed frustration that the DMs were not authorized to process many forms of crimes, such as "crimes against patrimony." When burglary accompanied a rape, for example, their hands were tied to prosecute the former. As a result, a measure was proposed to augment the jurisdiction of the DMs; a significant bill forwarding this goal for São Paulo (*decreto* 40.693.96) passed in 1996 (Santos 2001: 2).

35. I worked in Salvador's DM in 1990 (June–August) and from November 1992 through July 1993 (and continued to maintain contact through April 1994, during the period that I concentrated my research in residential neighborhoods); I again did fieldwork in the station during trips in 1995, 1999, and 2005. In addition, I visited specialized stations in the cities of Rio de Janeiro, Fortaleza, São Paulo, Porto Alegre, and Campo Grande.

36. Those requiring victim cooperation to proceed are either *ações privadas mediante representação,* or "private actions requiring [victim] representation," or *ações públicas condicionadas a representação,* public actions conditional on representation.

37. Although the terms *occorência* (occurrence) and *queixa* (complaint) were commonly used in Salvador's DM to distinguish between more and less severe offenses, respectively, they are not legitimate legal terms. Rather, the legal distinction is between the kind of action required by the state according to offense: crimes *"contra a vida"* (against life) obligate the state to prosecute regardless of whether the victim presses charges *(ações públicas incondicionadas),* whereas other offenses require the victim to press charges *(ações privadas mediante representação* and *ações públicas condicionadas a representação).* The first loosely correspond to DM's *ocorrências,* and the second to what are called *queixas* in the DM, although a persistent complainant for a *queixa* might see some result. But the DM was not able to pursue the processing of all *ocorrências,* as I have suggested.

38. A *delito* is simply a crime, but the term is employed in the DM to refer to more minor offenses, and is roughly equivalent to *queixa* as described above.

39. This figure, applicable for 1992 only, is based upon more extensive statistics than those represented in Table 4; five specialized and five conventional precincts were used to calculate a baseline.

40. Informe Nacional Brasil, PNUD 1998. http://www.undp.org/rblac/gender/campaign-spanish/brasil.htm [accessed March 3, 2005].

41. By 2005, two other municipalities in the state of Bahia had created specialized stations, but no action had been taken to install even specialized desks at other stations in Salvador.

42. Although this is a genuine shortcoming, in Brazil the civil police are specifically charged with the juridical work of investigating crimes while on-street

policing falls mainly to military police. This means that the work of civil police would already appear more desk-bound than that of their counterparts in the United States.

43. For São Paulo, investigations completed and forwarded to the court system were reported to be as high as 40 percent (Americas Watch 1991: 37) and 30 percent (Nelson 1996) for the early years, but these figures appear to be either erroneous or exceptionally above national norms.

44. See "Em gênero, número e grau." http://www.unicamp.br/unicamp/ unicamp_hoje/ju/outubro2002/unihoje_ju196pag06.html [accessed August 23, 2006]. Rio Grande do Sul's Jecrims compare favorably, however; Azevedo's (2001) analysis of these courts suggests they move away from adjudication and toward mediation in ways that productively instill democratic citizenship.

45. "Em gênero, número e grau." http://www.unicamp.br/unicamp/unicamp _hoje/ju/outubro2002/unihoje_ju196pag06.html [accessed August 23, 2006].

46. *National Post,* page A9, July 28, 2003.

47. "A lei Maria da Penha, finalmente." http://www.ciranda.net/spip/article 460.html [accessed January 2, 2007].

48. "All Women Police Stations Working in India." http://www.sameshield .com/news/awps.html [accessed March 10, 2005].

49. "Policewoman Wins Gender Parity Battle." http://www1.timesofindia .indiatimes.com/articleshow/450812221.cms [accessed March 20, 2005].

50. "Woman Crusader Dismissed." Times News Network, June 15, 2003. http:// timesofindia.indiatimes.com/articleshow/23762.cms [accessed March 24, 2005].

51. "Looking Back, Looking Forward," Geeta Seshu recalls the women of 2003. http://www.indiatogether.org/2003/dec/wom-year2003.htm [accessed April 7, 2005].

52. "An Interview with Chennai Police Commissioner (Tamil Nandu)." http://www.chennaionline.com/chennaicitizen/2001/kalimuthu1.asp [accessed March 10, 2005].

53. "Men Harassed at All Women Police Stations; Forced to Perform Sexual Acts," *The Hindu,* December 2, 2004. The "fellatio" reference here is puzzling; there was no mention of the officer being transgendered, so I assume the word *fellatio* is used more generally for oral sex in India, where in the United States the term *cunnilingus* would be used.

54. "Men Complain about Wives at Women-Only Police Station." http:// www.ananova.com/news/story/sm_688802.html?menu = news.quirkies [accessed March 18, 2005].

55. Sharma writes, "In Gwalior Mahila Thana, for instance, only 49 cases were filed in 1988. In Trivandrum's Vanitha Police Station, there had been a decline in the number of cases filed between 1985 and 1988. The number was 25 in 1985, 24 in 1986, 32 in 1987 and only 9 in 1988. Surprisingly, the decline had come at a time when the number of cases registered at other police stations in the state had

gone up." See "Investigative Techniques of Specialised Police Stations—All Women Police Stations (India)." www.wjin.net/Pubs/2304.pdf [accessed March 1, 2005]; a fuller version is available in Sharma (n.d.).

56. "First Women Police Station in Shambles." *Pakistan Press International,* December 22, 2003.

57. "Investigative Techniques of Specialised Police Stations—All Women Police Stations (India)." www.wjin.net/Pubs/2304.pdf [accessed March 1, 2005]; a fuller version is available in Sharma (n.d.)

58. "San Francisco." www.coastnews.com/dv1main.htm [accessed February 18, 2005].

59. As reported in "San Diego Domestic Violence Protocol." http://www .gov.ns.ca/just/Publications/russell/police.htm [accessed February 20, 2005].

60. "Europe: Domestic Violence—An All too Common Reality." http:// www.fidh.imaginet.fr/lettres/uk4–6.htm [accessed November 10, 2004].

61. "Europe: Domestic Violence—An All too Common Reality." http://www .fidh.imaginet.fr/lettres/uk4–6.htm [accessed November 10, 2004].

62. "U.S. Recaps Commitment to Women in Europe, Eurasia." http:/tokyo .usembassy.gov/e/p/tp-20040903–02 [accessed May 10, 2005].

FIVE. RELUCTANT CHAMPIONS

Epigraphs: Drª. Suzana Mª Ferreira, speaker at the Seminário Nacional: Violência contra a Mulher, São Paulo, May 30–31, 1994; J. Lorand Matory, *Black Atlantic Religion: Tradition, Transnationalism, and Matriarchy in the Afro-Brazilian Candomblé* (Princeton, NJ: Princeton University Press, 2005).

1. Neoliberal reforms are generally market oriented—geared toward boosting the private sector through the privatization of government enterprises and shrinking state expenditures through austerity measures such as cutting social programs.

2. *Gostar,* the word for "like," is more likely to be used than the verb *amar,* to love, in such a context as this *delgada's* inquiry. At the same time, the word *gostar* carries more weighty implications than "to like" in English: Here, its usage verges not only on "to love," but also carries the sense of "to choose." To admit *gosta* is often to admit choice of desiring to be with someone.

3. From the Conselho Nacional dos Direitos da Mulher booklet entitled *Guia de Defesa das Mulheres Contra a Violência.*

4. Technically, there is a division of labor in each platoon of seven: a "team chief," one "clerk" *(escrivã),* a person to attend the police radio, a person in charge of delivering summons, a (male) "*motorista*" who drives with the "summoner," and two "generic" agents. I found, however, that in practice this division was often set aside. Organization appeared extremely flexible; everyone did some of all duties without rigid adherence to the stated assignments.

5. Daily personnel included the detective squad *(vigilância e investigação)*, the head and assistant *delegadas*, and clerical staff.

6. A 1989 U.S. Survey on Human Rights discussing police violence in Brazil states that most instances of police brutality involve crimes where suspects bear arms, or where torture is used to exact information [*W. Post* 2/16/89]. Salvador's DM rarely contends with cases of this sort.

7. "Delegacias Circunscricionais da Capital e Região Metropolitana de Salvador." http://www.bahia.ba.gov.br/ssp/ [accessed June 5, 2005].

8. Weber describes charismatic authority as, "the absolutely personal devotion and personal confidence in revelation, heroism, or other qualities of individual leadership." Examples he offers of charismatic domination include powerful prophets, popular war lords, and rulers who gain power by vote or populist movements. Weber observed that in traditional societies charisma provided the sole means to authority, and thus he saw a movement away from exclusive reliance on charisma as a hallmark of modernity (1958 [1919]: 79).

9. Referring to public figures by their first name only is common in Brazil and is seen more frequently than last name alone.

10. "Iracema contraria o estereótipo da delegada grosseira" (Iracema contradicts the stereotype of the coarse delegada), *Journal da Bahia*, May 1, 1988.

11. The *delegada titular* in 1990 was quoted as saying, "[Brazilian] men are still machista, and it's the fault of their own mothers." "Delegacia de Mulheres não se vê na tevê" (Delegacia de Mulheres is not seen on TV), *Tribuna da Bahia*, January 22, 1990.

12. One reason for this responsiveness is that the acting Secretary of Public Security, Dr. Francisco Neto, was, for the first time police could remember, actually a *delegado* of police himself, whereas previously secretaries had not come to the position through police ranks. Perhaps related is the fact that Francisco Neto had undertaken an extensive research project on the history and experience of policewomen in the Bahian Civil Police Force to earn a masters at UFBa (Neto 1992).

13. In places in the following discussion, I treat the terms *sex* and *gender* interchangeably, so as not to translate informants' use of the word *sex* into *gender*, because they did not use the Portuguese word for *gender (gênero)*. Social scientists would usually use *gender* for what informants here are calling *sex*, a practice on the increase in Brazilian organizations and activism as well.

14. I strongly concur with scholars (e.g., Fontaine et al. 1985) who mandate that, contrary to earlier approaches, race cannot be adequately treated as an adjunct of class. Nonetheless, in the specific context of the staff of Salvador's Delegacia de Proteção à Mulher (DPM; title until 2002), the two are highly correlative: there is a marked lightening of complexion as one moves up the administrative hierarchy. Until 2002, only two of the *delegadas* were (notably) of Afro-Brazilian descent, even though the overwhelming majority of the agents have been Afro-Brazilian.

15. Relatives (parents and siblings) of *delegadas* were attorneys and *delegados,* doctors, dentists, professors, and teachers, to give some examples. Those of agents were merchants (many), domestic workers, homemakers, accountants, bookkeepers, tailors, nurses, petty bureaucrats, taxi and bus drivers, painters, machinists, and secretaries.

16. A male official at the Bahian Order of Attorneys said, "Law is the one field in Brazil where women experience absolutely no discrimination." Although this is an overstatement, it is probable that female lawyers experience less discrimination than female police. The tighter the class barriers to entry as one moves to higher occupational levels, the less sexual discrimination occurs.

17. Since this questionnaire was first administered in 1990, the *delegadas* Célia Miranda, Isabel Alice de Pinho, and other DM police who had become more involved with the women's movement have grown more likely to identify themselves as feminist.

18. Actually, just such a movement has arisen in the state of Minas Gerais, whose members declare allegiance to the "*Movimento Machista Mineiro*" (Movement of Machos Mineiros). Their reactionary, flamboyant diatribes against anything smacking of gender progressiveness—and particularly targeting declared feminists ("feminists have foot smell *[chulé]*" was the title of one letter to a newspaper editor penned by the group)—include just enough hyperbole that no one takes them particularly seriously.

On the opposite pole of men's positioning regarding feminism, a pro-feminist men's movement is taking shape in Brazil, especially anchored by men working to end men's violence against women through the international, grassroots White Ribbon Campaign (see *Campanha Brasileira Laço Branco,* http://www.laco branco.org.br/) [accessed December 29, 2006].

19. The state organ is Conselho Estadual dos Direitos da Mulher (Bahia); the munipical counterpart is the Superintendência Especial de Políticas para Mulheres (SPM).

20. Tensions have existed between the competing goals of a shelter versus a reference center, based upon the notion that a shelter can accommodate so few of the underserved complainants that it was unjustifiable in the absence of a referral center, which could serve more (Hautzinger 1997a).

21. Santos (2004) is doubtlessly invoking the intertextual link to Alvarez's titles (1989a; 1990), which use "engendering" as applied to a broader treatment of Brazilian gender politics in redemocratization.

CONCLUSION AND EPILOGUE

1. Barbosa (1995: 36) actually provides several glosses for the Brazilian *jeitinho,* including "institutional bypass." In verb form, she glosses *dar um jeitinho* as "to pull a string" or "to cut through red tape," stressing that it need not mean breaking rules.

2. Amado also wrote the novel *Gabriela,* discussed in chapter 2.

3. In this position DaMatta is joined by other Brazilian anthropologists, many of whom contrast these Brazilian qualities favorably to aspects of cultural life in the United States: this is evidenced in Oliven's work on contradictions (1989), money (1995), and popular music (1984a); Oliven, Tesser, and Chaves's work on money in popular music (1999); Barbosa's work on the *jeitinho* (1995); Kottack's on competitive (and not-so-competitive) swimming (1995); and Kant de Lima's on respective legal systems (1995). Linger (2001) makes similar comparisons about Brazilian warmth as contrasted with that of Japanese coolness, and Payne and Fits (1993) compare ambiguity in Brazilian and Spanish-speaking Latin American literature.

4. "Seus Direitos." http://mixbrasil.uol.com.br/pride/seusdireitos/delegada/delegada.shtm [accessed February 10, 2005]. "Relatorio sobre a Situação dos Direitos Humanos no Brazil. Chapter IX: Discriminação Racial." http://www.cidh.org/countryrep/brazil-port/Cap%209%20.htm [accessed August 3, 2006]. "Em Gênero, Número e Grau. http://www.unicamp.br/unicamp/unicamp_hoje/ju/outubro2002/unihoje_ju196page06.html [accessed August 23, 2006].

5. "Standoff Ends Tragically as Father Kills Son, Self." *Denver Post,* August 8, 2006, p. A1.

GLOSSARY OF PORTUGUESE TERMS

ABAFADO   overwhelmed

ABARÁ   fried or steamed bean cakes

ACARAJÉ   fried bean cakes

ACOMODADOS   men who relaxed and lost their vigilance with their wives

AFILHADO   godson

ALTO   hill

ALUCINDADA   possessed with passion

AMIGADO   in an informal conjugal union

APANHAR   to be beaten

ASSISTÊNCIALISMO   mentality of dependence on charity

ASSOCIAÇÕES DE MORADORES   neighborhood associations

BABALORIXÁ   a *pai de santo*, male Candomblé leader

BAIANA DE ACARAJÉ   a woman who sells *acarajé* and *abará*, fried or steamed bean cakes, on Salvador's streets. Usually a *mãe* or a *filha de santo* of Candomblé as well

BAIANO/A   Bahian (male/female)

BANANA   messy situation

BARONA   baroness, or rich woman

BARRACÃO   literally "big shed"

BLOCOS DE CARNIVAL   carnival clubs

BRIGA fight

BÚZIOS see JOGO DOS BÚZIOS

CACHAÇA liquor made from sugar

CAIPIRA hick, bumpkin

CANDOMBLÉ the primary Afro-Brazilian religion of Bahia, based on spirit possession by *orixá* deities

CARTEIRA ASSINADA literally signed card; refers to working legally, paying into the Brazilian equivalent of social security, working "above the table"

CARURU an okra stew; also a party held in commitment to a religious promise where carurú is served

CASA house or home

CASEIRO the "house man"; also *homem caseiro*

CHEIRO smell; to "*tomar um cheiro*" is to take a whiff of someone; a common form of affection

CIDADE BAIXA lower city

CIPÓ a woody, creeping vine, about an inch thick

CIÚME jealousy; "sick jealousy" is *ciúme doentio*

CLUBES DE MÃES mother's clubs

COBRAR to nag; nagging, charging

COMADRE "co-mother"; term for the godmother of one's child

COMPADRE "co-father"; term for the godfather of one's child

FANTASIA costume, as in for Carnaval

GATO "cat"; an illegal hook-up into water or electric lines

GUIAS literally "guide"; long strands of beads worn by devotees of Candomblé to indicate which *orixá* they serve

HOMEM CASEIRO the "house man"

IANSÃ warrior-woman *orixá* of the wind and storms; syncretized with Saint Barbara

IBEJIS twin spirits in Candomblé, syncretized with the twin saints Cosme and Damiã in Catholicism

IEMENJÁ female *orixá* of the sea; syncretized with Saint Ann

ILUSÃO illusion

ÍNDIO indigenous person

INFERNOS fires of hell

IYALORIXÁ a *mãe de santo*, female Candomblé leader

JEITINHO little string-pull

JOGO DOS BÚZIOS   a Candomblé method of divination performed by multiple casts of cowrie shells, *búzios*

KANGA   sarong for the beach

LADO DE LÁ   the side over there; a parallel relationship

LAVAGEM   washing

LIGAR   to be connected, to care

MACHISMO   the complex of *machista* values and behaviors

MACHISTA   adjective for a macho man or attitude

MACHO   a macho man

MADRINA   godmother

MÃE   mother

MÃE DE SANTO   a female Candomblé leader, *mãe de santo*

MALAGÜETA   hot Bahian pepper

MARGINAL   a criminal

MARGINALIDADE   criminality

MARIANISMO   Catholic ideology of female moral superiority and force

MARIDO   husband

MATO FECHADO   closed jungle

MELINDROSA   affected, coy

METER A COLHER   literally, dip the spoon; to get involved

MOÇA   maiden

MOCAMBO   a quilombo near Salvador or other Bahian town

MOLE   soft, weak

MULHER   woman

MULHER DE CASA   woman at home, wife

MULHER DA RUA   woman of the street, "other" woman

MULHER DECENTE   decent woman

MULHERENGO   womanizing man

NAMORAR   to be romantically involved; to make love

NAMORO   romantic affair

NEGÃO   big black man

NEGRO/A   black person (male/female)

NORMAL   normal, fine, natural

NÚMERO UM   number one, wife

ORELHÃO   public phone; literally "big ear" because of its shape

ORIXÁS   deities of Candomblé; saints

OTÁS   stones dedicated to individual *orixás,* through which they are "fed" with blood or food to their liking

OUTRA   other woman

OXALÁ   father of all *orixás*, ruler of peace and harmony

PAI DE FAMÍLIA   family man

PAI DE SANTO   Candomblé leader, babalorixá

PALAFITA   a house built on stilts over a mud flat

PAPO FORMAL   a formal talk

PAQUEIRA   flirtation, affair

PARTEIRA   midwife

PARTIR PARA A IGNORÁNCIA   "to go off into ignorance"; to become violent

PEGADO/A DEMAIS   too attached

PEJI   altar in Candomblé

PERIGROSOS   dangerous men

PICOLÉ   popsickle

POPULAR   humble, non-elite, of the people

PORRADA   literally, semen; punches

POVO   the people, the masses

PRAÇA   plaza

PREJUDICAR   to hurt, to bias

PSICÓLOGO   psychologist

QUADRILHA   folk dance similar to a square dance

QUILOMBO   a Brazilian maroon community; or settlement of escaped slaves

REAL   Brazilian currency since 1995

REBOCOU POR DENTRO   "plastered from within"; internal scarring from assaults

RECUPERAÇÃO   rehabilitation or recuperation

REDUÇÃO   reduction, a reading

RESPEITO   respect

REVOLTADA   revolted

RUA   street

SÃO JOÃO   Saint John, usually refers to the saint's day on June 23

SAPATONA   "big shoe"; pejorative for lesbian

SAUDADES   missing, longing

SENHOR/A   sir or ma'am; polite second-person address (you)

SOGRA   mother-in-law

SOLTEIRA   single woman

SUBURBIA   suburb; usually a poor neighborhood on city's periphery

SUPERMERCADO   supermarket

TAIPA   lath and plaster

TAPAS   slaps

TERREIRO DE CANDOMBLÉ   Candomblé house or temple

TOMAR PROVIDÊNCIA   "take providence"; to take advantage of a chance

TRABALHO   "work"; can refer to a spell or work of sorcery in Candomblé

REFERENCES

Adelman, Madelaine. 2003. "The Military, Militarism and the Militarization of Domestic Violence." *Violence against Women: An Interdisciplinary and International Journal, Special Issue: Violence against Women Associated with the Military* 9(9): 1118–1152.

Adelman, Madelaine, Edna Erez, and Nadera Shalhoub-Kevorkian. 2003. "Policing Violence against Minority Women in Multicultural Societies: 'Community' and the Politics of Exclusion." *Police and Society: An Interdisciplinary Journal of Law Enforcement and Criminology* 7: 105–133.

Albano, Celia. 1985. "Consideraciones sobre la experiencia del Centro de Defesa dos Direitos da Mulher de Belo Horizonte." Presented at the Encuentro sobre Feminismo en America Latina in Lima.

Albrecht, Terrance L., Gerianne M. Johnson, and Joseph B. Walther. 1993. "Understanding Communication Processes in Focus Groups." In *Successful Focus Groups,* edited by David L. Morgan. Newbury Park, CA: Sage Publications.

Alvarez, Sonia. 1989a. "Politicizing Gender and Engendering Democracy." In *Democratizing Brazil: Problems of Transition and Consolidation,* edited by Alfred Stepan. New York: Oxford University Press.

———. 1989b. "Women's Movements and Gender Politics in the Brazilian Transition." In *The Women's Movement in Latin America: Feminism and the Transition to* Democracy, edited by Jane S. Jaquette. Boston: Unwin Hyman.

———. 1990. *Engendering Democracy in Brazil: Women's Movements in Transition Politics.* Princeton: Princeton University Press.

———. 1998. "Latin American Feminisms Go Global." In *Cultures of Politics, Pol-*

itics of Cultures: Re-visioning Latin American Social Movements, edited by S. Alvarez, E. Dagnino, and A. Escobar. Boulder, CO: Westview Press.

Alves, Maria Helena Moreira. 1985. *State and Opposition in Military Brazil.* Austin: University of Texas Press.

Amado, Jorge. 1962. *Gabriela: Clove and Cinnamon.* New York: Alfred A. Knopf.

———. 1969. *Dona Flor and Her Two Husbands: A Moral and Amorous Tale.* New York: Knopf.

Americas Watch. 1991. *Criminal Injustice: Violence against Women in Brazil.* New York: Human Rights Watch.

Anderson, Benedict. 1983. *Imagined Communities: Reflections on the Origin and Spread of Nationalism.* London: Verso.

Anderson, Kristin L. 1997. "Gender, Status, and Domestic Violence: An Integration of Feminist and Family Violence Approaches." *Journal of Marriage and Family* 59(3): 655–670.

———. 2002. "Perpetrator or Victim? Relationships between Intimate Partner Violence and Well-Being." *Journal of Marriage and Family* 64(4): 851–863.

Ardaillon, Danielle, and Guita Grin Debert. 1987. *Quando a vítima é mulher: análise de julgamentos de crimes de estupro, espancamento e homicídio.* Brasília: Conselho Nacional dos Direitos da Mulher.

Avakame, Edem F. 1999. "Females' Labor Force Participation and Intimate Femicide: An Empirical Assessment of the Backlash Hypothesis." *Violence against Women* 5(11): 1321–1342.

Azevedo, Maria Amelia. 1985. *Mulheres espancadas: a violência denunciada.* São Paulo: Cortez.

———. 1987. *A Violência contra a mulher em questão na sociedade brasileira.* São Paulo: Núcleo Mulher da Universidade de São Paulo.

Azevedo, Rodrigo Ghiringhelli de. 2001. "Juizados especiais criminais: Uma abordagem sociológica sobre a informalização da justiça penal no Brasil." *Revista Brasileira de Ciências Sociais* 16(47): 97–110.

Bacelar, Jeferson. 1989. *Etnicidade Ser Negro em Salvador.* Penba: Ianamã.

Barbosa, Lívia Neves de H. 1995. "The Brazilian Jeitinho: An Exercise in National Identity." In *The Brazilian Puzzle: Culture on the Borderlands of the Western World,* edited by David Hess and Roberto da Matta, 35–48. New York: Columbia University Press.

Barker, Gary, and Irene Loewenstein. 1997. "Where the Boys Are: Attitudes Related to Masculinity, Fatherhood, and Violence among Low-Income Adolescent and Young Adult Males in Rio de Janeiro, Brazil." *Youth and Society* 29(2): 166–196.

Barnes, Sandra, ed. 1989. *Africa's Ogun: Old World and New.* Bloomington: Indiana University Press.

Bastide, Roger. 1996. "The Other *Quilombos.*" In *Maroon Societies: Rebel Slave*

Communities in the Americas, edited by Richard Price. Baltimore: Johns Hopkins University Press.

Berkovitz, Nitza. 1999. "The Emergence and Transformation of the International Women's Movement." In *Constructing World Culture: International Non-governmental Organizations Since 1875*, edited by J. Boli and G. Thomas. Stanford, CA: Stanford University Press.

Berman, Laine. 1999. "Dignity in Tragedy: How Javanese Women Speak of Emotion." In *Languages of Sentiment: Cultural Constructions of Emotional Substrates*, edited by Gary B. Palmer and Debra J. Occhi, et al., 65–105. Philadelphia: J. Benjamins.

Besse, Susan. 1989. "Crimes Passionais: A Campanha Contra os Assassinatos de Mulheres no Brasil: 1910–1940." *Revista Brasileira de História* 9(18): 181–197.

Besson, Jean. 1993. "Reputation and Respectability Reconsidered: A New Perspective on Afro-Caribbean Peasant Women." In *Women and Change in the Caribbean*, edited by J. Momsen. London: J. Curry.

Blay, Eva Alterman. 2003. "Violência Contra a Mulher e Políticas Públicas." *Estudos Avançados* 17(49): 87–98.

Borges, D. 1992. *The Family in Bahia, Brazil, 1870–1945*. Stanford: Stanford University Press.

Boselli. Giane. 2004. *Delegacia de Defesa das Mulheres: permanências e desafios.* Brasília: CFEMEA.

Boulding, Elise. 2000. *Cultures of Peace: The Hidden Side of History.* Syracuse: Syracuse University Press.

Bourdieu, Pierre. 1977. *Outline of a Theory of Practice.* Cambridge: Cambridge University Press.

———. 2001. *Masculine Domination.* Translated by Richard Nice. Stanford: Stanford University Press.

Bourgois, Philippe. 1995. *In Search of Respect: Selling Crack in El Barrio.* Cambridge: Cambridge University Press.

Bowker, Lee H. 1993. "A Battered Woman's Problems Are Social, Not Psychological." In *Current Controversies in Family Violence*, edited by Richard J. Gelles and Donileen R. Loseke. Newbury Park, CA: Sage Publications.

Brown, Judith K. 1999. "Introduction: Definitions, Assumptions, Themes, and Issues." In *To Have and to Hit: Cultural Perspectives on Wife Beating*, 2nd ed., edited by Dorothy A. Counts, Judith K. Brown, and Jacquelyn C. Campbell. Urbana: University of Illinois Press.

Buffon, Roseli. 1990. "Mudanças no Padrão de Masculinidade: quando a encenação da virilidade deve desenrolar-se sob um novo scripto." Paper presented at Universidade Federal de Santa Catarina, Brazil.

Burbank, Virginia. 1999. "Fight! Fight! Men, Women, and Interpersonal Aggression in an Australian Aboriginal Community. In *To Have and to Hit: Cul-*

tural Perspectives on Wife Beating, 2nd ed., edited by Dorothy A. Counts, Judith K. Brown, and Jacquelyn C. Campbell. Urbana: University of Illinois Press.

Burdick, John. 1990. "Gossip and Secrecy: Women's Articulation of Domestic Conflict in Three Religions of Urban Brazil." *Sociological Analysis* 51(2): 153–170.

Burton, Barbara. 2000. "Brutality and Bureaucracy: Human Rights, Intimate Violence, and the Role of Feminist Ethnography." *Political and Legal Anthropology Review* 23(1): 138–147.

Butler, Judith. 1990. *Gender Trouble: Feminism and the Subversion of Identity*. New York: Routledge.

Butler, Kim. 1998a. "Afterword: Ginga Baiana, the Politics of Race, Class, Culture, and Power in Salvador, Bahia." In *Afro-Brazilian Culture and Politics: Bahia, 1790s to 1990s*, edited by Hendirk Kraay. Armonk, NY: M. E. Sharpe.

———. 1998b. *Freedoms Given, Freedoms Won:Afro-Brazilians in Post-Abolition, São Paulo and Salvador*. New Brunswick, NJ: Rutgers University Press.

Calazans, Márcia Esteves de. 2004. "Mulheres no Policiamento Ostensivo e a Perspectiva de uma Segurança Cidadã." *São Paulo em Perspectiva* 18(1): 142–150.

Caldeira, Teresa P. R. 2001. *City of Walls: Crime, Segregation, and Citizenship in São Paulo*. Berkeley: University of California Press.

Campbell, Jacquelyn C. 1999. "Wife-Battering: Cultural Contexts versus Social Sciences." In *To Have and to Hit: Cultural Perspectives on Wife Beating*, 2nd ed., edited by Dorothy A. Counts, Judith K. Brown, and Jacquelyn C. Campbell. Urbana: University of Illinois Press.

———. 2004. "Helping Women Understand Their Risk in Situations of Intimate Partner Violence." *Journal of Interpersonal Violence* 12(19): 1464–1478.

CEPIA-Brasil (Ciudadanía, Estudo, Pesquisa, Informação e Ação-Brasil) (Barsted, Leila Linhares, coordinator). 1993. *Violência contra a Mulher e Cidadania: Uma avaliação das políticas públicas*. Rio de Janeiro: CEPIA-Brasil.

CHAME (Centro Humanitario de Apoio à Mulher). 1998. *O Que é que a Bahia Tem: O Outro Lado do Turismo em Salvador*. Salvador: Projeto CHAME/NEIM/UFBa.

Chauí, Marilena, Maria Celia Paoli, and S. O. S. Mulher (Bila Sorj, Pauloa Montero, Lígia Rodrigues, e Rita Andréa). 1984. *Perspectivas Antropológicas da Mulher 4: Sobre Mulher e Violência*. Rio de Janeiro: Zahar.

Chevigny, Paul. 1995. *Edge of the Knife: Police Violence in the Americas*. New York: New Press.

Clarke, R. 1995. "Situational Crime Prevention." In *Building a Safer Society: Strategic Approaches to Crime Prevention*, edited by M. Tonry and D. Farrington, 91–150. Chicago: University of Chicago Press.

Cole, Sally. 1994. "Introduction: Ruth Landes in Brazil; Writing, Race, and

Gender in 1930s American Anthropology." In *The City of Women* [1947], by Ruth Landes. Albuquerque: University of New Mexico Press.

Collier, Jane, and Sylvia Yanagisako. 1987. *Gender and Kinship: Essays toward a Unified Analysis*. Palo Alto: Stanford University Press.

Connell, Robert W. 1995. *Masculinities*. Berkeley: University of California Press.

Cornwall, Andrea. 1994. "Gendered Identities and Gender Ambiguity Among *Travestis* in Salvador, Brazil." In *Dislocating Masculinity*, edited by Andrea Cornwall and Nancy Lindisfarne. London: Routledge.

Corrêa, Mariza. 1983. *Morte em Familia: representações jurídicas de papéis sexuais*. Rio de Janeiro: Edições Graal.

Counts, Dorothy Ayers. 1999. "Preface." In *To Have and to Hit: Cultural Perspectives on Wife Beating*, 2nd ed., edited by Dorothy A. Counts, Judith K. Brown, and Jacquelyn C. Campbell. Urbana: University of Illinois Press.

Counts, Dorothy A., Judith K. Brown, and Jacquelyn C. Campbell, eds. 1999. *To Have and to Hit: Cultural Perspectives on Wife Beating*, 2nd ed. Urbana: University of Illinois Press.

Cubbins, Lisa A., and Dana Vannoy. 2005. "Socioeconomic Resources, Gender Traditionalism, and Wife Abuse in Urban Russian Couples." *Journal of Marriage and Family* 67(1): 37–52.

Cunha, Roberto Salles. 1989. *Os Novos Diretos da Mulher*. São Paulo: Atlas.

DaMatta, Roberto. 1982. *Violência Brasileira*. São Paulo: Brasiliense.

———. 1991. *Carnivals, Rogues, and Heroes: An Interpretation of the Brazilian Dilemma*. Notre Dame: University of Notre Dame Press.

———. 1995. "For an Anthropology of the Brazilian Tradition; or A Virtude está no Meio." In *The Brazilian Puzzle: Culture on the Borderlands of the Western World*, edited by David Hess and Roberto da Matta, 270–292. New York: Columbia University Press.

Daniel, E. Valentine. 1996. *Charred Lullabies: Chapters in an Anthropography of Violence*. Princeton: Princeton University Press.

Das, Veena, Arthur Kleinman, Mamphela Ramphele, and Pamela Reynolds. 2000. *Violence and Subjectivity*. Berkeley: University of California Press.

Dasgupta, Shamita Das. 2002. "A Framework for Understanding Women's Use of Nonlethal Violence in Intimate Heterosexual Relationships." *Violence Against Women* 8(11): 1364–1389.

de Aquino, Sílva. 2001. *Dores Visíveis: Violências em Delegacias da Mulher no Nordeste*. Salvador, Bahia, Brasil: REDOR/NEGIF/UFC.

Degler, Carl N. 1971. *Neither Black nor White: Slavery and Race Relations in Brazil and the United States*. New York: Macmillan.

de Oliveira, Neuza Maria. 1994. *Damas de Paus: O fogo Aberto dos Travestis no Espelho da Mulher*. Salvador: Universidade Federal da Bahia.

Dijaci, D. O., E. C. Geraldes, and R. B. Lima. 1998. *Primavera Já Partiu: Retrato dos homicídios femininos no Brasil*. Brasília: Movimento Nacional de Direitos Humanos.

di Leonardo, Micaela. 1991. "Introduction." In *Gender at the Crossroads of Knowledge*, edited by Micaela di Leonardo. Berkeley: University of California Press.

Dobash, R. Emerson, and Russell P. Dobash. 1992. *Women, Violence and Social Change*. London: Routledge.

d'Oliveira, Ana Flávia P. L., and Lilia B. Schraiber. 2005. "Violence against Women in Brazil: Overview, Gaps and Challenges." Presented at the expert group meeting: Violence against Women: A Statistical Overview, Challenges and Gaps in Data Collection and Methodology and Approaches for Overcoming Them. Geneva, Switzerland. (Available at http://www.un.org/women watch/daw/egm/vaw-stat-2005/docs/expert-papers/d_Oliveira.pdf).

Dunn, Christopher. 2001. *Brutality Garden: Tropicália and the Emergence of a Brazilian Counterculture*. Chapel Hill: University of North Carolina Press.

Ehlers, Tracy Bachrach. 1991. "Debunking Marianismo: Economic Vulnerability and Survival Strategies among Guatemalan Wives." *Ethnology* 30(1): 1–16.

———. 2000. *Silent Looms: Women and Production in a Guatemalan Town*. Austin: University of Texas Press.

Espinheira, Carlos G. d'Andrea. 1971. *Comunidade do Maciel*. Salvador: Secretaria de Educação e Cultura Fudação do Patrimônio Artistico e Cultural da Bahia.

———. 1984. *Divergência e Prostituição*. Rio de Janeiro: Tempo Brasileiro.

Fagan, Jeff. 1997. "The Myth of Classlessness in Domestic Violence." *New York Times*, March 31: A12.

Faludi, Susan. 1991. *Backlash: The Undeclared War against American Women*. New York: Crown.

———. 1999. *Stiffed: The Betrayal of the American Man*. New York: William Morrow and Co.

Feiguin, D. E. B. Trinidade, M. Aparecida, and M. E. Paternostro, eds. 1987. *Um Retrato da Violência Contra a Mulher: 2083 boletins de ocorrência*. São Paulo: SEADE/CECF.

Feldman, Allen. 1991. *Formations of Violence: The Narrative of the Body and Political Terror in Northern Ireland*. Chicago: University of Chicago Press.

Fernandez, James. 1982. *Bwiti: An Ethnography of the Religious Imagination in Africa*. Princeton: Princeton University Press.

Ferreira, M. I. Caetano, and W. P. Izumino. n.d. "Autoritarismo Socialente Implantado: Violência contra Mulher e Violência Familiar." Final Research Report. São Paulo: Núcleo de Estudos da Violência, USP.

Flake, Dallan F. 2005. "Individual, Family, and Community Risk Markers for Domestic Violence in Peru." *Violence Against Women* 11(3): 353–373.

Flynn, C. P. (1990). "Relationship Violence by Women: Issues and Implications." *Family Relations* 36: 295–299.

Fontaine, Pierre-Michel, ed. 1985. *Race, Class, and Power in Brazil.* Los Angeles: Center for Afro-American Studies, University of California.

Foucault, Michel. 1980. *Power/knowledge: Selected Interviews and Other Writings, 1972–1977.* Hemel Hempstead, U.K.: Harvester Wheatsheaf.

Freire, Paulo. 1978. *Pedagogia do Oprimido*, 10th ed. Rio de Janeiro: Paz e Terra.

Freyre, Gilberto. 1946. *Casa Grande e Senzala.* Rio de Janeiro: José Olympio.

Fuss, Diana. 1989. *Essentially Speaking: Feminism, Nature, and Difference.* New York: Routledge.

Geertz, Clifford. 1973. *The Interpretation of Cultures.* New York: Basic Books.

Gelles, Richard J., and Donileen R. Loseke. 1993. "Introduction." In *Current Controversies in Family Violence,* edited by Richard J. Gelles and Donileen R. Loseke. Newbury Park, CA: Sage Publications.

Giddens, Anthony. 1991. *Modernity and Self-Identity: Society in the Late Modern Age.* Stanford: Stanford University Press.

Gilmore, David D. 1990. *Manhood in the Making: Cultural Concepts of Masculinity.* New Haven, CT: Yale University Press.

Goldstein, Donna M. 2003. *Laughter out of Place: Race, Class, Violence, and Sexuality in a Rio Shantytown.* Berkeley: University of California Press.

Graden, Dale T. 1998. "So Much Superstition among These People!: Candomblé and the Dilemmas of Afro-Bahian Intellectuals, 1864–1871." In *Afro-Brazilian Culture and Politics: Bahia, 1790s to 1990s,* edited by Hendirk Kraay. Armonk, NY: M. E. Sharpe.

Gramsci, A. 1971. *Selections from the Prison Notebooks.* New York: International.

Greenfield, Sidney. 1994. "Moral and Ethical Standards in West African Yoruba and Brazilian Candomblé." Presented at the 93rd annual meeting of the American Anthropological Association.

Gregori, Maria Filomena. 1993. "Cenas e Queixas: mulheres e relações violentas." *Novos Estudos CEBRAP* (23).

Grossi, Miriam Pillar. 1991. "Vítimas ou Cumplices? Dos diferentes caminhos da produção acadêmica sobre violência contra a mulher no Brasil." Presented at the XV Encontro Anual da ANPOCS.

Gutmann, Matthew. 1996. *The Meanings of Macho: Being a Man in Mexico City.* Berkeley: University of California Press.

———. 1997. "Trafficking in Men: The Anthropology of Masculinity." *Annual Review of Anthropology* 26:385–409.

———, ed. 2003. *Changing Men and Masculinities in Latin America.* Durham: Duke University Press.

Hahner, June. 1990. *Emancipating the Female Sex: The Struggle for Women's Rights in Brazil, 1850–1940.* Durham: Duke University Press.

Hanchard, Michael. 1994. *Orpheus and Power: The Movimento Negro of Rio de Janeiro and São Paulo, Brazil.* Princeton: Princeton University Press.

Handwerker, W. Penn. 1998. "Why Violence? A Test of Hypotheses Representing Three Discourses of the Roots of Domestic Violence." *Human Organization* 57(2): 200–208.

Hanmer Jalna, Jill Radford, and Elizabeth Stanko. 1989. *Women, Policing, and Male Violence.* London: Routledge.

Harazim, Dorrit. 1998. "A Face do Silêncio: A violência doméstica atinge não apenas a mulher, mas toda a sociedade." *Veja,* July 1: 81–87.

Harding, Rachel. 2000. *A Refuge in Thunder: Candomblé and Alternative Spaces of Blackness.* Bloomington: University of Indiana Press.

Harris, Marvin. 1970. "Referential Ambiguity in the Calculus of Brazilian Racial Identity." *Southwestern Journal of Anthropology* 26: 1–14.

Hasenbalg, Carlos A. 1985. "Race and Socioeconomic Inequalities in Brazil." In *Race, Class, and Power in Brazil,* edited by Pierre-Michel Fontaine, 25–41. Los Angeles: Center for Afro-American Studies, University of California.

Hasenbalg, Carlos, and Nelson do Valle Silva. 1999. "Notes on Racial and Political Inequality in Brazil." In *Racial Politics in Contemporary Brazil,* edited by M. G. Hanchard. Durham: Duke University Press.

Hautzinger, Sarah. 1997a. "Da Delegacia Específica à Casa-Abrigo: Novo Passo no Combate à Violência Contra Mulher." *Bahia Análise and Dados* 7(2): 190–197.

———. 1997b. "The Powers and Pitfalls of Gender Essentialism: Policing Male-to-Female Violence in Brazil." *Political and Legal Anthropology Review* 20(2): 34–46.

———. 1997c. "Calling a State a State: Feminist Politics and the Policing of Violence against Women in Brazil." *Feminist Issues* 1–2: 3–30.

———. 2002. "Criminalising Male Violence in Brazil's Women's Police Stations: From Flawed Essentialism to Imagined Communities." *Journal of Gender Studies* 11(3): 243–251.

———. 2003. "Researching Men's Violence: Personal Reflections on Ethnographic Data." *Men and Masculinities* 6(1): 93–106.

———. 2004. "Here the Cock Does Not Crow, for He Is Not the Lord of the Land: Machismo, Insecurity, and Male Violence in Brazil." In *Cultural Shaping of Violence,* edited by M. Anderson. West Lafayette, Indiana: Purdue University Press.

Hearn, Jeff. 2004. "From Hegemonic Masculinity to the Hegemony of Men." *Feminist Theory* 5(1): 49–72.

Heise, Lori. 1998. "Violence against Women: An Integrated, Ecological Framework." *Violence against Women* 4(3): 262–291.

Heise, L., M. Ellsberg, and M. Gottemoeller. 1999. "Ending Violence against Women." *Population Reports,* L(11). Baltimore: Johns Hopkins University School of Public Health Press.

Hess, David, and Roberto DaMatta. 1995. "Introduction." In *The Brazilian Puzzle: Culture on the Borderlands of the Western World,* edited by David Hess and Roberto da Matta, 1–30. New York: Columbia University Press.

Honigmann, John. 1947. Review of *The City of Women*. *Social Forces* 26: 227.

hooks, bell. 1994. "Essentialism and Experience." In *Teaching to Transgress*. New York: Routledge.

Huggins, M. K., M. Haritos-Fatouros, and P. G. Zimbardo. 2002. *Violence Workers: Police Tortures and Murders Reconstruct Brazilian Atrocities*. Los Angeles: University of California Press.

Ilé Axé Opô Afonjá. 1999. "*Iansã* Is Not Saint Barbara." In *The Brazil Reader: History, Culture, Politics*, edited by Robert M. Levine and John J. Crocitti. Durham: Duke University Press.

Izumino, Wânia Pasinato. 1998. *Justiça e violência contra a mulher: o papel do sistema judiciário na solução dos conflitos de gênero*. São Paulo: Annablume, Fapesp.

Jaquette, Jane S., ed. 1989. *The Women's Movement in Latin America: Feminism and the Transition to Democracy*. Boston: Unwin Hyman.

Johnson, Michael P. 1995. "Patriarchal Terrorism and Common Couple Violence: Two Forms of Violence against Women." *Journal of Marriage and Family* 57(2): 283–295.

Johnson, Michael P., and Kathleen J. Ferraro. 2000. "Research on Domestic Violence in the 1990s: Making Distinctions." *Journal of Marriage and Family* 62(4): 948–963.

Johnson, Michael P., and Janel M. Leone. 2005. "The Differential Effects of Intimate Terrorism and Situational Couple Violence: Findings From the National Violence Against Women Survey." *Journal of Family Issues* 26(3): 322–350.

Johnson, Paul C. 2002. *Secrets, Gossip, and Gods: The Transformation of Brazilian Candomblé*. Oxford: Oxford University Press.

Jurema, Solange Bentes. 2001. "Ações e estratégias do CNDM para o 'empoderamento' das mulheres." *Revista Estudos Feminista* 9(1): 207–212.

Kandaswamy, Deepa. 2005. "Indian Policewomen Practice Policing and Politicking: All-Female Battalions Focus on Crimes against Women." *Ms.,* Spring. http://www.msmagazine.com/spring2005/indianpolicewomen.asp.

Kandiyoti, Denise. 1988. "Bargaining with Patriarchy." *Gender and Society* 2: 274–290.

Kant de Lima, Roberto. 1995. "Bureaucratic Rationality in Brazil and in the United States: Criminal Justice Systems in Comparative Perspective." In *The Brazilian Puzzle: Culture on the Borderlands of the Western World*, edited by David Hess and Roberto DaMatta, 241–269. New York: Columbia University Press.

Keck, M. Emily. 1989. "The New Unionism in the Brazilian Tradition." In *Democratizing Brazil: Problems of Transition and Consolidation*, edited by Alfred Stepan. New York: Oxford University Press.

Kerns, Virginia. 1997. *Women and the Ancestors: Black Carib Kinship and Ritual*. Urbana: University of Illinois Press.

———. 1999. "Preventing Violence against Women: A Central American Case." In *To Have and to Hit: Cultural Perspectives on Wife Beating*, 2nd ed., edited by Dorothy A. Counts, Judith K. Brown, and Jacquelyn C. Campbell. Urbana: University of Illinois Press.

Kirk, Gwyn, and Margo Okazawa-Rey. 2000. *Women's Lives: Multicultural Perspectives*, 2nd ed. Mountain View, CA: Mayfield.

Kottak, Conrad. 1992. *Assault on Paradise: Social Change in a Brazilian Village*, 2nd ed. New York: McGraw-Hill.

———. 1995. "Swimming in Cross-Cultural Currents." In *The Brazilian Puzzle: Culture on the Borderlands of the Western World*, edited by David Hess and Roberto da Matta, 49–58. New York: Columbia University Press.

Krauft, Bruce M. 1987. "Reconsidering Violence in Simple Societies." *Current Anthropology* 28(4): 457–500

Kulick, Don. 1998. *Travesti: Sex, Gender, and Culture among Brazilian Transgendered Prostitutes.* Chicago: University of Chicago Press.

Kurz, Demie. 1993. "Physical Assaults by Husbands: A Major Social Problem." In *Current Controversies in Family Violence*, edited by Richard J. Gelles and Donileen Loseke. Newbury Park, CA: Sage Publications.

Lancaster, Roger N. 1992. *Life Is Hard: Machismo, Danger, and the Intimacy of Power in Nicaragua.* Berkeley: University of California Press.

Landes, Ruth. 1940. "A Cult Matriarchate and Male Homosexuality." *Journal of Abnormal and Social Psychology* 35: 386–397.

———. 1994 [1947]. *The City of Women.* Albuquerque: University of New Mexico Press.

Lazarus-Black, Mindie. 2001. "Law and the Pragmatics of Inclusion: Governing Domestic Violence in Trinidad and Tobago." *American Ethnologist* 28(2): 388–416.

Lazarus-Black, Mindie, and Susan Hirsh, eds. 1994. *Contested States Law, Hegemony and Resistance.* New York: Routledge.

Lepowsky, Maria. 1999. "Women, Men and Aggression in an Egalitarian Society." In *Gender, Culture, and Ethnicity: Current Research about Men and Women*, edited by L. A. Peplau, S. C. DeBro, R. C. Veniegas, and P. L. Taylor, 284–289. Mountain View, CA: Mayfield.

Levinson, David. 1989. *Family Violence in Cross-Cultural Perspective.* Newbury Park, CA: Sage Publications.

Lima, Vivaldo da Costa. 1977. "A Família-de-Santo nos Candomblés Jeje-Nagos da Bahia: Um Estudo de Relações Intra-Grupais." M.A. thesis: Universidade Federal da Bahia.

Linger, Daniel. 1990. "Essential Outlines of Crime and Madness: Man-Fights in São Luís." *Cultural Anthropology* 5(1): 62–77.

———. 1992. *Dangerous Encounters: Meanings of Violence in a Brazilian City.* Stanford: Stanford University Press.

———. 1993. "The Hegemony of Discontent." *American Ethnologist* 21(1): 3–24.

———. 2001. *No One Home: Brazilian Selves Remade in Japan.* Stanford: Stanford University Press.

London, Scott. 1997. "Conciliation and Domestic Violence in Senegal, West Africa." *Political and Legal Anthropology Review* 20(2): 83–91.

Loseke, Donileen R. 1989. "'Violence Is Violence' . . . or Is It? The Social Construction of 'Wife Abuse' and Public Policy." In *Images and Issues*, edited by Joel Best. New York: Aldine de Gruyter.

Lowenthal, Ira. 1989. *Marriage Is 20, Children Are 21.* Ph.D. Dissertation. Baltimore: The Johns Hopkins University.

Machado, Eduardo Paes, and Ceci Vilar Noronha. 2002. "The Police of the Poor: The Violence of Police against Urban Popular Classes." *Sociologias* 7: 188–221.

Machado, Lia Zanota. n.d. *Eficácia e Desafios das Delegacias Especialzadas no Atendimento à Mulheres: O Futuro da Não-violência.* Brasília: Conselho Nacional dos Direitos da Mulher.

Majdalani, May. 1996. "Strategies for Identifying and Countering Domestic Violence." *Al-Raida* 13(74/75): 38–40.

MacKinnon, Catharine. 1989. *Toward a Feminist Theory of the State.* Cambridge, MA: Harvard University Press.

MacMillan, Ross, and Rosemary Gartner. 1999. "When She Brings Home the Bacon: Labor Force Participation and the Risk of Spousal Violence against Women." *Journal of Marriage and Family* 61(Nov.): 947–958.

Malone, Jean, Andrea Tyree, and Dan O'Leary. 1989. "Generalization and Containment: Different Effects of Past Aggression for Wives and Husbands." *Journal of Marriage and Family* 51(3): 687–697.

Marques-Pereira, B., and F. Raes. 2005. "Women's Movements: From Local Action to Internationalization of the Repertoire." In *Collective Action and Radicalism in Brazil*, edited by M. Duquette, M. Galdino, C. Levy, B. Marques-Pereira, and F. Raes. Toronto: University of Toronto Press.

Martin, Susan. 1989. *Breaking and Entering: Policewomen on Patrol.* Berkeley: University of California Press.

Matory, J. Lorand. 1994. *Sex and the Empire that Is No More: Gender and the Politics of Metaphor in Oyo Yoruba Religion.* Minneapolis: University of Minnesota Press.

———. 2005. *Black Atlantic Religion: Tradition, Transnationalism, and Matriarchy in the Afro-Brazilian Candomblé.* Princeton, NJ: Princeton University Press.

Mattos, Waldemar. 1979. *História da Polícia Civil da Bahia.* Salvador: Empresa Gráfica da Bahia.

Mayo, Yolando Q., and Rosa P. Resnick. 1996. "The Impact of Machismo on Hispanic Women." *Affilia: Journal of Women and Social Work* 11(3): 257–278.

McCall, George J., and N. M. Shields. 1986. "Social and Structural Factors in

Family Violence." In *Violence in the Home: Interdisciplinary Perspectives*, edited by Mary Lystad. New York: Brunner/Mazel.

McClusky, Laura. 2001. *Here, Our Culture Is Hard: Stories of Domestic Violence from a Mayan Community in Belize*. Austin: Texas University Press.

McCoid, Catherine H., and Manisha Desai. 1989. "Violence Against Women in South India and the United States." Paper presented to the American Anthropological Association.

McElhinny, Bonnie. 1994. "An Economy of Affect: Objectivity, Masculinity, and the Gendering of Police Work." In *Dislocating Masculinity: Comparative Ethnographies*, edited by Andrea Cornwall and Nancy Lindisfarne. London: Routledge.

Melzer, Scott. 2002. "Gender, Work, and Intimate Violence: Men's Occupational Violence Spillover and Compensatory Violence." *Journal of Marriage and Family* 64(4): 820–833.

Merry, Sally E. 1994. "Courts as Performances: Domestic Violence Hearings in a Hawai'i Family Court." In *Contested States: Law, Hegemony, and Resistance*, edited by Mindie Lazarus-Black and Susan F. Hirsch. New York: Routledge.

———. 2000. *Colonizing Hawai'i: The Cultural Power of Law*. Princeton: Princeton University Press.

Miller, Laura. 1997. "Not Just Weapons of the Weak: Gender Harassment as a Form of Protest for Army Men." *Social Psychology Quarterly* 60(1):32–51.

Mintz, Sidney W. 1971a. "Men, Women, and Trade." *Comparative Studies in Society and History* 13(3): 247–269.

———. 1971b. "Toward an Afro-American History." *Journal of World History (Cahiers d'Histoire Mondiale)* XIII(2):317–331.

———. 1974. *Caribbean Transformations*. Baltimore: Johns Hopkins University Press.

———. 1981. "Economic Role and Cultural Tradition." In *Black Women Cross-Culturally*, edited by Filomina C. Steady. Cambridge: Schenkman.

———. 1985. *Sweetness and Power*. Boston: Beacon Press.

Mintz, Sidney, and Richard Price. 1992 [1976]. *The Birth of African American Culture: An Anthropological Perspective*. Boston: Beacon Press.

Mishnun, Virginia. 1947. "Review of *The City of Women*." *The Nation* 165: 128.

Mitchell, William E. 1999. "Why Wape Men Don't Beat Their Wives: Constraints toward Domestic Tranquility in a New Guinea Society." In *To Have and to Hit: Cultural Perspectives on Wife Beating*, 2nd ed., edited by Dorothy A. Counts, Judith K. Brown, and Jacquelyn C. Campbell. Urbana: University of Illinois Press.

Mohanty, C. T. 1991. "Introduction: Cartographies of Struggle." In *Third World Women and the Politics of Feminism*, edited by C. T. Mohanty, A. Russo, and L. Torres. Bloomington: Indiana University Press.

Molyneux, Maxine. 1985. "Mobilisation Without Emancipation? Women's Interests, the State and Revolution in Nicaragua." *Feminist Studies* 11: 227–254.

Monagan, Alfrieta Parks. 1985. "Rethinking 'Matrifocality.'" *Phylon* 46(4): 353–372.

Moore, Henrietta. 1988. *Feminism and Anthropology*. Cambridge: Polity.

———. 1994. "The Problem of Explaining Violence in the Social Sciences." In *Sex and Violence: Issues in Representation and Experience*, edited by Penelope Harvey and Peter Gow. Routledge: London.

Mtintso, Thenjiwe. 2003. "Representivity: False Sisterhood or Universal Women's Interests? The South African Experience." *Feminist Studies* 29(3): 569–580.

Mueggler, Erik. 2001. *The Age of Wild Ghosts Memory, Violence, and Place in Southwest China*. Berkeley: University of California Press.

Muir, William Ker, Jr. 1977. *Police: Streetcorner Politicians*. Chicago: University of Chicago Press.

Naccache, Tina. 1996. "Violence." *Al-Raida* 13(74/75): 41–44.

Nanda, Serena. 1990. *Neither Man nor Woman: The Hijras of India*. Belmont, CA: Wadsworth.

Natarajan, Mangai. 2001. "Women Police in a Traditional Society: Test of a Western Model of Integration." *International Journal of Comparative Sociology* 42(1–2): 211–233.

Navarro, Marysa. 2002. "Against *Marianismo*." In *Gender's Place: Feminist Anthropologies of Latin America*. New York: Palgrave Macmillan. 257–272.

Nelson, Sara. 1996. "Constructing and Negotiating Gender in Women's Police Stations in Brazil." *Latin American Perspectives* 23(1): 131–148.

Neto, Francisco. 1992. *As Mulheres na Polícia Civil da Bahia*. Masters Thesis. Salvador: Univerisdade Federal da Bahia.

Neuhouser, Kevin. 1989. "Sources of Women's Power and Status among the Urban Poor in Contemporary Brazil." *Signs* 14(3): 685–702.

Nobre, Miriam. 2003. "Women's Rights to Employment and Fair Wages." *Rede Social de justiça e direitos humanos*. http://www.social.org.br/relatorio2003 ingles/relatorio029.htm.

Nogueira, Claudia M. 2004. *A Feminização no Mundo do Trabalho*. São Paulo, Brasil: Editora Autores Associados.

Nolasco, Sócrates. 1993. *O Mito da Masculinidade*. Rio de Janiero: Rocco.

O'Donnell, Guillermo. 1993. "On the State, Democratization and Some Conceptual Problems: A Latin American View with Glances at Some Postcommunist Countries." *World Development* 21(8): 1355–1369.

Oetzel, John, and Bonnie Duran. 2004. "Intimate Partner Violence in American Indian and/or Alaska Native Communities: A Social Ecological Framework of Determinants and Interventions." *American Indian and Alaska Native Mental Health Research: The Journal of the National Center* 11(3): 49–68.

Okum, Lewis. 1986. *Woman Abuse, Myth Replacing Fact.* Albany: State University of New York Press.

Oliveira, Neuza Maria de. 1994. *Damas de Paus: O fogo Aberto dos Travestis no Espelho da Mulher.* Salvador: Universidade Federal da Bahia.

Oliven, Ruben George. 1984a. "A Malandragem na Musica Popular Brasileira." *Latin American Music Review* 5: 1.

———. 1984b. "State and Culture in Brazil." *Latin American Perspectives.* 11(1): 3–137.

———. 1989. "Anthropology and Brazilian Society." *Current Anthropology* 30(4): 510–514.

———. 1995. "Looking at Money in America." *Critique of Anthropology* 18(1): 35–59.

Oliven, Ruben, George Tesser, and Carmen Chaves. 1999. "Money in Brazilian Popular Music." *Studies in Latin American Popular Culture* 18: 115–138.

Omari-Tunkara, M. S. 2005. *Manipulating the Sacred: Yorùbá Art, Ritual, and Resistance in Brazilian Candomblé.* Detroit: Wayne State University Press.

Ortner, Sherry B. 2003. *New Jersey Dreaming: Capital, Culture, and the Class of '58.* Durham: Duke University Press.

Ostermann, Ana Cristina. 2003a. "Communities of Practice at Work: Gender, Facework, and the Power of Habitus at an All-Female Police Station and a Feminist Crisis Intervention Center in Brazil." *Discourse and Society* 14(4): 473–506.

———. 2003b. "Localizing Power and Solidarity: Pronoun Alternation at al All-Female Police Station and a Feminist Crisis Intervention Center in Brazil." *Language in Society* 32(3): 351–382.

Palazzini, Karen. 1995. "Formal Employment or Informal Employment: Women's Decisions in Lauro de Freitas, Bahia." Paper presented at the annual meetings of the Latin American Studies Association.

Pan-American Health Organization. 1999. "Proyecto ACTIVA Data." *Revista Panamericana de Salud Pública* 5(4/5): 347–356.

Paoli, Maria Célia M. 1982. *Desenvolvimento e marginalidade: Um Estudo de Caso.* São Paulo: Livraria Pioneira Editora.

Parker, Richard G. 1991. *Bodies, Pleasures, and Passions: Sexual Culture in Contemporary Brazil.* Boston: Beacon Press.

Parks Monagan, Alfrieta. 1985. "Rethinking 'Matrifocality.'" *Phylon* 46(4): 353–372.

Patai, Daphne. 1988. *Brazilian Women Speak: Contemporary Life Stories.* New Brunswick, NJ: Rutgers University Press.

———. 1991. "Women and the New Brazilian Constitution." *Feminist Studies* 17(3): 550.

Payne, J., and E. Fits. 1993. *Ambiguity and Gender in the New Novel of Brazil and Spanish America.* Iowa City: University of Iowa Press.

Perlman, Janice. 1976. *The Myth of Marginality: Urban Poverty and Politics in Rio de Janeiro*. Berkeley: University of California Press.

———. 2006. "The Metamorphosis of Marginality: Four Generations in the Favelas of Rio de Janeiro." *The Annals of the American Academy of Political and Social Science* 606: 154–177.

Perry, Richard W. 2000. "City of Walls: A Discussion with Teresa Caldeira." *Political and Legal Anthropology Review* 23(1): 122–137.

Peterson, V. Spike, and Anne S. Runyan. 1994. "A Stark Picture: Gendered Politics in a Global Context." *Harvard International Review* (16)4: 38–42.

Pinheiro, Paulo Sérgio. 1996. "Democracies without Citizenship." *North American Council on Latin America* 30(2): 17–23.

Pitt-Rivers, J. 1968. "Honor." In *International Encyclopedia of the Social Sciences*, edited by D. Sills. New York: Macmillan.

Porto Filho, Ubaldo Marques. 1991. Rio Vermelho. Salvador: AMARV.

Prandi, J. Reginaldo. 1991. *Os candomblés de São Paulo: a velha magia na metrópole nova*. São Paulo: Editora Hucitec: Editora de Universidade de São Paulo.

Purushothaman, Sangeetha. 1998. *The Empowerment of Women in India: Grassroots Women's Networks and the State*. New Delhi and Thousand Oaks, CA: Sage Publications.

Quintas, Fátima. 1986. *Sexo e Marginalidade: um estudo sobre a sexualidade feminina em camadas de baixa renda*. Petrópolis: Editora Vozes Ltda.

Ramirez, Francisco O., Yasemin Soysal, and Suzanne Shanahan. 1997. "The Changing Logic of Political Citizenship: Cross-National Acquisition of Women's Suffrage Rights, 1890 to 1990." *American Sociological Review* 62: 735–745.

Ray, Ella Maria. 1998. Standing in the Lion's Shadow: Jamaican Rastafari Women Constructing Their African Identity. Ph.D. Dissertation. Baltimore: Johns Hopkins University.

Rebhun, Linda-Anne. 1999. *The Heart Is Unknown Country: Love in the Changing Economy of Northeast Brazil*. Stanford, CA: Stanford University Press.

Reddy, Gayatri. 2005. *With Respect to Sex: Negotiating Hijra Identity in South India*. Chicago: University of Chicago Press.

Rego, Waldeloir. 1993. "Mitos e Ritos Africanos da Bahia." In *Os Deuses Africanos no Candomblé da Bahia*. Salvador: Bigraf.

Ribeiro, Darcy. 1995. *O Povo Brasileiro: A formação e o Sentido do Brasil*, 2nd ed. São Paulo: Companhia das Letras.

Riches, David, ed. 1986. *The Anthropology of Violence*. Oxford: Basil Blackwell.

Rohter, Larry. 2001. "Brazil Passes Equal Rights for Its Women: After a Long Battle, Patriarchy Yielding." *New York Times*, August 19: Y10.

Rodrigues, Nelson. 1974. *Elas Gostam de Apanhar*. Rio de Janeiro: Bloch Editores.

Safa, Helen I. 1995. *The Myth of the Male Breadwinner: Women and Industrialization in the Caribbean*. Boulder: Westview Press.

Saffiotti, Heleieth. 1976. "Relationships of Sex and Social Class in Brazil." In *Sex and Class in Latin America*, edited by J. Nash and H. Safa. New York: Praeger.

———. 1987. "Feminismos e seus frutos no Brasil." In *Movimentos Sociais na Transição Democrática*, edited by Emir Sader et al. São Paulo: Cortez.

———. 1994. "Violência de gênero do Brasil contemporâneo." Report to UNICEF, CNPq, and the Ford Foundation.

———. 2004. *Gênero, patriarcado, violência*. São Paulo: Editora Fundação Perseu Abramo.

Sanjek, Roger. 1971. "Brazilian Racial Terms: Some Aspects of Meaning and Learning." *American Anthropologist* 73(5): 1126–1143.

Sansone, Livio. 2003. *Blackness without Ethnicity: Constructing Race in Brazil*. New York: Palgrave MacMillan.

Santos, Cecília MacDowell. 2001. "Delegacias Da Mulher em São Paulo: Percurso e Percalços." *Direitos Humanos no Brasil 2001*. Rede Social de Justiça e Direitos Humanos. http://www.dhnet.org.br/denunciar/brasil_2001/cap4_delegacia.htm.

———. 2004. "En-gendering the Police: Women's Police Stations and Feminism in São Paulo." *Latin American Research Review* 29(3): 29–55.

Sardenberg, M. Cecília B., and Ana Alice A. Costa. 1994. "Feminismos, Feministas e Movimentos Sociais." *Estudos Feministas* 3(2): 387–400.

Scheper-Hughes, Nancy. 1992. *Death without Weeping: The Violence of Everyday Life in Brazil*. Berkeley: University of California Press.

Schneider, Ronald M. 1996. *Brazil: Culture and Politics in a New Industrial Powerhouse*. Boulder: Westview Press.

Schwartz, Stuart. 1986. *Sugar Plantations in the Formation of Brazilian Society: Bahia, 1550–1835*. New York: Cambridge University Press.

———. 1996. "The *Mocambo*: Slave Resistance in Colonial Brazil." In *Maroon Societies: Rebel Slave Communities in the Americas*, edited by R. Price. Baltimore: Johns Hopkins University Press.

Scott, James C. 1985. *Weapons of the Weak: Everyday Forms of Peasant Resistance*. New Haven: Yale University Press.

Seremetakis, C. Nadia. 1991. *The Last Word: Women, Death, and Divination in Inner Mali*. Chicago: University of Chicago Press.

Shapiro, Dolores. 1995. "Blood, Oil, Honey, and Water: Symbolism in Spirit Possession Sects in Northeastern Brazil." *American Ethnologist* 22(4): 828–847.

Sharma, O. C. 1994. *Crimes against Women*. New Delhi: Ashish Publishing House.

———. 2002. "Investigative Techniques by Specialised Units in Police Stations—Womens Crime Cells (India)." Available at http://www.wjin.net/Pubs/2305.pdf.

———. n.d. "Crimes against Women." In "Police and Crimes against Women: Some Emerging Issues and Challenges." (Unpublished ms.)

Sheriff, Robin. 2000. "Exposing Silence as Cultural Censorship: A Brazilian Case." *American Anthropologist* 102 (1): 114.

Silva, Hélio. 1993. *Travesti: A Invenção do Feminino*. Rio de Janeiro: Relume Dumará.

Silva, Kelly Cristiane. n.d. *Pesquisa Nacional sobre as Condições de Funciona-mento das Delegacias Especializadas no Atendimento às Mulheres.* Brasília: Conselho Nacional dos Direitos da Mulher.

Silva, Marlise Vinagre. 1992. *Violência Contra a Mulher: Quem Mete a Colher?* São Paulo: Cortez.

Silva, Nelson do Valle. 1985. "Updating the Cost of Not Being White in Brazil." In *Race, Class, and Power in Brazil,* edited by Pierre-Michel Fontaine, 42–55. Los Angeles: Center for Afro-American Studies, University of California.

Silverstein, Leni. 1995 "The Celebration of Our Lord of the Good End: Changing State, Church, and Afro-Brazilian Relations in Bahia." In *The Brazilian Puzzle: Culture on the Borderlands of the Western World,* edited by David Hess and Roberto da Matta, 114–133. New York: Columbia University Press.

Simpson, Amelia. 1993. *Xuxa: The Mega-Marketing of Gender, Race, and Modernity.* Philadelphia: Temple University Press.

Skidmore, Thomas E. 1974. *Black into White; Race and Nationality in Brazilian Thought.* New York: Oxford University Press.

Smith, Raymond T. 1973. "The Matrifocal Family." In *The Character of Kinship,* edited by Jack Goody. Cambridge: Cambridge University Press.

Snider, Laureen. 1998. "Toward Safer Societies: Punishment, Masculinities, and Violence against Women." *British Journal of Criminology* 38(1): 1–39.

Soares, Barbara Musumeci. 1999. *Mulheres Invisíveis: Violência conjugal e as novas políticas de segurança.* Rio de Janeiro: Civilização Brasileira.

Sorj, Bila, and Paula Montero. 1984. "SOS-Mulher e a Luta contra a Violência." In *Perspectivas Antropológicas da Mulher 4: Sobre Mulher e Violência,* edited by Bruna Franchetto, M. L. V. C. Cavalcanti, and M. L. Heilborn. Rio de Janeiro: Zahar.

Stanko, Elizabeth A. 1985. *Intimate Intrusions: Women's Experience of Male Violence.* Routledge and Kegan Paul, London.

Steeves, H. Leslie. 1993. "Creating Imagined Communities: Development Communication and the Challenge of Feminism." *Journal of Communication* 43(3): 218–229.

Steinmetz, Suzanne K. 1978. "The Battered Husband Syndrome." *Victimology* 2: 499–509.

Stepan, Alfred. 1988. *Rethinking Military Politics: Brazil and the Southern Cone.* Princeton: Princeton University Press.

Stevens, Evelyn P. 1973a. "The Prospects for a Women's Liberation Movement in Latin America." *Journal of Marriage and Family* 35(2): 313–312.

———. 19973b. "Marianismo: The Other Face of 'Machismo' in Latin America." In *Female and Male in Latin America,* edited by Ann Pescatello, 89–110. Pittsburgh: University of Pittsburgh.

Stewart, Pamela J., and Andrew Strathern. 2002. *Violence: Theory and Ethnography.* London and New York: Continuum.

Stolcke, Verena. 1991. "The Social Impact of the Crisis of Development." In *Eight Essays on the Crisis of Development in Latin America,* edited by Gonzales Casanova et al. Amsterdam: CEDLA.

Strathern, Marilyn. 1988. *The Gender of the Gift: Problems with Women and Problems with Society in Melanesia.* Berkeley: University of California Press.

Straus, Murray A. 1983. "Societal Morphogenesis and Intrafamily Violence in Cross-Cultural Perspective." In *International Perspectives on Family Violence,* edited by Richard J. Gelles and Claire P. Cornell. Lexington, MA: Lexington Books.

———. 1993. "Physical Assaults by Wives: A Major Social Problem." In *Current Controversies in Family Violence,* edited by Richard J. Gelles and Donileen Loseke. Newbury Park, CA: Sage Publications.

Tafari-Ama, Imani M. 1998. "Rastawoman as Rebel: Case Studies in Jamaica." In *Chanting Down Babylon: The Rastafari Reader,* edited by Nathaniel S. Murrell, William D. Spencer, and Adrian A. McFarlane. Philadelphia: Temple University Press.

Taussig, Michael T. 1986 [1980]. *The Devil and Commodity Fetishism in South America.* Chapel Hill: University of North Carolina Press.

Tinsman, Heidi. 1997. "Household *Patrones*: Wife-Beating and Sexual Control in Rural Chile, 1964–1988." In *The Gendered Worlds of Latin American Women Workers: From Household and Factory to the Union Hall and Ballot Box,* edited by John D. French and Daniel James. Durham: Duke University Press.

Tjaden, P., and N. Thoennes. 2000. *Extent, Nature, and Consequences of Intimate Partner Violence: Findings from the National Violence against Women Survey.* Washington, D.C.: U.S. Department of Justice. (Available from www.ojp.usdoj.gov/nij/pubs-sum/181867.htm)

Torstrick, 2000. *The Limits of Coexistence: Identity Politics in Israel.* Ann Arbor: University of Michigan Press.

Tuzin, Donald. 1997. *The Cassawary's Revenge: Life and Death of Masculinity in a New Guinean Society.* Chicago: University of Chicago Press.

Twine, Francine Winddance. 1998. *Racism in a Racial Democracy: The Maintenance of White Supremacy in Brazil.* New Brunswick, NJ: Rutgers University Press.

Ulrich, Laurel T. 1980. *Good Wives: Image and Reality in the Lives of Women in Northern New England, 1650–1750.* New York: Oxford University Press.

United Nations. 2000. *The World's Women, 2000: Trends and Statistics,* 3rd ed. New York: United Nations.

Ventura, Lois A., and Gabrielle Davis. 2005. "Domestic Violence." *Violence Against Women* 11(2): 255–277.

Verdery, Katherine. 1991. *Nationalist Ideology under Socialism: Identity and Cultural Politics in Ceausescu's Romania.* Berkeley: University of California Press.

Verger, Pierre. 1993. "Orixás da Bahia." In *Os Deuses Africanos no Candomblé da Bahia*. Salvador: Bigraf.

Wade, Peter. 1994. "Man the Hunter: Gender and Violence in Music and Drinking Contexts in Colombia." In *Sex and Violence: Issues in Representation and Experience*, edited by Penelope Harvey and Peter Gow. Routledge: London.

Weber, Max. 1958 [1919]. *"Politics as a Vocation."* In *From Max Weber: Essays in Sociology*, edited by H. H. Gerth and C. Wright Mills. New York: Oxfor University Press. 77–128.

Werken, Tiffany van de. 2002. "Domestic Violence—Policing the 'New Crime' in the Northern Territory." *Police in Australia—Issues and Innovations in Australian Policing (Case Studies)*. Australian Institue of Criminology. http://aic.gov.au./policing/case_studies/domestic.html.

Wilson, Peter. 1973. *Crab Antics: The Social Anthropology of English-Speaking Negro Societies in the Caribbean*. New Haven: Yale University Press.

Wimberly, Fayette. 1998. *"The Expansion of Afro-Bahian Religious Practices in Nineteenth-Century Cachoeira."* In *Afro-Brazilian Culture and Politics: Bahia, 1790s to 1990s*, edited by Hendirk Kraay. Armonk, NY: M. E. Sharpe.

Wimmer, Franz. 1961. *Michaelis: Dicionário Ilustrado*. São Paulo: Melhoramentos.

Wolf, Diane L. 1992. *Factory Daughters: Gender, Household Dynamics, and Rural Industrialization in Java*. Berkeley: University of California Press.

Woortmann, Klaas. 1987. *A Família das Mulheres*. Rio de Janeiro: Tempo Brasileiro.

Yanagisako, Sylivia, and Carol Delaney. 1995. Naturalizing Power: Essays in Feminist Cultural Analysis. New York: Routlege.

Yllö, Kersti. 1983. "Sexual Equality and Violence against Wives in American States." *Journal of Comparative Family Studies* 14: 67–86.

———. 1984. "The Status of Women, Marital Equality, and Violence against Wives: A Contextual Analysis." *Journal of Family Issues* 5: 307–320.

———. 1993. "Through a Feminist Lens: Gender, Power, and Violence." In R. Gelles and D. Loseke, eds. *Current Controversies in Family Violence*. Newbury Park: Sage Publications.

INDEX

Chico, 74–76, 97, 167–71, 285n9
child abuse: and *audiências*, 163; and
    Bomfim family, xii, 63–64, 98–99;
    and informal interventions, 146
child care, 2, 23, 278n3
child custody/support, 154, 169, 196, 206
Chile, xv, 131–32, 281n31
churches, 17, 144, 288n4
Cida, 145
Cilene, 145–46
"citizenship of gender," 215, 263–65
City Council's Commission for Women's
    Rights (CDMCM), 241
City of Walls (Caldeira), 278–79n12
"City of Women," xvi, 7, 9–10, 257–58,
    262
City of Women, The (Landes), 6, 21
classism, 26–27, 42, 47, 85, 284–85n8; and
    DMs (Delegacias da Mulher), 196,
    298n14; and *outras* (other women), 101
classlessness, myth of, 34, 280n27
class spatialization, 13–15, 15 *table*, 278–
    79nn11–13
"*clube dos machō*" (big machos club),
    114–18
clubes de mães (mother's clubs), 17
code of individuals, 259–60
code of inviolate household privacy, 150
code of persons, 259
Coelho, Nilo, 239
Cole, Sally, 6–7
Coletivo do Ventro Livre (São Paulo),
    278n4
collective solidarity, 149, 151
Collor de Mello, Fernando, 239–40
Colombia, 182, 184, 281nn31–32
colonial past, 7, 10–11, 39
Columbine school massacre, 275
comadres (co-mothers), xii, xvii, 29, 90, 97,
    110, 139
Comisarias de Mujer y la Niñez (Nicara-
    gua), 184
*Comissão dos Direitos da Mulher da Câmera
    Municipal*, 241
comissárias, 170, 226, 288n5
Common Couple Violence (CCV), 178–79
compadres (godfathers), xii–xiii, 97, 108,
    139, 270

Companhia de Polícia Feminina (military),
    191
compartmentalization, institutional,
    215–16
compensatory violence, 31, 43, 45, 84, 95,
    129–33
Conçessão, 10
condoms, 278n4
Conflict Tactic Scale, 177
confusão (confusion), 106–7
Connell, Robert W., 133
conquistas (successes), 141, 292n11
consanguinity, 81, 91, 276
Conselho Estadual da Condição Feminina
    (São Paulo), 186
Conselho Estadual dos Direitos da Mulher
    (Bahia), 299n19
Constitution of Brazil (1988), 3, 201–2
consumerist fetishism, 85
contestatory patterns of violence, 43, 264;
    and *audiências*, 47, 151–52, 170, 180; and
    DMs (Delegacias da Mulher), 205; vs.
    dominance-driven violence, 174–76, 175
    table, 181, 290n17; and "family violence"
    vs. "violence-against-women" research,
    178–79
corn harvest, 139–40
corno (cuckold), 112, 115–16, 118–20, 127,
    134
corruption, police, 212, 238–40, 265
Cosme and Damião, 60
cost-benefit analyses, 44, 282n39
crack trade, 130
credible-force mandate, 95, 118, 120, 122,
    126, 130, 222–23
Cremilda, 146
crentes (born-again Protestant Christians),
    41, 157–59
Creuza, 53, 63, 68, 73, 82, 156
"crimes against a person," 202, 238
"crimes against custom," 201–2
criminalization of partner violence: cross-
    cultural perspective on, 34–35; and DMs
    (Delegacias da Mulher), 137, 186, 191,
    196–203, 200 *table*, 206–11, 216,
    295nn34,36; and exchange theory, 44;
    and limits of cultural change, 125–26;
    and masculinity, 46–47, 95, 110–11, 114,

120–22, 287n12; and nonintervention, 151; and policewomen, 225–29; and resource theory, 43

criminals. See *marginais* (criminals; underclass)

crisis-response teams, 216

Cristina, 228

cross-cultural perspective on violence, 32–37, 254, 280nn24–25, 282n38

crowding, 282–83n40

cruzado novo/cruzeiro novo, 59, 164, 284n4

cuckolded men, 112, 115–16, 118–20, 127, 134

"cult matriarchate," 6

cultural capital, 65

cultural change, 110, 125–26

cultural "codes"/"scripts," 4, 113, 120, 122

cultural reproduction theory, 43–44

"cultural showcase" cities, 14

cultural tolerance of violence: and *audiências,* 180; and DMs (Delegacias da Mulher), 217; and domination vs. contestatory violence, 176; and informal interventions, 144–47; and masculinity, 110–11, 122, 126, 130, 134

culture of poverty, 34, 280n28

Cunha, Roberto Salles, 202

cunnilingus, 296n53

currency, Brazilian, 59–60, 284n4

custom vs. modernity, 113

Dahl, Robert, 255

DaMatta, Roberto, 259–61, 263, 300n3

Damião. See Cosme and Damião

dança folclórica, 139–44

Danino, 84

day care centers, 2, 278n3

de Alves, Katía, 251–52

DEAM (Delegacia Especial de Atendimento à Mulher), 227 *fig.,* 252 *fig.,* 277–78n2, 292n11. See also DMs (Delegacias da Mulher)

de Aquino, Sílva, 253

death threats, 152, 157, 163, 199, 200 *table*

Debert, Guita, 209

decision making, domestic, 32, 37, 282–83n40

"deep play," 259

"defense of honor," 186

defensive violence, 237

deindustrialization, 130

Delegacia da Mulher (television show), 188–89, 248

Delegacia de Polícia de Defesa da Mulher (DPDM), 290n16

Delegacia de Proteção à Mulher (DPM), 173

delegacias, 2, 4, 92, 277–78n2; as ethnographic site, 5–6, 18, 50; and mythological allusions, 40; and representations of violence, 29, 31–32; as subject of male focus groups, 125. See also *audiências* (hearings); DMs (Delegacias da Mulher)

delegadas (police chiefs/magistrates), 139, 151–71, 288n5; and ambiguous mission of DMs, 199, 202–3; and backlog/overload of DMs, 206–8; careers of, 238–40, 298n11; and Celeste-Ediundo *audiência,* 152–57; and early signs of trouble in DMs, 193, 196; and essentialism, 217–18; and feminist activism, 241–42, 298n12; and gender identity, 244–46; and gender ideology, 248, 250, 299n17; and gender segregation, 214; and Janaína-Jorge *audiência,* 162–67; and Jecrims system, 209–11; and Joana-Chico *audiência,* 167–71; and Judete-Edilson *audiência,* 157–62; and *marginais* (criminals; underclass), 226, 227 *fig.;* and police violence, 233–35; and redemocratization, 186, 188; and revictimization of complainants, 230; and using police as reprisal, 173, 290n16; work schedule of, 233

delegitimation of male violence, 31, 34, 151

democratization, 2, 278n3. *See also* redemocratization

desabafar (purge, blowing off steam), 152, 289n8

destructive-yet-productive paradox of violence, 33

deterrent effect of DMs, 151, 173, 176, 208, 217

diabetes, 65

Diana, 49–51, 54–56, 82–83

Dinerges, 147–49

Diniz, Angela, 185

Dique de Tororó, 142, 142 *fig.*

discrimination. *See* classism; racism; sexism

Disque-Denúncia (Dial-Denounce), 252

divorce: and *audiências,* 153, 170; and compensatory violence, 129, 132; from cross-cultural perspective, 32, 37; and feminist theory, 283–84n41

DMs (Delegacias da Mulher), 1–2, 4–5, 47–48, 137–38, 182–220, 277–78nn1–2, 288n1; ambiguous mission of, 198–203, 200 *table;* and *audiências,* 139, 151–71, 288n5; and backlog/overload, 203–8, 204 *table,* 242, 295nn37–39, 295–96nn41–44; division of labor in, 233, 297n4, 298n5; and domination vs. contestatory violence, 174–76, 175 *table,* 290n17; early signs of trouble in, 193–98, 294n30, 295n34; engendering of, 254–56, 267, 299n21; and essentialism, 217–20; as ethnographic site, 5–6, 7, 64, 198–99, 295n35; and gendering of citizenship, 263–65; and gender segregation, 185, 189, 210–11, 214–17, 220, 294n22; ghetto-ization effects of, 203–8, 215–16; and Jecrims system, 200 *table,* 207, 209–11, 266, 296n44; leadership of, 251–54, 252 *fig.;* and pre-*delegacias* settings, 138–51; and redemocratization, 185–89, 293–94nn12,17,21; and symbolic feminization of police, 189–93; and using police as reprisal, 171–74, 290n16; and Zizi, 90–91, 137. *See also* policewomen

Domestic Violence Council, 216

Domestic Worker's Union, 68

dominance-driven violence, 22; and *audiências,* 47, 155; and Bomfim family, 54; as classic model, 31, 173; vs. contesta-tory patterns of violence, 43, 174–76, 175 *table,* 181, 290n17; cross-cultural/global perspectives on, 34, 37; and ecological theory, 282–83n40; and "family vio-lence" vs. "violence-against-women" research, 177–79; and feminist theory, 44, 283–84n41; and masculinity, 94, 127, 130, 133; and status-consistency/backlash thesis, 290–91n18

dona da cabeça (owner of head), 42, 67, 80–81, 87, 94

Donalda, 145, 149–50, 172

Dória, 189

double standards, sexual: and *audiências,* 160–61; from cross-cultural perspective, 32; and masculinity, 100–101, 112–13, 115, 133; and policewomen, 244

dowry deaths, 183, 213

drug dealing/trafficking, 130, 229, 272, 275

drug use, 86, 119, 153, 155, 168, 229–30, 258

Duarte, Nestor, 7–8

Dumont, Louis, 260

East Harlem (New York City), 130

ecological theory, 44, 282–83n40

economic activity of women, 3, 22–25, 279n20; and Jorginho, 101; and mas-culinity, 124, 129, 131–32; and status-consistency/backlash thesis, 290–91n18; and Yancí, 84–86, 285n14

economic crises, Brazilian, 22, 279n18. *See also* poverty

Edilson, 157–62, 289n11

Ediundo, 152–57

egalitarianism, 33–34, 45, 259–60

Ehlers, Tracy Bachrach, 67

Eliene, 68

elitism, 35, 220. *See also* classism

emasculation, 21, 128, 130, 223

embezzlement, 240

encompassment, 260, 263

engendering, 254–56, 267, 299n21

"entre tapas e beijos" (between slaps and kisses), 47, 136, 142, 144, 148, 179–80

epic romances, 61

equality/inequality, gender: and DMs (Delegacias da Mulher), 5, 201, 214; and "family violence" vs. "violence-against-women" research, 177; and feminist theory, 44–45, 283–84n41; and mas-culinity, 111, 130; in Nicaragua, 184, 292n10; and status-consistency/backlash thesis, 290–91n18

Espiritismo, 42, 91, 166–67, 288n4

essentialism: and DMs (Delegacias da Mulher), 217–20, 249; and gender difference, 47; and inversion dynamics,

imagined communities, 151, 218–20

Imperatriz, 230

impotence, 128, 223

impunity, male, 31, 42, 114, 130; and DMs (Delegacias da Mulher), 2, 4, 150, 186, 198, 208–9, 211, 216, 219

indentured servants, 53, 289n13

India, 35, 44, 182–85, 211–14, 216, 220, 280–81n29, 296–97n55

indios (indigenous people), 19–20, 25, 26 *table,* 32, 51, 162, 285n11

individualism, 79–80, 264

inequality. *See* equality/inequality, gender

infanticide, 209

informal economy, 12, 23, 55, 65, 124

informal interventions, 144–47, 288n4

insecurity of men, 34, 94–95, 128–34

insider-outsider perspectives, 7, 242

internalized racism, 65

International Day for Combating Violence against Women, 243

International Women's Day, 241

International Year of Women (1979), 3

interventions: and *audiências,* 151–71; and cross-cultural perspective on violence, 33; and DMs (Delegacias da Mulher), 47, 137, 195–98; and feminist theory, 283–84n41; and male focus groups, 123; and nonintervention, 147–51; in pre-*delegacia* settings, 138, 144–47; and Yancí, 82–83

Intimate Terrorism (IT), 178

inversion dynamics, 258–62, 300n3

Iracema, 239, 246, 250, 254

Isabel Alice (Doutora), 227 *fig.,* 251–53, 266, 299n17

Itamar, 119, 121

Izumino, Wânia Pasinato, 277–78n2

Jaldo, 148–49

Janaína, 151, 162–67, 171–72, 289–90n14

Jandiara, 155–56

jealousy, sexual: and *audiências,* 161, 169–70; and Bomfim family, 58, 62–63, 72; and masculinity, 112, 131–32

Jecrims system, 200 *table,* 207, 209–11, 266, 296n44

Jehovah's Witnesses, 41, 68, 158, 288n4

jeitinhos (little string-pulls), 259, 261, 263, 299n1, 300n3

Jeje culture, 9, 19–20, 279n16

Jesus Christ, 38, 190, 288n3

Jesus de Pinho, Isabel Alice. *See* Isabel Alice (Doutora)

Joana, 151, 167–71, 172

jogo dos búzios consultations, 41, 76–77, 282n36

Johnson, Michael P., 176–78

Johnson, Paul C., 40

Jorge, 52 *fig.,* 73, 99, 162–67, 171, 269–71, 289–90n14

Jorginho, xii–xiv, xvii, 52 *fig.;* and domination vs. contestatory violence, 176; and mother/daughter/in-law triangle, 49, 51, 53, 56–64, 72–77, 80, 90–91; as son/brother/husband, 94–110, 112, 114–19, 121–22, 133, 268–70, 274

Josi, xii, 52 *fig.,* 73, 107, 115, 202

Judete, 151, 157–62, 171–72, 289n11

Kant de Lima, Roberto, 300n3

Kardec, Allan, 166

Katía, 251–52

Katiana, 150

Kenya, 182, 184

kidnappings, 14, 32

Kottak, Conrad, 300n3

Ku Klux Klan, 275

Kulick, Don, 261–62

labor market, 3, 22–23, 279n20

ladeiras (steep walkways), 142, 143 *fig.*

Lancaster, Roger N., 130

Landes, Ruth, xvi, 6–10, 21–22, 257

land shortages, 162

Latin America, xv, 17, 22, 31, 36–37, 182, 184, 216, 281n31

laundry services, 50, 54–57, 60, 63, 73

Lawyers for Human Rights and Legal Aid, 213

legal system, Brazilian, 185–86

Leila, 139

Leone, Janel M., 178

Lepowsky, Maria, 33

lesbians, 243

upward class mobility, 27, 85
U.S. Army, 128
Uttar Pradesh (India), 280–81n29
uxorilocality (living with wives' families), 145

Valdinho, 51, 52 fig., 81–82
Vani, 53
Vânia, 236, 247, 250
vasectomies, 84
vengeance, xvi, 120, 146, 236
victimization, 31, 43; and *audiências,* 151–52; and Bomfim family, 54, 69, 80, 89–90; vs. contestatory patterns of violence, 180–81; and DMs (Delegacias da Mulher), 214, 223–24; and domination vs. contestatory violence, 174, 176; and informal interventions, 146; and police-women, 229–32, 244; and redemocratization, 187; and symbolic feminization of police, 190–91
vigilante law, xv, 16, 120
Vinaya, N. A., 212
violence-against-women researchers, 177–78
violence theory, 33, 280n26
"violent emotion" as legal defense strategy, 186
Virgin Mary, 66–67, 190, 288n3
virgins, 202–3
virilocality (living with husbands' families), 145

wage gap, 84, 124, 285n14
walls, invisible, 10–16, 278–79nn11–13
Wape people (Papua New Guinea), 280–81n29
washerwomen, 50, 54–57, 60, 63, 73
wash-honor-with-blood mandate, 112–14, 119–22
wealth, control of, 37, 85, 282–83n40
Weber, Max, 191, 238, 298n8
White Ribbon Campaign, 299n18
wifeliness, 39–40
wife-murder, 113–14
witchcraft, 76, 184
witnessing of violence, 28–29; as a child, 282–83n40

Wolf, Diane L., 132
"woman," 100, 186n4
women's councils, 3, 192, 294n27
"women's desks," 182
women's movements. *See* feminist activism
women's police stations, xv–xvii, 1–2, 4, 277–78nn1–2. See also *delegacias;* DMs (Delegacias da Mulher)
women's rights, 4, 111
Woortmann, Klaas, 21–22, 24
Worker's Party. *See* PT (Partido dos Trabalhadores)
work ethic, 12, 66, 84
working married women, 167, 171, 290–91n18
working poor, 157
World Bank, 37
World Conference on Women (Beijing), 3, 293n18
World Health Organization, 36

Xangô (god of thunder), 9, 38–40, 67, 133–34, 257

Yancí, xii, 38, 52 fig., 258, 262–63, 269, 274, 276, 279n17; as Dona Yasmín, 81–89, 285nn13,16; and informal interventions, 147, 156; and Jorginho as son/brother/husband, 100, 106, 121; and mother/daughter/in-law triangle, 46, 53–54, 59, 61, 64–74, 78–80, 89
Yanomami, 33, 280n25
Yasmín, Dona, 86–89. *See also* Yancí
Yemanjá Assaba, 39, 73, 94

zero-sum model of power, 123–25, 128, 132
Zilda, 198
Zizi, xii–xiii, xvii, 52 fig., 262, 269–70, 272–74; defined as battered woman, 29, 156; and DMs (Delegacias da Mulher), 90–91, 137, 156, 161–62, 217, 273; and domination vs. contestatory violence, 175–76; and Jorginho as son/brother/husband, 96–101, 103–4, 106–10, 114–15, 125; and mother/daughter/in-law triangle, 46, 49–51, 53–64, 72–74, 77, 80–81, 83, 89–90
Zumbi, 52 fig., 19, 51, 105, 279n15

Text:	11.25/13.5 Adobe Garamond
Display:	Perpetua, Adobe Garamond
Compositor:	BookMatters, Berkeley
Indexer:	Sharon Sweeney
Cartographer:	Bill Nelson
Printer and binder:	Maple-Vail Manufacturing Group